The Phonology-Syntax Connection

CENTER FOR THE STUDY
OF LANGUAGE
AND INFORMATION

The Phonology-Syntax Connection

X ——————————————————— X

Edited by
Sharon Inkelas and Draga Zec

X X X

The University of Chicago Press

Chicago and London

Sharon Inkelas is assistant professor of linguistics at the University of Maryland. Draga Zec is assistant professor of linguistics at Yale University and is a coeditor of *Working Papers in Grammatical Theory and Discourse Structure,* published by CSLI in 1988 and distributed by the Press.

The University of Chicago Press, Chicago 60637
The University of Chicago Press, Ltd., London
© 1990 by the Center for the Study of Language and Information
Leland Stanford Junior University
All rights reserved. Published 1990
Printed in the United States of America

99 98 97 96 95 94 93 92 91 90   54321

The Phonology-syntax connection / edited by Sharon Inkelas
and Draga Zec.
    p.   cm.
Includes bibliographical references.
    ISBN 0-226-38100-5. — ISBN 0-226-38101-3 (pbk.)
    1. Grammar, Comparative and general—Phonology. 2. Grammar,
Comparative and general—Syntax. I. Inkelas, Sharon. II. Zec,
Draga. III. Center for the Study of Language and Information (U.S.)
P217.3P54 1990
415—dc20   89-20582
                            CIP

Contents

Contributors

LEE BICKMORE is currently a Lecturer at the University of Texas at Austin. He recently completed his dissertation, entitled "Kinyambo Prosody," at UCLA.

MATTHEW Y. CHEN is Professor of Linguistics at the University of California, San Diego. His current research interests include tonology and syntax-phonology interface.

YOUNG-MEE YU CHO is a graduate student at Stanford University. She is writing a dissertation entitled "Parameters of Consonantal Assimilation".

CLEO CONDORAVDI is a graduate student at Yale University. Her area of specialty is syntax and semantics.

BRUCE HAYES is Professor of Linguistics at UCLA. His research interests beyond the topic of this volume include metrical stress theory, segment structure, and the theory of meter.

LARRY M. HYMAN is Professor of Linguistics at the University of California, Berkeley. He has worked extensively on prosodic phenomena and varied synchronic and diachronic issues in the phonology and grammar of a wide range of Niger-Congo languages.

SHARON INKELAS is Assistant Professor of Linguistics at the University of Maryland. Her Stanford University dissertation addresses the interactions between prosodic, morphological and syntactic structure.

ELLEN M. KAISSE is Associate Professor of Linguistics at the University of Washington. She is the author of *Connected Speech: the Interaction of Syntax and Phonology* and other works on the postlexical phonology of Greek, Turkish and English.

JONNI M. KANERVA is Assistant Professor of Linguistics at Indiana University. His Stanford University dissertation is entitled *Focus and Phrasing in Chicheŵa Phonology;* he also has interests in phonetics and syntax.

ISTVÁN KENESEI is Associate Professor at the Unversity of Szeged, Hungary. His main interest is syntax, and he has edited two collections of papers on the syntax of Hungarian.

MICHAEL KENSTOWICZ is Professor of Linguistics at the University of Urbana-Champaign. He has research interests in the phonology and syntax of Slavic, Semitic and African languages.

LUKOWA KIDIMA is a graduate student at UCLA. He is completing a dissertation on tone and accent in Kiyaka.

CHARLES W. KISSEBERTH is Professor of Linguistics at the University of Illinois, Urbana-Champaign. His work in recent years has emphasized the tonal/accentual structure of Eastern and Southern Bantu languages.

BRIAN MCHUGH is Assistant Professor at Temple University. His UCLA dissertation concerns phrasal cyclicity in Kivunjo Chaga and its implications for Prosodic Hierarchy theory.

MARINA NESPOR is Associate Professor at the University of Amsterdam. She works primarily on the interaction of the different (sub)components of the grammar.

DAVID ODDEN is Assistant Professor in the Department of Linguistics at Ohio State University. He is currently working on a descriptive grammar of Kimatuumbi.

WILLIAM POSER is Assistant Professor of Linguistics at Stanford University. His default interests are the phonetics/phonology interface, the formal properties of phonological rules, and Japanese.

KEREN RICE is Associate Professor of Linguistics at the University of Toronto. Her work is largely in the area of phonological theory and Athapaskan languages; she is the author of *A Grammar of Slave* (Northern Athapaskan).

ELISABETH SELKIRK is Professor of Linguistics at the University of Massachusetts at Amherst. Her publications *Phonology and Syntax: The Relation between Sound and Structure* (MIT Press, 1984), *The Syntax of Words* (MIT Press, 1982) and "Derived Domains in Sentence Phonology" (Phonology Yearbook 3, 1986) reflect her longstanding interest in the interface between phonology, morphology and syntax.

TONG SHEN is Assistant Research Fellow at the Research Institute of Linguistics, the Chinese Academy of Social Sciences, Beijing, China, and a Ph.D. candidate at the University of Massachusetts at Amherst. He specializes in phonology, Chinese linguistics and dialectology.

IRENE VOGEL is Associate Professor of Linguistics at the University of Delaware. She is currently working on a project on the lexical and postlexical phonology of Italian.

DRAGA ZEC is Assistant Professor of Linguistics at Yale University. The title of her Stanford University dissertation is *Sonority Constraints on Prosodic Structure.*

ARNOLD ZWICKY is University Professor of Linguistics at the Ohio State University and Visiting Professor of Linguistics at Stanford University. He publishes widely on the interfaces between syntax, morphology, and phonology and on linguistic theory in general.

Preface

This volume emerged from a workshop on the phonology-syntax connection, held in May, 1988 at the Center for the Study of Language and Information at Stanford University. The design of the workshop was to assemble for the first time contributors to the growing field of phonology-syntax interaction, with the stated aim of evaluating the role of the prosodic hierarchy therein.

Sponsorship for the workshop came from two CSLI projects: Grammatical Theory and Discourse Structure (part of the Relational Theories of Language and Action project), and Phonetics and Phonology. The workshop's ultimate success is due to the collaborative efforts of the extended Stanford linguistics community. Of particular help in organizing the events of the workshop were Elizabeth Bratt, Junko Itô, Smita Joshi, Marcy Macken, K. P. Mohanan, Tara Mohanan, and Bach-Hong Tran. For sharing the substantial burden of preparing the volume for publication, Jennifer Cole, Kristin Hanson, Kathryn Henniss and John Stonham deserve special tribute.

Our final acknowledgment belongs to two sets of people: to Joan Bresnan and Paul Kiparsky, for nourishing the original seeds of the workshop; and to Dikran Karagueuzian and Emma Pease, for helping to harvest the book.

Introduction

This collection of papers deals with the interrelatedness of syntax and phonology and, more generally, with the issue of interaction among the components of linguistic structure. It has long been recognized that phonology and syntax interact in non-trivial ways; what is currently under debate is the actual range of such interactions, and their most appropriate formal representation in the grammar.

The papers in this volume address these general issues, as well as a number of more specific topics relevant to its main theme—the phonology-syntax connection. In the introduction, we will focus mainly on the issue of whether or not phonology needs to have direct access to syntax. The stated theme of the workshop from which this book arose, this issue is touched upon, either explicitly or implicitly, in practically every paper herein. The volume as a whole throws some new light on this relatively old controversy.

The amount of information present in syntax is enormously rich, as shown by, among others, Zwicky's contribution. In a direct reference model with an unconstrained view of phonology-syntax interactions, all this information should in principle be available to phonology. By contrast, proponents of the prosodic approach believe that the range of syntactic information needed for the purposes of phonology can be restricted in a principled fashion. Their proposal consists of positing a new level of representation, prosodic structure, which serves as a mediator between the two components of phonology and syntax, and provides a locale for stating restrictions on their interaction. Prosodic structure is typically motivated on the following grounds: (a) the syntactic information relevant for phonology exhibits recurring patterns, and (b) these patterns do not always obtain a straightforward syntactic characterization (see, for example, Selkirk 1978, and Nespor and Vogel 1986). The information deemed necessary for syntax-phonology mapping amounts to information about arboreal configuration and phrasal rank bracketed structure; conspicuously absent is information about syntactic categories, or about morphological specifications of the terminal elements.

A number of papers in the present volume offer empirical support for the prosodic view. We find such confirming evidence as Bickmore's analysis of the effects of branching in the phrasal phonology of Kinyambo; Cho's analysis of Korean external sandhi domains; Condoravdi's analysis of juncture rules in Modern Greek; Hyman's analysis of boundary tones in Luganda and Kinande; Kanerva's analysis of the influence of syntactic focus on phrasing in Chicheŵa; Kenstowicz and Kisseberth's demonstration of phrasal rules in Chizigula; Kidima's account of tonal domains in Kiyaka; McHugh's analysis of phrasal domains for the tonal rules in Chaga; Nespor's move to derive metrical grid structure by a mapping from prosodic structure; Poser's analysis of "Aoyagi prefixes" in Japanese; Rice's reanalysis of Turkish and Sanskrit; and Selkirk and Shen's account of tonal domains in Shanghai Chinese. The authors may diverge regarding the actual mechanics within the prosodic component, but these minor differences do not diminish what appears to be quite an impressive set of results granting support to the prosodic view.

This volume provides evidence of yet another sort for indirect reference as well. Several papers argue against direct reference as a viable hypothesis by showing that certain phenomena can be captured only in prosodic terms. The first argument concerns the c-command relation, postulated in Kaisse 1985 as sufficient to provide direct structural syntactic characterization of phonological rule domains. Cho shows that the patternings of syntactic information for the purposes of external sandhi rules in Korean can be characterized in prosodic terms, but not in terms of c-command. The next argument against direct reference comes from the paper by Poser, who argues that a group of Japanese prefixes is lexically specified to introduce a (postlexical) prosodic phrase break. Under a direct reference approach, phonological rules which apply within these phrases would need to have access not only to the relevant syntactic information but also to the internal structure of words; this, however, is not necessary under the indirect reference approach. Third, Selkirk and Shen show that the mapping of function words into phonological words is not predictable from their syntactic status, but that it does follow from the mapping procedures for creating higher-level prosodic constituents. Next, Zec and Inkelas show that clitics need to be characterized in terms of prosodic subcategorization frames; and that certain dislocated syntactic constituents have to satisfy minimal size constraints expressible solely in prosodic terms. Finally, Condoravdi observes cases where lexical insertion is governed by prosodic conditions. In sum, prosodic structure appears to be the only appropriate component for stating the conditions on a number of widely varying processes.

The view opposed to this one is that the array of syntactic information needed for phonological rule domains is too varied to yield to any successful generalizations. Odden and Chen, in particular, point to a number of cases in which the syntactic properties of phonological rule domains elude the kinds of generalizations commonly made in the prosodic framework.

Chen argues for the relevance of the distinction between arguments and adjuncts in the creation of Xiamen tone groups, a distinction which cannot be derived from any other syntactic properties, while Odden presents several syntactically conditioned phonological rules in Kimatuumbi whose environments appear to be simply random collections of syntactic properties.

In light of this, it becomes obvious that one of the potential problems for the proponents of prosodic phonology is that the highly regular relation between syntax and phonology which they propose does not cover all the known cases of syntax phonology interface. This problem is addressed by Hayes, who offers an independent account for the residual cases, those which the prosodic phonology cannot account for, thus salvaging the results that this framework has achieved. In his precompiled phonology, Hayes proposes a principled distinction between rules that make direct reference to syntactic structure, and those which apply on prosodic domains: the former class is reanalyzed by Hayes as lexical rules whose application is constrained by lexically specified syntactic frames.

The syntax-phonology interface has been viewed mainly from the perspective of syntactic influences on phonological rules. A natural question to ask is whether phonological rule domains circumscribe the range of syntax-phonology interface, or whether the interface has a wider scope. In fact, several of the papers in this volume go beyond phonological rule domains in exploring the interface of syntax and phonology. Cho and Kidima argue persuasively that facts about prosodic structure, or about the mapping which relates syntactic and prosodic structure, can serve as a diagnostic for syntactic constituency. Kidima shows that, by virtue of phrase bounded tonal rules in Kiyaka, it is possible to detect whether a constituent is located within the VP or in postposed position. Furthermore, Cho argues for the syntactic VP constituent, whose existence in Korean is an area of controversy, solely on the basis of prosodic evidence.

The exact nature of the relation between the syntactic and the prosodic components is addressed by Vogel and Kenesei, and by Zec and Inkelas. Vogel and Kenesei contend that this relation is strictly unidirectional, that syntax can influence phonology but phonology cannot influence syntax. In contraposition, Zec and Inkelas argue for a bidirectional relation between the two structures. Vogel and Kenesei's proposal is couched within a transformational framework, while Zec and Inkelas's proposal is articulated within a nonderivational model in which the components of the grammar are co-present rather than transformationally related.

This volume thus suggests some new trends in the study of the phonology-syntax connection. In doing so it provides a concerted response to the justifiable skepticism of proponents of the direct reference approach, who have challenged adherents of prosodic phonology to provide arguments for the new level of representation that go beyond the avoidance of redundancy in stating rule domains.

1

Branching Nodes and Prosodic Categories: Evidence from Kinyambo

LEE BICKMORE

CURRENTLY TWO MAIN APPROACHES are taken in dealing with phonological rules which refer to phrasal junctures. The first approach maintains that phonological rules have access to the syntactic phrase marker, and simply include the relevant aspects of the phrase marker in the structural description of the given phonological rule. This 'direct' approach has been advocated by Clements 1978, Kaisse 1985, Odden 1987, and others. Though one can propose constraints on just how much of the syntax is available to the phonology, certain linguists have felt that direct access to syntax renders the phonological component much too powerful. This uneasiness has led some to propose that phonological rules have direct access not to syntax, but rather to prosodic phrases (and phrase boundaries) which have been constructed on the basis of the syntax, but which are not necessarily identical to any existing syntactic phrase. One such approach is the theory of the prosodic hierarchy.

This theory was developed by Selkirk 1981a, 1986, and has received subsequent attention in Nespor and Vogel 1982, 1983, 1986, Hayes 1989, Shih 1986, and others. Some theorists allow a block of direct-reference rules to apply before the prosodic ones. A somewhat stronger hypothesis involves the elimination of all direct-reference rules, the non-prosodic phrasal phenomena being handled by other means, such as precompilation (see Hayes (this volume)).

In this paper I describe several aspects of the phrasal phonology of Kinyambo within a specific version of the theory of the prosodic hierarchy.

In particular, I will show that the notion of branchingness plays a crucial role in the construction of certain phonological phrase boundaries which are referred to in the postlexical phonology of Kinyambo.

The outline of the paper is as follows. First, I will briefly describe the theory of the prosodic hierarchy assumed here. Second, I will discuss phonological phrases in particular, and suggest how this level in the prosodic hierarchy might be defined cross-linguistically. Finally, I will present some data from Kinyambo and show how they bear on the formulation of a parameterized universal phonological phrase construction rule.

1   Description of the Prosodic Hierarchy

In the theory of the prosodic hierarchy, the phonological string is exhaustively divided up into prosodic phrases based upon certain fundamental aspects of the string and its syntactic phrase marker (for example, reference to X, X′, X″). These prosodic phrases are in turn exhaustively combined into larger phrases, which are in turn combined into still larger phrases, etc., until the entire string is exhaustively parsed on every prosodic level. In this way a hierarchy of prosodic levels is obtained. Given the constraints that the string is exhaustively parsed at every level, and that a phrase on one level may belong to one and only one phrase on the next higher level, the phrases are said to be 'strictly layered' (Selkirk 1984).

What, then, are the various prosodic levels, and how many are there? Different linguists have proposed different numbers of levels. I will assume that there are five levels, starting with the word. This is shown below. (For language-specific examples showing independent justification of each level, see Nespor and Vogel 1986.)

(1) The Prosodic Hierarchy:

   a. Utterance

   b. Intonational Phrase

   c. Phonological Phrase

   d. Clitic Group

   e. Word

A schematic example of an utterance parsed into prosodic levels is given in (2):

(2) Utterance	U							
Intonational Phrase	I1			I2			I3	
Phonological Phrase	P1	P2		P3		P4	P5	
Clitic Group	C1	C2		C3	C4	C5		C6
Word	w1	w2	w3	w4	w5	w6	w7	w8

The claim is that phonological rules may make use of these phrases in their structural descriptions, but may not refer directly to any aspect of the syntax. For example, a rule could be said to apply within a certain prosodic phrase, or at the boundary of two prosodic phrases. This type of theory makes the claim that the phrasal phonological rules of a given language will not each make individual reference to arbitrary and distinct aspects of the syntax, but rather that the rules will tend to cluster into a small number of groups, each group referring to the same syntactically constructed phrase.

The final and perhaps most interesting claim that this theory makes is that the syntactic characterization of the different prosodic phrases may be able to be cross-linguistically specified, or at least parameterized. In this paper I wish to pursue this idea with respect to the phonological phrase (1c).

2   A Cross-linguistic Survey of Phonological Phrases

Let us now examine the types of phonological phrases which have been proposed in the literature. Nespor and Vogel 1986 examine rules from a number of languages which refer to phonological phrases, stating that all phonological phrases minimally include a head X and all elements on the non-recursive side of the head which are still within X^{max}. (For example, in head-initial languages, all the material on the left side of the head within X^{max} would be included with the head in a single phrase.) In addition, Nespor and Vogel suggest two parameters along which languages might differ. First, a language may obligatorily include, optionally include, or obligatorily not include the first complement of the head X located on the recursive side of the head. Second, this complement either may or may not branch. This is summarized below.

(3) *Phonological phrase construction rule* (adapted from Nespor and Vogel 1986)

Phonological phrases contain: a head X and all elements on the non-recursive side of the head which are still within X^{max}.

Parameters:

a. obligatory, optional, or prohibited inclusion of the first complement on the recursive side of X

b. this complement may branch or not

Given the above phonological phrase construction rule, there are five logical possibilities into which languages might fall, according to their selection of values of each of the two parameters. These are summarized below, each possibility being followed by a list of rules which Nespor and Vogel claim necessitate a phonological phrase construction rule of that type.

(4) Five logical possibilities (page numbers from Nespor and Vogel 1986):

    a. [prohibited complement]

      Liaison in colloquial French (p. 179)
      Extra high tone distribution in Ewe (p. 180)
      Word-initial voicing assimilation in Quechua (p. 183)
      Tone assignment, tone shifting, and reduction in Japanese
        (p. 183)

    b. [optional complement, −branching]

      Raddoppiamento Sintattico in Italian (p. 165)
      Stress retraction in Italian (p. 174)
      Rhythm rule in English (p. 177)
      Final lengthening in English (p. 178)
      Monosyllable rule in English (p. 178)

    c. [obligatory complement, +branching]

      Vowel Shortening in Chimwiini (p. 180)
      Certain rules in Kimatuumbi (p. 182)

    d. [optional complement, +branching]
      (none?)

    e. [obligatory complement, −branching]
      (none?)

It is interesting that Nespor and Vogel found no rules which would necessitate phonological phrases of the type (4d) and (4e). One might wonder, given this apparent gap, whether branchingness might be predictable on the basis of the optionality/obligatoriness of the complement.

    Selkirk 1986 has also suggested a possible cross-linguistic parameterization of a phonological phrase construction rule. Instead of describing how phrases are built up from heads, Selkirk maintains that phonological phrases are best described in terms of their endpoints. In this end-based approach she suggests two parameters, each having two possible values. The first parameter determines whether it is the right or the left edge of a constituent which is relevant to the construction rule. The second parameter specifies the nature of the constituent itself, with possible values of X^{max} or X^{head}. These parameters are summarized in (5):

(5) *Phonological phrases* contain the material between

    a. the right or left edges of

    b. X^{max} or X^{head}

The parameters in (5) describe four logically possible phrasing types into which languages might fall:

(6) Four logical possibilities:

    a. Right-edge X^{max}

       Tone sandhi in Xiamen (Selkirk 1986)
       Vowel shortening in Chimwiini (Selkirk 1986)
       Tonal phrasing in Papago (Hale and Selkirk 1987)

    b. Left-edge X^{max}

       Tone sandhi in Ewe (Selkirk 1986)
       Tone sandhi in Shanghai (Hale and Selkirk 1987)

    c. Right-edge X^{head}

       Liaison in French (Selkirk 1986)

    d. Left-edge X^{head}

       (no examples given)

Now that I have briefly interpreted two different approaches toward establishing a cross-linguistic phonological phrase construction rule, let us consider the notion of branchingness and its possible relevance to such a rule. In the approach taken by Nespor and Vogel, branchingness is appealed to directly in the formulation of the second parameter (3b), which states that the complement of the head X either may or may not branch. Thus, the languages listed under (4b) select the value [− branching complement], while those in (4c) select the value [+ branching complement].

By contrast, in the approach taken by Selkirk 1986, branchingness is not appealed to at all. The phonological phrase construction rule is based solely on the edge and type of constituent. In a recent article, however, Cowper and Rice (1987) claim that branchingness should be able to be referenced in Selkirk's end-based approach. Based upon certain facts from Mende, Cowper and Rice postulate that the branchingness of an X^{max} constituent should be a third parameter (in addition to (5a) and (5b)) in the end-based approach. I will briefly summarize their argument below.

The relevant phonological rule in Mende involves a fairly complex structural change and is simply dubbed Consonant Mutation. The rule essentially states that the initial consonant of a word undergoes some type of lenition (e.g., $p \rightarrow w$, $mb \rightarrow m$, $f \rightarrow v$) when preceded by another word in the same phonological phrase. Mende phonological phrase boundaries correspond to the parameter settings of left edge (see (5a)) and X^{max} (see (5b))—with one additional (and crucial) stipulation: X^{max} must be branching (X^{max-b}, in their notation). For specific examples of the application and non-application of Consonant Mutation, the reader is referred to Cowper and Rice 1987. Example (7) illustrates some syntactic environments in which Consonant Mutation (CM) does and does not apply.

(7) Consonant Mutation in Mende

	Application of CM		*Non-application of CM*
a.	[NP [**V**]$_{VP}$]$_S$	g.	[NP [**V** PP]$_{VP}$]$_S$
b.	[P [**N**]$_{NP}$]$_{PP}$	h.	[P [**N** Det]$_{NP}$]$_{PP}$
c.	[N [**A**]$_{AP}$]$_{NP}$		
d.	[NP **V**]$_{VP}$		
e.	[[NP **N**] Det]$_{NP}$		
f.	[NP **P**]$_{PP}$		

Note that in every case above where CM applies to the bold word, the item immediately to the left is within the same phonological phrase. In the two cases in which CM does not apply, a phonological phrase boundary intervenes between the underlined target item and the trigger which precedes it, so that the structural description of the rule is not met. Branchingess is crucial in distinguishing the cases in (7a-c) from those in (7g-h).[1]

3   Phonological Phrases in Kinyambo

I will now present evidence from Kinyambo which supports the claim that branchingness is crucial in any attempt to formulate a parameterized cross-linguistic phonological phrase construction rule.

Kinyambo is a Bantu language spoken in the Karagwe district in north-western Tanzania. It is closely related to Haya, Runyankore, Rukiga and Kikerewe. The data presented here have been compiled from elicitation sessions with R. Adewole, a native speaker of Kinyambo.

Table 1 contains examples of Kinyambo nouns in their isolation forms, listed according to number of syllables and tone pattern. There are three surface tones in Kinyambo: High (á), Low (a), and Falling (áa). Nouns have the following morphological structure: Preprefix – Prefix – Noun Root (e.g., *o-mu-sogoro* 'bean leaf'). Hyphens in the table indicate morphological boundaries.

Several generalizations can be noted on the basis of these surface isolation forms. First, there is a maximum of one non-Low tone per noun. Second, the non-Low tone never appears on the final syllable. Third, the non-Low tone may appear on the prefix or preprefix only when the root is monosyllabic (e.g., *é-m-bwa* 'dog,' *o-mú-twe* 'head').

I propose the following underlying representations for the above forms. First, the roots of those surface forms containing a non-Low tone will have a floating High tone underlyingly; this tone is subsequently associated to

---

[1] I should note here that Cowper and Rice's analysis has recently come under criticism by Tateishi 1987, 1988, who suggests that Consonant Mutation in Mende is not constrained by X^{max-b} boundaries at all. Rather, he argues that the rule is instead morphologically conditioned, triggered by an agreement prefix which indicates that the head takes a nominal element in its own maximal projection.

Syllables in stem	Total syllables	All Low	One High	One Falling
1	2	e-n-te 'cow'	é-m-bwa 'dog'	(táata 'my father')
1	3	o-mu-ti 'tree'	o-mú-twe 'head'	
2	3	e-n-goma 'drum'	e-n-jóki 'bee'	o-mw-áana 'child'
2	4	e-ki-tabo 'book'	o-mu-kóno 'arm'	o-bu-háango 'bigness'
3	4		e-n-kókora 'cough'	
3	5	o-mu-sogoro 'bean leaf'	o-mu-rúmuna 'sibling'	
4	5		o-mw-íjukuru 'grandchild'	

Table I

the leftmost mora of the root, by a standard left-to-right tone association convention.[2] Second, class prefixes and preprefixes are underlyingly
toneless although they sometimes surface as High (e.g., *émbwa* 'dog' and
omútwe 'head'), due to a leftward tone shift rule to be discussed below.
Finally, preprefixes, although underlyingly toneless, also become High
phrase-medially by a rule of High Insertion which will not be formalized
here. I will note here that only High tones are present in the underlying
representation. All surface Lows are the result of a late rule of default
Low tone insertion (also not formalized here).

Note that exactly in the case of monosyllabic High-toned roots, the
High surfaces not on the root but on the prefix or preprefix containing
the immediately preceding mora.

(8) é-m-bwa   'dog' (isolation)
     o-mú-nya   'lizard' (isolation)

However, this phenomenon is crucially constrained by phonological phrasing; when the word is not phrase-final, no tone shift occurs, and the surface
form is identical to the underlying form, as shown in (9).

(9) embwá zirungi   'good dogs'
     omunyá gurungi   'good lizard'

---

[2]In the text which follows I have chosen not to complicate the derivations by illustrating the left-to-right tone association which takes place straightforwardly in each
case where the root has a High tone associated with it. Thus what is given as the underlying representation will contain the association lines added by the above-mentioned
convention.

To account for this, I propose a rule of Phrase-final Leftward Tone Shift. This rule delinks a High tone from a phrase-final mora, relinking it to the mora immediately to the left:

(10) μ μ / — //   Phrase-final Leftward Tone Shift
       ⎺⎺⎽≢
        H

The derivation of the isolation form of *omúnya* 'lizard' (see (9)) is shown in 11:

(11)   o-mu-nya   UR
         |
         H

       o-mú-nya   Phrase-final Leftward Tone Shift (10)
         ⎺⎺⎽≢
          H

The phrase boundary at which this rule applies is the intonational phrase (see (1b)). Cross-linguistically, intonational phrase boundaries occur at the edges of a laundry list of constructions, including parentheticals, tag questions, vocatives, expletives, and pre- and post-posed constituents. Impressionistically, these seem to be the strongest boundaries possible while continuing in the same utterance. However, in syntactic formalism it is very difficult to give a unified account of the intonational phrase.

The examples below show that the rule of Phrase-final Leftward Tone Shift occurs at the end of an intonational phrase, but not internal to one.[3]

(12)   [Arajun'   ékíjwi]$_I$ [Káto]$_I$ [ekijwí   change]$_I$
       He-will-help   knee   Kato (voc.)   knee   my
       'He will help the knee, Kato.'   'my knee'

(13)   [Omúnya]$_I$ [nibanágara]$_I$ [omunyá   gurungi]$_I$
       lizard (voc.) they-sleep   lizard   good
       'Lizard, they are sleeping.'   'good lizard'

Below I give examples of the underlying representations of the isolation forms of various other types of nouns found in Table I.

(14)   omukóno   o-mu-kono   'arm'   UR
       'arm' (isolation) |
                            H

(15)   obuháango   o-bu-haango   'bigness'   UR
       'bigness' (isolation) |
                               H

---

[3]It should be noted in (12) that unlike Haya (Hyman and Byarushengo 1984:57), there is no High tone on the final syllable of a word preceding a vocative boundary (e.g., *Arajun' ékíjwí Káto).

(16) omurúmuna   o-mu-rumuna   'sibling'   UR
      'sibling' (isolation) |
                          H

Given this brief analysis of the underlying representation of Kinyambo nouns, we are now in a position to examine a phonological rule which I claim is bounded by the phonological phrase of the prosodic hierarchy (see (1c)). This rule, High Deletion, states that a High tone in one word will cause the deletion of the rightmost High tone in the word to its left, if the two words are both part of the same phonological phrase.[4] This is formalized below.

(17) High Deletion

$$H \rightarrow \emptyset / [\ldots [\ldots \underline{\quad} \ldots]_W [\ldots H \ldots]_W \ldots]_\phi$$

(W = word, ϕ = phonological phrase)

The application of High Deletion is illustrated in the derivation in (18):

(18)   [[o-mu-kama]$_W$ [mu-kazi]$_W$]$_\phi$ UR
            | |
           H   H
        chief   old

      o-mu-kama mu-kazi   High Deletion
              |
             H

      o-mu-kama mu kazi   Default Low Tone Insertion
      | | | | | | |
      L L L L   L H L

      omukama mukázi   Surface Form

'the old chief'

(cf. *omukáma* 'chief (isolation)')

In the above, High Deletion accounts for the fact that the High tone which appears on the first syllable of the root of *omukáma* 'chief' in isolation is not present when the same word precedes a word containing a High tone. Additionally, it must be the case that the deletion of a High tone is triggered by the presence of another High and not simply by the presence of a following word, as a High in one word does not delete

---

[4]I show in Bickmore (forthcoming) that the likelihood of application of Beat Deletion depends on the distance between the trigger and target Highs. In short, if the two Highs are on adjacent syllables, then High Deletion is obligatory; otherwise it is optional.

when the following word is toneless (e.g., /o-mu-káma mu-ruungi/ ⟶ *omukáma muruungi*).

The claim that this rule is bounded by the phonological phrase, and not simply the utterance, is based upon the fact that the rule applies in certain syntactic environments and not others.

In those cases where the rule does not apply I assume that there is a phonological phrase boundary between the trigger and the target of the rule which prevents the rule from applying. In those cases in which the rule does apply, I assume that there is no such prosodic boundary. The following is a representative, though certainly not comprehensive, list of environments in which High Deletion may and may not apply. I will discuss a subset of these environments in some details below.

(19) Environments in which High Deletion Applies

    a. [N [ADJ/NUM]$_{AP}$]$_{NP}$

    b. [N [CP + *a* NP]$_{PP}$]$_{NP}$ (noun-'associative'-noun)

    c. [V NP]$_{VP}$

    d. [V ADV]$_{VP}$

    e. [V PP]$_{VP}$

    f. [V [N]$_{NP}$ PP]$_{VP}$

    g. [V [N]$_{NP}$ ADV]$_{VP}$

    h. [V [N]$_{NP}$ NP]$_{VP}$

    i. [V [N]$_{NP}$ [N]$_{NP}$ ADV]$_{VP}$

    j. [A ADV]$_{AP}$

    k. [P NP]$_{PP}$

    l. [[X]$_{XP}$ *na/anga* XP]$_{XP}$ (X-conjunction 'and'/'or'-XP)

    m. [[N]$_{NP}$ VP]$_{S}$

    n. [[N]$_{NP}$ [*ni* X]$_{VP}$]$_{S}$ (subject-copula-NP)

(20) Environments in which High Deletion does not apply

    a. NP$_{VOC}$ —— S (vocative)

    b. [V [N PP]$_{NP}$ —— NP]$_{VP}$

    c. [V [N ADJ]$_{NP}$ —— ADV]$_{VP}$

    d. [V [N ADJ]$_{NP}$ —— NP]$_{VP}$

    e. [[N ADJ]$_{NP}$ —— *na/anga* NP]$_{NP}$
       (N-Adj-conjunction-NP)

    f. [[N ADJ]$_{NP}$ —— VP]$_{S}$

    g. [[N [CP + *a* NP]$_{PP}$]$_{NP}$ —— VP]$_{S}$
       (Assoc. NP as subject)

    h. [[N [CP + *a* NP]$_{PP}$]$_{NP}$ —— *na* NP]$_{NP}$
       (Assoc. NP in conjunction)

    i. [V [N […ADV]$_{S}$]$_{NP}$ —— ADV]$_{VP}$

Given these environments in which High Deletion does and does not apply, respectively, I propose that the phonological phrase construction rule for Kinyambo is as follows:

(21) Kinyambo phonological phrase boundaries are the right edges of branching maximal projections.

As Cowper and Rice claimed for Mende, I claim that for Kinyambo it is necessary to invoke directly the property of branchingness to correctly predict the location of phonological phrase boundaries. I will justify this claim in two stages. First I will show that assuming X^{max} instead of X^{max-b} as the relevant constituent for phonological phrase boundaries makes incorrect predictions. Then I will show that the rule is bounded by X^{max-b} and not simply the sentence or utterance.

To illustrate that reference to X^{max} would make incorrect predictions regarding phonological phrase boundaries, let us examine three different syntactic constructions. The first is a simple subject-verb sentence in which the subject NP and the verb are both unmodified. The structure of such a sentence is as follows:

(22) *Subject-Verb*

$$[[N]_{NP} [V]_{VP}]_S$$

If phonological phrase boundaries in Kinyambo were simply right-edge X^{max} brackets, as is the case in many languages (e.g., see (6a)) we would predict a phonological phrase boundary between the subject NP and the verb, since there is a right edge X^{max} bracket (namely $]_{NP}$) between the two constituents. Thus we would expect High Deletion not to apply. That it does is illustrated in the examples below.[5]

(23) abakózi   bákajúna   [abakozi bákajúna]$_\phi$
      'workers'   'they helped'   'the workers helped'
      (isolation) (isolation)

(24) omukáma   nejákwiija   [omukama nejákwiija]$_\phi$
      'chief'   'will come'   'the chief will come'

(25) omukázi   nejákwiija   [omukazi nejákwiija]$_\phi$
      'wife'   'will come'   'the wife will come'

The above examples are consistent with the claim that boundaries are right-edge X^{max-b} brackets. Since there is no branching maximal projection node between the subject and the verb, High Deletion is free

---

[5]Hyman and Byarushengo 1984 discuss a process of tone reduction in Haya which essentially has the effect of deleting all Highs in a VP except those in the last word. High Deletion in Kinyambo is not restricted to head-modifier/complement phrases, as seen in examples (23)-(25).

to apply, and a High tone in the verb causes an underlying High tone on the root of the subject NP to delete. As all finite verbs contain at least one High tone, it is not possible to contrast (23)-(25) with examples in which the subject NP is followed by a toneless VP. The only branching maximal projection in the examples above is $]_S$[6], which does not intervene between any two constituents. Thus the whole sentence is a phonological phrase (as well as an intonational phrase and utterance).

Next let us consider the case where a verb is followed by two unmodified objects. If phonological phrase boundaries were right-edge X^{max} boundaries, then we would expect High Deletion not to apply between the two objects, as there is a right-edge NP bracket intervening.

(26) *Verb-Object-Object*

$$[\text{V} [\text{N}]_{NP} [\text{N}]_{NP}]_{VP}$$

The rule of High Deletion does apply, however, as illustrated in the examples below.[7]

(27) Nejákwórecha   omukáma   émbwa
      'he will show'   'chief'   'dog'
      (isolation)   (isolation) (isolation)

      [Nejákworech' ómukam' émbwa]$_\phi$
      'He will show the chief the dog.'

(28) Nejákwórecha   omurúmuna   ekitébe
      'he will show'   'sibling'   'chair'

      [Nejákworech' ómurumun' ékitébe]$_\phi$
      'He will show the sibling the chair'

(29) Nejákúha   omutáhi   ebitóoke
      'he will give' 'friend'   'bananas'

      [Nejákuh' ómutah' ébitóoke]$_\phi$
      'He will give the friend bananas'

In (27) we see that the High tone on the first syllable of the second object *émbwa* has caused the deletion of the underlying High tone on the first syllable of the root of the first object *omukáma*.[8] The same is true

---

[6]S = IP (INFL Phrase), a maximal projection in the Barriers framework (Chomsky 1986).

[7]Apostrophes indicate the application of a rule of Vowel Elision, not discussed here.

[8]The High tone on the preprefix of the first object (e.g., *ómukam'* in (27)) is the result of a High Insertion rule, mentioned at the beginning of this section, but not discussed in detail. A High on a preprefix triggers High Deletion but never undergoes it. This matter, not discussed here because of limitations in space, is covered in detail in Bickmore 1989.

in (28) and (29), where in both cases a High tone in the second object triggers the deletion of the High tone on the root of the first object. In all of the examples, the High tone which surfaces on the preprefix of the first object precipitates the deletion of the High on the verb.

Thus, I claim that there is no phonological phrase boundary between the two objects. This follows automatically if phonological phrase boundaries correspond to X^{max-b} instead of simply to X^{max} boundaries. The only right-edge X^{max-b} boundary in the example above is that of S, and does not intervene between any two constituents.

Finally, let us consider a sentence in which the verb is followed by two objects and an adverb. Assuming a flat grammatical structure for VP, the bracketing of such a construction would be as follows:

(30) *Verb-Object-Object-Adverb*

$$[\text{V} [\text{N}]_{\text{NP}} [\text{N}]_{\text{NP}} [\text{ADV}]]_{\text{VP}}$$

Here, there are two right-edge X^{max} boundaries, namely the $]_{\text{NP}}$'s following each of the two objects. These, however, are not right-edge X^{max-b} boundaries, as neither object NP is modified. Thus, given the phonological phrase construction rule in (21), we would expect High Deletion to apply twice in the VP, once between the two objects and once between the second object and the following adverb. That this is the case is illustrated in the example below:

(31) a. Nejákúha   omukózi   ekitébe   mpóra
          'he will give' 'worker'   'chair'   'slowly'
          (isolation)   (isolation)   (isolation)

      b. [Nejákuh'   ómukoz'   ékitebe   mpóra]$_\phi$
          He-will-give   worker   chair   slowly
          'He will give the worker a chair slowly'

In (31b) the High tone on the adverb causes the deletion of the High tone on the first syllable of the root of *ekitébe*, while the High tone on the preprefix of the second object causes the deletion of the High tone in the root of the first object.

I have shown that phonological phrase boundaries in Kinyambo are not right-edge X^{max} brackets. I also pointed out that the data thus far presented are consistent with the claim that phonological phrase boundaries in Kinyambo are right-edge X^{max-b} brackets. However, based upon the examples given above it could plausibly be argued that High Deletion simply applies anywhere in the sentence so long as its phonological structural description is met. I will now show that such is not the case by providing examples of sentence-internal phonological phrase boundaries. In each case it will be shown that reference to X^{max-b} correctly predicts the location of the phonological phrase boundary.

Let us first consider the case where the subject noun is modified by an adjective. We will contrast this to the examples in (23)-(25), above where the noun was unmodified. The two structures are presented below.

(32) a. *Subject–Verb*

$$[\; [\; N \;]_{NP} \; [\; V \;]_{VP} \;]_S$$

b. *[Subject–Adj]–Verb*

$$[\; [\; N \; [\; A \;]_{AP} \;]_{NP} \; [\; V \;]_{VP} \;]_S$$

As we saw earlier, (32a) contains no internal right-edge X^{max-b} bracket, and hence High Deletion is free to apply within the entire sentence. In (32b) however, there is a right-edge X^{max-b} bracket in the sentence, namely $]_{NP}$. Whereas the right-edge NP bracket is a maximal projection in both cases, it is branching only in (32b). We thus predict that there will be a phonological phrase boundary between the adjective and the following verb, and hence High Deletion should not affect a High tone in the adjective. The relevant example is shown in (33):

(33) a. [abakozi   bákajúna]$_\phi$
     workers   they-helped
     'The workers helped.'

   b. [Abakozi   bakúru]$_\phi$ [bákajúna]$_\phi$
     workers   mature   they-helped
     'The mature workers helped.'

In (33a) we see that the High tone on the first syllable of the verb causes the deletion of the underlying High tone seen in the isolation form of *abakózi* 'workers.' In (33b) however, the High tone of *bakúru* 'mature' fails to delete in the presence of the High tone in the verb. Because the right-edge X^{max-b} bracket following the adjective constitutes a phonological phrase boundary, High Deletion is blocked from applying across it. Of course, the rule does apply in (33b) between the subject noun and the modifying adjective, which form a single phonological phrase.

It is possible to provide a minimal pair which contrasts with (33b), above. Let us consider a case in which there is a null subject followed by an adjective. In such cases, High Deletion may apply as shown below.

(34) [bakuru   bákajúna]$_\phi$ (cf. *bakúrú* 'mature')
    mature   they-helped
    'The mature ones helped.'

The example above, however, raises the interesting and controversial question regarding the role that empty categories play in phrasal phonology. If, for example, the structure of the subject NP in (34) is [*e* AP]$_{NP}$, then technically High Deletion should not apply, as a branching maximal projection (namely $]_{NP}$) intervenes between the adjective and the finite verbal form. The phonological phrase construction rule in Kinyambo, however, appears to ignore the existence of the empty category.

There are several possible solutions to this dilemma. One alternative is to assume that at the time of phonological phrase construction, the structure of the subject NP in (34) is either $[\text{ N }]_{NP}$ (i.e. a deadjectival noun) or simply $[\text{ A }]_{AP}$. Another alternative is to stipulate in the phonological phrase construction rule that boundaries are right-edge brackets of branching maximal projections containing at least two non-null words or, alternatively, à branching prosodic structure.[9] I leave the matter open for future research.

Next let us consider a case in which the first of two objects is modified by a prepositional phrase. We will contrast this construction with the double object construction presented earlier, in which neither is modified. The two structures are given in (34a-b):

(35) a. *Verb–Object–Object*

$$[V [N]_{NP} [N]_{NP}]_{VP}$$

b. *Verb–[Object PP]–Object*

$$[V [N [P [N]_{NP}]_{PP}]_{NP} [N]_{NP}]_{VP}$$

Example (35a) contains no sentence-internal right-edge X^{max-b} brackets, and High Deletion is predicted to apply throughout. In (35b), however, we find two such brackets: the right edge of the PP, and the right edge of the NP which contains it, both separate the object of the preposition from the second object of the verb. We thus predict a phonological phrase boundary there, blocking the application of High Deletion between the two string-adjacent nouns. This is illustrated in the example below.:

(36) a. [Nejákworech'   ábakoz'   émbwa]$_\phi$
       He-will-show   workers   dog
       'He will show the workers the dog.'

   cf. abakózi 'workers (isolation)'

   b. [Nejákworech'   ómukama   w'ábakózi]$_\phi$ [émbwa]$_\phi$
       He-will-show   chief   of workers   dog
       'He will show the chief of the workers the dog.'

Whereas in (36a) the High tone on *émbwa* 'dog' causes the the underlying High tone of abakózi 'workers (isolation)' to delete, the same word *émbwa* 'dog' in (36b) fails to affect the High tone in the preceding noun.

---

[9]This last possibility, of requiring both a branching syntactic and a branching prosodic structure, was suggested to me by Sharon Inkelas.

Note that in (36b) the phrase ... *ómukama w'ábakózi*..., termed an
'associative' construction by Bantuists, might be interpreted either as
N-PP (as I have given it) or as N-NP. However, both approaches are
consistent with my thesis. If the phrase were interpreted as N-NP, then
the following structure would result:

(37) [V [N [x-N]$_{NP}$]$_{NP}$ [N]$_{NP}$]$_{VP}$

    (where x represents the associative clitic)

Even in (37), a right-edge branching NP bracket still introduces a phonological phrase boundary between the final two nouns.

    Examples (33) and (36) show that High Deletion is bounded not simply
by the sentence or utterance, but rather by a prosodic phrase larger than
the word, but smaller than the utterance. This is consistent with my
claim that High Deletion is bounded by the phonological phrase, whose
boundaries coincide with right-edge X^{max-b} brackets.:

    To illustrate this point most clearly, let us finally consider a syntactic
minimal pair in which the string of lexical items is identical, but in which
the syntactic bracketing differs.

(38) Mbonir' [émbw' [[érire   muno   [Kénya]$_{NP}$]$_{VP}$]$_S$]$_{NP}$
      [Mbonir' émbw'   érire   muno   Kénya]$_\phi$
      I-saw   dog   REL-ate   well   Kenya
      'I saw the dog who, while in Kenya, ate well.'

(39) Mbonir' [émbw' [[érire   múno]$_{VP}$]$_S$]$_{NP}$ Kénya
      [Mbonir' émbw'   érire   múno]$_\phi$ [Kénya]$_\phi$
      I-saw   dog   REL-ate   well   Kenya
      'I saw, in Kenya, the dog who ate well.'

    The only difference between (38) and (39) lies in the element which the
locative adverb *Kénya* modifies. In (38) *Kénya* modifies the verb *okura*
'eat' of the relative clause modifying *émbwa* 'dog.' By contrast, in (39)
Kénya modifies the verb *okubona* 'see' of the matrix clause. In the second
case, there will be a right-edge X^{max-b} bracket between the adverb *múno*
'well' and *Kénya*, while in the second there is not (assuming, as we did in
(30), a flat structure for the VP). The resulting difference in phonological
phrasing explains why the High tone of *múno* 'well (isolation)' is deleted
in (38), but not in (39).:

4 Conclusion

In this analysis I have argued that phonological phrase boundaries in
Kinyambo are best described as the right edges of branching maximal
projections. The Kinyambo facts thus support the claim made by Cowper and Rice 1987 that the parameters of a cross-linguistic phonological
phrase construction rule must include branchingness. In the end-based

approach of Selkirk 1986, this means adding $X^{\text{max}-b}$ to the possible types of constituents whose right or left end constitutes a phonological phrase boundary. If this is done, the typology in (6) thus expands to include two new groups, both of which are now represented in the literature. This is summarized in (40):

(40) Extension of Selkirk Typology

      e. Left-edge $X^{\text{max}-b}$
         Consonant Mutation in Mende

      f. Right-edge $X^{\text{max}-b}$
         High Tone Deletion in Kinyambo

The Kinyambo and Mende facts do not fit as easily into the Nespor and Vogel typology outlined in (4). Kinyambo, for example, would nearly fit into category (4c), if the VP could be thought of as the complement of the subject (cf. (7a), (23)-(25)). But if phrases are always built around heads, as Nespor and Vogel suggest, then phonological phrases like those in (7a) and (23)-(25) will be unaccounted for. Additionally, the Nespor and Vogel parameters seem to suggest that at most one complement will be combined with a head to form a phonological phrase. Even if this combination is permitted to be recursive (as is needed to account for certain phrasing facts in Chaga (McHugh (this volume))) such a system would not account for the inclusion of two (or more) objects of a single verb into the same phonological phrase, which (27)-(29) show to be necessary in Kinyambo.

    In summary, it seems that we are still in search of a parameterized cross-linguistic phonological phrase construction rule with descriptive adequacy (let alone explanatory adequacy). The Nespor and Vogel parameters account for optional inclusion of complements into phonological phrases, needed for the phenomena in (4b), something that Selkirk's parameters do not handle directly. On the other hand, I have shown above that the Kinyambo facts fall neatly into the expanded Selkirk typology, but do not find a place as readily in the Nespor and Vogel typology. The thesis of this paper is simply that, to account for the Kinyambo (and Mende) facts, any cross-linguistic phonological phrase construction rule will have to be able to appeal to the property of branchingness.

2

What Must Phonology Know About Syntax?

MATTHEW Y. CHEN

AS WE THINK ABOUT the phonology-syntax connection, two basic questions recur. The first concerns the direct accessibility of syntactic information to phonological processes. The second addresses what grammatical properties are relevant to phonology. Given that grammatical information is conventionally coded in terms of labelled trees, there are two main aspects of syntactic representations: node labels and tree geometry. Node labels specify both categorial distinction (N, V, A, etc.) and categorial rank (X^0, X', X^{max}), while tree geometry encodes the I(mmediate) C(onstituent) hierarchy and, indirectly, such grammatical relations as head-complement, etc. The end-based (Selkirk 1986, Chen 1987c) and relation-based (Nespor and Vogel 1986, Hayes 1989) approaches to prosodic structure exploit these two aspects of grammatical structure, respectively.

I will answer the first of the two recurrent questions in the affirmative, bringing forth some supporting evidence in section 1. With respect to the second question, I will argue in section 2 that both end-based and relation-based approaches are needed. Where functional relation (e.g., subject-predicate, head-complement) and strictly tree-based structural configuration (e.g., constituency, c-command, adjacency) make different predictions, it is the former and not the latter that prevail, as shown in section 3. In section 4 I argue that phonology systematically discriminates between the grammatical relations of argument and adjunct. Concluding remarks follow in section 5.

1   Accessibility of Grammatical Information

Prosodic phonologists have made a persuasive case for a highly constrained model of the syntax-phonology interface, according to which
grammatical structure interacts with phonology only to the extent that it
determines the prosodic domains delimiting the operation of phonological
rules (Selkirk 1984, Hayes 1989, Hyman 1987). It should be noted that
even advocates of a 'syntax-blind' phonology, to borrow a felicitous term
from Selkirk, entertain the possibility of a class of phonological processes
that must make direct reference to one or another aspects of syntactic
structure (Selkirk's 'phonosyntactic rules,' roughly equivalent to the P1
or external sandhi rules of Kaisse 1985). In recent work Odden 1987 has
made the strongest case for a direct link between syntax and phonology. His argument rests on two observations: first, that the complexity
of syntactic conditions associated with sandhi contexts makes it difficult
to reduce them to any recognized prosodic entity; and second, that any
attempt to restate the syntactic conditions in prosodic terms would create
recursive prosodic constituents—in violation of the Strict Layer Hypothesis (Selkirk 1984).[1] Here I will document a case which seems to suggest
a direct link between syntax and phonology. The argument turns on the
fact that even after establishing a prosodic domain, it is necessary to
maintain intact some grammatical information in order for phonological
processes to operate properly.

The Mandarin dialect of Pingyao is spoken in the historic heartland
of North Central China, about 75 km south of Taiyuan, the capital city
of what is now the Shanxi province.[2] It has a relatively impoverished
tonal inventory, but a highly complex tone sandhi (henceforth TS) pattern. Its tonemic system comprises three citation or base tones (BT): LM,
HM, and MH (Low-Rising, High-Falling and High-Rising).[3] In connected

---

[1]Intersecting prosodic domains, or 'ambiprosodicity,' have also been documented in
Bamileke (Hyman 1985), Luganda (Hyman et al. 1987) and Xiamen (Chen 1987c). In
Chen 1987a I argued for the need to allow phonology to have direct access to syntax,
using data from Chongming tone sandhi. Since then I have discovered serious flaws
in the corpus of data due mainly to inconsistencies in the phonetic transcriptions. A
radical reanalysis of the Chongming data has been undertaken by H-M. Zhang 1988.

[2]The analysis presented here is based on published reports (Hou 1980-1982), supple-
mented by my own field notes taken during the winter of 1986-1987. Not surprisingly,
there are some differences between Hou's description and the pronunciation of my informant (Hu Youren, male, age 43); but nothing of theoretical significance hinges on
such subdialectal/idiolectal variations.

[3]Pingyao contrasts *checked* (ending in a glottal stop) vs. *free* syllables (all others,
including syllables closed off by a nasal). A syllable carrying the same tone (e.g., LM
or HM) may display different sandhi behavior depending on whether it is checked or
free. More importantly, in some instances the tone that appears in citation forms (i.e.,
separate from context) need not coincide with the underlying tone. Thus, the citation
tone LM comes from two historical sources (*ying-ping* vs. *yang-ping* in traditional
nomenclature), and gives rise to two different sandhi forms in accordance with their
historical tonal categories. I will gloss over these details, and refer the interested reader
to Hou 1980-1982 and Shen 1988.

speech what tonal sequences actually emerge depends both on the combination of the BTs as well as the grammatical relations holding between the tone-carrying units (morphemes, words, phrases) across the sandhi site. To simplify the picture somewhat, there are two classes of grammatical relations, type A and B. Subject-predicate and verb-object constructions belong to type A; all others fall under B. This syntax-based dichotomy in tone sandhi patterns is illustrated in (1). Notice, for instance, that the same LM-MH sequence emerges as ML-MH in a verb-object constructions like 'till soil,' but comes out as LM-LM in a lexical compound like 'cowpea.'[4]

(1)

Base tones		Sandhi tones for type A			Sandhi tones for type B		
LM	LM	LM	LM	jiao hua 'water flower'	ML	MH	cong hua 'onion flower'
MH	LM	LM	LM	mai hua 'sell flower'	MH	HM	gui hua 'cassia flower'
LM	MH	ML	MH	geng di 'till soil'	LM	LM	jiang dou 'cowpea'

The matter becomes even more intriguing when we consider the effect of TS on more complex structures exhibiting hierarchical structure and allowing for possible interaction between TSA and TSB (TS type A and B).[5] The null hypothesis is for TS rules to apply cyclically, with the grammatical relation holding at each cycle determining which of the two rules, TSA or TSB, is applicable at that point. The null hypothesis makes the correct prediction in cases like the following:

(2) a. 'to divide things'

divide	things			
[fen	[dong-xi]$_B$]$_A$			
LM	LM	LM		BT
	ML	MH		TSB
	N/A			TSA
LM	ML	MH		

---

[4]In citing most Chinese examples I will use the official *pinyin* transcription regardless of the actual phonetic values in the dialects in question. Dialectal forms are used only where no pinyin equivalent is available.

[5]TSA and TSB actually comprise two *sets* of rules, which combine to produce the outputs exemplified in (1). These rules were stated in the form of tables of correspondences between input and output tones by Hou 1980-1982, and reformulated in the more conventional format by Shen 1988. I will not go into the details of the rules, but ask the readers to assume that the appropriate rule(s) have been applied in the derivations to be given below.

b.   'toilet kit'

	comb	head	box	
	[[shu	tou]$_A$	he]$_B$	
	LM	LM	HM	BT
	N/A			TSA
		MH		TSB
	LM	MH	HM	

In the derivations above, the labelled brackets [...]$_A$ and [...]$_B$ stand for grammatical units of type A or B, which select for TSA and TSB respectively on each successive cycle. But the picture is considerably more complicated. A simple cyclic mode of application fails in other cases like (3):[6]

(3) a.   'the journey is long'

	journey	long	
	[[lu-dao]$_B$	chang]$_A$	
	MH MH	LM	BT
	HM		TSB
	N/A		TSA
	MH HM	LM	*

	LM		TSA
LM			TSA!
LM LM	LM		ok

b.   'very lucrative'

	very	make	money	
	[hen	[zhuan	qian]$_A$]$_B$	
	HM	MH	LM	BT
		LM		TSA
	N/A			
	HM	LM	LM	*

	N/A			TSB
		HM		TSB!
	HM	MH	HM	ok

The expected output of cyclic TS rules for (3a,b) is *MH-HM-LM and *HM-LM-LM respectively, both ungrammatical, as indicated on the last line of derivation above the double dashed lines. The correct derivation of (3a) requires that TS rules apply from right to left (R/L) and that it is TSA rather than TSB that applies to the inner-bracketed compound

---

[6]The exclamation mark (!) highlights unexpected rule selection (e.g., TSA instead of TSB, despite the grammatical relation type B holding between the two leftmost syllables).

lu-dao 'journey.' (3b) presents an exact mirror image: TS applies from left to right, and TSB rather than TSA applies to the inner bracket [...]$_A$. Without going into the details, and without citing further specific examples, the overall pattern is laid out in (4).

(4)

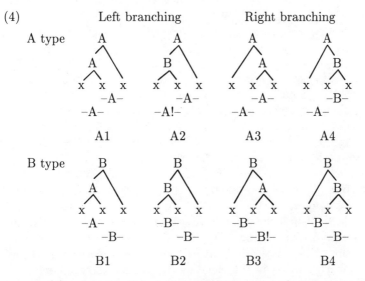

Diagram (4) exhausts all logical possibilities: right/left-branching, A/B-type of grammatical constructions on the inner/outer cycle. The trees represent the IC hierarchy in the usual manner, with node labels A/B indicating the construction types, and x's standing for the tone-carrying syllables. –A– and –B– indicate which TS rule applies to which pair of adjacent syllables. Thus case A2, instantiated by example (3a), signifies a right to left iterative application of TSA. The picture in (4) displays at once a striking symmetry and a curious paradox. The most promising and insightful analysis of this puzzling problem is one proposed by Shen 1988, for which I will attempt an exposition below, with certain paraphrases and modifications where necessary.[7] Central to her analysis is the idea of 'directional cyclicity,' a hybrid between cyclic and directional/iterative modes of rule application. I have revised and repackaged her complex idea into the following general principles (P1-5):

(5) Principles of Directional Cyclicity

> P1 TS applies to 2-3 syllable feet (see Foot-formation, section 3)
>
> P2 Directionality
> TS scans A constructions right to left
> TS scans B constructions left to right

---

[7]Hou's (1980-1982) account of 2- and 3-syllabic TS in Pingyao is purely taxonomic, consisting of tables of correspondences between base tones and sandhi tones, cross-classified by syntactic types. The systematic relationship between 2- and 3-syllabic TS processes had eluded all previous analyses.

P3 IC constraint
TS applies between ICs

P4 Rule selection
TSA/B apply to A/B constructions respectively

P5 Bracket erasure
When TS fails on account of P3, try the next larger construction (erasing inner structures in the process)

Evidence suggests that TS is limited to disyllabic and trisyllabic *feet*, with longer strings normally breaking up into prosodic units of 2-3 syllables (P1). This appears to be a typical pattern with all Mandarin dialects of Chinese (see Shih 1985, Hung 1987, and Chen 1986a,b). P2 captures the striking observation first made by Shen 1988, that TSA and TSB apply in opposite directions: R/L for TSA, and L/R for TSB. Her generalization is borne out quite clearly in (3). But unlike simple directional iterative rules, TS imposes an additional requirement that the syntactic structure be *congruent*, that is, branching in the same direction of rule application: right-branching for R/L scanning TSA, and left-branching for L/R scanning TSB, so that the TS applies only to ICs. This is stated as P3. In this sense, cases A3-4 and B1-2 have *congruent* tree structures, and TSA or TSB apply in the usual cyclic fashion, as stipulated by P4 and instantiated by derivations (2a,b). Where syntactic structures are *non-congruent*, as in the cases of A1-2 and B3-4, directional TS fails, and P5 comes into play. Bracket erasure turns a binary-hierarchical structure like A2 [[x x]$_B$ x]$_A$ into [x x x]$_A$. This accounts for the otherwise surprising observation that it is TSA and not TSB that applies between the first two syllables, since at the point TS applies, the inner brackets [x x]$_B$ have been removed and rendered invisible. The steps of the derivation of A2 (=(3a)) are detailed below in (6). The exact mirror image (3b) can be derived in like manner.

(6) 'the journey is long' (= (3a))

journey long
[[lu-dao]$_B$ chang]$_A$ foot = domain of TS (P1)
←————————   TSA scans right to left (P2)
        na   TSA blocked by IC Constraint (P3)

[lu-dao   chang]$_A$ bracket erasure (P5)
←————————   TSA scans right to left (P2)
MHMH   LM   BT
    LM   TSA (P4)
LM   TSA! (P4)
LMLM   LM   ok

Assuming that the analysis presented so far is correct, let us see what Pingyao TS has to say about the syntax-phonology interface. One might conclude that there are two types of TS: lexical (TSB) and postlexical (TSA), the former applying to lexical compounds and the latter to phrasal constructions. While not *a priori* implausible, this solution runs into a number of problems. On the one hand, TSB applies to such phrase-like strings as *lan se* 'blue color' and *fu qilai* '(to) pick up,' which are both semantically transparent and syntactically 'free' in the sense of permitting separation and various kinds of insertions (cf. *fu ta bu qilai* 'pick-him-not-up,' that is, 'cannot pick him up'). Conversely, constructions that exhibit semantic and syntactic properties of genuine lexical compounds undergo TSA rather than TSB. For instance, *tou teng* (lit. 'head aches') has the idiomatic meaning of 'troublesome' and, in contrast to genuine subject-predicate constructions like *shou teng* 'hand aches,' can take adverbial intensifiers like *hen* 'very' as in *hen tou teng* 'very troublesome' (compare: **hen shou teng* for 'the hand aches very much'). In addition, assigning TSB and TSA to the lexical and postlexical components entails the kind of interdigitation of lexical and postlexical rules (as required, for instance, in the derivations of (2a,b)) that are incompatible with the model of lexical phonology (Kiparsky 1982b, Mohanan 1982).

Noting the interdigitation of TSA and TSB, one might propose to put both types of TS processes in the lexical component to take advantage of the looping effect allowed for different phonological processes (TSA, TSB) operating in tandem with different morphological processes (in this case, A vs. B-type constructions).[8] Regardless of the desirability of the 'loop' in a stratum-ordered lexical phonology (see Mohanan 1986), this alternative is clearly not viable. The prediction is for TSA to apply in the wake of A-type compounding, and TSB to be triggered by a B-type word formation process. The net effect is that of the garden variety of cyclical application, with node labels selecting the appropriate phonological rules on a particular cycle, analogous to the interplay between the compound and nuclear stress rules in English (see SPE:21). This mode of application of TS rules has been shown to generate the wrong outputs in (3a,b).

The only remaining alternative is to put both TSA and TSB in the postlexical component. This does not necessarily mean that one must accept the inevitable conclusion that there exist syntax-sensitive postlexical rules (i.e., Selkirk's phonosyntactic rules or Kaisse's P-1 level external sandhi rules)—so long as there remains the option of redefining A- and B-types of syntactic constructions in prosodic terms. Unfortunately, this option is precluded in the current conception of prosodic structures. It becomes immediately obvious that one cannot merely set up intermediate entities, say phonological phrases and phonological words, corresponding to the A/B-bracketed constructions respectively, and restrict the scope of TSA and TSB accordingly, without creating recursive proso-

---

[8]This was suggested by B. Hayes at the Phonology-Syntax Connection workshop.

dic domains—in violation of the Strict Layer Hypothesis—as schematized below:

(7)   ...p-phrase

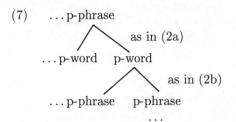

as in (2a)

...p-word   p-word

as in (2b)

...p-phrase   p-phrase

...

Pingyao TS, therefore, strongly suggests that phonology must directly reference syntax. What is even more striking is that Pingyao TS requires *both prosodic and syntactic* information. As noted before, the mode of operation of TS (cyclic, iterative, L/R or R/L) is determined by A- vs. B-type of constructions. But such notions as the cycle and directionality are relevant only to trisyllabic or longer strings. Thus the foot constitutes the domain within which TS operates (= P1). However, having established the prosodic foot, one cannot simply discard all syntactic information. The prosodic foot must retain two types of syntactic information: (a) tree geometry or IC hierarchy—to ascertain whether two adjacent tone-carrying units satisfy the IC constraint (= P3); and (b) grammatical relation (e.g., subject-predicate, verb-object, modifier-head)—to determine the direction of scanning (= P2) and to select the appropriate rule type (= P4).

In brief, Pingyao TS suggests an intricate syntax-phonology interface: prosodic structure (the foot) delimits the scope of TS operation, while syntactic properties within the prosodic domain determine the two aspects of the actual implementation of phonological processes, namely 'traffic control' (directionality of scanning) and 'menu selection' (TSA vs. TSB).

2   End-based Prosodic Domains

We turn now to the second major issue relating to the phonology-syntax connection. Regardless of the position one takes with respect to the direct accessibility of syntax to phonology, there remains the question of what kinds of grammatical information are relevant to phonology, either in directly conditioning the phonological rule itself, or for the purpose of creating the intermediate prosodic entities that in turn define the scope of phonological operations. As we noted in the introduction, one aspect of syntactic representation consists of node labels, which specify categorial distinction as well as categorial rank. It has been observed that phonology generally disregards categorial distinctions in syntax[9] but heeds categorial rank, systematically exploiting the X^0 (word) vs. X^{max} (phrase)

---

[9]See Kaisse and Zwicky 1987 for the most recent expression of this near-consensus. It is well known, of course, that English stress rules treat nouns differently from verbs

dichotomy for the purpose of delimiting phonological domains. Selkirk 1986 proposes a particularly elegant theory which promises to provide a principled basis for an array of prosodic entities that have proliferated in recent literature.[10] According to Selkirk 1986:389, a prosodic unit can be defined solely by reference to two parameters: rank and directionality:

(8) End parameter settings

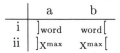

Tone sandhi phenomena in Chinese offer strong evidence corroborating the core idea underlying (8). Xiamen and Wenzhou exemplify the two diametrically opposite types, (i-b) and (ii-a). A tone group (TG) in Xiamen is derived quite straightforwardly by demarcating the right end of X^{max}, as illustrated in (9):[11]

(9) 'The old lady doesn't believe that parrots can talk'
　　old　　lady　　　　Neg　　believe　　　parrot　　can　　talk
　　lao　　tsim-a-po　 # m　 siong-sin　 ying-ko　 # e　 kong-we
　　　　　　　　　]NP　　　　　　　　　　　　　]NP　　　　　]VP,S'
　　(　　　　　　)　(　　　　　　　　　　　　)　(　　　　　)

TS is limited to the string bounded by parentheses (. . .), and its application is blocked across TG boundaries (#).[12] The southern Wu dialect of Wenzhou, on the other hand, derives its prosodic domain (roughly equivalent to the clitic group) by marking the beginning of a content word (X^0). This has the effect of cliticizing all nonlexical items or function words uniquely in the leftward direction, regardless of the constituency relations. Where there is no content word on the left to cliticize to, function words adjoin to the host on the right by default—as in (10c). The asymmetry between syntactic and prosodic units is apparent in the following examples. Square brackets indicate syntactic constituency, while a slash separates clitic groups.[13]

---

and adjectives. But this apparent category-sensitive stress assignment is reinterpreted as a matter of lexical representations, which redundantly mark certain segments or syllables as extrametrical.

　　Mandarin treats reduplicated verbs (with a strong-weak pattern, e.g., *kan-kan* 'look-look, take a look') quite differently from reduplicated adjectives/adverbs (which carry a characteristic weak-strong rhythm, e.g., *man-man*, 'slow-slow, slowly'). Although the details remain unclear, work in progress on such dialects as Pingyao (N. Mandarin) and Chongming (N. Wu) suggests that tone sandhi rules discriminate between reduplicated nouns, verbs, adjectives, measure words, etc., (see Chen 1987a, Zhang 1988).

[10] As of last count, there are seven: syllable, foot, phonological word, clitic group, phonological phrase, intonational phrase and utterance (see Nespor and Vogel 1986, Hayes 1989).

[11] In all subsequent examples, the symbols =, # stand for the application and blockage of phonological process under discussion (in this case, tone sandhi).

[12] For details, see Chen 1987c.

[13] Incidentally, Wenzhou constitutes a counterexample to the principle of 'shared category membership' proposed by Hayes 1989 for determining the directionality of

(10) a. 'one cannot use up the money'

money   use   not   finish

chaopiao   [yong   [bu   wan]]

xx   / x   − / x

b. 'things are cheaper than in the U.S.'

things   than   U.S.   cheap

dongxi   [[bi   meiguo] pianyi]

xx   −   / xx /   xx

c. 'pull the tricycle to the gate'

OM   tricycle   pull   to   gate

ba   sanlunche [la   [dao   menkou]]

−   xxx   /   x   − /   xx

Wenzhou has a tonal neutralization rule which deletes the underlying tone of function words such as *bu* 'not,' *bi* 'than,' the object marker *ba*, and *dao* 'to.' Tone loss sets the well-formedness conditions in motion: the atonal syllables (symbolized as '−') assimilate to the closest tonic, i.e., tone-carrying syllable to the left (symbolized as 'x'). Pretonic syllables, on the other hand, are realized uniformly with a Low(-Falling) tone.[14]

There is no doubt that the end-based theory captures exactly the underlying principle that is operative in languages like Xiamen and Wenzhou. However, the end-based theory is not without problems. Consider the following example from French. '=' indicates a site for the rule of Liaison, while '#' symbolizes the blockage of the same process in conversational style:[15]

(11) 'a dark little place'

un petit = endroit # obscur

    ]$_{A,AP}$]$_N$]$_{A,AP,NP}$

(   ) (   ) (   )   X^0

(   ) (   ) (   )   X^{max}

If the end parameter is set to X^0, the prediction is that no liaison applies at all (beyond the clitic group). Under the assumption that all complements are X^{max}, *petit* constitutes an AP; this wrongly predicts that liaison applies across *endroit* and *obscur*, but not across *petit* and *endroit*—exactly the opposite of what actually takes place. Suppose we ignore for the moment the possibility of internal structure (albeit of limited scope) within the prehead modifier (e.g., *un [[tout petit] endroit] ...*) and analyze *petit* not as a fully fledged phrasal construction, but a bare A

---

clitic adjunction to a neighboring host. Wenzhou function words behave like *directional clitics* (see Nespor and Vogel 1986).

[14]The Wenzhou data are based on work in progress (see also Chen 1988). My principal source for the Wenzhou data is Pan Wuyun.

[15]I take it for granted that the languages under discussion in this section set the end parameter to the right edge.

(a sort of *XP-redux*). The expected end-based prosodic structure would be as follows:

(12)   un petit = endroit # obscur

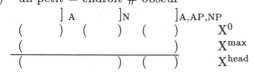

X^0 and X^{max} settings would still derive incorrect liaison domains. It is, therefore, necessary to introduce the notion of X^{head}. It should be obvious that the notion of the 'head' is a relational one, and not, properly speaking, a matter of categorial rank as reflected in X-bar notation. The relationship between X^0 and X^{head} is analogous to that between NP and subject. An X^0 (in this instance, both *petit* and *endroit*) may or may not be the head, just as an NP may or may not be the subject, depending on its function within a phrase or clause. To include X^{head} among X^0, X'...X^{max} is to mix two different kinds of entities. The notion of X^{head} has no place in a strictly end-based theory. One way to infer the notion of the head directly from the X-bar notation is to assume that "The head of a phrase is the only daughter of the phrase that is not a maximal projection" (Di Sciullo and Williams 1987:23). This means that the prehead adjunct *petit* must be an X^{max}, leaving *endroit* as the only non-maximal projection within the NP. Since analyzing *petit* as an AP leads to undesirable consequences in terms of derived prosodic structures, the only remaining alternative is to construe *petit-endroit* as some sort of compound, i.e., a single lexical unit, as suggested by Selkirk 1986:

(13)   un petit=endroit # obscur

$\quad\quad\quad\quad\quad]_N \quad\quad\quad]_{A,AP,NP}$

$\quad\quad (\quad\quad\quad\quad) \quad (\quad\quad) \quad\quad\quad X^0 = X^{head}$

However, this analysis stretches the notion of the compound to a point where a nominal compound is, by definition, synonymous with any modifier + noun construction. More importantly, if (14) is construed as containing a nominal compound *petits-endroits*, i.e., a unitary syntactic word, its word-internal inflectional morphology would be totally unexpected, since inflection is generally regarded as a syntactic relation holding between words.

(14)   des petits=endroits # obscurs

$\quad\quad\quad\quad\quad\quad]_N \quad\quad\quad\quad]_{A,AP,NP}$

Even if we can somehow get around the difficulties associated with the notion of X^{head} (within the X-bar theory) and with prehead modifier structures, it is possible to find other critical contexts in which the end-based (à la Selkirk 1986, Chen 1987c) and relation-based (à la Nespor and Vogel 1986, Hayes 1989) approaches to prosodic phonology make testably

different predictions. Consider the following case (15), instantiated by
the Italian example in (16). H,C stand for head and complement (i.e.,
argument or adjunct) respectively:

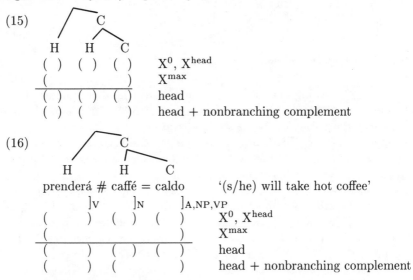

(15)

    H   H   C
    ( )   ( )   ( ) X^0, X^{head}
    (   ) X^{max}
    ───────────────
    ( )   ( )   ( )   head
    ( )   (   )   head + nonbranching complement

(16)

    H   H   C
    prenderá # caffé = caldo   '(s/he) will take hot coffee'
          ]v   ]n   ]A,NP,VP
    (   )   (   )   (   ) X^0, X^{head}
    (   ) X^{max}
    ──────────────────────
    (   )   (   )   (   )   head
    (   )   (   )   head + nonbranching complement

The end-based theory predicts that the phrasal rule of word-initial consonant gemination (*raddoppiamento sintattico*, or RS) either applies everywhere (within a prosodic unit defined by the right edge of X^{max}) or
nowhere (within a unit defined by X^0 or X^{head}). One cannot freely adjoin
short (nonbranching), X^0-defined prosodic units into larger ones, without making reference to the relational concept of head-complement, for
otherwise there is no way to prevent (17) or (18):

(17)   prenderá # caffé = caldo
        (   )   (   )   (   ) X^0, X^{head}
      *(   )   (   )   adjoin X^0-based prosodic units

(18)   (tre) cani = blu # misteriosi   '(three) mysterious blue dogs'
            ]N   ]A,AP   ]A,AP,NP
        ( )   ( )   (   ) X^0, X^{head}
      *( )   (   )

3   Relation-based Prosodic Mapping

What seems clear is that while the end-based theory nicely captures certain mapping relations between syntactic and prosodic structures, it fails
to account for some other facts in natural languages. The following Mandarin example, taken from Hung 1987:182, shows the four ways of cutting
up the sentence into prosodic units in accordance with the four logically
possible end parameter settings.

(19)   'the dog bit the pony'
                  dog   bite   small horse
                [[gou]   [yao   [xiao-ma]]]
                   3   3   3   3   BT
     a.   *   (3   # (3   # (2   3 $_{\text{X}^{\max}}$[
     b.   *   3) #   2   2   3)   ]$_{\text{X}^{\max}}$
     c.   *   (3   # (3   # (2   3   Word[
     d.   *   3) #   3) #   2   3   )   ]Word
     e.   ok   (2   3)   (2   3)

Each of the syllables of (19) carries an underlying Low tone 3. A tone sandhi rule turns tone 3 into a High-Rising tone 2 when followed by another tone 3. Assuming that this TS process is domain-bounded, TS should be blocked at the junctures marked by #. This prediction is wrong in each case (hence marked *). The correct reading presupposes a division of (19) into a prosodic representation consisting of two feet, as shown in (19e). This division is not predicted by any of the logical possibilities of the end-setting parameters. Example (19e) is derivable in accordance with the following relation-based principles:[16]

(20) Foot Formation Rule (FFR)

    a. Immediate Constituency (IC): Link immediate constituents into disyllabic feet.

    b. Duple Meter (DM): Scanning from left to right, string together unpaired syllables into binary feet, unless they branch to the opposite direction.

    c. Triple Meter (TM): Join any leftover monosyllable to a neighboring binary foot to form a 'superfoot' according to the direction of syntactic branching.

In accordance with FFR, we derive the two-foot prosodic structure:

(21) 'the dog bit the pony'

     dog   bite   small horse
     [[gou] [yao   [xiao-ma]]]
      3   3   (3   3)   by FFR-a
     (3   3)   (3   3)   by FFR-b
     (2   3)   (2   3)   by TS within feet
     (2   2)   (2   3)   by TS across feet (optional)

It should be obvious that FFR treats S-structures as unlabelled trees: it focuses on bracketing/branching alone, and is indifferent to node labels. End-setting, therefore, has no meaning in such a system.

---

[16]FFR first arose out of a need to relate the syntactic structure of a line to the metrical template of classical Chinese poetry (see M. Chen 1984). It has proven to be a fundamental principle underlying the prosodic organization underlying phrasal tonology, as richly documented in Shih's 1985 dissertation.

As Shih 1985 has amply demonstrated, FFR works reasonably well for an impressive array of bewildering facts that had previously resisted analysis. Nevertheless, such a strictly tree-based analysis still leaves a large number of unresolved problems. Consider the following contrasts, some of which were first brought to light by Hung 1987:

(22) a. 'a small umbrella'

	small	rain umbrella	
	xiao	[yu-san]	
	3	3 3	BT
	(3	(2 3))	unmarked
	(2	2 3)	marked (allegro only)

b. 'raise a puppy'

	raise	small	dog	
	yang	[xiao	gou]	
	3	3	3	BT
	(3	(2	3))	unmarked
	(2	2	3)	marked (allegro only)

(23) a. 'the dog bit me'

	dog	bite	I	
	gou	[yao	wo]	
	3	3	3	BT
	(3	(2	3))	unmarked
	((2	2)	3)	unmarked

b. 'always eager to go'

	always	want	go	
	zong	[xiang	zou]	
	3	3	3	BT
	(3	(2	3))	unmarked
	((2	2)	3)	unmarked

Despite the fact that all the examples in (22,23) exhibit identically right-branching trees, (22) behaves quite differently from (23) in terms of TS: (22a,b) clearly favor a [3-2-3] reading, while (23a,b) seem neutral between [3-2-3] and [2-2-3]. If tree geometry is the only factor that determines FFR, then what explains this difference? Hung argues that it is not the IC cut or, equivalently, tree geometry, but what Selkirk 1984 calls the 'Sense Unit Condition' (SUC) that determines FFR. In a nutshell, SUC says that two words (more generally, two constituents) form a sense unit if they stand in a head-argument or head-adjunct relation. SUC was originally formulated as a constraint on intonational phrasing. We may extend this SUC and substitute it for FFR:

(24) Sense Unit Condition (SUC)

Members of a prosodic unit must satisfy the Sense Unit Condition

Accordingly, there is only one way to construe (22a,b), namely (x (x x)), which is isomorphic to the syntactic bracketing, since neither *xiao yu* 'small rain' nor *yang xiao* 'raise small' yields a head/complement reading.[17] At the unmarked tempo, TS applies cyclically, first on the binary foot, then on the ternary (super-)foot.[18] This potentially bleeding mode of rule application yields the unmarked reading [3-2-3]. In fast speech, the internal structure of the ternary feet (occasionally longer strings) is disregarded, calling for a simultaneous (or left-to-right iterative) rule application, giving rise to the marked [2-2-3] reading which is characteristic of allegro speech. In contrast, (23a,b) lend themselves to two alternative prosodic structures, both consistent with SUC, since in addition to *yao wo* 'bit me' and *xiang zou* 'want to go,' *gou yao* 'dog bite' and *zong xiang* 'always want' stand in an argument-head and adjunct-head relation, respectively, even though they are non-constituents from the standpoint of the conventional tree representation. The cyclical application of TS to ((3 3) 3) first yields ((2 3) 3), then ((2 2) 3), as one of the alternative readings at the normal rate of speech. To further substantiate the need for a relation-based definition of prosodic units, more relevant examples are given below:

(25) a. 'I want to buy books'

I	want	buy	book	
wo	[xiang	[mai	shu]]	
3	3	3	1	BT
(2	3)	(3	1)	TS within feet
(2	2)	(3	1)	TS across feet (optional)

b. '(he) also writes novels'

also	write	novel		
ye	[xie	[xiao-shuo]]		
3	3	3	1	BT
(2	3)	(3	1)	TS within feet
(2	2)	(3	1)	TS across feet (optional)

Here *wo xiang* 'I want' and *ye xie* 'also write' satisfy the SUC, and consequently form disyllabic feet, with automatic phonetic consequences. Now, contrast (25) with the examples in (26), which also display a uniformly right-branching syntactic tree structure. In these cases, the sentence cannot be evenly split into two disyllabic feet, since neither *qing lao* 'hire old' nor *zhao xiao* 'look for small' form sense units. The only possible prosodic organization is the one shown on the bottom line of (26a,b), consisting

---

[17]For convenience, I am employing the word 'complement' as a cover term for both adjunct and argument. Where 'complement' is used interchangeably with 'argument,' the usage will be made clear.

[18]The assumption is that at the moderate, normal rate of speech, Standard Mandarin TS applies cyclically foot-internally, and then optionally across the feet. As tempo quickens, however, TS ignores foot-internal brackets and, in extreme cases, divisions between the feet. For details, see Shih 1985.

of a 'defective' monosyllabic foot, followed by a ternary foot. The application of TS within the ternary foot bleeds the optional TS between two feet, producing the expected phonetic output.

(26) a. 'hire an old cashier'

	hire	old	cashier		
	qing	[lao	[zhang-gui]]		
	3	3	3	4	BT
*	(2	3)	(3	4)	TS within feet
*	(2	2)	(3	4)	TS across feet
ok	(3)	(2	(3	4))	

b. 'look for small wine bottles'

	look-for	small	wine	bottle	
	zhao	[xiao	[jiu	ping]]	
	3	3	3	2	
*	(2	3)	(3	2)	TS within feet
*	(2	2)	(3	2)	TS across feet
ok	(3)	(2	(3	2))	

A relation-based principle of foot-formation is better able to deal with other tree configurations as well. (27a) is left-branching, and (27b,c) have a nested structure.

(27) a. 'this kind of wine is good'

	this	kind	wine	good	
	[[zhei	zhong]	jiu]	hao	
	4	3	3	3	BT
	(4	3)	(2	3)	
	((4	2)	2)	(3)	

b. 'the cat is smaller than the dog'

	cat	compare	dog	small	
	mao	[[bi	gou]	xiao]	
	1	3	3	3	BT
	(1	3)	(2	3)	
	(1)	((2	2)	3)	

c. 'he walked toward the north'

	he	face	north	walk	
	ta	[[wang	bei]	zou]	
	1	3	3	3	BT
	(1	3)	(2	3)	
	(1)	((2	2)	3)	

In (27a), the nominal head *jiu* 'wine' forms a prosodic unit with the predicate *hao* 'good,' consistent with SUC. Intrapodal TS bleeds interpodal TS, producing as output [4-3-2-3]. Alternatively, (27a) is organized in a manner that is isomorphic to its morphosyntactic structure: $(((xx)x)x)$ yields [4-2-2-3] as the output of cyclic TS. (27b,c) are somewhat more complicated. *Bi gou* 'than dog' and *wang bei* 'toward the north' are syntactically bracketed as prepositional phrases which function as the degree or directional complements of *xiao* 'small' and *zou* 'walk,' respectively. However, as Hung 1987:21 argues, *bi* and *wang* can function as ordinary verbs as well, meaning 'to compare' and 'to face,' respectively. This interpretation of (27b,c) makes it possible to construe *mao bi* 'cat compare' and *ta wang* 'he face' as subject/predicate, sanctioning them as legitimate prosodic units.[19] This explains the alternative reading with the tonal sequence [1-3-2-3]. Such an alternative is not open to the sentences in (28):

(28) a.   'it's better to elect me'

		elect		me	good	
		[[xuan-ju]		wo]	hao	
		3	3	3	31	BT
	*	(2	3)	(2	3)	
	ok	((2	2)	2)	(3)	

   b.   'to carry two pails of water'

		carry	two		pails	water	
		tiao	[[liang		tong]	shui]	
		1	3		3	3	BT
	*	(1		3)	(2	3)	
	ok	(1)	((2		2)	3)	

Again, it is the SUC that rules out the possibility of linking *wo hao* 'I good' and *tiao liang* 'carry two' into bona fide prosodic feet, and explains the starred readings in (28a,b).

SUC is not without problems of its own, however. Here is a class of critical examples that lends itself to a straightforward prosodic analysis in

---

[19]According to this construal, (27b,c) are more accurately translated as 'The cat (when) compared with the dog is smaller' and 'He walked (while) facing the north.' These additional observations lend support to Hung's argument. Coverbs like *bi*, for instance, behave like ordinary verbs in that they can function as the main verb (a), and take complements of various sorts (b) and aspectual markers (c):

(a) tamen bi   fenshu
    they   compare grade
    'they are comparing grades'

(b) Lao Wang bi-bu-shang   Lao Li
               compare-Neg-Pot
    'Lao Wang cannot compare with Lao Li'
    ('Lao Wang is no match for Lao Li')

(c) xiaqi women bi-guo   liang ci
    chess we   compare-Asp two   times
    'we have competed with each other at chess twice'

a syntactic tree-based model but poses a serious problem for the semantic relation-based approach:

(29)   'I am very satisfied'
           I   very   satisfied
           wo   [hen   [man-yi]
           3   3   3   4   BT
       a. (2   3)   (3   4)   ok
       b. (2   2)   (3   4)   ok
       c. (3   (2   (3   4))   ok

(30)   'I keep a dog to watch the gate'
           I   keep   dog   watch   gate
           wo   [yang   [gou] [shou   men]]
           3   3   3   3   2   BT
       a. (3   (2   3))   (3   2)   ok
       b. ((2   2)   3)   (3   2)   ok
       c. (2   3)   ((2   3)   2)   *
       d. (2   3)   (2   (3   2))   *

FFR predicts (29a) as the unmarked reading and (29b) as the allegro version. One must appeal to considerations such as focus or topicalization to somehow override FFR-b (Duple Meter) and produce the desired effect of (29c). The SUC, on the other hand, incorrectly rules out (29a), since there is no plausible way to construe *wo hen* 'I very' as a sense unit. As for (30), the IC-driven FFR predicts that the sentence will be uniquely parsed into two prosodic feet, as shown in (30a). Reading (30b) is consistent with FFR in allegro speech (since internal structure of the first foot will be ignored). The SUC, on the other hand, predicts that all four alternative prosodic structures are possible. What provisos can be added to eliminate (30c) and (30d) remain to be worked out.

Selkirk 1986 correctly distinguishes two sorts of prosodic units:

a. those that have independent phonological properties, such as the syllable and the foot on the one end of the prosodic hierarchy, and the intonational phrase, on the other;

b. those that have no *raison d'être* other than serving to circumscribe the scope of phonological processes.

This second set of prosodic entities comprises the phonological word, the clitic group, and the phonological phrase. She hypothesizes that an exclusively end-based theory can adequately account for all scope-defining prosodic entities of type (b) above the foot and below the intonational phrase. Specifically, she rejects a relation-based approach to derived prosodic domains (exemplified by Nespor and Vogel 1986 and Hayes 1989, among others) as too powerful.

In this context, the facts of Mandarin TS take on an added significance. The prosodic domain we have been calling the foot (following the tradition of M. Chen 1984, Shih 1985, and Hung 1987) cannot be identified with the word-internal foot, replaceable by the metrical grid (at least in the grid-only account of Prince 1983 and Selkirk 1984), since foot formation can cross any syntactic juncture, including that between the subject and the predicate. Nor can our prosodic foot be equated with the intonation phrase on the other end of the prosodic hierarchy. For one thing, the intonational phrase is signalled by (potential) pause and characteristic intonational contours. The prosodic unit we have been calling the foot in Mandarin exhibits no such properties. In addition, IPs purport to be the maximal domain of phonological rules. It is clear that TS freely crosses foot boundaries in Mandarin. Therefore, the foot in Mandarin is clearly a prosodic entity of type (b): it is a theoretical construct, having no other purpose than to define the scope of TS. Yet, an end-based theory or, for that matter, an exclusively structure-based theory, is alone quite incapable of insightfully deriving the notion of foot in Mandarin. The facts of Mandarin TS clearly point to the need to generalize a relation-based principle like the SUC beyond the intonational phrase, and extend it perhaps to both types of prosodic units.

4   Argument vs. Adjunct Phrases

So far we have taken the SUC to be neutral between argument and adjunct. There is, however, evidence that phonology must distinguish between argument and adjunct structures. In my formulation of the Xiamen Tone Group (TG) formation rule, the closing bracket of an X^{max} ($=$ XP) marks the end of one TG and the beginning of another—with one important exception, namely when this X^{max} is a (c-commanding) adjunct phrase. This proviso correctly distinguishes the permissible TS sites (signalled, as before, by '$=$') from those junctures blocking TS (marked by '$\#$'). This point can be illustrated by the well-known example first noticed by Cheng 1968:

(31) a. mua-a $\#$ tua e sio-piah
      sesame-seed big E bun
      'buns with big sesame seeds'

    b. mua-a $=$ tua e sio-piah
      sesame-seed big E bun
      'buns the size of sesame seeds' (tiny buns)[20]

In (31a) *mua-a* 'sesame seed' plays the role of the subject of the relative clause, whereas the same word functions as the degree adjunct of the

---

[20]This *e*, which I parse simply as E, is variously described as a subordinator, nominalizer, relative clause marker, complementizer, etc., and has a function corresponding to Mandarin *de*. X can modify Y with or without the intervening *e/de* in Chinese.

adjective *tua* 'big' in (31b). Similar minimal pairs are not hard to find.

(32) a. gin-a # le   huan, # bien ts'ap   yi
       child   Asp irrational don't pay-attention he
       'The child is acting irrationally; don't pay him any attention'

   b. yi a   le   gin-a = huan
      he still Asp child   irrational
      'He is still acting irrationally like a child'

(33) a. tsit tiam-tsing # goo k'oo
       one hour   five dollar
       'five dollars an hour'

   b. tsit tiam-tsing = ku
      one hour   long
      'an hour long'

In all these cases the NPs *gin-a* 'child' and *tsit tiam-tsing* 'one hour' either function as the subject and block TS, or function as an adjunct and allow TS to take place. The TS-blocking XP is not limited to the subject position. Where a pre-head argument is allowed, TS is blocked, as predicted:

(34) a. p'ue # sia-liao-loo
       letter   write-Asp
       'has written the letter'

   b. tua-mng # ao-piaq
      gate   behind
      'behind the gate'

   c. tsin ku # yi-tsing
      very long   before
      'very long ago'

   d. tsiaq-pa # yi-ao
      eat-Asp   after
      'after having eaten'

In (34a) an object NP, *p'ue* 'letter,' precedes the verb *xia* 'write.' Noting that the unmarked word order in Xiamen is VO, one may argue that what accounts for the TS blockage is not its object role, but the fact that the object NP has been moved or topicalized to a pre-verbal position.[21] Such an explanation is not available for (34b-d). In terms of word-order typology, Chinese is a mixed language in that despite its VO order, it is a

---

[21]Nespor and Vogel 1986:188 observe that moved elements such as topicalized and extraposed expressions obligatorily constitute separate intonational phrases.

post-positional language. Therefore, the complements (i.e., arguments) of the post-positional phrases (34b-d) occupy their normal pre-head position.

Let us look at an alternative analysis that dispenses with the functional notions of adjunct and argument. One approach is to distinguish the recursive (expandable) and non-recursive (non-expandable) sides of a phrasal construction relative to the head. All elements on the non-recursive side join the head to form a phonological phrase; they are in effect regarded not as 'fully-fledged' complement phrases, but as specifiers or some sort of XP redux, as it were, a position espoused in its various forms by Kaisse 1985, Nespor and Vogel 1986, and Selkirk 1986, among others.[22] According to this approach, the nominal expressions *mua-a* 'sesame seed,' *gin-a* 'child,' and *tsit tiam-tsing* 'one hour' are parsed not as full NPs in (31a,32a,33a) but as bare nouns in (31b,32b,33b). The XP redux notion is based on the observation that prehead complements are typically limited to single words, not phrases. Thus adjectives and adverbs in Ewe do not participate in the bar-system as nouns and verbs, in that they can neither be modified nor take complements of their own (Clements 1978). The XP redux hypothesis in its strong form is easily falsifiable, as some prehead elements may have at least limited internal phrase-like structure, as:

(35) a. [chiaramente e beatamente] contenta
      'clearly and blissfully happy'

      b. la [più vecchia] città
      'the oldest city,

There is no doubt that the nonrecursive side of a phrasal construction exhibits certain syntactic restrictions.[23]

---

[22]Interestingly, this idea goes all the way back to SPE, which implicitly assumes that prehead modifiers are non-phrasal categories. As is well known, SPE derives phonological constituents by flanking X^0 and X^{max} with a boundary #. If we assume that the prenominal adjective *unlikely* is a fully-fledged X^{max}, we would cut up the following sentence into four strings (corresponding to what has become known as the clitic group) separated by two or more #s:

(a) * [the [book]] ## [was [in [an ## [[unlikely]] ## [place]]]]

The only way to derive the correct phonological partitioning (b) is to analyze *unlikely* as a non-phrasal X^0:

(b) [the [book]] ## [was [in [an [unlikely] ## [place]]]] (See SPE:366ff)

[23]One of the more interesting restrictions is the 'Head-final filter' on prenominal modifiers pointed out in Di Sciullo and Williams 1987:51, according to which prenominal modifiers must terminate in the head, as illustrated by the unacceptability of (b):

(a) the [very proud] man

(b) *the [proud of his children] man

However, the notion of a reduced, nonphrasal construction on the nonrecursive side of the head is unlikely to replace the argument/adjunct distinction. For one thing, some languages exhibit a uniformly branching phrase structure, where the distinction between recursive and nonrecursive sides is irrelevant. For instance, the Basque VP is uniformly head-final, with all complements branching to the left.[24]

The canonical form of VP is (36), where X, Y ... = complement structures:

(36)   VP = (X), (Y)... V (Aux)

Now contrast (37a) and (37b):

(37)   a.   hark [liburua ong(i) = irakurri zuen]
        he   book   well   read   Aux
        'He read the book well'

     b.   hark [liburua # arin   irakurri zuen]
        he   book   quickly read   Aux
        'He read the book quickly'

Vowel degemination applies in (37a), changing *ongi irakurri* to *ong irakurri*. The same rule fails in (37b), leaving the sequence *liburua # arin* intact. The Basque data seem to preclude alternative analyses that do not make crucial reference to the argument/adjunct dichotomy. One such alternative is to hypothesize that Basque sets the end-parameter to X^{max}[on the left. This allows us to derive the following prosodic units (38a,b), correctly allowing vowel degemination in the former, but blocking it in the latter:

(38)   a.   hark   [liburua   ong(i)   =   irakurri   zuen]
        he   book   well   read   Aux
        ( ) (   ) (   )

     b.   hark   [liburua   #   arin   irakurri   zuen]
        he   book   quickly   read   Aux
        ( ) (   )   (   )

However, the left-end setting incorrectly predicts the following prosodic structure, failing to block the application of vowel degemination between *ipuina* and *azaldu*.

(39)   zuk [bere anaiari # ipuina # azaldu iezaiokezu]
      you his   brother   story   explain Aux
      *( ) (   ) (   )
      'You may explain this story to his brother'

---

[24]The exception is negative constructions. I owe all the Basque data cited in this paper to Dois-Bienzobas (1988 and personal communication).

The word-final vowels in *anaiari* and *ipuina* are both immune to degemination. A second alternative, also ruled out, is the notion that adverbial constructions are somehow restricted and impoverished. This is depicted in the following example, where the complex bracketed AdvP in no way inhibits vowel degemination, which deletes the final vowel of the adverbial head *geroago:*

(40) liburua [hiru ordu eta erdi geroag(o)] = osatu   zuen
    book   three hour and half later   complete Aux
    'He finished the book three hours and a half later'

The only plausible way to capture the grammatical condition of vowel degemination is to say that it applies between an adjunct and its head, but not between an argument and its head. Unlike Basque, Xiamen VPs may have complements on either side of the V. Interestingly, regardless of its relative position to the head, the complement blocks TS if it functions as an argument, permitting TS if it functions as an adjunct. The four logically possible relations holding between the italic elements (2 positions × 2 functions) are given below:

(41)   a.   Argument + Head

> Ong sian-sih # [*huat-bun* # *kong* kaq   tsin liu-li]
> Ong Mr.   French   speak COMP very fluently
> 'Mr. Ong speaks French fluently'

  b.   Adjunct + Head

> Ong sian-sih # [*t'iao-kang* = *kong* peq-ts'at]
>   purposefully   tell   lie
> 'Mr. Ong purposefully lied'

  c.   Head + Argument

> A-bing # [*sang*   *tang-oq*   # k'i ts'ia-tsam]
> A-bing   accompany classmate   to station
> 'A-bing accompanies his classmate to the station'

  d.   Head + Adjunct

> A-bing # [*k'uah puah tiam-tsing ku* = tian-si tsiat-boq
>   watch half hour   long TV   program
> 'A-bing watches TV for half an hour'

In (41a,b) the complements occupy a pre-head position; in (41c,d) the complements occur in the post-head slot. If the distinction between recursive vs. nonrecursive sides is the relevant factor, one expects TS to apply in (41a,b) but not in (41c,d)—or vice versa, depending on which side is considered to be recursive. The fact is that TS applies in (41b,d) but is blocked in (41a,c). This clearly suggests that the relevant conditioning factor is the functional dichotomy between arguments and adjuncts.

Finally, TS in Fuzhou, a northern Min dialect of Chinese, supplies further corroborating evidence in support of the relevance of the phonological contrast between argument and adjunct. As described by Hung 1987, Fuzhou TS displays a curious asymmetry in that it is permitted between a pre-head adjunct and the head, and between the head and a posthead argument, but disallowed between a prehead argument and the head and between the head and a posthead adjunct.

(42) Fuzhou TS

    adjunct   = head
    argument # head
              head = argument
              head # adjunct

Critical examples follow:[25]

(43) adjunct = head

    a. tuai = po-lo
       'big grapes'

    b. kuo = lo-riʔ
       'too honest'

    c. tse =   k'au
       together go
       'to go together'

(44) argument # head

    a. tsy   # tseing kui
       book   very   expensive
       'books are very expensive'

    b. i   # le-k'oung
       he   Asp-sleep
       'he is sleeping'

(45) head = argument

    a. k'ang = tieng-ning
       see   movie
       'see a movie'

    b. e =   siu-zui
       know swim
       'know how to swim'

---

[25]Fuzhou TS is foot-bound, i.e., limited to two- or three-syllable (right-branching) feet. Hence the short examples. All Fuzhou examples are taken, with minor modifications, from Hung 1987.

(46) head # adjunct

    a. keing # loey zuo
        tall   six foot
        'six feet tall'

    b. si # ts'uo le
        die   house LOC
        'die at home'

    c. t'iu # ia eing
        'jump very high'

It seems doubtful that a theory that is blind to the functional distinction between argument and adjunct can adequately account for the array of external sandhi facts taken from such diverse languages as Chinese and Basque.

5   Concluding Remarks

To recapitulate, here are some of the chief findings together with some comments:

(a) Syntax and phonology may interact in a manner that is both direct and complex: syntax-based prosodic domains delimit the scope of phonological rule operation, while syntactic properties within the prosodic domain determine *which* phonological processes are implemented (e.g., which of the two types of TS rules, TSA or TSB) and *how* this is accomplished (left to right, or right to left).

The likelihood that at least some phonological processes must directly reference syntax creates a 'residue' to the more highly constrained theory of prosodic mediation. It remains to be seen how a theory of the residue—like 'precompiled phonology,' proposed by Hayes (this volume)—handles cases like Pingyao (see section 1), Kimatuumbi (Odden 1987) and, perhaps, Chongming (Chen 1987a, Zhang 1988).

(b) There are two major types of principles which derive prosodic domains from syntactic structures: one refers to the ends/edges of syntactic constituents (i.e., the end-based approach); the other focuses on the grammatical relations holding between two adjacent constituents (i.e., the relation-based theory).

These two mapping relations between syntactic and prosodic structures may be seen as two basic principles of speech organization: demarcation, and grouping. Demarcation highlights the endpoints of grammatically important constituents, e.g., word, phrase, clause. Thus the Wu dialects (e.g., Shanghai) of Chinese are known to be left-prominent in the sense that only the left-most syllable of a content word retains its base tone, spreading it across the entire phonological word (or, more precisely, the clitic group). It seems quite natural for such languages to exploit the end-based strategy, creating a pattern like that in (47), where X marks phonological prominence and $_w$[signals the beginning of a content word (as opposed to function words or, loosely speaking, grammatical particles).

(47)   X x x... X x x... X x x...
   $_w$[$_w$[$_w$[

Grouping, on the other hand, links grammatically related items to form a unit of speech production. Hence the relation-based mapping principle.

The coexistence of end-based and relation-based prosodic units does not necessarily mean an embarrassment of riches of an overly powerful theory; rather, it reflects two aspects of speech organization. One plausible hypothesis is this: phonological processes serving a demarcative function tend to operate within end-base derived prosodic domains, while coarticulation effects typically occur within a relation-based unit of processing. We have already seen an example of a primarily demarcative phonological rule in Shanghai. Wenzhou, another Wu dialect, is a mirror image of Shanghai in that it is right-prominent: only the rightmost syllable of a content word keeps its base tone, while all other syllables lose their underlying tones and eventually become associated either with the tone of the prominent syllable (by tone assimilation), or with a Low-Falling tone by default (see Chen 1988). Xiamen TS, as it may be recalled, turns every tone except the last of a tone group (TG) into a corresponding sandhi form. The net effect is for the appearance of a base tone to mark the end of every TG, which coincides with the end of an X^{max} (see Chen 1987c). Viewed in this light, tone sandhi in these dialects can be viewed as the functional equivalent of 'tonal punctuation,' whereby the base tone marks the beginning or the end of a grammatical unit (namely a content word, or an X^{max}). In contrast, TS processes in most Mandarin dialects, like Beijing (see Shih 1986, Hung 1987) and Tianjin (see Hung 1987; Chen 1986b, 1987b), have a different motivation: TS typically serves to dissimilate adjacent tones. Thus in Beijing, the first of two adjacent Low tones becomes High-Rising. This tone dissimilation is extended to other tones in Tianjin, as shown in (48):[26]

(48)   base tones   sandhi tones
   21-21   213-21
   213-213   45-213
   53-53   21-53

Clearly, tone sandhi in Beijing and Tianjin serves a different purpose, and is phonetically motivated. It operates within a prosodic domain derived

---

[26]The numerals 1 to 5 indicate pitch levels on a 5-point scale, with 5 being the highest. Thus [53] means High-Falling, and [213] means Low Fall-Rising, etc.

by the mechanism of relation-based grouping. I suspect that phonetically motivated processes of coarticulation (broadly defined) such as assimilation, dissimilation, and syllable restructuring, tend to operate within units of speech planning, namely prosodic entities created out of a group of syntactically or semantically related elements. French Liaison and Italian *raddoppiamento sintattico* are both instances of resyllabification.[27] It is not surprising that both processes operate within a prosodic domain defined as head plus pre-head specifiers and modifiers, or as head plus post-head short (non-branching) complements.

(c) Where tree-geometry and functional relations make different predictions about phonological phrasing, it is the latter that prevails. Among the functional relations that play a role in determining the operation of phonology is the argument/adjunct dichotomy.

Since conventional tree representation is designed precisely to encode such meaning relations as head/complement, it is only natural that prosodic mapping rules based on tree structure per se, as well as those based on functional relations, should make equivalent predictions for the most part. In section 3 we have seen ample evidence that where the two mapping principles diverge, the semantic/functional relations turn out to be a better predictor of phonological phrasing. The argument/adjunct asymmetry is one aspect in which tree geometry either underdifferentiates or misrepresents (from the phonological viewpoint) functional relations. (49a,b) instantiate a case of underdifferentiation, where tree geometry alone cannot distinguish between argument and adjunct:[28]

(49) a. me = swoʔ pun
          buy   one   volume

      b. keing # loey zuo
          tall   six   foot
          'taller by six feet'

Fuzhou TS applies in (49a), while failing to apply in (49b), as noted before. One way to encode this argument/adjunct dichotomy in tree-structural terms is to consider arguments as X'-level complements, while attaching adjuncts to a higher X" node (see Jackendoff 1977). (49a,b) will thus be reconfigured as (50a,b) respectively. The applicability of TS is now a function of the 'distance' between two adjacent elements across the TS site, as measured in terms of the number of nodes or connecting branches intervening between the two elements.[29]

---

[27]Consonant gemination may be seen as a case where the word-initial consonant becomes ambisyllabic, that is, shared by adjacent syllables across the word boundary. Thus *caffé caldo* 'hot coffee' undergoes the following change, [ka.fe # kal.do] → [ka.fek.kal.do].

[28](49a) is adapted from Wright 1983:362.

[29]For more on depth of branching, see Clements 1978.

(50) a.

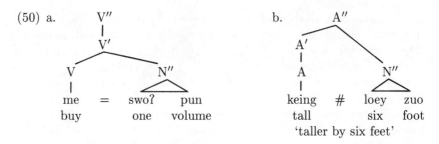

b.

While this solution works for (50), the ploy to encode functional distinctions in terms of tree geometry makes exactly the wrong prediction for the Xiamen facts as shown in (51):

(51) a.

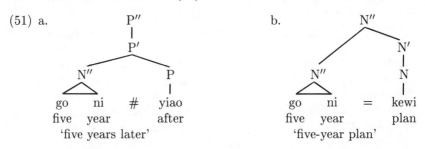

b.

If one counts the connecting nodes/branches, one must conclude that *go ni,* when functioning as a prenominal adjunct, is more distantly related to *kewi* in (51b) than it is to *yiao* in (51a), where the same NP functions as an argument of the postpositional head. The prediction is that phonological processes, TS in this case, are more likely to apply in (51a) than in (51b). The facts are exactly the opposite. Phonology, therefore, must be able to read off the functional roles of the complements, regardless of how these are represented in tree-structural terms. In this connection, it is of some interest to observe the increasing interest that the adjunct/non-adjunct asymmetry is generating among students of syntax and semantics (see Lasnik and Uriagereka 1988, inter alia).

3

Syntax and Phrasing in Korean

YOUNG-MEE YU CHO

A THEORY OF THE phonology-syntax connection starts with the identification of phonological rules whose domains are larger than the phonological word. Among these phrasal rules, some are sensitive to syntactic bracketing. In earlier papers (Cho 1987a, 1987b), I identified and defined the domains of several syntax-sensitive phrasal rules in Korean, as well as a postlexical rule that applies throughout the utterance when no pause intervenes.

This paper provides new data on syntax-sensitive rules, involving complex NP constructions and scrambled sentences, and argues that currently available theories need be revised to accommodate the Korean facts. A set of phrase formation rules is formulated to accommodate the data presented in the paper. In the final section, I put forward arguments, based on phrasing, for treating the verb phrase as a maximal projection, thus providing phonological evidence for the configurational nature of Korean.[1]

1 Obstruent Voicing in Simplex Sentences

In this section I present the rule of Obstruent Voicing (henceforth OV), which voices plain consonants but not aspirated or tense consonants. Two other rules, Stop Nasalization and Homorganic Nasal Assimilation, have

I would like to thank E. J. Baek, Joan Bresnan, C.-W. Kim, Paul Kiparsky, William Poser, and Michael Wescoat for helpful discussions and comments. I am especially grateful to K. Hong for answering all my questions on Korean syntax.

[1]See, for instance, Choe 1985, Hale 1985, Whitman 1986 for discussions of the configurational-nonconfigurational parameter.

also been argued to apply on the same domain as OV (Cho 1987a), but this paper will analyze only OV in detail.[2]

The rule is formulated in (1).

(1) Obstruent Voicing

$$\begin{bmatrix} -\text{cont} \\ -\text{asp} \\ -\text{tense} \end{bmatrix} \longrightarrow [+\text{voice}]/[+\text{voice}]\_[+\text{voice}]$$

Now I present the data that are crucial in determining the domain of its application. Various simple phrases in which OV applies are listed in (2).[3] Whereas monomorphemic adjectives and adverbs are analyzed as non-phrasal, adjective and adverb phrases have sentential characteristics in Korean and therefore will not be dealt with in this section.

(2) a. phonological word
        apəci → abəji   N
        'father'

     b. Determiner-Noun
        kɨ cip → kɨjip   NP
        'that house'   Det   N

     c. Adjective-Noun
        motɨn kɨlim → modɨn gɨrim   NP
        'every picture'   Adj   N

     d. Possessive Noun-Noun
        Suni-ɨy cip→ Suniɨy jip   NP
        'Suni's house'   NP   N

     e. Verb of Relative Clause-Noun
        kɨ-ka   mək-nɨn   pap   NP
        he-Sub   eat-Mod   rice   S'
          → kɨga məŋnɨn bap   NP VP N
        'the rice he is eating.'

     f. Object-Verb
        kɨlim-ɨl   pota → kɨrimɨl boda   VP
        picture-Acc   see   NP   V
        'look at the picture'

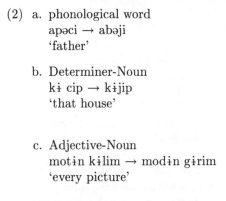

---

[2] The effect of OV is the most salient, due to the fact that all case markers, which are suffixed to an NP, end with a voiced segment, such as a vowel or a sonorant.

[3] In addition to OV, a postlexical rule applies to change /l/ into [r] in the syllable onset position, as in [gɨrim] (2c, 2f).

kɨ-eke   poita   → kɨege boida
he-Dat   show
'show him'

g. Verb-Verb
cap-a pota → caba boda
'try holding'

Next, consider the phrases in (3), in which the application of OV is blocked. (In these sentences it is crucial that no word bears intonational emphasis, since any word with emphasis obligatorily starts a new phonological phrase.[4] The influence of focus on phrasing will be dealt with later.[5])

(3) a. Subject-Verb
        kæ-ka   canta
        dog-Nom   sleep
        → kæga/ canda
        'The dog is sleeping'

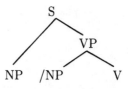

     b. Subject-Object
        kæ-ka   pap-ɨl   məknɨnta
        dog-Nom   rice-ACC eat
        → kæga/ pabɨl məŋnɨnda
        'The dog is eating rice.'

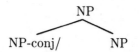

     c. Object-Object
        ai-eke   kwaca-lɨl   cunta
        child-Dat candy-Acc   give
        → aiege/ kwajarɨl junda
        'He gives a candy to the child.'

     d. NP-conj-NP
        horaŋi-wa koyaŋi
        → horaŋiwa/ koyaŋi
        'the tiger and the cat'

[4]This is similar to the Hausa case discussed in Inkelas, Leben and Cobler 1986.

[5]It is well-known that intonational emphasis affects phrasing in several ways that are not well understood. All of the data used in this paper, other than the sentences involving focus, were read by a native speaker with a most 'neutral intonation.' It should be mentioned that the actual phonological phrases of a given sentence might be different from those proposed in this paper, due to the size of the phrases, the location of emphasis, and so forth.

e. Topic NP-S'
   sakwa-nɨn   pəlinta
   apple-Top   throw
   → sagwanɨn/ pərinda
   'Apples, they throw away.'

S
  NP/   NP   VP
  S'

f. Subject-Sentential Adverb-Verb
   Suni-ka   kithɨkhake cip-e   kass-ta
   Suni-Nom good   home-Loc go-past
   → suniga/ kithɨkhake/ cibe gat∗ta
   'It was good that Suni went home.'

S
  NP   /Adv   /VP

Given the above data, the domain of OV might well be definable in accordance with some of the algorithms proposed in the literature, shown in (4):

(4) a. The relation-based theory

(Selkirk 1984, Nespor and Vogel 1986, Hayes 1989) The phonological phrase is formed by adjoining the head and its adjacent complement in the maximal projection.

b. The end-based theory (Selkirk 1986)

$$X^{max}[\ldots$$

c. The direct syntax approach (Kaisse 1985)

External sandhi applies between a sequence of two words a and b when b domain c-commands a.

The three theories exemplified in (4) predict the same result in analyzing the above data. Example (5) shows the output of each algorithm:

(5) a. The relation-based theory

The head and its adjacent complement form a phonological phrase.

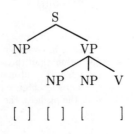

b. The end-based theory

Choose the left end of a maximal projection.

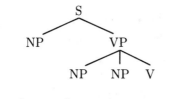

$X^{max}[\quad X^{max}[\quad X^{max}[\dots$

$[\quad]_p\ [\quad]_p\ [\qquad]_p$

c. The direct syntax approach

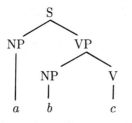

b does not domain c-command a.

c domain c-commands b. (b and c are a sandhi pair.)

At this point one argument against the direct syntax approach can be raised. As one can see from the example sentences in (3), OV is a 'domain-span' rule in the typology of sandhi rules proposed in Selkirk 1980a. That is, the rule applies word-internally as well as between two words. Since the direct syntax approach does not identify any independent phonological domain, the word-internal application of a rule is not accounted for by such syntactic notions as the c-command relation and the edge condition (Vogel and Kenesei (this volume)). One way to solve this problem is to apply the rule twice, once in the lexicon and again postlexically. The problem with this solution, however, is not only the undesirability of the double application of the rule but also that marking the feature [voice] in the lexicon would be a violation of structure preservation (Kiparsky 1982b), since the voicing of obstruents is not distinctive in Korean.[6]

2 More Data on OV

We have seen that the three theories make the same claims concerning simplex sentences. However, the predictions of the theories diverge when

---

[6]It has been argued independently by Kaisse 1985 and Rice (this volume) that P1 rules are neutralizing. However, OV constitutes a counter-example: this allophonic rule clearly applies before the highest level of the prosodic hierarchy. Even though OV contributes a non-distinct feature, its domain should be smaller than the utterance in the hierarchy.

more complex structures are considered. In this section I will present three cases which make it possible to compare the theories, and propose some modifications.

First, let us look at the cases illustrated in (6).

(6) a.

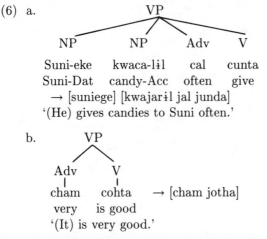

Suni-eke   kwaca-lɨl   cal   cunta
Suni-Dat   candy-Acc   often   give
→ [suniege] [kwajarɨl jal junda]
'(He) gives candies to Suni often.'

b.

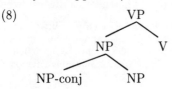

'(It) is very good.'

Within both the end-based theory and the direct syntax approach, the correct phrasing obtains. However, to phrase the adverb with the verb and the second NP in (6a), the relation-based theory needs to be revised to refer to 'the closest complement' rather than to 'the adjacent complement.' Example (6b) is a case where there is no XP complement within the maximal projection. The revised algorithm needed to get both cases right is proposed in (7).

(7) Phonological Phrase Formation

    a. The head is joined with its closest XP complement.

    b. If there is no XP complement, combine the head and all the material within the maximal projection.

    c. All words unaffected by the above clause form phonological phrases of their own.

What is expressed disjunctively in the first two clauses of (7) is an automatic consequence, for a head-final language like Korean, of the left-end setting of the maximal projection in the end-based theory.

Second, consider a case where a conjoined NP precedes a matrix verb. As observed in Selkirk 1986, this is a case where the relation-based theory makes a different prediction from the end-based theory (and from the direct syntax approach).

(8)

In a structure like (8) the relation-based theory predicts one phrasing that covers the whole VP, since the verb, which is the head, forms a phonological phrase with the entire conjoined NP. On the other hand, the end-based theory predicts that the verb will join with the right-hand conjunct to form a phonological phrase, as shown in (9). By marking the left-end of a maximal projection the end-based theory yields two phrases, which is correct for Korean.

(9) $_X$max [NP-conj $_X$max [NP V

     [NP-conj]   [NP V]

The direct syntax approach also predicts this same result. Since the words inside of the two conjoined NPs are not in a c-command relation, phrasal rules should not apply between the two.

The Korean data falsify the prediction made by the relation-based theory, as illustrated in (10).

(10) Holaŋi-wa   koyaŋi-lɨl   po-ass-ta.
    tiger-and   cat -Acc   see-Past-VE
    → [horaŋiwa] [koyaŋirɨl boatt*a]
    '(I) saw tigers and cats'

One way of salvaging the relation-based theory would be to stipulate a 'bottom-up' condition to phonological phrase formation of (7), which guarantees that the phrasing will start from the most embedded maximal projections. This condition also plays a crucial role in analyzing the phrasal phonology of English and Hausa (Zec and Inkelas 1987, Inkelas 1988). With this new condition, the relation-based theory predicts that two conjoined NPs do not form a phrase. Since the two conjoined NPs are not in the head-complement relation, no phrasing takes place in the entire conjoined NP. Instead the algorithm selects the next higher maximal projection, VP in this case, combining the head V and the closest NP.

Third, consider sentences involving complex NPs.

(11) a. [[John] [saw [the cat [that
            [caught [the rat [that [stole [the cheese]]]]]]]]]
       [John saw the cat]   [that
            caught the rat] [that stole the cheese.]
      ......]$_X$max ....
      ....]$_X$max

    b. [[na-nɨn] [[[[[[koyaŋi-lɨl] c*oc-nɨn]
        I-top   cat-Acc   chase-Rel
     kaŋaci-lɨl] t*æli-n] salam-ɨl] poassta.]]]
     puppy-Acc beat-Rel man-Acc saw

     [nanɨn] [koyŋirɨl c*onnɨn] [kaŋajirɨl t*ærin] [saramɨl boatt*a]
     'I saw a man who beat the puppy that was chasing the cat.'

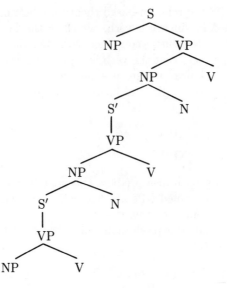

$\chi^{max}[\chi^{max}[\ldots\ldots\ldots\ldots$

The end-based theory predicts only two phrases for both Korean and English, whereas the actual number of possible phrases should be three in (11a) and four in (11b). In a left-branching language, a complex NP has only one left end of X^{max}, while in a right-branching language like English, it contains only one right end.

Now let us attempt to modify the assumptions of the end-based theory to accommodate the data involving embedded structure. Given the syntactic phrasing in (11a,b), it seems that S′ has the effect of blocking the phrasing. In order to get the intended phrasing, it seems necessary to add a condition that S′ obligatorily starts a new phrase. However, this condition proves insufficient for the following Korean sentences.

(12) a. [[John]   [saw [a cat [that [was smiling.]]]]]
         ....]χ^{max}..........S′ [..................]χ^{max}
          [John]   [saw a cat] [that was smiling]

     b. [[Suni-nɨn] [[[[us-nɨn]] koyaŋi-lɨl] poass-ta.]]]]
          Suni-Top   smile-rel cat-Acc   saw.
        χ^{max}[.......... χ^{max}[.........]S′......................

        *[Sunɨnin] [unnɨn] [koyaŋirɨl boat*ta]   (not acceptable)
        [Sunɨnin] [unnɨn goyaŋirɨl] [poat*ta]   (actual phrasing)

What (12b) shows is that, in contrast to English, the head noun and the verb of the relative clause form a phonological phrase across the S′ boundary when the relative clause contains a non-branching VP. In this case, S′ does not block the phrasing. Thus, it seems difficult to revise the end-based theory to get the right result. If reference has to be made to the right edge of a specific phrasal category, such as NP in this case, the prime virtue of the end-based theory disappears; i.e., sentence phonology can no longer refer just to a restricted body of syntactic information, such as the location of the ends of syntactic constituents of designated types in the X′ hierarchy.

Similar to the result obtained in the end-based theory, the direct syntax approach predicts that sandhi will occur everywhere within the VP, since every word contained in the matrix VP is c-commanded by the following word. Here again we must introduce a condition that would block the formation of a sandhi-pair across the S′ boundary in English, but not in Korean.

The relation-based theory, on the other hand, fails to make a definite prediction in phrasing, because it relies crucially on the head of a phrase, and there is more than one head in the matrix VP. If the phrasing starts from the highest node, the resulting phrases number exactly two, as in the two other theories. By contrast, if phrasing starts from the innermost maximal projections, observing the revised version of Phonological Phrase Formation, the desired result obtains for both sentences (11b) and (12b), which correspond to (13a) and (13b), respectively.

(13) a. [[[NP] [[[NP V]] N] V]]] N] V]]
          [NP]   [NP V] [N V]   [N V]

   b. [[NP] [[[[V]] N] V]]
          [NP]   [V   N] [V]

Thus, with the provision that the phrasing starts from the innermost maximal projection, an assumption necessary to account for the coordinate structure as well, the relation-based theory makes the correct prediction.

Example (14) summarizes the above findings.

(14)	Domain-span rule	Non-Complement	Coordination	Relative Clause
R-based	OK	revision to 'the closest XP'	a 'bottom-up' condition	OK with revision
E-based	OK	OK	OK	English: S′[Korean: ???
DSA	reapplication SP violation	OK	OK	English: S′ blocking Korean: ???

Since an immediate solution is available only within the relation-based theory, I will continue to express Korean Phrase Formation in terms of that theory in the next section.

3   Semantic Information on Phrasing

The data presented in previous sections deal with sentences lacking emphatic or contrastive stress. In this section, I will show that the semantic notion of focus, together with its phonological realization as high pitch, plays a crucial role in phrasing. The data show that the determination of prosodic structure is not entirely dependent on syntactic notions. In defining the contexts for phonological rules, we need more than a basic rule whose effect is adjoining material to the head within maximal projections.

Most notably, interrogative pronouns and words with an emphatic or contrastive accent form a phonological phrase with the following word, even when the two words are contained in different maximal projections. This happens only when the following word itself is not accented, as in the multiple question construction, and only when the following word has not been incorporated into a phonological phrase with some other element.

First consider the behavior of interrogative pronouns. In Korean, wh-words and corresponding indefinite quantifiers have the same morphological form, as shown in (15).

(15) a.   nuku   'who'   'someone'
           muəs   'what'   'something'
           ənce   'when'   'sometime'
           əti   'where'   'somewhere'
           ət*əhke   'how'   'somehow'
           wæ   'why'   —

      b.   nu(ku)-ka   ka-ni?
           who-Nom   go

           i. 'Who is going?'

           ii. 'Is anyone going?'

The sentence in (15b) is a wh-question if the pronoun *nuku* bears High pitch and a yes-no question if *nuku* bears low pitch. The distinction between the interrogative pronoun and the indefinite pronoun is made solely on the basis of phonetic prominence (Martin 1951).

I believe that this distinction is due to the intonational configuration, rather than to lexical tone specification, for two reasons. First, if it is assumed that interrogative pronouns have High tone specified lexically, then the question arises as to why these are the only words with lexical tones. Second, it is not only interrogative pronouns but also words with emphatic or contrastive stress that behave this way in the determination of phrasing.

Next, consider how the presence of focus affects phrasing. Example (16) provides some relevant data.

(16) a. nuka   'who(Nom)' [+high]

      [núga   gayo]
      who   goes
      'Who is going?'

   b. [Súni-ga gayo]
      'Suni is going.' (in answer to (a))

   c. [Suni-ga]   [kayo]
      Suni-Nom   goes (normal declarative sentence)
      'Suni is going.'

   d. nuka   'someone(Nom)'
      [nuga] [kayo]
      'Is someone going?'

   e. [núga]   [cibe   gayo]
      who   home   go
      'Who goes home?'

   f. [Súni-nɨn   gaji-man],   [Súja-nɨn   jayo]
      Suni-Cont   go-but   Suja-Cont   sleep
      'Suni is going but Suja is sleeping.'

As shown in (16a) and (16f), the accented subject gets phrased with the non-branching verb phrase. In view of the above fact, it is necessary to include one more clause in the rule of Phonological Phrase Formation; that is, words with the feature [+accent] form a phonological phrase with an unphrased word.[7]

The final version of Phonological Phrase Formation is stated below:

(17) Apply the following rules cyclically to all maximal projections, proceeding from the bottom up. At any given stage (a) applies before (b). Let the maximal projection under consideration on a given cycle be M.

    a. If M branches, combine the head of M into a phonological phrase with all adjacent unphrased material, up to and including the closest XP, or if no such phrase is present, the left edge of M.

    b. Phrase any focused word with the next word, unless that word is already phrased.

    After (a) and (b) have applied in all possible environments, (c) applies.

    c. Unphrased words form phonological phrases of their own.

---

[7]This is very similar to Selkirk's Focus Rules, which restructure the phonological phrases already formed.

4   The Status of VP

Whether in a simplex or in a complex sentence, one observes that an unstressed subject NP never joins the verb to form a phonological phrase, whereas the object NP and verbal adverbs freely join the verb in phrasing. In this section, I will argue that this difference in behavior can best be explained by treating VP as a maximal projection, and by defining the subject as the daughter of S and the object as the daughter of VP. I thus provide phonological evidence for the syntactic category VP. The existence of VP in Korean has been a source of some debate in the syntax literature. There exists a body of work in which Korean has been argued to be a nonconfigurational language (Whitman 1986, Hale 1985), as well as many studies that assume the more traditional configurational approach.

First, I will propose what I believe to be a more accurate phrase structure for the sentences presented in the previous sections. Then I will argue that what appears to be a subject/object asymmetry in neutral sentences is in fact a consequence of their characteristic phrase structures. Finally, I will show that a genuine argument for the VP constituent as a maximal projection comes from 'scrambled sentences.'

Before I introduce the data involving scrambled sentences, a comment is in order regarding the relationship between an NP's pragmatic function, its case marker, and its phonological characteristics. Example (18) summarizes this relationship.

(18) case-markers for Subject (Sohn 1980, Choi 1984)

nɨn	Unmarked Topic	Contrastive Focus
	unstressed	stressed
ka	Marked Topic	Exhaustive Listing Focus
	unstressed	stressed

As with the interrogative pronouns, morphologically identical case markers are disambiguated by means of stress. One recalls, moreover, that this phonetic prominence plays a role in phrasing.

In (18), one can see that there is no neutral subject in simplex sentences in Korean, unlike in English.[8] The expressed subject must take one of the above four pragmatic functions. Even though it has been traditionally assumed that *ka* marks the neutral subject when not bearing the function of exhaustive listing, Sohn, Choi, and others have noted that *ka* should be regarded as signalling a marked topic and that the neutral subject is dropped on the surface. These dropped NPs are what are often called 'zero pronominals' (Kameyama 1985, Chang 1986, Whitman 1987); they retain all of the subject properties, e.g., those pertaining to reflexive binding and control.[9]

---

[8] It seems possible to express a subject with no pragmatic function in embedded clauses. There is, however, no detailed syntax work on this subject.

[9] The differences between marked and unmarked topics have not been well defined

Given the assumptions made in the literature, I conclude that the subject, if it is realized on the surface, is either a topic or a focus. Following the widely accepted tree structures for Korean, I will assume that the relevant phrase structures are those shown in (19).

(19)

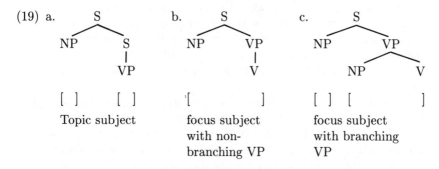

a. Topic subject

b. focus subject with non-branching VP

c. focus subject with branching VP

Example (19) illustrates two surface realizations of the subject: as a topic, in (19a), and as a focus, in (19b) and (19c). At this point one may entertain the idea that the subject/object asymmetry observed in the data could be accounted for in a theory that assumes no VP. A nonconfigurational theory would posit the structures shown in (20), as opposed to the configurational structures in (19).

(20)

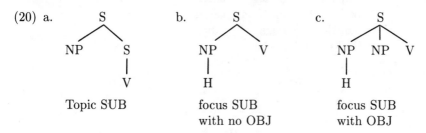

a. Topic SUB

b. focus SUB with no OBJ

c. focus SUB with OBJ

Given the structures in (20), it can be assumed that the head is combined with the closest NP within the maximal projection. In (20a), because of the intervening S node, the topic subject does not form a phrase with the verb, but the focus subject in (20b) does so when there is no object NP. It seems in this case that the phrasing does not differentiate the subject from the object; instead, the crucial factor in phrasing is to combine the V and the closest NP within a maximal projection, in this case, the S node. One might conclude that what appears at first sight to be a case of subject/object asymmetry is in fact a direct consequence of the particular characteristics of the phrase structure, which has been established on purely syntactic grounds. The data that include only so-called 'neutral sentences' are thus consistent with both of the theories. In these sentences, a nonconfigurational account actually seems simpler,

---

in the literature. Roughly, the marked topic is used when the whole situation is topicalized, in contrast to the unmarked topic which picks a single NP as a topic (Ki-Sun Hong, personal communication).

since phrasing is sensitive only to the adjacency of the verb and the NP, but not to any phonological information. In a configurational account, not only adjacency but also the notion of focus is needed.

Crucial evidence in favor of a VP constituent in Korean comes from scrambled sentences. Positing a VP as a maximal projection yields the right phrasing in sentences with a topicalized object. By contrast, a nonconfigurational approach, lacking VP, needs to refer not only to the maximal projection and the head and complement relation but also to other information, such as an NP's grammatical function. The data shown in (21) elucidate this point.

Whether one takes sentences with a fronted object to be derived through NP movement or to be base-generated, (21d) is the structure widely accepted in the syntax literature. Just as the nonscrambled sentences do not exhibit the subject/object asymmetry, neither do the sentences in (21a,b), phrasing in exactly the same way.

(21) a. Cuni-ka   koŋ-il   capa.
         Cuni-Nom   ball-Acc   catch
         [cuniga]   [koŋil   jaba]
         'Cuni catches balls.'

    b.   koŋ-il   Cuni-ka   capa
         ball-Acc   Cuni-Nom   catch
         [koŋil]   [cuniga   jaba]
         'Balls, Cuni catches.'

    c.
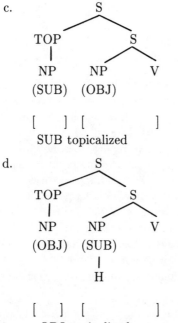

    d.

Now I will present an argument for the existence of a maximal projection that contains the object and the verbal adverb but not the subject, as shown in (22). The only difference between the sentences in (21) and those of (22) is an added verbal adverb. When an adverb is added, the resultant phrasings are different. In sentences with a topicalized object NP, the subject NP precedes the adverb, as shown in (22a). Here, the subject NP is phrased separately from the following adverb and the verb.

On the other hand, when the subject is topicalized, the object NP forms a phrase with the following material. This difference can be readily explained if one posits a node that contains the object and the adverb, as shown in (23). However, in an account that does not set up a VP node, as in (24), one obviously needs more than a structural configuration. One might attempt to solve this problem by referring to grammatical functions such as SUB and OBJ. Even with this additional apparatus, however, it is not clear how the requisite phrase formation rule can be formulated. For example, one ad hoc rule might be formulated as follows: (a) Starting from the verb, combine it with everything to its left up to, but not including, an NP that bears a subject grammatical function or a sentential adverb; (b) if there is no material between the verb and the subject, combine the two.

(22) a. Cuni-ka   koŋ-ɨl   cap∗alli   capa.
         Cuni-Nom   ball-Acc   fast   catch
         [cuniga]   [koŋɨl   jæp∗alli   jaba]
         'Speaking of Cuni, he catches balls quick.'

    b. koŋ-ɨl   Cuni-ka   cap∗alli   capa.
         ball-Acc   Cuni-Nom   fast   catch
         [konɨl]   [cuniga]   [cæp∗alli   jaba]
         'Balls Cuni catches quick.'

(23) a.   b.

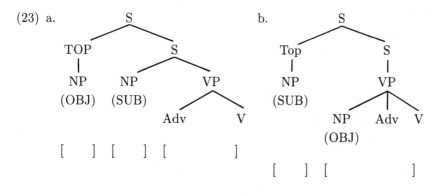

(24) a.

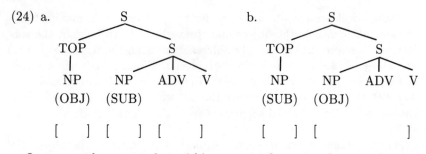

In sum, we have seen that within a nonconfigurational approach, very ad hoc assumptions are needed to get the right phrasing facts, whereas those same facts follow naturally from positing a VP node.

5   Conclusion

In this paper I have argued for two things. First, in view of the parsing of complex sentences, the relation-based theory does a better job than the end-based theory of formulating phonological phrases in Korean. Second, the evidence from Korean phrasal phonology supports a configurational approach to Korean syntax over a nonconfigurational one.

4

Sandhi Rules of Greek and Prosodic Theory

CLEO CONDORAVDI

THE THEORY OF PROSODIC phonology, designed as a theory of phrasal phonology, has contributed insights about the interaction between syntax and phonology and postlexical rule application. As developed in Selkirk 1980a, 1984, 1986; Nespor and Vogel 1982, 1986; and Hayes 1989, the theory makes the following basic claims:

(1) a. The domains for postlexical rule application are provided by the hierarchically organized prosodic structure, the *prosodic hierarchy*.

   b. The role syntax plays in sentence phonology is indirect. The extent of the influence of syntactic structure on phonology is in determining prosodic structure.

   c. The mapping between syntactic and prosodic structure is highly constrained.[1]

Optimally, then, there should be no phonological rules whose domain of application is provided directly by the syntax. Although some apparent

Thanks to S. Inkelas, P. Kiparsky, and D. Zec for many useful discussions, and to the NELS audience, E. Selkirk and K. Rice in particular, for their comments on an oral presentation of this work. I am grateful to D. Odden, who first prompted me to look at the sandhi phenomena of Modern Greek, and to W. Poser, whose class on Phrasal Phonology renewed my interest in these issues.

[1]Though proponents for a direct influence of syntax on phonology would dispute (1a) and (1b), they would still adhere to an appropriately formulated version of (1c). Phonological rules would be allowed to have only limited access to syntactic structure, preferably one that would be systematic across languages as well.

cases of direct syntax-phonology interaction have been successfully reanalyzed either within a prosodic framework (cf. *Phonology Yearbook* **4**) or as precompiled lexical rules (Hayes (this volume)), problematic cases still remain. The external sandhi rules of Modern Greek constitute one such case, resilient as they have been to a prosodic treatment.

Greek has three distinct rules which delete an unstressed non-high word-final vowel if it is followed by a vowel-initial word. In the discussions of Greek sandhi so far, the problem appears particularly intriguing. Which of the three rules applies to a given pair of words depends on the syntactic relation between the two words; this relation, however, has been argued to be of a rather whimsical nature, hard to express even syntactically in any general and sufficiently abstract terms.

In this paper, I reexamine the Greek sandhi rules and show that they are, in fact, amenable to a prosodic treatment. The mapping between syntax and phonology in Greek turns out to be easily expressible within the edge-based approach introduced in Selkirk 1986 and Chen 1987c. Furthermore, as I show, the Greek facts have implications for the organization of postlexical phonology and for the nature of prosodic subcategorization and phrasal allomorphy. In the course of the analysis, I argue for the introduction of a new prosodic category, which I call the *minimal phrase,* and for a partly bottom-up, partly top-down phrasing. The new prosodic constituent is motivated on two independent grounds: (a) it constitutes a postlexical rule domain; (b) it serves as the environment of phrasal allomorphy. That phrasing cannot be strictly bottom-up is shown by the effect of focused elements on phrasing. If phrasing is partly top-down, then the building of prosodic structure cannot be done successively for each prosodic category and cannot be intertwined with the phonology. As a consequence some theories of phrasal phonology are filtered out.

1   External Sandhi Rules

The sandhi phenomena have had a long history in the linguistic literature on Modern Greek, starting with Hadzidakis's 1905 original analysis. Yet the realization that the different processes of vowel coalescence are sensitive to the syntactic configuration of the words involved was late to come.[2] The sandhi phenomena were systematically discussed in Kaisse 1977a, where seven rules were shown to be operative, three of them syntactically conditioned deletion rules:[3] First Vowel Deletion (Rule 1), Un-

---

[2] In the absence of this realization, the exact number of the vowel coalescence processes has been a point of disagreement. As Malikouti-Drachman and Drachman 1978 have pointed out, the contradiction in the vowel hierarchy, already noted by Hadzidakis, and the ensuing debates would in many cases have been avoided had the syntactic configuration of the words been taken into account: "The crucial point is that the synchronic material of the vowel coalescence processes that demonstrate the hierarchy is heterogeneous syntactically and stylistically" (p. 185, my translation).

[3] One of the remaining four, the rule of contraction, applies between clitics and their host, while the other three are not syntactically conditioned rules. One of them, the

rounded First Vowel Deletion (Rule 2) and Less Sonorant First Vowel Deletion (Rule 3).[4]s

All three rules have the following in common: they do not delete high vowels, they do not delete stressed vowels, and they are blocked if the deletion of a vowel would cause two stressed syllables to become adjacent.[5] The First Vowel Deletion Rule, illustrated in (2), deletes the final vowel of the first word regardless of the nature of the initial vowel of the second word.[6]

(2) a. to áloγo   érxète   → to áloγ' érxete   o e
the horse-sg. come-sg.

b. ta áloγa   érxonde → ta áloγ' érxonde   a e
the horse-pl. come-pl.

Unrounded First Vowel Deletion, illustrated in (3), is similar to First Vowel Deletion except that the vowel o is not deleted.

(3) a. to frésko   elafró   frúto   → *to frésk' elafró frúto   *o e
the fresh-sg. light-sg. fruit-sg

b. ta fréska   elafrá   frúta   → ta frésk' elafrá frúta   a e
the fresh-sg. light-sg. fruit-sg

Less Sonorant First Vowel Deletion, illustrated in (5), differs from the previous two rules in that the second vowel, as well as the first, must meet certain requirements. Traditional grammarians, as well as Kaisse, have

---

rule of vowel degemination, will figure in our discussion later.

[4]I adopt Kaisse's naming for the three rules and her analysis of them as deletion rules since the exact phonological process involved is not crucial to the analysis. The dialect described in Kaisse 1977a and in this work is the Athenian dialect. I must note that there is great dialect variation in the number of rules, and in terms of the elements affected and the incurring change (see Thumb 1912, Newton 1972, Malikouti-Drachman and Drachman 1978, and references therein).

[5]The relevant pairs consist of a penultimately stressed word followed by an initially stressed word:

(a) i   γáta érγete   → *i γát' érγete (Rule 1 blocked)
the cat   come-3sg.

(b) fréska   órima   fruta   → *frésk' órima fruta (Rule 2 blocked)
fresh-pl. ripe-pl. fruit-pl.

(c) ta   frúta   óla   → *ta frút' óla (Rule 3 blocked)
the fruit-pl. all-pl.

Interestingly, a sequence of two adjacent stressed syllables is not otherwise blocked in the language; there is no equivalent to the English Rhythm Rule in Greek:

(e) δekatrís ánθropi
thirteen people

(f) *δékatris ánθropi

[6]The site of deletion is marked with an apostrophe.

appealed to a so-called "strength" hierarchy of vowels shown in (4).[7] Less Sonorant First Vowel Deletion, then, deletes the final vowel of the first word if it is "weaker", that is lower on the hierarchy, than the following vowel.

(4)   o   a   u   i   e

$\longleftarrow\!\!\!\!\longrightarrow$

   "strong"   "weak"

   e may delete before o, a, u, i
   a may delete before u, i, e
   o may *not* delete

The three rules apply in different environments. Examples (2) and (3) distinguish Rule 1 from Rule 2. The crucial vowel sequences are marked next to each sentence. In the subject-verb sequence of (2), both o and a delete before e. Therefore, Rule 1 applies in this environment. In the adjective-adjective sequence of (3), however, o does *not* delete before e while a does. Rule 2 applies in this environment.

Examples (3) and (5) distinguish Rule 2 from Rule 3. In the noun-postnominal modifier sequence of (5a) and (5b), or in the verb-complement sequence of (5c) and (5d) ,a does *not* delete before e, but it does delete before o. Rule 3 applies in these environments.

(5)   a. ta   kómata ekína → *ta kómat' ekína   *a   e
         the parties those

      b. ta   kómata óla → ta kómat' óla   a   o
         the parties all

      c. kítaksa   eftá eláfya → *kítaks' eftá eláfya   *a   e
         looked-at-1sg. seven deer

      d. kítaksa   oxtó eláfya → kítaks' oxtó eláfya   a   o
         looked-at-1sg. eight deer

The rules are sensitive to the syntactic configuration of the words involved, rather than, as Kaisse 1977a argues, their lexical category specification. (6a) and (6b) contain an identical sequence of adjectives, but each sequence is the site of a different sandhi rule. In (6a) the two adjectives are within the same NP, whereas in (6b) the first belongs to an NP, while the second one belongs to an adjunct adjectival phrase. In (6a) Rule 2 applies; in (6b) Rule 1 applies.

(6)   a. to   frésko akálipto   frúto → *to frésk' akálipto frúto
         the fresh   uncovered fruit

---

[7]It is unclear what the phonological justification for this particular hierarchy is. I will, nevertheless, refer to it for descriptive purposes.

b. to peδi servire to   fruto to   frésko akálipto

→ ... frésk' akálipto

the child served the fruit   the fresh   uncovered

'The child$_i$ served the fresh fruit$_j$ uncovered$_{i/j}$.'

All three rules operate *across* phonological words. Notice that *within* phonological words, as in the postlexically formed phonological words of (7), traditionally known as clitic groups, hiatus is resolved in rather different ways. For example, a high vowel may delete, as in (7a); **a** does not delete before **o** (7b); and the second vowel in a sequence, or a stressed vowel, may delete (7c).[8]

(7) a. m**u**   a**γ**órase   → m' a**γ**órase
        to-me bought-3sg.

    b. t**a**   oδí**γ**isa   → *t' oδí**γ**isa
        them led-1sg.

    c. t**u**   ípa   → t**ú** 'pa
        to-him said-1sg.

Kaisse 1985:124–125 gives the following formulation for the domains of application of the three rules:

(8) a. *Unconditional First Vowel Deletion* applies between any two words separated by an S bracket; and between a nonverb and any adjacent word not in the same phrase.

---

[8]Kaisse 1977a discusses this rule under the name of contraction, and Nespor and Vogel 1986 assume that it is a *w* juncture rule having the clitic group as its domain. Actually, the vowel coalescence phenomena between clitics and their hosts are not the result of a fully productive postlexical rule having the phonological word or the clitic group as its domain. Whether a vowel deletes, given an appropriate vowel sequence, depends on the identity of the lexical item or the clitic the vowel belongs to. For example, the second vowel in a sequence may delete only if it is an augment or belongs to some particular lexical item (for a list of these see Mackridge 1985:34): observe the contrast between (7c) above and (a) below. Also, the high vowel **u** may delete before **a** if it belongs to a gen.-sg. article, or a 1st or 2nd person clitic pronoun, but not if it belongs to a 3rd person clitic pronoun: (7a) and (b), (c) (below) thus contrast with (d) (below).

(a) t**u**   iposçéθika   → *t**u** 'posçéθika
        to-him promised-1sg.

(b) s**u**   a**γ**órase   → s' a**γ**órase
        to-you-sg. bought-3sg.

(c) t**u**   a**γ**oryú   → t' a**γ**oryú
        the-gen.-sg. boy-gen-sg.

(d) t**u**   a**γ**órase   → *t' a**γ**órase
        to-him bought-3sg.

b. *Less Sonorant First Vowel Deletion* applies between a verb and its complements, but is bled by Unrounded First Vowel Deletion.

c. *Unrounded First Vowel Deletion* applies between a noun and its preceding complements and specifiers, and between a verb or preposition and its (following) complements (including, optionally, adverbs).

Given this formulation, the rules seem to require non-overlapping disjunctive domains and an extrinsic ordering stipulation. The theory that Kaisse develops admits a segregation of postlexical phonology into a P1 and a P2 component. The sandhi rules naturally fall into the P1 component given their dependency on syntactic structure. The prediction of such a model is that no purely phonological rule may interact with the sandhi rules. The prediction is not unique to this particular model. It follows from any model in which phonosyntactic rules (rules sensitive to syntactic structure) form a subcomponent distinct from subcomponents of purely phonological rules, such as, for example, the model outlined in Selkirk 1986.

That prediction, however, is not borne out in Greek. The allophonic rule of palatalization interacts with the sandhi rules in an unexpected fashion (Kaisse (this volume)). In Greek, the alternation between palatals and velars is not distinctive; velar consonants palatalize when they are followed by a front vowel:

(9) γ^jelyo γ^jipsos   vs. γala γoma γulya
     'laughter' 'plaster'   'milk'   'eraser'   'sip'

     çeri   çiros   vs.   xari   xora   axuri
     'hand'   'pig'   'favor'   'country'   'barn'

     k^jeri k^jirios   vs.   kapa   kora   kuvas
     'candle'   'gentleman'   'cape'   'crust'   'bucket'

The interaction between palatalization and the sandhi rules has the following two surprising properties: (a) a vowel exercises its palatalizing effect *before* it is eliminated by sandhi (10a), and (b) the vowel of the following word has no effect on the consonant left final after sandhi (10b).

(10) a. to kreas pu etroγ^je   axnize   → ... etroγ^j axnize
          the meat that ate-imp.-3sg. was-steaming-3sg.
          'The meat that he was eating was steaming.'

      b. to kreas pu etroγa   itan nostimo → ... etroγ itan ...
          the meat that ate-imp.-1sg. was delicious
          'The meat that I was eating was delicious.'

The interaction of the sandhi rules with the allophonic rule of palatalization also shows that we cannot "push" the sandhi rules into the lexicon, treating them as precompiled rules, in the sense of Hayes (this volume).

So far, then, we have seen that the sandhi rules are sensitive to syntactic structure, and yet, given their interaction with an allophonic rule, they cannot be phonosyntactic rules if we are to take seriously any reasonably restrictive model of postlexical phonology, which would place phonosyntactic rules earlier in the derivation than purely phonological rules. Luckily, the paradox we are faced with is only an apparent one. The domains of application of the sandhi rules are, in reality, provided by the prosodic hierarchy, enriched, however, with a new prosodic category, intermediate between the phonological word and the phonological phrase.

First Vowel Deletion applies in the following syntactic environments:

(11) **First Vowel Deletion**
   NP – V (Su – V)
   NP – Adv (D.O. – Adv)
   NP – S (topicalization)
   $\left. \begin{array}{l} \text{NP} \\ \text{S} \end{array} \right\}$ – Conj
   NP – PP
   NP – NP (I.O. – D.O.)
   NP – S′ (S′:complement or adjunct)
   NP – AdjP
   AdjP – NP

What these environments have in common is that they all involve the edge of a maximal projection: the first word belongs to a maximal projection which does not include the second word. A matching of an X^{max} edge with a prosodic constituent edge has already been demonstrated for several languages. It has been given theoretical justification by Selkirk 1986 and Chen 1987c, who argue that the syntactic information available for prosodic phrasing is describable in terms of the right or left end of the constituents of the X-bar hierarchy and the different levels those constituents correspond to. For Greek then, X^{max} and right edge are the parameter settings for the delimitation of the prosodic constituent *phonological phrase*. First Vowel Deletion applies across phonological phrases.

Let us now look at the environments of the other two rules:[9]

(12) **Unrounded First Vowel Deletion**
   Between prenominal modifiers in an NP
   Between a prenominal modifier and the head N in an NP
   Adv – V[10]

---

[9]Prepositions do not appear in the list since it is impossible to discern which rule they would undergo. Most prepositions are clitics. The remainder, with one exception, end either in a consonant or a stressed vowel. The only preposition eligible to undergo sandhi is *isame* 'up to'. Its final **e** would be deleted by all three sandhi rules.

[10]Kaisse 1977a assumes that such a sequence is a site of Unconditional First Vowel Deletion but acknowledges that there is not sufficient evidence to distinguish between Unconditional First Vowel Deletion and Unrounded First Vowel Deletion. As it happens, there are a few adverbs in Greek that end in -o, and these provide sufficient

(13) **Less Sonorant First Vowel Deletion**
   V – Adv
   V – NP (Su, D.O., I.O.)
   V – AdjP
   V – adverbial clause
   V – S′
   V – PP
   N – postnominal modifier[11]

The environments show a remarkable complementarity. Rule 2 applies across words up to a lexical head, while Rule 3 applies between a lexical head and material following it within the same maximal projection.[12] Heads, therefore, as well as maximal projections, are crucial in phrasing. The prosodic category delimited by heads can be neither the phonological word[13] nor the phonological phrase, since the parameter setting for the latter is $X^{\max}$. Therefore, a new prosodic category is needed, one higher in the hierarchy than the phonological word w and lower than the phonological phrase ϕ. This new category I will call *minimal phrase* and symbolize with z. Its parameter settings are: X^{head} and right end.[14] The Phrasing Algorithm that I propose for Greek is stated in (14).

---

evidence in favor of the classification of Adv – V under Unrounded First Vowel Deletion:

(a) liγo erxotan   → *liγ' erxotan
   little come-imp.-3sg.
   'He was rarely coming.'

(b) oloena   erxotan   → oloen' erxotan
   all-the-time come-imp.-3sg.
   'He was coming all the time.'

[11]Such cases are not discussed in Kaisse's studies. See examples (5a) and (5b) above.

[12]In a review of Kaisse 1985, Rice 1987:309 makes a brief suggestion for the accommodation of the Greek facts into a prosodic framework: "Using the framework laid out by Selkirk 1986, it appears that the domain of Less Sonorant First Vowel Deletion and Unrounded First Vowel Deletion can be characterized as that obtained by marking the right edge of maximal projections. ...Unconditional First Vowel Deletion seems to be a rule of a larger domain, perhaps the utterance." According to this suggestion, there are two domains, two of the rules having the same domain. But what further information could distinguish the proper environments for these two rules within the domain delimited by the right edge of a maximal projection? An analysis recognizing only two domains for the three sandhi rules fails to capture the complementarity between elements preceding the head and those following it within the same maximal projection.

[13]Following Zec and Inkelas (this volume), I am assuming that the postlexically formed phonological word includes clitics and their host. The facts of stress, stop voicing (see the discussion of the clitic group in Greek in Nespor and Vogel 1986), and palatalization provide ample evidence that this prosodic category is distinct from any prosodic category constituting the domain of a sandhi rule.

[14]I am assuming that adjectives and adverbs do not have phrasal projections when used as modifiers, an assumption that is common in discussions of phrasing across languages. I leave it as an open question whether this really reflects something about the syntax of adjectives and adverbs (not projecting to phrasal categories), or whether

(14) a. From left to right map all material up to and including the lexical head of a maximal projection into a minimal phrase z.

  b. From left to right map all material up to the right end of a maximal projection into a phonological phrase ϕ.

  c. Map all unassociated material within a ϕ into a z.

Clauses (14a) and (14b) take priority over clause (14c). Essentially, the effect of the phrasing algorithm is the following: strings of w's are grouped into z's and ϕ's, and remaining material within a ϕ is then incorporated into prosodic structure by forming its own z. The way the algorithm works is illustrated in (15).

(15) a. [[freska$_A$ fruta$_N$] elafra$_A$]   'fresh light fruit'

  b. (freska)$_\omega$ (fruta)$_\omega$ (elafra)$_\omega$

  c. [(freska)$_\omega$ (fruta)$_\omega$]$_z$ (elafra)$_\omega$ (by (15a))

  d. [[(freska)$_\omega$ (fruta)$_\omega$]$_z$ (elafra)$_\omega$]$_\phi$ (by (15b))

  e. [[(freska)$_\omega$ (fruta)$_\omega$]$_z$ [(elafra)$_\omega$]$_z$]$_\phi$ (by (15c))

The three sandhi rules are as follows (I have abstracted away from the particular features of the vowels deleted in each case): Unrounded First Vowel Deletion applies between w's in the domain of the minimal phrase; Less Sonorant First Vowel Deletion applies between minimal phrases in the domain of the phonological phrase; First Vowel Deletion applies between phonological phrases within a "large" domain (U-domain).

(16) Unrounded First Vowel Deletion:
    $V \rightarrow \emptyset /$ __ $]_w [_w$ V   domain z

  Less Sonorant First Vowel Deletion:
    $V \rightarrow \emptyset /$ __ $]_z [_z$ V   domain ϕ

  First Vowel Deletion:
    $V \rightarrow \emptyset /$ __ $]_\phi [_\phi$ V   domain U

All three rules are juncture rules, with an interesting property: the type of the juncture depends on the domain of the rule. More specifically, if α is the domain of the rule and β the category of the juncture, then β is immediately dominated by α in the prosodic hierarchy. Thus all we need to know about a rule is its domain and whether it is a juncture rule. It is important to note that the need for three distinct domains is independent of the analysis of the actual phonological processes involved in the sandhi phenomena. Even if the sandhi rules are the result of resyllabification

---

adjectives and adverbs don't count as heads *for the purposes of phrasing*—that is, whether a completely cross-categorial syntax-phonology mapping is tenable.

and degemination, one would still have to contend with three domains. Palatalization, I am assuming, is a word-level allophonic rule.

Although the mapping between syntactic and prosodic structure in Greek turns out to be rather unsurprising, Greek still provides an interesting case for theories of syntax-phonology interaction in the following three ways.

a. Both X^{head} and X^{max} are implicated in phrasing. In exploring the implications of the end-based approach, Selkirk 1986 surmised that X^{head} might play a role in phrasing, in determining, for example, the edge of a *small phonological phrase*.[15] Whether X^{head} is an alternative parameter setting for the delimitation of a phonological phrase, or whether it delimits a new prosodic category, was left unclear. What has not been shown up to now is a case where both the maximal and the small phonological phrases are needed, and that is precisely what Greek provides.

b. What forms a minimal phrase in Greek is not a compound word but a full-fledged syntactic phrase prosodically composed of full phonological words. That is, a minimal phrase in Greek may contain any number of full phonological words.

c. While the left side of a NP in Greek is a recursive side, all material on that side phrases together with the head;[16] furthermore, if a specifier follows the head, the phrasing breaks it off from the head. In other words, in Greek we have a real case of edge-to-edge mapping, rather than a relational type.

According to relational theories of mapping, heads are phrased together with all elements on their non-recursive side within the same maximal projection (Nespor and Vogel 1986, Hayes 1989). Theories relying on a relational-type mapping and those relying on an edge-based mapping make similar predictions in most cases but they are crucially distinguished in some. Test cases arise in a configuration in which a word is between two heads but forms a maximal projection with neither of them. In the configuration in (17a), relational theories would, in principle, allow w_2 to form a prosodic constituent p of its own (see (17b)), or join the prosodic constituent p on its left (see (17c)), but would exclude the phrasing shown in (17d). Edge-based theories, on the other hand, predict that (17a) would phrase as in (17d).

(17) a. [Y^{head} Z [W X^{head}]$_{X^{\text{max}}}$]$_{Y^{\text{max}}}$

---

[15]In that work, the small phonological phrase is assumed to be the domain of 'unmarked' liaison in colloquial French.

[16]For Nespor and Vogel 1986, the recursive side with respect to the head of a phrase is the unmarked position for complements of the head. Even from that standpoint, the left side of a NP, being the unmarked position for modifiers, is a recursive side: unlike Romance languages, in Greek there are no limitations on the number or type of adjectives appearing to the left of a nominal head.

b. $[_p \; w_1 \;] \; [_p \; w_2 \;] \; [_p \; w_3 \; w_4 \;]$

c. $[_p \; w_1 \; w_2 \;] \; [_p \; w_3 \; w_4 \;]$

d. $[_p \; w_1 \;] \; [_p \; w_2 \; w_3 \; w_4 \;]$

In Greek, a V – Adv – [$_{NP}$ Adj N] sequence, which instantiates the schema in (17a), is organized into z's in the way predicted by the edge-based approach: the adverb belongs to the z delimited by the nominal head. As seen in (18), the sandhi rule applying between the adverb and the numeral modifier in the object NP is Unrounded First Vowel Deletion.

(18) a. klotsise   aγarba enya kolones   → ...aγarb' enya...
         kicked-3sg. clumsily nine pillars
         'He clumsily kicked nine pillars.'

      b. klotsise   apo   liγo enya kolones   → *...liγ' enya...
          kicked-3sg DISTR little nine pillars
          'He kicked nine pillars a little each.'

2   The Prosodic Category z

In this section, I provide independent evidence for the inclusion of the minimal phrase in the inventory of prosodic categories in Greek by arguing that the environment of some phrasal allomorphy requires reference to the minimal phrase.

A long-standing puzzle for Greek has been the distribution of the -n-final masc.-acc.-sing. form of certain pronominal elements. These include the following pronouns and pronominal modifiers:[17] *pyos* 'who, which', *aftos* 'he, this', *tutos* 'this', *ekinos* 'he, that', *kapyos* 'someone, some', *olos* 'all, whole', *alos* '(someone) else, other/another', *enas* 'someone, one', *opyos* 'who/whichever', *tosos* 'such, so/as/that much/many', *osos* 'as much/many as'.[18] The n-final forms of these pronominals are obligatory when the following word begins either with a vowel or a voiceless stop, as in (19a,b), (20a,b) and (21a,b). Mysteriously, however, it is also obligatory in some other environments as well. Consider *pyos*. While in (19d) the form without the final n is acceptable, final n is obligatory in (19c) and (19e). An identical contrast can be observed for *enas* between (20d) and (20c,e), and for *opyos* between (21d) and (21c,e).

(19) a. pyon/*pyo andra?
         'which-acc. man-acc.?'

      b. pyon/*pyo kafe?
         'which-acc. coffee-acc.?'

---

[17]In Greek there is no distinction between free pronouns and pronominal modifiers; *pyos*, for example, means both 'who-masc.' and 'which-masc.'

[18]The pronominal elements are listed in the masc. nom. sing. form.

c. pyon/*pyo voiθises?
'which-acc. did you help?' or 'which-acc. one did you help?'

d. pyo filo su?
'which-acc. friend-acc. of yours?'

e. filo su pyon/*pyo voiθises?
'which-acc. friend-acc. of yours did you help?'

(20) a. enan/*ena andra
'one-acc. man-acc.'

b. enan/*ena kafe
'one-acc. coffee-acc.'

c. iδa enan/*ena na kapnizi
'I saw someone-acc. smoking'
or 'I saw one-acc. (of those) smoking'

d. ena filo su
'one-acc. friend-acc. of yours'

e. δose apo enan/*ena sta peδya
'give the children one-acc. (of those) each'

(21) a. opyon/*opyo andra
'whichever-acc. man-acc.'

b. opyon/*opyo kafe
'whichever-acc. coffee-acc.'

c. opyon/*opyo δyaforetiko vris
'whoever-acc. different you find'
or 'whichever-acc. one different you find'[19]

d. opyo δyaforetiko δromo
'whichever-acc. different-acc. road-acc.'

e. δromo opyon/*opyo vris
'whichever-acc. road-acc. you find'

The generalization is that the *n*-final form is obligatory when the element is (a) a pronoun, (b) a modifier following the nominal head, or (c) a modifier immediately preceding a null head.[20] But why should the generalization require a three-way disjunctive statement? Syntactically (a), (b), and (c) have nothing in common. In prosodic terms, however, they can be unified as follows:

---

[19] A proper translation of this in English is: whoever/whichever one you might find that is different.

[20] The equivalent of the English nominal pro-form *one* is a null pro-form. This null element constitutes a nominal head and, crucially, it must be visible in phrasing.

> The n-final form is obligatory when the pronominal element
> is at the right end of a minimal phrase.[21]

This prosodic generalization accounts for the distribution of the final-n form in environments (a-c) as follows. If a pronominal element is a free pronoun, then it constitutes the head of a NP. Since heads induce a minimal phrase break on their right, it follows that, if overt, they end up at the right end of a minimal phrase; if the head is null, the immediately preceding modifier ends up at the right end of a minimal phrase. This covers environments (a) and (c). Finally, given clause (14c) of the phrasing algorithm, material to the right of the head within a maximal projection constitutes its own minimal phrase; therefore, if a single word, it is at the right end of a minimal phrase. This covers environment (b).

If the clustering of (a), (b), and (c) is not accidental, then we should expect that a description of the distribution of other elements would include either (a), (b), and (c) together, or their complement, but not an arbitrary combination, say, (a) and (c) and something else. This is precisely what we find. The restricted allomorphs of *ólon* 'all-gen.-pl.' and *ekínon* 'them-gen.-pl., those-gen.-pl.' provide the desired case. *ólon* has an allomorph with a more restricted distribution (*olonón*) and so does *ekínon* (*ekinón*). As can be seen in examples (22) and (23), *olonón* appears in the familiar constellation, (a) and (b) but not (c), while *ekinón* appears everywhere else. In other words, *olonón* can appear only z-finally, while *ekinón* can appear only in a position that is final-it not z-final.

(22) a. ton filon olon/olonón
          'all-gen.-pl. the-gen.-pl. friends-gen.'

      b. dose olon/olonón psomi
          'give all-gen.-pl. bread'

      c. olon/*olonón ton filon
          'all-gen.-pl. the-gen.-pl. friends-gen.'

(23) a. ekinón ton filon
          'those friends-gen.'

      b. *ton filon ekinón
          'those friends-gen.'

      c. *dose ekinón psomi
          'give those people bread'

---

[21] Of all the attempts to characterize the obligatory occurrence of the n-final form, the most insightful is that of Triandaphyllidis 1941:82 (my translation and italics): "The final n is preserved in the masc.-acc.-sing. of several pronouns and pronominal adjectives when they *are not closely connected with the following word* or when it [the following word] starts with a vowel or stop consonant." The analysis that I offer can be seen as making the notion of "not closely connected" precise: two words are not closely connected if they are not part of the same z. This analysis also accounts for the case when the relevant pronominal element is utterance final.

The formalization of these generalizations raises some interesting theoretical questions. While the alternations discussed implicate a postlexical prosodic category, they don't arise through any postlexical rule application. After all, they involve only a class of pronominal elements and some isolated forms like *ólon* and *ekínon*. The proper characterization of these alternations must be as *lexically precompiled phrasal allomorphy*, in the sense of Hayes (this volume). Hayes, in an effort to eliminate all syntax-sensitive rules from postlexical phonology, develops a theory of lexically precompiled rules, that is, lexical rules which create allomorphs for insertion in certain phrasal contexts (hence the term 'precompiling'). While the cases of phrasal allomorphy discussed in Hayes (this volume) all involve some rather idiosyncratic syntactic environments, the cases of Greek allomorphy are, in a sense, better behaved, in that they exploit a prosodic category, allowing for a simply stated environment.[22] There is nothing surprising about this as long as we assume that lexical insertion is subject both to syntactic and to prosodic well-formedness conditions. In other words, at the point of lexical insertion both syntactic and prosodic structures have been created, and lexical insertion must be in accord with well-formedness conditions on both structures.[23] The prosodic requirements of allomorphs can be represented by the familiar subcategorization frames. *Olonón* and *ekinón*, therefore, would be accompanied by the following subcategorization frames in their lexical specification:

(24) *olonón*   —]$_z$
     ekinón   — w

If subcategorized information must be local, then the specification — w would exclude anything intervening between the relevant lexical item and the next w.[24]

For the class of pronominal elements showing the $n/\emptyset$ alternation, we can utilize Hayes's phonological instantiation frames and assume that the n-final form is inserted in Frame 1.

(25) Frame 1:   —]$_z$

We have seen that postlexical prosodic categories enter the lexicon as phrasal environments. Inkelas 1988, 1989a has argued for the need of prosodic categories in the lexicon, both lexical and postlexical, but in her view prosodic subcategorization is a property solely of affixes and clitics.

---

[22] As Hayes points out, these idiosyncratic environments are the result of a restructuring of the residue of at one point exceptionless postlexical rules. There is no reason, in principle, why restructuring of an environment should not exploit the prosodic inventory of the language and thus create a more regular pattern.

[23] In a more general vein, Zec and Inkelas (this volume) argue for bidirectionality in syntax-phonology interactions, always mediated by prosodic structure.

[24] This case of allomorphy is interesting for another reason. The more restricted allomorph does not induce blocking. The non-restricted forms *ólon* and *ekínon* are not simply the *elsewhere* case but the *anywhere* case.

In other words, prosodic subcategorization is tied to prosodic dependence. The analysis of the Greek facts forces a different view: prosodic subcategorization subsumes but is not identical to prosodic dependence. More precisely, prosodic subcategorization is a representation of two things: (a) prosodic dependence, in which case it is interpreted as building prosodic constituency, (b) prosodic allomorphy, in which case it serves as a well-formedness condition on lexical insertion.

3 A New View on Phrasing

The formulation of the Greek phrasing algorithm reflects both a bottom-up type of phrasing (clauses (14a,b)), and a top-down type of phrasing (clause (14c)). This will be justified in the present section.

In the common view of phrasing, every language has a phrasing algorithm *per* prosodic category[25] and, crucially, a string is submitted to a series of *successive full* parses with respect to each prosodic category. In other words, when category X^n is to be constructed, all categories of lower type, X^{n-m}, $m = 1, 2, \ldots, n$ must have already been constructed. For some theorists, furthermore, phonological rules having as their domains categories of lower type have already applied when X^n is to be constructed. The phonology is thus interspersed with prosodic structure formation. (For an explicit proposal, see McHugh (this volume)).

Underlying the view of exclusively bottom-up parsing is the assumption that the formation of one prosodic category does not interact with that of any other category, except for the grouping of prosodic constituents of type X^{n-1} into constituents of type X^n. In this section, I will show that this assumption is untenable: the way a string is parsed with respect to a given prosodic category *may* depend on the way it is parsed with respect to a higher prosodic category. These *top-down effects* are of the following two types: (a) a prosodic category may be constructed, either fully or partially, *within* the domain of a higher prosodic category, and (b) the conditions defining the span of a given prosodic category may be overridden by those defining the span of a higher prosodic category.

I will present three cases to this effect; the first two are of type (a), and the third is of type (b). I will further show that top-down effects entail that any exclusively bottom-up phrasing algorithm will yield well-formed structures only at the cost of redundancy and unnecessary complexity. The argument is independent of the way prosodic phrasing is expressed. Even if we reconstruct phrasing algorithms as constraints imposed on prosodic parsing, it is only at the price of great duplication that the well-formedness conditions for a category X^n can be stated with reference to X^{n-1} exclusively.

In (26) are listed the necessary properties of well-formed prosodic structures:

---

[25] At least for those categories that are operative in the language.

(26) a. *Exhaustiveness of parse*: a string is exhaustively parsed with respect to each prosodic category.

   b. *Strict Layering*: A prosodic constituent of type X^n dominates constituents of type X^{n-1} (the immediately lower category in the prosodic hierarchy) and every prosodic constituent of type X^n is exhaustively contained in a constituent of type X^{n+1}.

   c. Prosodic structure constitutes a well-formed tree structure.

Although the validity of the conditions in (26) is a basic assumption of prosodic theory, their status remains an open question. Are they *independent* constraints on phrasing algorithms or constraints governing prosodic parsing, or do they follow from such algorithms or constraints? And if the latter, are all three independent of each other?[26] I raise and discuss these questions in some length as a preliminary to the exposition of the empirical evidence because a discussion of top-down phenomena and their consequences is meaningful only if they have been settled.

Selkirk 1986 hypothesized that these necessary properties of prosodic structure follow from the edge-based approach to the mapping between syntactic and prosodic structure: "this simple end-based theory of derived domains, appropriately generalized, constitutes both a theory of the relation between syntactic structure and prosodic or phonological structure *and a theory of that prosodic structure itself*" (p. 386, my italics). Selkirk's claim is not simply that the edge-based mapping is subject to the conditions in (26), but that it is inherently such that it would never yield offending configurations.

An end-based mapping alone, however, does not always yield structures satisfying the conditions in (26) because, by itself, it does not guarantee exhaustiveness of parse.[27] Given that exhaustiveness of parse does not necessarily follow from an end-based mapping, the conditions of Strict Layering and tree structure well-formedness do not follow either. To see this consider the configuration in (27a).

(27) a. $[\, Y \, X^{\text{head}} \, Z \,]_{X^{\text{max}}} \, W$

   b. $[\, w_1 \, w_2 \,]_z \, w_3 \,]_\phi \, w_4$

   c. $*[\, [\, w_1 \, w_2 \,]_z \, [\, w_3 \,]_\phi \, w_4 \,]_z$

How would (27a) phrase given the parameter setting $[\, X^{\text{head}}, \text{right} \,]$ for z and $[\, X^{\text{max}}, \text{right} \,]$ for ϕ?[28] Notice first that a strictly end-to-end mapping unsupplemented by any other principles would leave w_3 unphrased

---

[26]For discussion of these issues see also Inkelas 1989a, especially Chapter 9.

[27]If exhaustiveness of parse indeed followed from the end-based mapping, then Strict Layering would follow as well, given "the hierarchy of syntactic categories themselves (in the end-settings) and . . . the simple-minded way the tree is scanned for instances of these ends" (Selkirk 1986:388). If prosodic structure observes the Strict Layering condition, it is a well-formed tree structure.

[28]See Selkirk and Shen (this volume) for a discussion of cases of this type.

with respect to z. Only a condition of the type in (26a) would guarantee that w_3 must be parsed with respect to that category too. Assuming we construe (26a) as a condition of maximal parse up to satisfaction of the end-based specifications, then we must still guarantee in some way that the result is a tree structure. Otherwise nothing would rule out the ill-formed structure shown in (27c). An additional condition of type (26b) would guarantee strict layering of prosodic constituents and, consequently, the well-formedness of tree structure. If, on the other hand, (26a) is incorporated directly into a phrasing algorithm, making explicit provisions for unphrased elements identified within a higher constituent, as is the case with w_3 in (27b), then the resulting structures will observe (26b).[29]

We have established, therefore, that (26a) and (26b) must supplement an end-based mapping as additional mapping clauses in phrasing algorithms or as constraints on the resulting representations. The first case of top-down effects appears precisely in mapping clauses incorporating (26a) and can be characterized as follows: material unparsed with respect to some prosodic category is identified within the domain of an immediately higher category.

Clause (14c) in the phrasing algorithm proposed for Greek in section 1 guarantees that a string is parsed exhaustively with respect to the category z. As seen in (15) and schematically in (27) above, exhaustiveness of parse is not achieved by the end-to-end mapping alone. The algorithm proposed departs from the usual assumptions about phrasing in that it accommodates both the minimal phrase and the phonological phrase and in that it reflects both a bottom-up type of phrasing (clauses (14a,b)), and a top-down type of phrasing (clause (14c)). Given the priority of clause (14b) over clause (14c), the ϕ domain is already defined when unassociated w's are to be mapped into z's.

Let us compare the "mixed" algorithm proposed above with the pair of algorithms conforming to the common assumptions:

(28) *Minimal Phrase*

    a. From left to right map all material up to and including the lexical head of a maximal projection into a minimal phrase z.

    b. Map all unassociated material within the same maximal projection into a z.

(29) *Phonological Phrase*
From left to right map all material up to the right end of a maximal projection into a phonological phrase ϕ.

Clause (28b) guarantees the well-formedness of the prosodic tree structure by anticipating the effect of the phonological phrase formation rule.

---

[29]Whether such a construal of (26a) would result in automatic satisfaction of (26b) in the general case I leave as an open question. See Inkelas 1989a for a positive suggestion.

The redundancy between clause (28b) of the minimal phrase formation and the phonological phrase formation arises because the string must have already been parsed fully with respect to all lower prosodic categories and because the prosodic structure must form a tree structure. The "mixed" algorithm avoids this redundancy; the well-formedness of the tree structure is achieved by the ordering of clauses (14b) and (14c).[30]

In sum, prosodic structure is built in a way that makes available more than one prosodic category at once; "unassociated material" is unassociated material *within* a domain, or, more precisely, a part of a string may be unparsed with respect to some prosodic category while being already incorporated into prosodic structure within a higher prosodic category. This is, in effect, an instance of top-down phrasing.

The second case of top-down phrasing, involving a prosodic category which is defined within a larger domain, has been discussed by Selkirk and Tateishi 1988a, who have shown that the minor phrase in Japanese is defined within the domain of the major phrase. Selkirk and Tateishi have argued that the well-formedness conditions on minor phrases[31] are not checked strictly locally: one must have access to the arrangement of a sentence into prosodic words, minor phrases *and* major phrases. Given that in Japanese, major phrases are delimited by the left edge of a maximal projection, one could state the well-formedness conditions on minor phrases with reference to edges of maximal projections. This, however, would duplicate the conditions on the formation of major phrases[32] and would make the formulation of the conditions of minor phrases very cumbersome.[33]

The third case, involving focused elements, provides an even more compelling argument for top-down phrasing. The effect of focused elements on prosodic structure formation demonstrates that the specifications for the construction of a prosodic category α may override those of a prosodic category β, where α is higher on the prosodic hierarchy than β. That focus plays a special role in phrasing has already been shown for several languages by Vogel and Kenesei 1987, Inkelas 1988, Cho (this volume), Kanerva (this volume), Vogel and Kenesei (this volume), and Zec and Inkelas (this volume), among others. In Greek, as well, the phrasing requirements of focused elements supersede those of the regular mapping

---

[30]This ordering, as we will see later, is not particular to this phrasing algorithm but follows from a basic difference between the two types of clauses.

[31]One such condition is the peripherality constraint which, as formulated by Selkirk and Tateishi, states that an unaccented prosodic word at the periphery of major phrases must be dominated by the same minor phrase as an adjacent prosodic word.

[32]If, for instance, major phrases in Japanese were not delimited by reference to maximal projections in syntactic representation, then, everything else being equal, maximal projections would not play a role in the delimitation of minor phrases either.

[33]Complications would arise, for example, because the peripherality constraint holds for both ends of a major phrase, but the right end of a major phrase does not necessarily coincide with the right edge of a maximal projection. The right edge of a maximal projection coincides with that of a major phrase only if it is immediately followed by the left edge of a maximal projection, or if it is sentence final.

principles in the language. Crucially, however, focus does not impose a special requirement in the phrasing of either the minimal phrase or the phonological phrase. More specifically, a focused word does not form either a minimal phrase or a phonological phrase on its own,[34] nor does it introduce a minimal phrase or a phonological phrase break. Rather, a focused element introduces a U break at its left end.

To appreciate the effect of focus we must see in what ways the construction of prosodic structure by the regular (syntax-sensitive) mapping principles gets disrupted in the presence of a focused element. We can determine the organization of focused elements and adjacent material into prosodic structure in Greek using the three sandhi rules with their respective successively larger domains as a diagnostic. As we see in (30a), there is no z boundary between the focused adjective and the unfocused noun, which would have been the case if the focused element constituted its own z, or if it introduced a z break immediately after it. If there were a z boundary between the focused and the unfocused words, **a** would not delete before **e**, Less Sonorant First Vowel Deletion being the rule applying across a z juncture. Instead, the two words belong to the same minimal phrase a and Unrounded First Vowel Deletion applies as usual (see (30b)). As we see in (30c), there is no ϕ boundary between the focused verb and the unfocused direct object, which would have been the case if the focused element constituted its own ϕ, or if it introduced a ϕ break immediately after it. If there were a ϕ boundary between the focused and the unfocused words, **a** would delete before **e**, First Vowel Deletion being the rule operating across ϕ boundaries. Instead, the three words form two minimal phrases belonging to the same phonological phrase and Less Sonorant First Vowel Deletion applies as usual (see (30d)).

(30) a. γipsin**a** **e**lafya → γipsin' elafya
         [+FOC]
         'plaster deer(pl.)'

     b. γipsin**o** **e**lafi → *γipsin' elafi
         [+FOC]
         'a plaster deer'

     c. aγoras**a** **e**fta elafya → *aγoras' efta elafya
         [+FOC]
         'bought-1sg. seven deer'

     d. aγoras**a** **o**xto elafya → aγoras' oxto elafya
         [+FOC]
         'bought-1sg. eight deer'

---

[34]This would be the equivalent of the effect of focus in Hausa, where, according to Zec and Inkelas (this volume), prominent elements constitute their own phonological phrase.

So far we have seen that focus has no effect on the relation between the focused element and material on its right. A focused word and a following unfocused word are phrased as usual without any disruption. The effect of focus appears between the focused element and material on its left and consists in splitting material which would otherwise phrase together. In other words, whereas by the regular mapping principles some elements would be dominated by one and the same prosodic constituent, the presence of a focused element splits them apart into two prosodic constituents.

The break a focused element introduces at its left end is not simply a z break, for Less Sonorant First Vowel Deletion, the rule operating between z junctures, does not apply in sequences as in (31a). Nor is it a ϕ break, for First Vowel Deletion, the rule operating between ϕ junctures, does not apply in the sequence of (31a) or (31b).

(31) a. ascima onira → *ascim' onira
           [+FOC]
       'bad dreams'

    b. ton   anθropo   ekinon   → *ton anθrop' ekinon
       the-acc. person-acc. that-acc.
                     [+FOC]
       'that person'

More generally, no sandhi rules apply between an unfocused and a focused word. To see that the break introduced by a focused element is specifically a U break, we must consider the rule of vowel degemination, which, as argued in Nespor 1987, has U as its largest domain.[35] Between a focused and an unfocused element the rule applies, as shown in (32a), both elements, therefore, are within the same U. On the other hand, as shown in (32b), the rule does not apply between an unfocused and a focused element, even when those would ordinarily belong to the same z. Therefore, there must be a U break between them.[36]

(32) a. γipsina aγalmata → γipsin' aγalmata
        [+FOC]
       'plaster statues'

    b. γipsina aγalmata → *γipsin' aγalmata
        [+FOC]

---

[35]The vowel degemination rule applies between any two words in a sentence (but not within a word), and, in some cases, even across sentences (see ex. (7) in Nespor 1987:65). In the analysis of Nespor, the rule deletes the second vowel in a sequence if it is unstressed. I think the rule should be characterized as deleting the first vowel if it is unstressed and if the resulting sequence would not result in two stressed syllables being adjacent (the same constraint as on sandhi rules).

[36]There is no perceptible pause at the U break, that is between the focused and the preceding element.

The importance of the phrasing of focused elements in Greek lies precisely in showing that top-down phrasing does not simply delimit the construction of lower categories with respect to higher ones so as to yield structures of the appropriate kind but it also delimits higher categories in ways that are inconsistent with the delimitation of lower categories by the regular mapping principles. If (30), (31) and (32) are to be parsed fully with respect to z and ϕ before they are incorporated into U, then we must ensure that a z break and a ϕ break are introduced before the focused word by adding the necessary specifications in the algorithms for z and ϕ. But is the complication in the algorithms for z and ϕ necessary? The additional specifications simply anticipate the eventual introduction of a U break at that site.

How do we eliminate the redundancy from prosodic structure formation while still capturing the interactions between prosodic categories discussed above? Suppose that phrasing algorithms consist of three types of clauses: overriding structure clauses, regular mapping clauses, and clauses accommodating unassociated material. The phrasing requirements of prominent elements are accommodated by the overriding structure clauses, the prosodic structure built by reference to syntactic structure is accommodated by the regular mapping clauses, and material unaccounted for by either of the former two types of clauses is accommodated by the third type of clause. Unassociated material arises in two ways: the syntax-sensitive clauses leave unassociated material within a certain domain, or the overriding structure clauses create a split, leaving unphrased material which would otherwise be assigned prosodic structure by the regular mapping clauses. Prosodic structure is built in two passes: through *primary* parsing governed by the specifications of the overriding structure and the regular mapping clauses, and through a *mop up* operation. Within primary parsing the overriding structure clauses constitute the special case, and the regular mapping clauses constitute the elsewhere case.[37] From this perspective, we can also reconstruct Nespor and Vogel's (1986) optional restructuring as the availability of alternative strategies (stray adjunction vs. formation of a new constituent) within a language for achieving exhaustiveness of parse. Such a move would provide some justification for the existence of so-called restructuring, it would unify all phenomena involving alternative prosodic representations, and it would afford an interesting prediction with respect to the exact site of "restructuring" and the categories involved. If apparent cases of restructuring are the result of the availability of alternative mopp-up operations, then they should appear only in configurations where some material is left unparsed by primary mapping.

Top-down effects in which the specifications of a higher category su-

---

[37]My conjecture is that there are no inconsistencies in the specification of the prosodic categories within each clause type. Inconsistencies in the specification of prosodic categories within a clause type would, in effect, amount to the superiority of some categories over others.

persede those of a lower category have a further consequence: the whole of prosodic structure must be present when phonological rules apply. Therefore, phonology is not taking place in tandem with prosodic structure building, either in a strong form (the cyclic application that McHugh (this volume) has advocated) or in a weaker form (category to category as, for example, Rice (this volume) presupposes). As we saw in the discussion of focus in Greek, not only is vowel degemination blocked in the presence of a U break, but so are the sandhi rules. An analysis assuming interspersing of prosodic structure formation with phonological rule application would consistently make the wrong predictions with respect to these facts. The reason is that, in reconciling the top-down effects in phrasing with phonological rules having access to intermediate prosodic representations, the wrong domains are identified for the application of rules. For example, if such an analysis is to capture top-down effects in Greek by resorting to restructuring—that is, if z and ϕ are to be built according to the regular edge-based specifications and later split apart in the presence of a U break—it would predict that the w juncture and z juncture sandhi rules should apply between an unfocused and a focused word. Or, if it is to specify a z and a ϕ break before a focused word, then it would predict that the z juncture and the ϕ juncture sandhi rules should apply between a focused and an unfocused word.

While much of this section was devoted to demonstrating the existence of top-down effects, we still have not addressed the question: why do top-down effects arise? The perspective on phrasing that I consider in this section suggests that top-down effects are in essence repair mechanisms. The configurations in which such repair mechanisms are needed have two possible sources: they arise from special mapping requirements of particular elements in a language, *and* from the way prosodic parsing is organized, namely the separation between primary and mop-up parsing operations.

5

Precompiled Phrasal Phonology

Bruce Hayes

WHAT IS THE MECHANISM by which syntax affects phonological rule application? A very restrictive hypothesis is the following:

(1) Syntax has phonological effects only insofar as it determines phonological phrasing.

By phonological phrasing I mean the theory of the prosodic domains developed in work by Selkirk 1980a, 1981a, 1986; Nespor and Vogel 1982, 1986; Hayes 1989; and others. The basic idea is that the output of the syntactic component is submitted to a set of phonological phrasing rules, which rebracket and relabel the structure to form a new, purely phonological bracketing which I will refer to as the 'prosodic hierarchy.' To give an example, the sentence whose syntactic structure is given in (2a) would be assigned the prosodic structure under (2b).

Phonological rules may refer to the prosodic hierarchy in three ways (Selkirk 1980a): they may be *bounded* by a particular domain, they may refer to the right or left edge of a domain in their structural descriptions, and they may refer to domain-internal junctures of the form][. A crucial element of the theory is the Strict Layer Hypothesis (Selkirk 1981a): each non-terminal category in the hierarchy dominates only categories of the immediately lower level. Thus U dominates only I, I only P, and so on.

I would like to thank Sharon Inkelas, Ellen Kaisse, Patricia Keating, and members of the Phonology-Syntax Connection workshop audience for helpful comments and discussion on an earlier version of this article. Thanks also to Koichi Tateishi for providing me with copies of his forthcoming work on Mende, from which my own discussion of this language has greatly benefited.

(2) a.

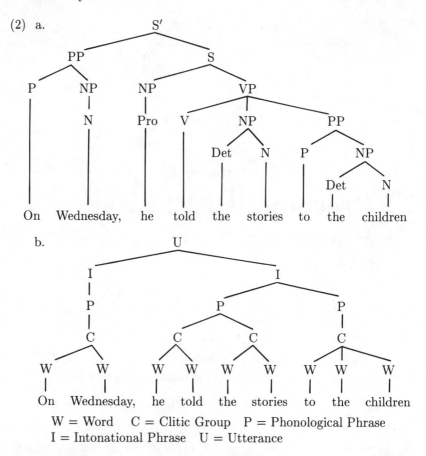

b.

W = Word   C = Clitic Group   P = Phonological Phrase
I = Intonational Phrase   U = Utterance

When combined with a requirement that the string be parsed exhaustively at all levels, this means that all expressions have exactly the same number of levels of embedding.

The basic support for the prosodic hierarchy lies in the fact that there are many phonological rules that refer to phrasal domains that are not syntactic constituents. This and other arguments are presented in a growing body of research; cf. *Phonology Yearbook 4,* several of the papers in this volume, and the references cited therein. I review some of the arguments below in section 8. Although problems and possible counterexamples exist in various languages, my view is that prosodic hierarchy theory has had enough descriptive and explanatory success so far that it constitutes the most promising research program for the study of phrasal phonology.

1   Shortcomings of Prosodic Hierarchy Theory, and a Proposal

It is clear, however, that the prosodic hierarchy cannot serve as a complete theory of the phonological phenomena that are syntax-dependent. That is, the slogan under (1) has been clearly shown not to be true. I give some counterexamples below.

(3) a. *Ewe* (Clements 1978): A High tone verb acquires Rising tone following High or Rising tone if the immediately following noun root bears Mid or Low tone on its first syllable.

    b. *French* (Selkirk 1972): In colloquial style (*conversation familière*), liaison occurs between an adjective or quantifier and a following noun, but not between an adverb and a following verb or adjective.

    c. *Hausa* (Kraft and Kirk-Green 1973): A verb-final long vowel is shortened immediately before an object NP.

Rules like these refer to very specific syntactic information, and do not generalize across X' categories as phonological phrasing characteristically does. Thus it is unlikely that a successful account of such rules based on phonological phrasing could be maintained. I will refer to rules like (3a-c) as 'direct-syntax rules.' Selkirk 1980a and Nespor and Vogel 1986:32–3 note the existence of such rules, and observe that they fall outside the scope of prosodic hierarchy theory.

The existence of direct-syntax rules is a problem for prosodic hierarchy theory, since when a rule doesn't fit the predictions of the theory, we can usually reclassify it as a direct-syntax rule. This seriously reduces the falsifiability, hence the predictive value, of the theory.

An option that may be workable here is to develop a theory of the *residue* left unaccounted for by prosodic hierarchy theory. That is, the phenomena that elude successful treatment in prosodic hierarchy theory may have their own regularities that can be insightfully accounted for under a completely different theory.

In this paper I propose a theory of this sort, based in part on work by Zwicky 1985d, 1987a; Pullum and Zwicky 1988 (forthcoming); and Spencer 1988. My claim is that all phonological rules fall into one of two classes: (a) truly phrasal rules, which apply postsyntactically and may refer only to the levels of the prosodic hierarchy; (b) lexical rules, which apply presyntactically within the lexicon. Of the latter, a subset are 'precompiled rules,' which derive multiple diacritically-marked allomorphs for certain classes of words. At the interface of syntax and phrasal phonology, the appropriate diacritically-marked allomorphs are inserted in the relevant syntactic contexts.

A central claim of the theory is that direct-syntax rules do not exist. The theory reanalyzes most such rules as precompiled rules. The reanalysis is not just a notational translation, because the conditions under which rules may be precompiled are limited in specific ways. Thus my proposal makes empirical predictions that are not made by a theory under which direct-syntax rules are allowed.

I will refer to my proposal as precompilation theory. My conjecture is that precompilation theory and prosodic hierarchy theory together form most of an adequate account of syntactic effects in phonology.[1]

The outline of this paper is as follows. I first discuss some proposals made earlier in the literature that serve as ingredients of precompilation theory, then the theory itself, then arguments in favor of it. Finally, I discuss the role of the prosodic hierarchy in the general theory of phrasal alternations, and diagnostics that indicate whether a rule is precompiled or truly phrasal.

2   An Example of Precompilation: Inflection

I assume the following outline of grammatical structure, which indicates the directions in which representations flow through the various components. Semantics is excluded here, since there is little agreement as to where it belongs (cf. Woodbury 1987).

(4)

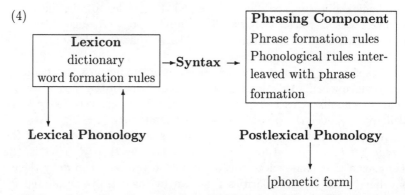

Lexicon		**Phrasing Component**
dictionary →Syntax →	Phrase formation rules
word formation rules	Phonological rules inter-leaved with phrase formation

Lexical Phonology   **Postlexical Phonology**

[phonetic form]

The configuration above leads to an ordering paradox concerning inflectional morphology. I will suggest that a frequently-proposed answer to this paradox (Lieber 1980, Williams 1981, and Lapointe 1981) can be extended as the answer to the problem of direct-syntax phonological rules.

The inflectional ordering paradox is as follows. The distribution of inflection is determined syntactically, through processes such as agreement and concord. Nonetheless, in its morphological manifestation inflection can involve the kinds of irregularity and idiosyncrasy that we associate

---

[1]The quibble "most of" appears in the preceding sentence because some direct-syntax rules in the literature must be reanalyzed by other means than precompilation theory. Two such cases are: (a) rules triggered by particular morphemes, such as the vowel merger process triggered by the Puerto Rican Spanish future marker -á, documented in Mercado 1981 and Kaisse 1985; (b) rules that are analyzable as syntactically-distributed floating morphemes. An example of the latter is Odden's 1987:21–6 rule of Phrasal Tone Insertion in Kimatuumbi: the data he describes suggest that no such rule exists; rather, Kimatuumbi has a floating High tone particle, which is distributed syntactically and whose meaning corresponds to a grammaticized version of the English continuation rise intonation.

with lexical phonology and morphology. A good example here is the case of Slavic languages, in which inflection can be manifested by fully abstract jer vowels, can be involved in cyclic rule application, and can involve suppletion or even paradigm gaps (Lightner 1972, Halle 1973, Pesetsky 1985, Kenstowicz and Rubach 1987).

The paradox resolves itself under a precompilation theory of inflection. The basic idea here (cf. Robins 1959, Matthews 1972) is that inflectional systems involve a finite, predetermined structure, with a specific and limited set of inflectional categories; i.e., of cross-classified 'slots' arranged in paradigms, which are filled by individual inflected words. Anderson 1982 formalizes this idea with the device of a 'morphosyntactic representation,' a (possibly layered) set of inflectional features that indicates the inflectional category of each word.[2]

Assuming morphosyntactic representation, the paradox is resolved as follows: morphosyntactic representations are created in the lexicon, and the lexical morphology and phonology create the word forms that fill the paradigm slots that morphosyntactic representations define. Because inflection is carried out lexically, all of the phenomena that we associate with the lexicon (irregularity, suppletion, cyclic rule application, etc.) can be associated with inflection as well as with derivation.

In the syntax, feature values are assigned to terminal nodes by rules such as agreement. At the stage of lexical insertion, inflected words are inserted into frames such that their morphosyntactic representations are featurally non-distinct from the values borne by the terminal nodes into which they are inserted. Thus the choice of inflected form used is determined syntactically, while the phonological form of the inflected word is determined by the morphological and phonological rules of the lexicon.

At first glance, this looks like a cheat; the morphosyntactic representations are being used solely to allow us to order lexical operations before syntactic ones. But more careful thought suggests that it is correct. In particular, it correctly predicts that inflectional categories, unlike syntactic structures, are bounded in scope. Individual languages may include colossal numbers of inflected forms (Odden 1981b estimates 16 trillion forms for the Shona verb), but they do not have an *infinite* number; the large numbers are due to the geometric combinatorial possibilities of independent inflectional categories. If inflection had direct access to syntax, with its essentially unbounded character, we would expect to find unbounded inflectional systems, such as an affix that is added to a Wh-word each time it crosses a bounding node. By invoking the admittedly global device of morphosyntactic representation, we correctly predict the non-existence of such cases. Moreover, we are able to characterize both morphology and syntax by the rather distinct principles that each requires.

---

[2]However, Anderson would not subscribe to the notion of precompiled inflection, described below.

I have dealt with this idea at some length because it illustrates the mechanism of *precompilation*: inflectional morphology may precede syntax because each inflected form is precompiled in the lexicon, accompanied by a frame indicating where it may be inserted. It is the same strategy I will suggest for direct-syntax rules in phonology.

The notion of precompilation should not be confused with the notion of lexical listing. As Aronoff 1976 has made clear, lexical rules have two functions, that of generating new words and that of expressing the pattern of existing words. It is quite possible that a lexically precompiled inflected form could be generated 'on line' as a neologism; in fact, in languages with rich morphologies this will very often be the case. The crucial point is that inflected forms are *derived in the lexicon,* which allows us to account for forms that show classically lexical behavior.

3   Allomorphy Rules

As is well known, there exist cases of morphological alternation that are not insightfully derivable by phonological rules. For example, in Yidiɲ, an Australian language (Dixon 1977), the ergative suffix appears as -*ŋgu* after vowel-final stems and as -*du* after consonant-final stems. There is no justification anywhere else in the grammar of Yidiɲ for a phonological rule having the effects of either (5a) or (5b):

(5) a. d ⟶ ŋg / V —

    b. ŋg ⟶ d / C —

Moreover, neither rule can be construed as a general phonological process in Yidiɲ, as both /Vd/ and /Cŋg/ sequences exist. In fact, neither (5a) nor (5b) was ever a phonological rule at any stage in the history of the language (Dixon 1980:318–20, Hale 1976).

If we wish to distinguish regularities that are properties of individual morphemes from general properties of a sound system, then the most reasonable account would be to characterize the Yidiɲ ergative not with phonological rules but with rules of allomorphy (Aronoff 1976). Schematic rules would be as follows:

(6) a. Insert /ŋgu/ / V —$]_{[+Ergative]}$

    b. Insert /du/ / C —$]_{[+Ergative]}$

Cross-linguistically, rules of allomorphy have diverse structural conditions: they may refer to phonological environments, to inflectional features, and to the identity of individual morphemes (as in cases where a given affix appears on an arbitrary subset of stems).

4   Phonological Instantiation

Pullum and Zwicky (forthcoming) argue that syntactic rules may not make reference to phonological properties. That is, we do not expect to find rules that front noun phrases consisting of two heavy syllables, that delete resumptive pronouns if they contain a coronal, that enforce a verb-second constraint for high-voweled verbs, and so on.[3]

What is striking about Pullum and Zwicky's principle is the following: syntactic rules clearly can make reference to properties of particular words. For instance, in various languages only certain verbs permit long-distance dependencies to extend into their complement clauses, only certain verbs permit clause union in causative constructions, and only certain verb-preposition sequences permit preposition stranding in cases of Wh-movement. Although treatments vary, I believe that reference by rules to individual morphemes would be required in some form in all syntactic frameworks.

What this suggests is that words appear in syntactic representations in rather abstract form, consisting of a kind of place marker, lacking in phonological content. More specifically, we can posit that what we think of as 'lexical insertion' is actually two processes: (a) insertion into syntactic trees of abstract place markers, indicating the identity of a word and its syntactic properties; (b) post-syntactic *phonological instantiation* of abstract markers with phonemic material. The following is a crude example of this scheme:

(7) a. Abstract   b. Index Insertion   c. Phonological
     Phrase   Instantiation
     Marker   728 = index of *John*   (Postsyntactic)
                     142 = index of *saw*
                     986 = index of *Bill*

```
        S                    S                       S
       / \                  / \                     / \
     NP   VP              NP   VP                  NP   VP
     |   /  \             |    / \                 |    / \
     N  V    NP           N   V   NP               N   V   NP
              |           |   |   |                |   |   |
              N          728 142  N               jan  sɔ  N
                                  |                        |
                                 986                      bɪl
```

---

[3] The work of Zec and Inkelas (this volume) is a serious challenge to this principle. A line of reasoning that preserves the principle is as follows. The phonological properties to which syntax apparently makes reference are precisely the properties to which rules of phonological phrasing may refer; i.e., branchingness, heaviness, and the like. This suggests that Zec and Inkelas's ill-formed examples should not be ruled out in the syntactic component, but rather are ill-formed because the rules of phonological phrasing are unable to assign them a well-formed structure. This predicts, correctly I think, that for phonological properties that cannot be accessed by rules of phrasing (e.g., [high] or [coronal]), there will be no cases in which syntactic rules give the appearance of referring to this property.

The intent of this proposal should be clear: to allow syntactic rules to refer to lexical information, with the exception of phonological content.

5   Precompilation Theory

With this background, my proposal can be stated more precisely: there are no true phonological rules that make reference to syntactic representations. Rather, most of the rules that have in the past been analyzed as such should be characterized as 'phrasal allomorphy'; that is, as the selection of the appropriate precompiled allomorph for phonological instantiation. The idea of phrasal allomorphy has been developed and argued for in earlier work by Zwicky 1985d, 1987a and by Pullum and Zwicky 1988 (forthcoming).

The more novel aspect of my proposal will be as follows: phrasal allomorphs may be derived by phonological rule within the lexical phonology, so that whole classes of words will have multiple precompiled allomorphs.

I begin with a very simple example, the alternation of the indefinite article *a/an* in English, as in (8):

(8) a pear   an apple   an edible pear   an apparently ripe pear

Although this alternation may have originally been due to a phrasal phonological rule (responsible for other alternations like *thine eyes ~ thy face*), synchronically it is completely isolated. Since only one morpheme alternates, it makes little sense to analyze the alternation in phonological terms; an account positing allomorphy is more accurate. The notion of phonological instantiation provides a straightforward account, as follows:

(9) 999 ⟶ ən   / __V   where 999 = index of the indefinite
                                            article

       ə   / elsewhere

In what follows, it will be useful to regard the environments for phonological instantiation as similar in form to syntactic subcategorization frames. Under such a view, the lexical entry for the indefinite article would appear as follows:

(10)
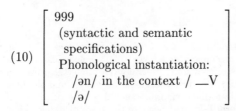

$$\begin{bmatrix} 999 \\ \text{(syntactic and semantic} \\ \text{specifications)} \\ \text{Phonological instantiation:} \\ \text{/ən/ in the context / \_\_V} \\ \text{/ə/} \end{bmatrix}$$

To ensure the selection of the *ən* allomorph over *ə* in prevocalic position, I posit that phonological instantiation is governed by the Elsewhere Condition (cf. Pāṇini, Anderson 1969, Kiparsky 1973b), which insures that the most specific insertion context that is applicable in any particular environment takes precedence over more general insertion contexts.

A more interesting case, because it refers to syntax, is the alternation in the Spanish feminine definite article *la* (Pullum and Zwicky 1988), which appears as *el* before certain nouns beginning in stressed /á/ (see Posner 1987 for details).

(11)   la tórre   'the tower'
       el água   'the water'   (N.B. *água* is feminine)
       la álta tórre   'the high tower'

The interesting example here is *la álta tórre,* which shows that the conditioning environment is partly syntactic. I express the allomorphs and their environments for phonological instantiation as follows:

$$(12) \quad \left[\begin{array}{l} /\text{el}/ \\ /\text{la}/ \end{array} \right. / \; —[_N \; \text{á} \; \left. \right]$$

The next step in the analysis proposed here is the crucial one: to allow for whole classes of words to acquire precompiled alternants. In this case, mere lexical listing will not suffice, since the form of the allomorphs is largely or completely predictable.

To illustrate the mechanism I will propose, it will be useful to go though a concrete example, namely the rule of Hausa noted under (3c). In Hausa, final long vowels of verbs appear as short when the verb precedes a full NP direct object. Here are sample data, taken from Kraft and Kirk-Green 1973:

(13)   ná: ká:mà: 'I have caught (it)'   (no object)

       ná: ká:mà: ší   'I have caught it'   (pronominal object)

       ná: ká:mà kí:fí: 'I have caught a fish'   (full NP object)

       ná: ká:mà: wà   'I have caught   (object does not
       Mú:sá: kí:fí: Musa a fish'   directly follow)

My proposal is as follows. A language's lexicon may include a set of 'phonological instantiation frames,' which serve as standardized contexts for the phonological instantiation of words. For instance, the following phonological instantiation frame is available in Hausa:

(14) *Frame 1:* / [$_{\text{VP}}$ __ NP ...], NP non-pronominal

This indicates that Hausa words (here necessarily verbs, given the frame) may have an extra allomorph marked to appear in this particular context.[4]

Second, I assume that for every word, the grammar automatically generates allomorphs marked for every applicable phonological instantiation frame. Thus for every Hausa verb there is generated a variant marked [Frame 1]. In the case of *ká:mà:,* the two variants are generated as follows:

---

[4]Hausa also has a Frame 2, for verbs preceding dative objects, and possibly a Frame 3, for verbs preceding pronominal clitics.

(15)   ká:mà: input
       ká:mà:, ká:mà:[Frame 1]   outputs

Similar variants would be created for all other verbs of Hausa.

Third, I assume that lexical phonological rules may include phonological instantiation frames in their structural descriptions. The Hausa Shortening rule refers to [Frame 1]:

(16) Hausa Shortening

$$\text{V:} \longrightarrow \text{V} / [\cdots \underline{\hspace{1cm}}]_{[\text{Frame 1}]}$$

Shortening would apply to the forms of (15) as follows:

(17)   ká:mà: ká:mà:[Frame 1]   inputs (from (15))
       ká:mà: ká:mà[Frame 1]   outputs

Since Shortening is a lexical rule, its outputs count as lexical entries; both are available for phonological instantiation. When phonological instantiation takes place, the appropriate allomorph is inserted in each syntactic environment. Thus *ká:mà* will be inserted before lexical objects (following the Elsewhere Condition), and *ká:mà:* will be inserted elsewhere. This completes the analysis.

Two points are worth emphasizing. First, there is no loss of generality in treating the shortening alternation in the lexicon rather than at the phrasal level. Shortening has essentially the same environment that it would have if it were expressed as a direct-syntax rule, but this environment is expressed as a phonological instantiation frame rather than as a syntactic context. Second, the analysis does not commit us to the claim that Hausa speakers memorize two allomorphs for every verb. As Aronoff 1976 notes, lexical rules can apply productively as well as relating memorized forms. The situation is quite parallel to what is posited in lexical accounts of inflection (section 3), which likewise can be agnostic about the extent to which lexically derived forms are memorized.

Some additional facts about Hausa further illustrate the precompilation analysis. In particular, Shortening is not the only lexical rule of Hausa that is triggered by [Frame 1]. A particular lexical class of verbs (the 'Grade II' verbs of Parsons 1960) also undergo a change in vowel quality, as exemplified below:

(18)   a.   ná: sàyá: 'I bought (it)'
       b.   ná: sàyí àbíncí   'I bought food'

I would account for this by positing a second rule that includes [Frame 1] in its structural description:

(19) Hausa Raising

$$a \longrightarrow i / [\cdots \underline{\hspace{1cm}}] \begin{bmatrix} \text{Grade II} \\ \text{Frame 1} \end{bmatrix}$$

The fact that this rule is restricted to a particular diacritic lexical class supports the claim that it is lexical, since such restrictions are characteristic of lexical rules, but not of true phrasal phonology.

In fact, [Frame 1] governs alternations in Hausa that are almost completely isolated in the grammar. In particular, a handful of verbs show irregular allomorphs in the [Frame 1] environment:

(20) a. ná: gání: 'I see'
        ná: gá Áúdù 'I see Audu'

   b. sánì: 'know (isolation)'
       sán   'know (pre-object)'

   c. bárì: 'permit (isolation)'
       bár   'permit (pre-object)'

   d. bá: 'give (isolation)'
       bá:̀   'give (pre-object)'

These would plausibly be listed in the lexicon, along the following lines:

(21) 'see': /gá/[Frame 1]   /gání/

The overall picture is that [Frame 1] serves as an organizing principle for the Hausa lexicon, determining in part the verbal allomorphs that the lexical rules derive.

I would add that this account of Hausa Shortening is largely a formalization of what appears in the Hausa literature (e.g., Parsons 1960, Leben 1971, Newman 1973, McHugh 1981). Hausaists typically treat the verbal allomorphs as members of a paradigm, isolated from their phrasal context.[5]

At this point I summarize the general claim I am making: there are no rules of true phrasal phonology that refer directly to syntax. Instead, most apparent cases of syntax-sensitive phonology are appropriately analyzed as cases of precompilation. Precompilation sometimes takes the form of lexical listing, as in English *a/an*. Where it involves a more general alternation, the alternants are derived by lexical rules, which make reference to phonological instantiation frames. In phonological instantiation, which intervenes between syntax and true phrasal phonology, the appropriate allomorph is selected for insertion, following the Elsewhere Principle.

To give further examples, here are the other two apparent direct-syntax rules of (3), reanalyzed as precompiled.

---

[5] A reviewer notes two further complications in the Hausa data: (a) Frame 1 must be modified to allow for certain particles to intervene optionally between verb and object; (b) as one might expect in a lexical rule, Shortening has exceptions, i.e. verbs which have final long vowels across the board. The same reviewer's suggestion that we replace Shortening with a Lengthening rule (applying before object pronouns) seems unworkable, since it fails to account for vowel length in isolation forms.

(22) a. *Ewe* (Clements 1978): A High tone verb acquires Rising tone following High or Rising tone if the immediately following noun root bears Mid or Low tone on its first syllable.

$$\text{H} \longrightarrow \text{R} \ / \ [_V \ [-\text{Lopitch}] \ \underline{\quad}]_{[\text{Frame 1}]}$$

Frame 1: $/ \ \underline{\quad}[_N \ [-\text{Hipitch}] \ \dots]$

b. *French* (Selkirk 1972): In colloquial style (*conversation familière*), liaison occurs between adjectives and quantifiers and a following noun, but not between an adverb and a following verb or adjective.

$$\text{C} \longrightarrow [+\text{extrasyllabic}] \ / \ [_{\{A,Q\}} \ \cdots \underline{\quad}]_{[\text{Frame 1}]}$$

Frame 1: $/ \ [_{X'} \ \underline{\quad}X^0 \ \dots]$

For the theoretical background to (22b), see Clements and Keyser 1983:96–114.

6   Arguments for Precompilation Theory

So far, I have proposed that precompilation theory provides a workable alternative to a theory that allows direct-syntax rules. In this section, I argue that there are explanatory advantages in treating the relevant phenomena with precompilation rather than with direct-syntax rules.

6.1   Structure Preservation

Precompilation theory derives phrasal alternations with lexical rules, whereas in a direct-syntax approach, the rules must be postlexical. If precompilation theory is correct, then the conditions that are met by ordinary lexical rules should hold for precompiled rules as well.

It is widely believed that lexical rules are subject to a requirement of 'structure preservation' (Kiparsky 1985b): their outputs must be segments that already exist in the phonemic inventory of the language. Mohanan and Mohanan 1984 weaken this requirement somewhat, arguing on the basis of Malayalam for a 'lexical alphabet' that contains a few sounds not present in the underlying alphabet. Nonetheless, the basic spirit of structure preservation is maintained in their proposal, in that lexical rules may have as their outputs only segments from a strictly limited inventory. This is obviously not the case with postlexical rules, which in every language derive a vast array of phonetic segments on the surface.

The crucial point is this: to my knowledge, all the rules that have been argued to require direct reference to syntax share the property of structure preservation, deriving segments that exist independently in the phonemic inventory of the language. This is predicted by precompilation theory: rules previously described as direct-syntax rules are treated as precompiled rules in the lexicon, where structure preservation holds. The predictions of precompilation theory would be falsified if, for example, the rules of English that assign shades of vowel length, or which nasalize vowels in the neighborhood of nasals, or which front velars near front vowels, etc., were shown to refer to particular syntactic environments rather than to phonological phrasing.

I am aware of one potential counterexample to the prediction of structure preservation for precompiled rules. Tateishi 1987 suggests that the Consonant Mutation rule of Mende, which I argue below is precompiled, violates structure preservation. Tateishi's contention is that the segments [b], [g], and [gb] are derived only by Mutation and are not in the lexical alphabet of Mende. The references on Mende I have read, however, suggest that this is quite unlikely. The sections in Innes's 1969 Mende dictionary for words beginning with non-derived *b*, *g*, and *gb* are very ample, forming about 8% of the total vocabulary. Non-alternating /b/, /g/, and /gb/ occur in commonplace expressions of greeting and thanks (Innes 1967:9); and as the entries in Innes 1969 indicate, words with non-alternating /b/, /g/, and /gb/ freely participate in Mende affixational processes. Etymologically, no /b/, /g/, or /gb/ is of ancient origin, but synchronically this is irrelevant: through borrowing and other mechanisms, these originally allophonic sounds have been restructured as phonemes of Mende.

6.2 Rule Ordering: Precompiled Precedes Postlexical

Precompilation theory divides phrasal phonology (broadly construed) into two very separate parts: precompiled phrasal phonology, which resides in the lexicon, and true phrasal phonology, which follows syntax and respects the prosodic hierarchy. Necessarily, the two lie in a rigid ordering relation: true phrasal phonology may refer to information derived by precompiled phonology, but not vice versa. To my knowledge, this expectation is confirmed.

A possible exception is the interesting situation in Turkish described by Kaisse 1986, (this volume). For many speakers of Turkish, there are three distinct categories of voicing in stops: invariantly voiceless, invariantly voiced, and alternating. The latter are voiced in surface syllable-initial position, voiceless syllable-finally. The interest of this case lies in the fact that that Turkish surface syllabification is determined in part by a clearly postlexical rule that resyllabifies consonants across word boundaries.

Kaisse's example presents an ordering paradox if we assume that the distribution of voicing in stops must be carried out by lexical rules; i.e., that the voicing alternations are precompiled. This is not clear, however. I believe that any adequate analysis of the facts would require us to adopt the following assumption or some notational equivalent of it: the Turkish stops group into three phonemic categories, [+voice], [−voice], and [0 voice], with the rule for voicing applying only to the third, alternating category. Given this, the distribution of voicing could just as well be carried out by an exceptionless postlexical rule. Such an analysis involves no precompiled rules, so that the ordering paradox disappears.

The kind of ternary distinction on which the analysis depends is disallowed under a number of theories, but nonetheless appears to be widely attested in vowel harmony, tone, and elsewhere; for further defense of ternarity, see Goldsmith 1987b.

6.3   Rule Ordering: Precompiled May Precede Lexical

Precomplication theory makes another, rather striking prediction about rule ordering: that certain phonological rules that have heretofore been considered phrasal, namely the precompiled ones, can actually apply before lexical phonological rules. Three cases of this sort have been pointed out in the literature.

Hausa

In Hausa, the rule that shortens final vowels before a full NP object ((3c) above) interacts with the rule of Low Tone Raising (Leben 1971), which raises Low tone to High when it occupies a long final vowel and immediately follows another Low tone:

(23) Hausa Low Tone Raising

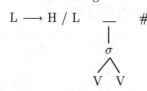

Low Tone Raising is arguably a lexical rule. It has a fair number of exceptions (McHugh 1981:18), and native speakers seem clearly aware of its effects. However, Low Tone Raising must be ordered after Shortening, because Low-toned vowels that are shortened are not raised. Under standard views, this should not be a possible ordering, since lexicon-internal processes must precede the concatenation of words into phrases. However, we noted above that Hausa Shortening would necessarily be a precompiled rule in our framework, owing to the quite explicit syntactic conditions on its application. If Shortening applies in the lexicon, then the fact that it precedes a lexical rule is not contradictory. Sample derivations, showing how this works, are shown below:

(24) /káràntà:/   /káràntà:/   'read' (underlying form)
      káràntà: káràntà:[Frame 1]   Free assignment of phonological
                                           instantiation frames
      —   káràntà[Frame 1]   Shortening
      káràntá: —   Low Tone Raising

The form *káràntà* will be inserted before NP objects, *káràntá:* elsewhere.

Mende

In Mende (Cowper and Rice 1987), there is a phrasal rule of Mutation, which lenites various word-initial consonants in certain syntactic environments. Cowper and Rice argue that the rule refers to the prosodic hierarchy. However, several facts cast doubt on this claim. First, the rule appears to be sensitive to certain empty syntactic categories (Cowper and Rice 1987, Tateishi 1988). Among others, Berendsen 1985 and McHugh 1987 have argued that true phrasal phonology is never trace-sensitive.[6] Second, Mutation has a fair number of lexical exceptions, found in borrowings, proper names, and certain kinship terms (Innes 1967:45–6). Such exceptions are characteristic of lexical rules, but typically not of true phrasal rules. Third, Innes 1962:8 mentions that in a few words, the mutated allomorph is different from what the phonological mutation rule would predict, requiring such forms to be lexically listed. For these reasons, I will assume that Mende Mutation is precompiled.

In this respect it is striking that Mutation must be ordered before reduplication, which is generally agreed to be a lexical process. The following data illustrate this (Innes 1967:108):

(25) a.   táa   fɛmbé-ma
          he   shake-prog.
          'He is shaking (it)'
          (base form of verb)

  b.   táa   mbomɛí   vɛmbé-ma
       he   hammock shake-prog.
       'He is shaking the hammock'
       (initial consonant of verb mutated)

  c.   táa   fɛmbɛ-fémbɛ-ma
       he   redup.-shake-prog.
       'He is repeatedly shaking (it)'
       (reduplicated form)

  d.   táa   mbomɛí   vɛmbɛ-vémbɛ-ma
       he   hammock redup.-shake-prog.
       'He is repeatedly shaking the hammock'
       (mutated consonant copied in reduplication)

The crucial datum here is the verb *vɛmbɛ-vémbɛ-ma* in (25d), where the initial /f/ must first be mutated to /v/, then copied to yield the surface form.

Under precompilation theory, this result can be derived. Mutation is a precompiled rule, which applies lexically to words marked for [Frame 1], as in (26).

---

[6]It is possible to analyze Mende Mutation without the use of empty elements, but only at the cost of referring to very specific syntactic or morphological categories, such as unaccusative verbs and inalienably possessed nouns (Tateishi 1987). The argument against a prosodic hierarchy account holds under either analysis.

(26) a. *Mende Mutation:*   C ⟶ [+mutated] / [—...]$_{[Frame\ 1]}$

   b. *Frame 1:* [N^X [—]$_{X^0}$ ...]$_{X'}$ where N^X is some projection of N

Justification for the formulation of Frame 1 can be found in the work of Tateishi 1988, who has independently made the argument from reduplication for the lexical status of mutation. The ad hoc feature [+mutated] stands for a rather heterogeneous set of phonological changes, described in the work cited above.

Being lexical, Mutation may precede the lexical process of reduplication. Schematic derivations for the verbs of (25c) and (25d) are as follows:

(27) a. /fɛmbɛ/   b. /fɛmbɛ/   underlying form of
                                                      stem 'shake'

   fɛmbɛ$_{[Frame\ 1]}$ fɛmbɛ   free assignment of
                                                      instantiation frames

   vɛmbɛ$_{[Frame\ 1]}$ —   Mutation

   vɛmbɛvɛmbɛ$_{[Frame\ 1]}$ fɛmbɛfɛmbɛ   Reduplication

The outputs that result are inserted following an NP object (27a), and elsewhere (27b). The upshot of the analysis is that there is no ordering paradox, since both Mutation and Reduplication are lexical processes.[7]

Kimatuumbi

The most striking case of precompiled phrasal rules preceding lexical rules is that provided by Odden 1986b, this volume (see also Odden 1981a, 1987). The data involve the well-known rule of Shortening in Kimatuumbi, which Odden 1986b states as being directly sensitive to syntax:

(28) a. Kimatuumbi Shortening

   VV ⟶ V / [[—]$_X$ Y]$_{X'}$ where Y contains phonetic material

   b. kɩkóloombe   'cleaning shell'
      kɩkólombe chaángu   'my cleaning shell'

Shortening interacts with a rule of Glide Formation, which converts a prevocalic high tense vowel (transcribed /ɩ, y/) to a glide, at the same time lengthening the following vowel:

(29) a. Kimatuumbi Glide Formation

   /ɩ,y/ + V ⟶ [y,w] VV

   b. /ly-até/ ⟶ lw-aaté   'banana hand'
      cf. ly-tóóña   'star'

---

[7]Innes 1962 notes that some speakers produce forms derivable by applying Mutation after Reduplication: *vɛmbɛ-fɛmbɛ*. Such forms are neutral with respect to the issues at stake. A precompilation account would assume that for these speakers, Reduplication precedes Mutation within the lexicon, since the ordering of lexical rules appears to be largely idiosyncratic.

Odden notes that this rule is word-bounded, citing cases like *iláatú itúumbwįįke* (**iláatwįįtúumbwįįke*) 'the shoes fell.' He also shows that Glide Formation does not affect long vowels, so long vowels may occur freely in prevocalic position.

Odden next shows that Glide Formation interacts in an interesting way with morphological levels. The levels he assumes for Kimatuumbi are shown schematically as follows (Odden 1986b, (3)):

(30) a. Levels for Kimatuumbi Verbs

   [subord. [subject – tense – object [ROOT – derivation]₁]₂]₃
     markers   marker   marker

   e.g., [pa [n – áa – kį [kalaang – įté]₁]₂]₃
         when I   past it   fried   perfective
         'when I fried it'

   b. Levels for Kimatuumbi Nouns

   [locative [Class 5 [noun class [ROOT – derivation]₁]₂]₃]₄

   e.g., [kų [[mw [aák – į]₁]₂]₃]₄
         to   Cl. 1 hunt er
         'to the hunter'

Within a given morphological level, Glide Formation applies level-finally, left-to-right. However, Glide Formation is also cyclic, in the sense that it applies successively at the end of each of the four morphological levels. As a result, the same underlying sequence of vowels can surface differently, depending on the morphological structure involved. For example, the form [mų į [ųtí]₁]₂ 'you should pull it' surfaces as *mwįįutí* (i.e., /ųįV/ ⟶ [wįįV]); whereas the form [mų [[į [úlá]₁]₂]₃]₄ 'in the frog' surfaces as *mųyuúlá* (i.e., /ųįV/ ⟶ [ųyV]). These forms are taken from Odden 1986b, (9–11); for full derivations, see this and other references by Odden cited above. The crucial point for present purposes is that Kimatuumbi Glide Formation shows the classical properties of a lexical rule: interleaving with morphology (i.e., cyclicity) and sensitivity to morphological levels.

Consider now the interaction of Glide Formation and Shortening. Odden's crucial observation is the following: the rule of Shortening, which is obviously phrasal, must be ordered right in the middle of the lexical phonology. In particular, it applies only at Level 1, ordered after Glide Formation. Therefore, it is *fed* by Level 1 applications of Glide Formation, but is *counterfed* by applications of Glide Formation at levels 2, 3, and 4.[8] In the derivation below (Odden 1986b, (23–4)) the vowel /aa/ derived at Level 1 from /į+a/ undergoes phrasal Shortening, but the vowel /aa/ derived at Level 2 from /ų+a/ does not.

---

[8] An additional fact noted in Odden 1981a is probably also relevant here: as a Level 1 rule, Shortening does not apply to underlying long vowels that occur in prefixes attached at levels 2, 3, and 4.

(31) [tʉ [ak-ị-an-a]₁]₂ ịtúumbili   'inf.-net hunt-for-recipr.-final
                                            vowel # monkeys' =
                                            'to net-hunt monkeys for each
                                            other'
        [ak-ị-an-a]₁   Level 1: affixation
        [akyaana]₁   Glide Formation
        [akyana]₁   Shortening (triggered
                                                    by phrasal context,
                                                    ịtúumbili)
        [tʉ akyana]₂   Level 2: affixation
        [twaakyana]₂   Glide Formation
            —   (Shortening is Level 1
                                                    only)
        twaakyana ịtúumbili   output

The lesson that Odden draws from these remarkable facts is that lexical rules and phrasal rules do not always interact in the expected fashion,
and that grammatical theory must be revised so that the lexical phonology
can apply after the syntax.

I agree fully with Odden's general point that the Kimatuumbi facts
require us to revise our conceptions of how lexical and phrasal phonology
are related. But there are problems with his specific account. Odden's
theory doesn't just reshuffle the components of the grammar, but it also
radically extends our notion of the phonological cycle. In particular, the
theory claims that in course of Level 1, the phonological rules have the
power to look *completely outside the word* to the phrasal context, in order
to establish whether Shortening is applicable. Once this is done, the
cycle returns to the word-internal context, applying to levels 2, 3, and 4.
This procedure violates the notion of cyclic rule application in the most
fundamental way: the rules on a given cycle may refer to information
that does not actually appear in the representation until several cycles
later in the derivation. If this is allowed, the whole notion of the cycle
becomes a much weaker one, allowing the grammar to access larger and
smaller domains in arbitrary order. Given what it entails, Odden's idea
of ordering the lexical phonology to follow the syntax is less appealing.

I believe that the Kimatuumbi facts should be taken instead to argue
for precompilation theory. Specifically, if we suppose that Shortening is a
precompiled rule, then its intimate ordering relations with the lexical rule
of Glide Formation immediately become unremarkable. The specific analysis goes as follows. Kimatuumbi permits the phonological instantiation
frame under (32).

(32) *Frame 1:* [... [—]ₓ Y]ₓ′   Y ≠ ∅

That is, special allomorphs are derived for insertion in head positions that
precede an overt complement.

Shortening is a lexical rule, which applies only at Level 1:

(33) Kimatuumbi Shortening (precompiled version)

$$VV \longrightarrow V \; / \; [\; \cdots \; - \; \cdots \;]_{[\text{Frame 1}]}$$

The derivation for the form *twaakyana įtúumbili* 'to net-hunt monkeys for each other' (from (31)) would proceed as follows. At Level 1, the stem *akįana* generates two allomorphs, one marked for [Frame 1], the other serving as the elsewhere case. The lexical derivation for the specially marked form proceeds essentially as Odden has it, with the exception that Shortening does not refer to a phrasal context (indeed, no such context yet exists, since we are still in the lexicon). Rather, Shortening refers to the phonological instantiation frame of (32), which restricts the output form to head positions followed by an overt complement. After phonological instantiation, this yields the correct result.

The upshot is that the basic idea of the cycle is maintained: no rule refers to information that is not yet present on the cycle on which the rule applies. The universal ordering of lexical before syntactic rules is also preserved.[9]

To summarize this section: a basic claim of precompilation theory is that many rules that have been called 'syntax sensitive' are actually lexical rules, which precompile allomorphs for insertion in particular phrasal contexts. A prediction of this is that this class of rules, being lexical, may apply before ordinary lexical rules. The prediction is confirmed by the facts of Hausa, Mende, and Kimatuumbi.

6.4   Summary of the Arguments

My overall argument is closely related to a proposal made by Kaisse 1985. Kaisse suggests that postlexical phonology is divisible into two rule components, called P1 and P2. P1 rules have all the properties of lexical rules other than confinement within word boundaries: they exhibit structure preservation, are subject to morphological restrictions, have lexical exceptions, and may apply cyclically. P2 rules are the classical postlexical rules, and lack all of these properties.

Precompilation theory accepts this bifurcation, but attempts to give it a principled basis by actually placing the P1 rules in the lexicon. My view is that the simplest explanation for why P1 rules act as if they were lexical is to assume that they *are* lexical.

7   Whither the Prosodic Hierarchy?

Since precompilation theory and prosodic hierarchy theory are both theories of phonological alternation at the phrasal level, one wonders whether

---

[9]Odden notes that Shortening has exceptions in borrowings: cf. *boóksį yaángu* 'my box' and *bakteélįya yaángu* 'my bacteria' (Odden 1986b, (25)). Since lexical rules often fail to apply to borrowed forms, these data support the claim (common to Odden's account and mine) that Shortening is a lexical rule.

the adoption of the former impinges on the validity of the latter. I believe this is not so, although admittedly a number of supporting cases for prosodic hierarchy theory disappear when reanalyzed as precompiled. Below, I briefly review the basic arguments for prosodic hierarchy theory, drawing on Selkirk 1980a, 1986; Nespor and Vogel 1982, 1986; and Hayes 1989.

a. In a number of languages, more than one rule refers to the same phrasal domains, where the domains are not equivalent to syntactic constituents. This suggests that syntactic effects in phonology can be mediated by a *structure*, for which the prosodic hierarchy appears to be an appropriate representation.

b. Typological patterns about junctural strength emerge naturally from the hierarchy. In particular, rules that apply before a juncture of a certain strength apply before all junctures of greater strength; and rules that apply across a given juncture strength apply across all junctures of weaker strength. These fall out under prosodic hierarchy theory from Strict Layering and from the ways rules are allowed to refer to edges (Selkirk 1980a).

c. Shih 1985 and McHugh (this volume, forthcoming) argue for Mandarin and Chaga respectively that phonological rules can apply cyclically at the level of the phrase. But the cycle that we find is not the cycle predicted by SPE, with rules reapplying on ever-larger syntactic constituents. Rather, the phrasal cycle is apparently the result of an interleaving of phonological rules with phrase formation rules, just as the word-internal cycle results in lexical phonology from the interleaving of phonological rules with rules of word formation.

d. The rules of phrase formation found in the world's languages show an encouraging family resemblance, suggesting that the theory is on the right track in isolating phrase formation as a level of abstraction at which valid generalizations can be made.

There are a number of cases in which adopting precompilation theory actually provides additional support for prosodic hierarchy theory, by removing apparent violations of the Strict Layer Hypothesis. For example, Chen 1987c points out that the domains required by Xiamen tone sandhi overlap with intonational phrases. Xiamen tone sandhi has two properties that suggest it is a precompiled rule (see below for discussion of these diagnostics): it may apply across pause, and it must have recourse to fairly rich syntactic information, in particular, the argument/adjunct distinction. A plausible precompilation analysis for Xiamen would insert 'basic' allomorphs at the right edges of non-adjunct maximal projections, 'sandhi' allomorphs elsewhere. These purely syntactic environments have no necessary connection with the prosodic principles that determine intonational phrasing in Xiamen. Thus the overlap of the tone sandhi 'domains' with intonational phrasing says nothing about the Strict Layer Hypothesis, because tone sandhi does not refer to a prosodic domain.

As S. Inkelas has pointed out to me, Hausa Shortening (16) is a similar case. The phonological phrases that would be diagnosed by Shortening if we regarded it as a true phrasal rule would contradict the phonological phrases diagnosed by other means, in particular by the distribution of the clitic *fa* (Inkelas 1988). The contradiction disappears when we recognize that Shortening is precompiled, whereas the distribution of *fa* is genuinely sensitive to phonological phrasing.

A third example, from Tiberian Hebrew, is pointed out by Dresher 1983. Here, the phonology of the construct state, which would plausibly be analyzed as precompiled, applies in overlapping domains with the truly phrasal phonology.

If both precompilation theory and prosodic hierarchy theory are valid, the obvious question that arises is which theory is relevant for a given rule. To put it another way, how do we determine in which component of the grammar (lexical vs. postlexical phonology) a rule creating phrasal alternations resides? Before we consider this question, it is worth examining the issue from the viewpoint of historical change.

8   Historical Change and Reanalysis

Consider the characteristic historical evolution of phonological rules (Anderson 1985:73–9), interpreted from the viewpoint of lexical phonology (Kiparsky 1982b:56–8). Typically rules originate phonetically, then crystallize as categorial, exceptionless postlexical rules. With the passage of time, they accumulate exceptions and irregularity, until at some critical point they are *restructured* by a new generation as lexical rules. Ultimately, through leveling and other processes, lexical rules disappear from the grammar.

The above account of restructuring is normally regarded as valid only for rules that apply within words, since phrasal alternations are held to be exclusively postlexical. But if precompilation theory is correct, then phrasal rules can be viewed as having essentially the same history: they originate phonetically, crystallize into categorial postlexical rules, acquire exceptions and irregularities, and at some crucial stage *restructure* as lexical rules–that is, as precompiled. Later, through leveling and other processes, they die out. The gradual death of precompiled rules can be seen in progress in the case of French liaison and the Celtic mutations.

Excursus: Inflectional Restructuring

Moribund precompiled alternations sometimes undergo a *second* restructuring: they become rules of inflectional morphology, which mark particular inflectional categories by phonological means. This is demonstrated clearly by Rotenberg 1978 for Modern Irish. In this language, certain tense-marking pre-verbal particles have dropped, so that the mutation they leave behind becomes the sole marker of verbal tense. Similarly, cases in which a noun in a particular case and gender triggers mutation on a following adjective get reanalyzed as adjective agreement, so that the adjective no longer has to immediately follow the noun to get mutated. Other cases of inflectional restructuring can be found in French liaison (Morin and Kaye 1982), English *n't* (Zwicky and Pullum 1983), and Italian inflected prepositions (Napoli and Nevis 1987).

E. Selkirk has suggested to me the possibility of treating *all* precompiled phonology as inflection. While this proposal has the merit of reducing the apparatus needed in the theory, I disagree with it because it would obscure important differences between precompiled phonology and inflection. First, inflectional morphology appears not to be influenced by the phonological form of nearby words in the string. Second, as Anderson 1988 and others have suggested, inflectional morphology is based on a fairly restricted set of syntactic structural relations, whereas precompiled phonology can involve rather haphazard environments that reflect its origins in true phrasal phonology. Third, precompiled phonology appears to be subject to a strict locality requirement: the triggering context for a precompiled allomorph must always lie in an adjacent word. Such a locality requirement clearly is not placed on inflection: for example, wh-words are often inflected according to the properties of a trace they bind elsewhere in the sentence.

The separation of inflection from precompiled phonology is supported by Rotenberg's 1978 work on Irish. His analysis suggests that the Irish mutations have been reanalyzed as inflection (hence as potentially nonlocal) in just those cases in which the data were amenable to syntactic reinterpretation as agreement or other inflectional processes. In the remaining contexts, mutation persists as a local process–in my terms, as precompiled phonology.

9   The Diagnosis Problem

To return to the main thread: the fact that precompiled phrasal rules originate historically as true phrasal phonology means that the diagnosis of a rule as precompiled or not is nontrivial. In particular, precompiled rules may look very much like they have prosodic environments, because they are restructured versions of older rules that did have prosodic environments.

Note that the diagnosis problem for phrasal rules is essentially parallel to the diagnosis problem (lexical vs. postlexical) for word-internal rules, itself a controversial and difficult topic.

As an initial attack on the problem, I suggest the following diagnostics for whether a phrasal rule is precompiled or postlexical.

Diagnostics for Precompiled Rules

a. Only precompiled rules can precede rules of lexical phonology (cf. Hausa and Kimatuumbi above).

b. Only precompiled rules can precede morphological rules (cf. Mende above, as well as the Leurbost Scots Gaelic case discussed in Thomas-Flinders 1981).

c. Only precompiled rules can treat parallel X′ categories differently (Hausa, French liaison).

d. If we assume (following Berendsen 1985, McHugh 1987) that traces and other empty categories are deleted prior to true phrasal phonology, then sensitivity to empty categories diagnoses a precompiled rule. Berendsen notes several phonological rules whose sensitivity to trace can be predicted depending on whether they are 'P1' or 'P2,' or in our terms depending on whether they are precompiled or true phrasal phonology.

Diagnostics for True Phrasal Phonology

a. Only true phrasal rules may follow postlexical rules.

b. Only true phrasal rules may violate structure preservation.

c. Only true phrasal rules may involve phrasal cyclicity; i.e., the interleaving of phonology and phrase construction.

d. Rules of phonological spreading, particularly spreading of autosegments over multiple syllables, would in many cases be impossible to treat as precompiled, and thus would have to be analyzed as true phrasal phonology. A good example is the tonal phonology of Chaga (McHugh (forthcoming)).

e. Assuming that phonological instantiation is insensitive to pause, then any rule blocked by pause is a rule of true phrasal phonology (cf. Rotenberg 1978).

f. Assuming that phonological instantiation is not sensitive to speaking rate, then rules that apply in larger domains at greater speaking rates must be true phrasal rules, and not precompiled.[10]

---

[10] Here it is worth noting the case of French liaison, which is highly unusual in that it expands its domain in slower, more careful speech styles. This is due, I believe, to the precompiled status of liaison: in careful speech, French speakers make use of largely obsolete phonological instantiation frames, which are artificially preserved by education and social pressure.

I am not sure if whether the converse of this diagnostic holds; i.e., whether if a rule applies in an invariant domain, it is precompiled. The phrasal rules of Chaga (McHugh (forthcoming)) cast doubt on this, in that they apply in invariant domains but by diagnostics (c) and (d) are true phrasal rules.

g. Assuming that phonological instantiation cannot access phonological phrasing, any rule that refers to the prosodic hierarchy, or follows a rule that refers to the prosodic hierarchy, is a true phrasal rule. Note that the background assumption is not a necessary consequence of the theory: both phonological instantiation and phrase formation fall within the 'interface component' that lies between syntax and true phrasal phonology. In principle, some forms of phonological instantiation might follow phrase formation within this component, and thus be able to refer to prosodic domains.

The joint effect of the diagnostics proposed above is that the theory is quite testable empirically: ideally, all of the diagnostics should agree for all of the rules. Note, however, that many of the diagnostics depend on additional assumptions about precompilation theory and prosodic hierarchy theory. I have tried to make these assumptions explicit above. Counterevidence must therefore be considered carefully for just what it counterexemplifies.

10   Conclusion

To summarize: my proposal is that all phrasal phonological phenomena can be analyzed either under prosodic hierarchy theory or under precompilation theory. As a result, the class of rules that refer directly to syntax in their structural descriptions can be eliminated from phonological theory.

On the surface, this is hardly an earth-shaking result. After all, in order to eliminate one class of rules from phonological theory, we have had to introduce two others. The real point is that taken together, prosodic hierarchy theory and precompilation theory form a *structured* account of the data: every phrasal rule must fit into one theory or the other, and for a rule to fit into a theory, it must meet specific requirements, as I have tried to show in the preceding section. Thus the overall approach has the virtue of making falsifiable predictions. In contrast, it is hard to imagine an observation that would falsify a theory that simply said that phonological rules may refer to syntactic structure.

This kind of compartmentalization has already borne fruit for word-internal rules, as the theory of lexical phonology. By adding precompilation theory to prosodic hierarchy theory, my intent is to develop an equally articulated, hence predictive theory of alternations at the phrasal level.

6

Boundary Tonology and the Prosodic Hierarchy
LARRY M. HYMAN

PHONOLOGISTS HAVE LONG BEEN interested in phonological rules that apply at the left or right edge of a constituent. The literature describes numerous processes affecting consonants and/or vowels at the beginning or end of a 'word,' 'phrase,' or other unit: 'initial' glottal stop insertion, 'final' devoicing, 'final' deletion and so forth. Selkirk 1980a,b; 1984, Nespor and Vogel 1986, and others have proposed that these constituents or 'prosodic domains' are organized into a phonological hierarchy which, going from smallest to largest domain, includes the phonological word (PW), clitic group (CG), phonological phrase (PP), intonational phrase (IP) and utterance (U).[1]

Processes which are restricted to the initial or final position of any such domain are termed 'domain-limit' rules. Instead of referring to the junctures or boundary symbols of earlier frameworks, domain-limit rules target the left or right edge of a constituent at any 'layer' of the above prosodic hierarchy.

Nowhere is the need for such domain-limit rules more evident than in the area of tone. Tone rules that apply at the beginning or end of a prosodic domain are extremely common and, as in the case of their segmental counterparts, tend to cluster around a few recurrent processes. In this study I shall refer collectively to such tonal domain-limit rules as 'boundary tonology.' Adopting the framework of Archangeli and Pulleyblank (to appear), some of the parameters of boundary tones are seen in (1).

---

[1]Though in this paper I am interested only in phrasal domains, it should be noted that the same authors propose that the hierarchy extends to the progressively smaller foot and syllable domains.

(1) a.   domain   : PW, CG, PP, IP, U
     b.   edge   : left, right
     c.   function   : insert, delete, spread, delink
     d.   trigger   : High, Low, etc.
     e.   target conditions   : specific tone(s) and/or tone-bearing
                                units (TBUs)

The first two parameters identify the relevant domain and its edge. A rule may thus target the left edge of a PW, the right edge of a PP and so forth. The remaining three parameters are needed for phonological rules in general. First, we must know if the rule inserts, deletes, spreads or delinks a feature or features. Second, in the case of tone, we must know which feature(s) trigger the rule—e.g., a H(igh) tone, or a L(ow) tone. Finally, we need to identify any phonological target condition(s) that must be met. The rule may require a specific adjacent tone (i.e., preceding or following it), and/or it may target a specific TBU. However, in the case of domain-limit rules, there may be *no* phonological target conditions (though there will still be domain and edge indications). This last possibility is manifested, for example, when a so-called boundary tone is inserted initially or finally within a domain, without reference to any surrounding phonological material.

In order to illustrate the application of parametric phonology to boundary tonology, let us consider two brief illustrations from Luganda.[2] There is a quite general rule according to which a High tone is lowered to Low when it is linked to a vowel that is initial within its CG. The so-called initial vowel (IV) morpheme is affected by this rule. In (2a) I have provided a set of 'non-tonic' nouns, i.e., those which in isolation surface without a High to Low pitch drop:[3]

(2) a.   ki-tabo   / e-ki-tabo   'book'
          mu-limi   / o-mu-limi   'farmer'
          ka-kulwe / a-ka-kulwe   'tadpole'

     b.   na = ki-tabo   'with a book'
          na = mu-limi   'with a framer'
          na = ka-kulwe   'with a tadpole'

     c.   na = é-kì-tabo
          na = ó-mù-limi
          na = á-kà-kulwe

Nouns appear both with and without an IV in Luganda, depending on a number of factors irrelevant to the present issue. In (2a) we see that whether the three phonetic IVs [e, o, a] appear or not, these forms are non-tonic. In (2b) we see that when the non-tonic proclitic *na=* 'with'

---

[2]Research on the prosodic structure of Luganda has been supported in part by National Science Foundation Grant No. BNS8719197.

[3]'Non-tonic' forms receive their surface pitches from the postlexical tonology.

is placed before non-tonic nouns lacking an IV, the whole CG remains non-tonic. However, as seen in (2c), where the nouns begin with the IV, a High to Low pitch drop occurs between the IV and the following noun class prefix.

To account for these tonal alternations, the IV morpheme must be set up with underlying High tone, but its High must be deleted whenever it is initial within its CG. Following the parameters given in (1), this rule is stated as in (3).

(3)   a.   domain   : CG
      b.   edge   : left
      c.   function   : delete
      d.   trigger   : H
      e.   target condition   : vocalic mora[4]

The second illustration concerns intonational High in Luganda. In all reference works, final non-tonic moras in Luganda are cited with High tone. However, depending on the intonation, these moras can be realized High *or* Low. Thus, consider the forms in (4), where $H_{//}$ indicates the intonational High tone in question:

(4) a.   à-gùl-à   / à-gúl-á   'he buys'
                         $H_{//}$
          à-gùl-ìl-à   / à-gúl-íl-á   'he buys for'
                          $H_{//}$
          à-gùl-ìl-ìl-à / à-gúl-íl-íl-á   'he bribes'
                            $H_{//}$

     b.   bá-gùl-à   / bá-gùl-á   'they buy'
          H L   H L $H_{//}$
          bá-gùl-ìl-à / bá-gùl-íl-á   'they buy for'
          H L   H L $H_{//}$
          bá-gùl-ìl-ìl-à / bá-gùl-íl-íl-á 'they bribe'
          H L   H L $H_{//}$

The forms in (4a) are all non-tonic (see footnote 3), with the subject prefix *a-* arguably having undergone rule 3. As seen, these non-tonic forms may be realized either with all Low tone, or they may be realized with a Low on the first mora and High tone on the remaining moras. In (4b) the subject prefix *ba-* has an underlying High tone, causing a pitch drop to Low on the following mora of the verb root *-gul-*. The remaining non-tonic moras may again be realized either with Low tone or with High tone, as seen. Consider now forms ending with a Low tone, rather than with one or more non-tonic moras. In (5a) we see that if the form ends with a single Low, the intonational High cannot surface; in (5b) we see that if there are at least two Low-toned moras, $H_{//}$ links to the last Low-toned mora.

---

[4]The exact statement of this target condition may vary according to one's view of the skeleton and syllable structure. What is intended in (3e) is that only a CG-initial onsetless mora is targeted.

(5) a. y-à-gúl-à / y-à-gúl-à   'he bought'
    H L   H L H∕∕

   b. y-à-gúl-ìl-à / y-à-gúl-ìl-á   'he bought for'
      H L L   H L L H∕∕
   y-à-gúl-ìl-ìl-à / y-à-gúl-ìl-ìl-á   'he bribed'
      H L L L   H L L L H∕∕

The rule inserting H∕∕ is given in (6).

(6)   a. domain   : IP
      b. edge   : right
      c. function   : insert
      d. trigger   : H
      e. target condition : none

As seen, a High boundary tone is inserted at the right edge of an intonational phrase. The absence of any target condition means that the High
comes in unlinked, and that it must link by the general properties of the
language—which, for example, do not allow it to link to a Low-toned mora
that is immediately preceded by a High-toned mora. The only additional
statement that need be made is that this insertion rule is optional. If it
does not apply, default Low tone will instead be assigned to all non-tonic
moras.

    The two Luganda rules in (3) and (6) illustrate boundary tonology
that is sensitive to a CG versus an IP and to the left edge versus right
edge of the domain. In addition, the rules illustrate the deletion versus
insertion parameters. Other tone languages provide examples of boundary
tonology involving other domains as well as the spreading and delinking
parameters.

    In the remainder of this paper I hope to do two things. First, I will
show from Kinande data in section 1 that the prosodic hierarchy makes
correct predictions concerning boundary tonology. Specifically, it will
be shown that in Kinande, the boundary tonology specific to a smaller
domain (the PP) must take place 'inside' the boundary tonology of a
larger domain (the IP). Second, in section 2, I will draw again on Luganda
and then on Gokana to examine some of the implications of the Kinande
analysis in section 2.

1   Kinande Boundary Tonology

In this section I will present the general properties of boundary tonology
in Kinande, a Bantu language spoken in Eastern Zaire.[5] In order to do so,
I will focus mostly on the tonal alternations characterizing the six noun

---

[5]I wish to thank N. Mutaka for his help in the study of Kinande, and M. Cohen,
Dean of Humanities at the University of Southern California, for his generous support
of Mr. Mutaka's graduate study in linguistics at USC.

tone patterns illustrated in (7) as they appear after all lexical tone rules
have applied:

(7)   a.   e-ki-ryatu   'shoe'   d.   e-ki-tabu   'book'
                                              H L
      b.   e-ki-rimu   'spirit'   e.   e-ki-saka   'bush'
           H L   H H L
      c.   e-ki-koba   'rope'   f.   e-ki-tsungu 'potato'
           H L L   L

As seen, the output of Kinande lexical tonology provides TBUs which
have High or Low tone or are toneless.[6] In (7) e- is the augment or IV
morpheme, as in Luganda, and ki- is a class 7 noun prefix. The surface
realization of these nouns varies according to context. We can define the
neutral environment to be one where no postlexical tone rules apply to
these nouns other than the assignment of a default Low to each toneless
mora. Such an environment is observed when these nouns occur phrase-
internally followed by a toneless mora, as in (8).

(8)   a.   è-kì-ryàtù kì-rítò   d.   è-kì-tábù kì-rítò
                     H%L//   H L   H%L//
      b.   è-kí-rìmù kì-rítò   e.   è-kí-sákà kì-rítò
           H L   H%L//   H H L   H%L//
      c.   è-kí-kòbà kì-rítò   f.   è-kì-tsùngù kì-rítò
           H L L   H%L//   L   H%L//

In (8) these nouns are followed by the adjective ki-rito 'heavy,' whose
underlying stem tone should be ignored at this point. As seen from the
tone markings above the vowels, the toneless moras have received a default
Low specification.

We now turn to the postlexical tonology that obtains in non-neutral
environments. For reasons that will become apparent, we shall first
demonstrate that a High tone can always override a Low tone in Kinande,
whether it is from a leftward High tone spreading within a phonological
phrase, leftward linking of a floating High tone, or linking of a H// boundary tone.

In (9) I illustrate the realization of the six nouns when followed by a
High TBU within the same phonological phrase:

(9)   a.   è-kì-ryàtú kí-nénè   d.   è-kì-tábú kí-nénè
                       H H%L//   H L   H H%L//
      b.   è-kí-rìmú kí-nénè   e.   è-kí-sáká kí-nénè
           H L   H H%L//   H H L   H H%L//
      c.   è-kí-kòbá kí-nénè   f.   è-kì-tsùngú kí-nénè
           H L L   H H%L//   L   H H%L//

---

[6]I ignore here apparent OCP violations, which are irrelevant to the concerns of this
paper.

Here the nouns are followed by the adjective *ki-nene* 'big' (whose stem tones can be disregarded). As seen, there is a postlexical rule of leftward High tone spreading that spreads the High of the adjective prefix *ki-* onto the last mora of the noun, whether it is toneless or has a lexical Low tone. Thus we have the first indication that a High can override a Low.

In (10) we see that a floating High tone can also override a Low tone:

(10)   a. è-kì-ryàtú kì-ryâ
                    H L H₉L͇₍₍
       b. è-kí-rìmú kì-ryâ
          H L   H L H₉L͇₍₍
       c. è-kí-kòbá kì-ryâ
          H L L H L H₉L͇₍₍

       d. è-kì-tábú kì-ryâ
          H L H L H₉L͇₍₍
       e. è-kí-sáká kì-ryâ
          H H L H L H₉L͇₍₍
       f. è-kì-tsùngú kì-ryâ
                   H L H₉L͇₍₍

The demonstrative *ki-rya* 'that' is preceded by a floating High tone which links to the last mora of the preceding noun.

Finally, in (11) we see that an interrogative H₍₍ boundary tone can also override a Low tone:

(11)   a. mw-á-tùm-à è-kì-ryátú
          H L   L   H₉H₍₍
       b. mw-á-tùm-à è-kí-rímú
          H L   L   H H₉H₍₍
       c. mw-á-tùm-à è-kí-kòbá
          H L   L   H L H₍₍

       d. mw-á-tùm-à è-kì-tábú
          H L   L   H H₍₍
       e. mw-á-tùm-à è-kí-sáká
          H L   L   H H H₍₍
       f. mw-á-tùm-à è-kì-tsùngú
          H L   L   H₍₍

These utterances are glossed 'did he send a shoe?', 'did he send a spirit?' and so forth. We are interested only in the last TBU of the noun, which invariably has taken on the phonetic High of the intonational boundary tone H₍₍. The observational generalizations seen from these forms are: (a) if the noun ends in a toneless mora, as in (11a,b), *two* boundary Highs are added (marked, respectively, H₉ and H₍₍); and (b) if a noun ends in a Low-toned mora, as in (11c-f), only *one* boundary High is added (namely, H₍₍).[7]

We have thus established two facts. First, within a phonological phrase, a High can override a Low (cf. (9), (10)). Second, before pause (or, more accurately, at the end of an IP), a High can override a Low (cf. (11)). The question that is now relevant is: what happens *across* phonological phrases? The PP can be informally defined for Kinande as in (12).

(12)

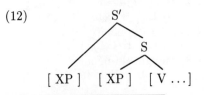

---

[7]For clarity, I have omitted from the representation of (11c-f) the final Low tone that is overridden by the High boundary tone.

Within tensed clauses, each daughter of S or S′ that precedes the verb constitutes a PP; on the other hand, all material following the verb within the same S joins with this verb to constitute a single PP.[8] An example of a sentence having three such PPs is given in (13).

(13) [ò-mù-tùtùtù] [è-kì-tsùngù] [kí-ryà-w-â]
      L   L H L   H%L//
    'in the morning a potato fell'

It should be noticed that the High of the verb *ki-rya-w-a* '(it) fell' does not spread leftwards onto the subject noun *e-ki-tsungu* 'potato.' In (14a) we see that the initial High of the subject noun *ka-tsuba* (proper name) does not spread onto the adverbial *o-mu-tututu* 'in the morning.'

(14) a. [ò-mù-tùtùtù] [ká-tsùbà] [á-lyà-w-â]
               L   H L L   H L H%L//
      'in the morning Katsuba fell'

      b. [tùm-á ká-tsùbà]   cf. [tùmà]
         L L H L L   L L
      'send Katsuba!'   'send'

From (13) and (14a) we conclude that leftward High tone spreading may not apply across a PP boundary onto material in a preceding PP. Thus, this rule can only apply within a single PP, as in (14b).

Finally, it should be noted in (15) that a floating High tone may, however, link leftwards onto a preceding PP:

(15) [ò-mù-tùtùtú] [kì-ryá] [kí-ryà-w-â]
      L   HL H%   H L   H%L//
    'in the morning that one fell'

We now turn to the phrasal boundary tone H% in (16).

(16) a. è-kì-ryàtú kì-kâ-w-â   d. è-kì-tábù kì-kâ-w-â
          H% HL   H%L//   H L   HL   H%L//
      b. è-kí-rìmú kì-kâ-w-â   e. è-kí-sákà kì-kâ-w-â
         H L H% HL   H%L//   H H L   HL   H%L//
      c. è-kí-kòbà kì-kâ-w-â   f. è-kì-tsùngù kì-kâ-w-â
         H L L   HL   H%L//   L HL   H%L//

While the toneless final moras of the subject nouns in (16a,b) show a final phrasal H% before the verb *ki-ka-w-a* '(it) is falling,' the final Low-toned moras of the subject nouns in (16c-f) do not become High. We know that this High cannot be a floating High coming from the verb, or it would be expected to link to both toneless and Low-toned preceding moras, as was seen in (15). We also cannot let this phrasal boundary tone

---

[8]This state of affairs, which is found with minor variations in many Bantu languages, is remarkably similar to the account given for the Athabaskan language Slave by Rice 1987.

be automatically inserted at the end of a PP or it would have the same properties as the $H_{//}$ intonational boundary tone, seen to override a Low tone in (11) above. Instead, $H_{\%}$ must only be inserted if the final mora of a PP is toneless, as formalized in (17).[9]

(17)   V →   V // —]PP
           |
           H

Or, within the parametric approach outlined in section 1, this rule would be stated as in (18).

(18)   a. domain   : PP
       b. edge   : right
       c. function   : insert
       d. trigger   : H
       e. target condition : toneless mora

In (19) we see that this rule applies to the last mora of a PP regardless of its category:

(19) a.   [è-kì-ryàtù   è-kyó]   [tù-ká-làngìr-á]   [kì-kâ-w-â]
                            $H_{\%}$ H $H_{\%}$ HL $H_{\%}L_{//}$
           shoe   that (rel)   we see   is falling

      b.   [è-kì-ryàtù   è-kyó]   [tw-á-lángìr-à]   [ky-á-w-à]
                            $H_{\%}$ H H L L   H   L
           shoe   that (rel)   we saw   is falling

      c.   tu-ka-langir-aa   vs.   tu-a-lang-ir-a
           H   H H   L L
           'we see'   'we saw'

In (19a,b) we see that the first $H_{\%}$ goes on the relative marker *e-kyo*. In these sentences, *e-ki-ryatu e-kyo* 'shoe that' is separated off as a single PP by virtue of its preceding the relative verbs *tu-ka-langir-a* 'we see' and *tw-a-langir-a* 'we saw.' In addition, the verb in the relative clause forms a separate PP from the verb that follows, as per the general algorithm in (12). In (19a) we see a second $H_{\%}$ on the relative verb that is lacking in (19b). The lexical outputs in (19c) show that this difference is directly attributable to the fact that the present tense ends in a toneless mora, while the chosen past tense ends in a Low tone. Thus, the $H_{\%}$ insertion rule in (18) targets the final mora of whatever word ends the phrase.

Consider now the realization of forms appearing prepausally in declarative utterances. The transcriptions in (20) show how our six nouns would appear both at the end of such an utterance and as citation forms.

---

[9]This rule is nearly identical to the phrasal tone insertion rule proposed by Odden 1987 for the Bantu language Kimatuumbi, although without the condition that the final mora be toneless. It might be noted at this point that the final Low of nouns such as *e-ki-tsungu* 'potato' in (16f) is motivated by the failure of that mora to receive a $H_{\%}$ phrasal tone.

(20)   a.   è-kì-ryátù   d.   è-kì-tábù
                H%L//   H L
        b.   è-kí-rími̥ù   e.   è-kí-sákà
                H H%L//   H H L
        c.   è-kí-kòbà   f.   è-kì-tsùngù
                H L L   L

Note that rule (18) assigns a H% to the nouns in (20a,b), which before
the application of (18) end in a toneless mora. Since the nouns in (20c-
f) end in a Low-toned mora, these do not acquire a phrasal H%. Now,
assuming these phrasal outputs, where only (20a,b) have a H% tone, a L//
intonational tone is inserted prepausally to mark completed assertions.
In (20a,b) this creates a sequence of two boundary tones, as seen in (21).

(21)   ....]PP ....]IP
             H%   L//

In (21) I identify the L// tone with the intonational phrase layer of the
prosodic hierarchy. As we shall see, an IP in Kinande is marked either
with a L// tone (when the IP occurs at the end of a completed assertion)
or else with a H// tone. The prosodic hierarchy makes the prediction that
the H% boundary tone, coming as it does at the end of a PP, must occur
within the L// (or H//) of the IP. The result is a H%L// sequence in (20a,b),
where H% (realized on the penultimate mora) is identical to the final H% we
saw in (16a,b). In other words, it is exactly the same forms showing a H%
on the last toneless mora of a PP that have a corresponding *penultimate*
H% in utterance-final position (cf. Hyman and Valinande 1985).
    Some derivations are given in (22).

(22)   a.   e-ki-ryatu   e-ki-ri̥mu   e-ki-koba
                                    H L   H L L
        b.   e-ki-ryatu   e-ki-ri̥mu   e-ki-koba
                H%   H L H%   H L L
        c.   è-kì-ryátù   è-kí-rími̥ù   è-kí-kòbà
                 ⸝⸜   │ ⸝⸜⸝   │ │ │
                H% L//   H L H% L//   H L L L//

Starting with the lexical representations in (22a), in (22b), rule (18) has
inserted the H% boundary tone onto the final toneless mora of the nouns *e-
ki-ryatu* 'shoe' and *e-ki-ri̥mu* 'spirit,' since they meet the target condition
of the rule. On the other hand, no H% is found on *e-ki-koba* 'rope,' since
this noun ends in a Low-toned mora. In (22c) the L// intonational tone is
inserted (by a rule yet to be formalized). In the first two columns this L//
causes the H% to delink from the final mora and relink to the penultimate
mora. In the last column, L// has no effect, since the last mora of *e-ki-koba*
is already Low.
    We now are in a position to derive the interrogative forms seen earlier
in (11). Sample derivations are given in (23).

(23)   a.   e-ki-ryatu   e-ki-rįmu   e-ki-koba
                                   H L   H L L

       b.   e-ki-ryatu   e-ki-rįmu   e-ki-koba
                 H%   H L H%   H L L

       c.   è-kì-ryátú   è-kí-rįmú   è-kí-kòbá

                 H% H//   H L H% H//   H L L H//

The lexical representations in (23a) are identical to those in (22a). The
forms obtained in (23b) by assigning the H% by rule (18) are also identical
to those seen in (22b). The only difference comes in (23c), where the intonational tone is H// rather than L//. As before, the intonational tone links
to the final mora, delinking the preceding tone. In the first two columns
the preceding tone is the phrasal H%, which then links to the penultimate
mora. In the case of *e-ki-rįmu* 'spirit,' the Low of this penultimate mora
is itself delinked and fails to have any phonetic effect. Similarly, when
the H// tone links to the final mora of *e-ki-koba*, the delinked Low has no
effect.

To summarize, we achieve the following results: if a form ends in a
toneless mora, its interrogative realization will be with High tones on its
final *two* moras; on the other hand, if a form ends in a Low-toned mora,
there will be only a single High tone on that final mora.[10]

A parameterized version of intonational boundary tone insertion is
now given in (24).

(24)   a.   domain   : IP
       b.   edge   : right
       c.   function   : insert
       d.   trigger   : Low, High
       e,   target condition : none

The inserted floating boundary tone will link up according to the general
properties of Kinande; i.e., there is no need to indicate the specific linking
and delinking operations seen in (22) and (23). In addition, since the

---

[10]One might object to a process where one High tone causes another High tone
to delink and then relink to the preceding mora. There are precious few cases in
non-boundary tonology, where the spreading of a tone displaces a like tone onto a
neighboring TBU. An alternative analysis of the Kinande facts is logically possible,
taking its inspiration from Hyman and Byarushengo's 1984 analysis of Haya. First,
there would be a rule of the form,

H%]PP]IP

which says that the phrasal H%, already linked to the final mora of its PP, spreads
leftwards onto the preceding mora in IP-final position. With the H% doubly linked, a
L// boundary tone would now delink the second of the two links of H%. With a doubly
linked H% we could say that when H// follows a final High-toned mora, it has no effect.
Thus we would have no need to say that L// or H// bump H% onto the penultimate
mora. I know of no Kinande-specific way of choosing between these two analyses.

choice of $L_{//}$ versus $H_{//}$ boundary tone is not phonologically conditioned, no target condition is given in (24e).

To summarize thus far, there is a $H_\%$ marking the right edge of a PP and either a $L_{//}$ or a $H_{//}$ marking the right edge of an IP. As expected, the $H_\%$ occurs to the left of the $L_{//}$ or $H_{//}$. Because of the 'prior' relationship imposed by the prosodic hierarchy, we have seen that the boundary tonology boundary tones of a larger domain may affect the boundary tonology of a smaller one, though the reverse should not be possible.

We now consider further justification of this claim.

The data in (25) now show that the $H_\%$ boundary tone is not found on the last PP within an 'imperative IP':

(25)   a. tùm-à è-kì-ryàtù   d. tùm-à è-kì-tábù
          L   L   L$_{//}$ L   L   H L
       b. tùm-à è-kí-rìmù   e. tùm-à è-kí-sákà
          L   L   H L L$_{//}$ L   L   H H L
       c. tùm-à è-kí-kòbà   f. tùm-à è-kì-tsùngù
          L   L   H L L   L   L   L

In (25) the imperative verb *tum-a* 'send!' is followed by each of our six nouns. The forms that are interesting to us are those in (25a,b), where we fail to obtain the expected **tùm-à è-kì-ryátù* 'send a shoe!' and **tùm-à è-kí-rímù* 'send a spirit!'. As indicated, these forms end with a simple $L_{//}$ tone, rather than with the expected $H_\% L_{//}$ sequence.

Before attempting an analysis, let us consider a few additional observations. (26) shows that despite morphological differences, the plural imperative works the same way as the corresponding singular:

(26) mù-túm-é è-kì-ryàtù   'send (pl.) a shoe!'
        H   H   L$_{//}$

The same effect can be seen on first or second person forms, if there is imperative force, as in (27a), which is interpreted as an order:

(27) a. à-túm-é è-kì-ryàtù   'let him send a shoe!'
        H   H   L$_{//}$

     b. à-túm-é è-kì-ryátù   'he can send a shoe!'
        H   H   H$_\%$L$_{//}$

On the other hand, in (27b), which is interpreted as a suggestion (e.g., in response to the question 'what might he do?'), the normal $H_\% L_{//}$ desinence is observed on *e-ki-ryatu*. In (28) we see that when the interrogative $H_{//}$ tone is superimposed, only the non-imperative tone pattern (with $H_\%$) is possible:

(28) nyì-túm-é è-kì-ryátú   'me send a shoe?'
        H   H   H$_\%$H$_{//}$

Finally, the negative imperative shows regular (non-imperative) boundary tonology, as seen in (29).

(29) í sì w-á-tùm-à è-kì-ryátù   'don't send a shoe!'
     H L H L L   H%L//

I will refer to the appropriate environments informally as 'imperative.' Our account requires that we either keep the H% from being assigned or that we have a later rule removing H% in the proper imperative forms. I will adopt the latter approach and propose that the H% of an imperative PP is deleted when the PP stands at the end of an IP (e.g., before pause):

(30) a. domain   : IP
      b. edge   : right
      c. function   : deletion
      d. trigger   : H
      e. target condition : final mora in imperative

The reason for this decision is that the H% *is* present in an imperative, if the imperative PP is not final within its IP. The imperative forms in (31) consist of one IP containing two PPs:

(31) a. [[tùm-à è-kì-ryàtú] [w-ás-è]]   'send a shoe and come!'
          L L   H%   H L

     b. [[tùm-à è-kí-rìmú] [w-ás-è]]   'send a spirit and come!'
          L L H L H%   H L

     c. [[tùm-à è-kí-kòbà] [w-ás-è]]   'send a rope and come!'
          L L H L L   H L

In (31a,b) we see the presence of a H% boundary tone on *e-ki-ryatu* and *e-ki-rimu*, the two nouns that end in a lexically toneless mora. In (31c), on the other hand, *e-ki-koba* does not show a final H%, because it ends in a lexical Low-toned mora. The H% tones are thus not affected by rule (30), because their respective PP is not final within the one imperative IP.

Perhaps the most interesting property of the system is the interaction between rule (30) and list intonation. As seen in (32), list intonation is marked exactly the same as question intonation, namely by the presence of a H// tone.[11]

(32) mó-tw-à-tùm-à è-kì-ryátú, nà è-kí-rímú, nà è-kí-kòbá, nà è-kì-tábú,
     H   L L L   H H%H//   H H%H//   H L H//   H H//
     nà è-kí-sáká, nà è-kì-tsùngú, nà è-kí-ndù
     H H H//   H//   H% L//
     'we brought a shoe... a spirit... a rope... a book... a bush... a potato... and a thing'

As seen in the gloss, this intonation pattern requires that a pause occur between each of the list NPs. The marker *na* 'and' separates each noun

---

[11]Thus, it might be more appropriate to speak of H// as being the mark of 'non-completion' and L// the mark of 'completion.'

from the preceding one. As in the case of question intonation in (11), the first two nouns (which end in a toneless mora) are characterized by a $H_\%$ phrasal tone followed by a $H_{//}$ intonational tone. The remaining non-final nouns, ending as they do in a Low-toned mora, receive only the $H_{//}$ intonational tone. (The added noun *e-ki-ndu* 'thing' is toneless, receiving the $H_\%$ $L_{//}$ tonal sequence appropriate at the end of an assertion.)

When we look at the same list intonation in an imperative utterance, a different tonal realization is observed:

(33) tùm-à è-kì-ryàtú, nà è-kí-rì̩mú, nà è-kí-kòbá, nà è-kì-tábú,
    L L $H_{//}$ H L $H_{//}$ H L $H_{//}$ H H $H_{//}$
    nà è-kí-sáká, nà è-kì-tsùngú, nà è-kì-ndù
    H H $H_{//}$ $H_{//}$ $L_{//}$

    'send a shoe... a spirit... a rope... a book... a bush... a potato... and a thing'

In (33) the first two nouns *e-ki-ryatu* and *e-ki-rịmu* appear with only the intonational $H_{//}$, rather than with the $H_\%H_{//}$ sequence seen in (32). Note also that the final noun *e-ki-ndu* is realized with a $H_\%L_{//}$ sequence in (32), but only with the $L_{//}$ intonational tone in (33). What this means is that the imperative has 'tonal scope' over all of these constituents. The proposal here is that (32) and (33) are divided into seven IPs. All IPs must be identified as 'imperative' in (33) so that rule (30) can apply to each IP, deleting the $H_\%$ that would otherwise appear.

Assuming that this is to be accomplished in a strictly phonological way, rather than by direct reference to the imperative construction, there seem to be two possible approaches. The first is to implement some kind of co-indexing. Perhaps the head IP of the U can transmit the feature 'imperative' to sister IPs. Or, adopting the idea that an IP can be (optionally) divided up into smaller IPs (see, among others, Nespor and Vogel 1986), perhaps (33) starts as one IP with its feature 'imperative,' and when it is broken up into smaller IPs, each one keeps the feature in question, satisfying the target condition in (30). This approach assumes that IPs are disjoint, as in (34a). The second approach claims that the IPs are instead self-embedded, as in (34b).

(34) a. ... [X]IP [Y]IP [Z]IP ...

     b. ... [[[X]IP Y]IP Z]IP ...

While rule (30) would apply to each IP in (34a) separately, requiring co-indexing of the feature 'imperative,' it would apply to (34b) in an ever-enlarging cyclic fashion, exactly as McHugh (this volume) has argued for Chaga. (34b) requires that the pauses in (32) and (33) mark right IP-ends, but not that each stretch so marked be an independent or disjoint sister IP. This second approach has some appeal, but of course violates the Strict Layer Hypothesis (Selkirk 1984).

2   Further implications

In the preceding section we saw that the prosodic hierarchy is strikingly confirmed in Kinande boundary tonology. Since Beckman and Pierrehumbert 1986 have shown that boundary tones are ordered by size of domain in the realization of English stress-accent and Japanese pitch-accent, the present study completes the picture by showing that boundary tones work the same way in a non-accentual tone system. At this point I would like to consider three implications of the Kinande study.

The first implication concerns the parameterized approach outlined in section 1 and further illustrated in section 2. There it was shown that boundary tonology can target a specific landing site either by requiring a particular tone or a particular TBU. Thus, Kinande $H_\%$ is inserted only if the final mora of a PP is toneless. What this means is that boundary tones need not come in as floating tones waiting to be linked to an appropriate TBU. Of course, the intonational $H_{//}$ in Luganda (section 1) and the intonational $H_{//}$ and $L_{//}$ in Kinande do have this property. In this framework, however, this is reflected merely by the presence versus absence of a phonological target condition.[12]

Now, given the possibility of phonological target conditions on boundary tone insertion, it should be possible for a landing site not to be adjacent to the relevant domain edge. Such an example is found in Luganda question intonation, where a S(uperhigh) is inserted onto the first Low-toned mora following the last High of an utterance:

(35) a. tu-ba-gulilila → tú-bǎ-gùlìlìlà   'are we bribing them?'
     H L   H S L LLL

    b. tw-aa-ba-labilila → tw-áá-bǎ-làbìlìlà   'did we look after them?'
     H L L LLL   H S L LLL

    c. a-ba-gulilila → à-bà-gùlìlìlà   'is he bribing them?'
     L L L LLL

Examples (35a,b) show that all moras after the target Superhigh mora are pronounced phonetically Low. Example (35c) shows that if an utterance lacks a High to Low pitch drop, Superhigh fails to be inserted and, instead, question intonation consists of a sequence of Low tones.[13] While it usually does not occur adjacent to the right edge of the U domain, Luganda Superhigh is still a boundary tone.

The second implication is that intonational boundary tones may be regarded as IP or U level morphemes in much the same way as the so-called affective particles, question markers and so forth used for similar

---

[12]In other words, I do not view rule (18) as a phonological rule having a grammatical condition and (24) as a morphological rule introducing a morpheme. It would be interesting to know, however, whether IP-level boundary tones tend to have fewer target conditions than PP-level boundary tones, as I in fact believe.

[13]The corresponding statement would normally have a single Low followed by all H TBUs, i.e., à-bá-gúlílílá 'he is bribing them,' as may be recalled from section 1. As before, apparent OCP violations should be disregarded.

purposes in different languages. In other words, besides the parallel in function, there may be important *structural* similarities between boundary tones and particles. In fact, the difference may be simply that the former lack segmental content, while the latter do not. If so, there should be cases where a phonological rule applies at domain p, before a 'boundary particle' is inserted by rule at domain $p + 1$. I will now cite one case from Gokana, a Cross-River language spoken in Eastern Nigeria.

Gokana has the morphologized Low spreading rule in (36a), which is responsible for derivations such as in (36b).

(36) a. [C   V]$_{verb}$ b.   ā è tù   'he took (it)'

L   H]$_{PP}$ ML H

A Low tone spreads and knocks off the High of a monomoraic verb in PP-final position. This rule does not apply when the verb is followed by an object within the same PP as in (37).

(37)   āè tú nɔ̄m   'he took an animal'
          [ML H M]$_{PP}$

In (38) we see that two particles are 'invisible' to the Low spreading rule in (36a):

(38) a. nwɛ́ɛ́ ɛ̀ tù ē ?   'who took (it)?'

H L H H   [who-PST-take-WH]

      b. nwín ē-ā-è tù ā   'the child that took (it)'

H MML H H   [child-REL-he-PST-take-REL]

In (38a) the WH particle /E/ cannot belong to the same PP as the verb *tu* 'take'; if it did, rule (36a) would not apply. Similarly, in (38b), the relative particle /a/ must not appear in the same PP as the preceding verb. I would like to suggest that /E/ and /a/ are inserted much in the same way as boundary tones. Rule (36a) applies at the PP level before the IP-level rules of /E/ and /a/ insertion which, like intonational boundary tones, target specific grammatical or pragmatic functions.[14]

Finally, the third implication of the Kinande study concerns my analysis of imperative tone. If this analysis is correct, then we should find parallel 'scope' effects in other languages. Consider again the Gokana /E/ particle appearing at the end of a WH-Q or focus Gokana focus construction. In (39),

---

[14]Another rule is responsible for the surface M(id) tone on /E/ and /a/ in (38).

(39) what   FOC-he-PST   take   open-with
     éé   ñ-á-è   (tú)   kùù-mà

door   WH   and   cut-with   meat   WH
nùtɔ   Ø   vàá   kpɔ́ɔ́-má   nɔm   έ
       έ   έ
  *   έ   Ø
  *   Ø   Ø

'with what did he open the door and cut meat?'

the /E/ particle must appear at the end of this complex sentence and may also appear optionally at the end of the first clause. It is ungrammatical to have /E/ only at the end of the first clause, or to have no /E/ at the end of either clause. The analysis I propose is that /E/ is required at the end of a WH-Q or focus IP. If the whole utterance in (39) is a single IP, there will be only one /E/ at its very end; if, on the other hand, there is an IP break after *nutɔ* 'door,' each IP will require a separate /E/. In other words, a rule of E-insertion will target IPs within the scope of the WH or focus element in exactly the same way as Kinande rule (30) targets IPs within the scope of an imperative.

It is safe to conclude, then, that parallels to the Kinande findings are found in both the tonal and segmental phonology of other languages.[15]

---

[15]In Hyman 1989 I describe a rule of Dagbani, a Gur language spoken in Northern Ghana, that inserts a glottal stop at the end of every IP under the scope of negation. In addition, B. Ladd has pointed out parallel interrelationships between IPs in English intonation. Finally, IP-final leftward tone spreading in Haya (Hyman and Byarushengo 1984) may be regarded as applying under the scope of assertion (cf. Byarushengo et al. 1976), via a 'McHugh cycle' applying to a self-embedded IP such as in (34b).

Summary of Tonal Realizations in Kinande

lexical representation (end of lex. phonology) e- "augment", ki- "class 7 prefix" + noun stem	neutral environment w/default Low / __ki-ḷto 'heavy'	end of phrase, e.g., as subject / __H%	end of assertion, e.g., citation form / __H%L//	question/list intonation / __H% H//
e-ki-ryatu 'shoe'	è-kì-ryàtù	è-kì-ryàtú H%	è-kì-ryátù H%L//	è-kì-ryátú H%H//
e-ki-rimụ 'spirit' H L	è-kí-rìmụ̀ H L	è-kí-rìmụ́ H L H%	è-kí-rímụ̀ H H%L//	è-kí-rímụ́ H H%H//
e-ki-koba 'rope' H L L	è-kí-kòbà H L L	è-kí-kòbà H L L	è-kí-kòbá H L L	è-kí-kòbá H L L
e-ki-tabu 'book' H L	è-kì-tábù H L	è-kì-tábù H L	è-kì-tábù H L	è-kì-tábù H H//
e-ki-saka 'bush' H H L	è-kì-sàkà H H L	è-kì-sàkà H H L	è-kì-sàkà H H L	è-kì-sàkà H H H//
e-ki-tsungu 'potato' L	è-kì-tsùngù L	è-kì-tsùngù L	è-kì-tsùngù L	è-kì-tsùngú H//

H% = phrasal tone; L//, H// = intonational tones (only tones that surface are indicated)

7

Toward a Typology of Postlexical Rules

ELLEN M. KAISSE

LEXICAL PHONOLOGY POSTULATES A fundamental dichotomy be-
tween lexical and postlexical rules application, that is, between operations
limited to strings found within the word and those which may apply
between words. In Kiparsky 1982b, 1985b and Mohanan 1982, 1986,
postlexical rule application is grossly characterized, I believe correctly,
as less phonologized and less grammaticized than its lexical counterpart,
in some cases even involving phonetic implementation. However, a point
made repeatedly in the papers in this volume is that postlexical rule application is a more complex phenomenon than the simple across-the-board
matter we once thought it might be. In this paper I will show the utility
of extending the lexical/postlexical dichotomy outside the lexicon, for the
characteristics differentiating lexical rules from postlexical rules may also
be found to cluster in one type of postlexical rule versus another. This
point is made briefly in Kiparsky 1985b, where contrasting treatment of
Vata and Akan postlexical vowel harmonies are given, and in Kaisse 1985
(chapter 1). I believe the idea that there is a dichotomy should be credited
to Rotenberg 1978, who distinguished between rules which require tem-
poral or phonetic adjacency and rules which have no such requirement
but instead require structural, grammatical adjacency. In Kaisse 1985 I
dubbed the former sort of rule, the one originally intended by Kiparsky
and Mohanan when they spoke of postlexical rules, 'P2' rules, referring
to the postlexical stratum in which they applied. P1 rules correspond to

Thanks to M. Beckman, S. Hargus, B. Hayes, T. Maes, K. Rice, and P. Young for
helpful discussion of many of the issues touched on in this paper. I am also grateful to
S. Karasu for his patient and creative help with the Turkish data.

the structure-sensitive rules of Rotenberg and, *ex hypothesi*, should apply
after all lexical rules and before all P2 rules.

Direct or Indirect?

Much of the debate on the phonology-syntax interface has come down
to what may be little more than a difference in orientation, for it asks
whether phonological rules access syntax directly or do so only through
the mediation of a prosodic hierarchy. I suspect that the P1 rules on which
I concentrated in Kaisse 1985 correspond for the most part to rules which
apply within phonological phrases in the prosodic hierarchy, however they
may be defined for the specific language under investigation.

I do not think that Selkirk's 1986 end-based algorithm for creating domains differs substantively from the c-command based approach of Kaisse
1985. Certainly some statements are more awkward to make in the c-
command version, but there is no mathematical difference in the information used or available in each algorithm since the end-based algorithm
looks for cases where c-command (based on maximal projections) holds in
one direction or the other and marks the end of a domain there, while the
c-command version (also based on maximal projections) allows or disal-
lows phonological interaction between strings of words based on whether
or not c-command obtains. The end-based theory is preferable in that
it allows a simple characterization of the entire span throughout which a
rule might apply, while the c-command version must state the extent of
the span iteratively from word to word; the end-based theory also deals
more gracefully with rules applying at the end of a span. But these are
differences in ease alone, not in predictive value. The c-command theory
has some advantages of its own, for it does not require the postulation of
constituents that are needed only to describe the sandhi phenomena in
question. (see Kaisse and Zwicky 1987). The existence of several rules applying within the same putative prosodic constituent does not necessarily
support a domain-based rather than a direct-syntax-based theory. Kaisse
1985 argues that the direct-syntax based sandhi rules are the local rules
of the postlexical phonology. When we find several local syntactic rules
in a language (e.g., Dative Movement and Particle Movement), we do
not feel compelled to set up new syntactic constituents encompassing the
units that undergo the rule; we simply follow Emonds 1976 in recognizing
a natural class of rules which operate between a non-phrasal constituent
and some other c-commanding constituent. Similarly, the existence of
several sandhi rules applying within strings of words satisfying the same
syntactic requirements need not argue that there is an actual prosodic
constituent within which these rules apply. To reiterate my position,
it may be more convenient to think in terms of domains than in terms
of syntactic relations, but I find no fundamental difference between the
two approaches. The excellent paper of Cho (this volume), which explicitly contrasts solutions couched within the direct-syntax, end-based, and

relation-based theories, is precisely the sort of work we need to undertake to see if empirical differences do emerge, but I do not find in that paper any phenomena in Korean which cannot be stated in any one of the theories, albeit awkwardly. For instance, Cho criticizes the direct-syntax approach because a Korean sandhi phenomenon occurs within words, although no c-command holds between the segments of a single word. But not all rules which require c-command also occur within words (the Modern Greek rules discussed below do not, for instance), so that any theory-driven simplification in the Korean statements entails a concomitant complication in the grammar of Greek. One can imagine quick-and-awkward fixes for the Korean case, such as stipulating that in this case what is required to prevent phonological interaction is the absence of c-command between words. As Selkirk 1986 observes, such statements are inelegant, but the mathematician will reply that what is awkward to state in words is not necessarily any less natural or simple.

In any case, I have no insuperable objections to stating sandhi rules in terms of domains derived through determining where command and government hold rather than in terms of command and government directly. However, I continue to see a difference in kind between rules operating on what we can grant to be clitic groups and phonological phrases on the one hand, and intonational phrase and utterances on the other. To put it more contentiously, I do not believe that these small groups belong to the same prosodic hierarchy. The larger domains can be restructured (Nespor and Vogel 1986): they are of variable size, tending to include larger syntactic constituents if those constituents contain few words or are spoken rapidly. In other words, the larger prosodic domains are less grammaticalized than clitic groups or phonological phrases. They are not nearly so intimately related to, nor derived from, syntactic categories and syntactic concepts.

Precompilation

I differ from Hayes (this volume) in maintaining that there are productive (not 'precompiled') postlexical rules which share with lexical rules non-gradience, existence of exceptions, and other characteristics which I shall detail shortly. While Hayes must surely be right in reanalyzing Kimatuumbi Vowel Shortening, which actually precedes clearly lexical rules, as a precompiled lexical rule, I do not think all P1 rules are properly so reanalyzed.

One case where precompilation seems unlikely to work involves one of the Modern Greek vowel deletion rules discussed at greater length in section 5. (The Greek rules are syntactically and phonologically complex, and I must refer the reader to Kaisse 1977a and 1977b for a more careful account.) The rule I call Less Sonorous Vowel Deletion meets Hayes's criterion for precompilation because its syntactic environment does not generalize across X-bar categories: it applies between a verb and its object but not between other head-complement types, and it applies between verb and adverb but not verb and prepositional phrase, thus requiring mention of category membership. As I understand the theory, the phonological requirements of the rule preclude precompilation. Verb-final /a/ or /e/ is deleted when the next word begins with a back vowel: any back vowel for the focus /e/, but only a non-high back vowel for the focus /a/. The phonological properties of the focus and the determinant word cannot be referred to simultaneously in a precompiled rule, nor can a frame refer to the underlying form of a word altered by precompilation. Yet in this case the possibility of deleting the first vowel depends on the features of both the first and the second vowel—if the deleted vowel was /e/, the vowelless allomorph can be inserted before a word beginning with /u/ but if the deleted vowel was /a/, the vowelless allomorph is incorrect. Thus, *iθel usiastika* may be the realization of *iθele usiastika* 'he actually wanted' but not of *iθela usiastika* 'I actually wanted.' It might be possible to salvage the precompilation analysis by splitting the deletion of the non-round, non-low vowels into two separate precompiled rules with identical syntactic insertion frames, but the repetition in the grammar of such a complex syntactic frame would entail a serious loss of generality.

Let us consider why there might be both precompiled and P1 rules. The most lexical of lexical rules occur at Stratum 1, while less lexical characteristics emerge as one travels 'down' towards the word level and the postlexical level(s). For instance, the last level of the lexical phonology may not exhibit strict cycle effects (Kiparsky 1985b) while the first level is the repository of the most exception-laden phonology and the morphology with the most noncompositional semantics. Thus, Hayes's well-taken observation that P1/precompiled rules exhibit lexical characteristics can follow naturally either from his contention that these rules really *are* lexical or from my contention that they are closest to the lexicon and thus share many characteristics with lexical rules. The historical progression from rules of phonetic implementation to Level 1 lexical rules can have many stages, I suspect, and a rule may pause at the P1 stratum before entering the lexicon proper. Precompiled rules might be partly diagnosable by their having lost even more phonetic motivation than P1 rules, and indeed the fact that several of Hayes's precompiled rules make a change in one word without reference to the phonology of the adjacent word supports this speculation. The most spectacular illustration of the existence of precompiled rules, Kimatuumbi Vowel Shortening, is quite odd phonologically: it shortens any vowel in the head of a phrase, and ignores the durational or rhythmic properties of the determinant word.

Just as not all lexical rules are well-behaved with respect to the predictions of Lexical Phonology, so a careful investigation of a postlexical phenomenon can turn up characteristics that are not what my theory would predict. Frankly, I would be surprised if the gradual lexicalization of a rule resulted in a perfect segregation of prototypically lexical versus postlexical characteristics. In the remainder of this paper, I will investigate two postlexical rules, Turkish Final Devoicing and English Iambic Reversal (aka the Rhythm Rule) to see how the criteria suggested by a strict dichotomy between P1 and P2 rules actually are distributed *in vivo*. I shall also discuss briefly a set of postlexical rules in Modern Greek which are acutely sensitive to syntactic information, but which are ordered incorrectly both for my theory and Hayes's because they apparently follow an automatic rule distributing allophonic information.

1   Typological Characteristics

If P1 rules correlated ideally with lexical rules and P2 rules with postlexical rules in the 'classical' sense, we would have the following segregation of characteristics:

P1 rules:

- sensitive primarily to syntactic information; syntactically local in a domain whose size is not variable; insensitive to intonational phrasing
- possibly requiring syntactic or lexical information beyond category-neutral, X-bar statements
- possibly cyclic
- neutralizing (structure-preserving)
- ingradient (categorical)
- style sensitive
- rate insensitive
- possibly having lexical exceptions
- having a lexicalizable output
- possibly showing strict cycle effects
- pause sensitive only if creating linked structures
- having an output available to rules of versification
- ordered before all P2 rules

Many of these characteristics are drawn from the canon of Lexical Phonology, since it is my conjecture that P1 rules will, in most ways, resemble lexical rules. (See Kaisse and Shaw 1985 for a more leisurely guide to the criteria.) Some of the litmus tests may be naive. For instance, it would never have occurred to me to separate sensitivity to intonational phrase from sensitivity to pause until I read Maes's contribution to this conference (Maes 1988). Maes argues that rules which create linked structures (such as French Liaison's creation of a link between a final consonant and a following onset slot) are sensitive to pause, regardless of whether they are P1 or P2, and thus that pause insertion is not a straightforward diagnostic of the P1/P2 dichotomy.

1.1   Syntax Sensitivity

Intended here is invariant sensitivity to largely syntactic factors. A characteristic mark of a P1 rule, or of a rule occurring within phonological phrases, is the failure to apply across syntactically not very distant but nonetheless recognizable structural junctures. Such inhibiting environments may include the juncture between the complements of a single verb or other head, between subject and verb, between an element which is part of a conjoined structure and some adjacent item, or between a head and an unsubcategorized element within its maximal projection.[1]

I have proposed (Kaisse 1985, chapter 1) that the ability of P1 rules to see syntactic bracketing, and the corresponding inability of P2 rules to refer to syntactic information, follow from a combination of their order within the grammar and the principle of Bracket Erasure.[2] Bracket Erasure states that the morphological organization of a string becomes invisible after one leaves the stratum at which it was created. In a simple model with only one postlexical stratum, no morphological information should be available, but all the syntactic bracketing should be accessible, since it is not created until words are inserted into phrase-markers. In the elaborated model I propose, this bracketing should be available to the P1 rules but should be erased when one leaves the P1 stratum.[3] Since the syntactic organization involves nested bracketing, some P1 rules may apply cyclically on syntactic constituents.

P1 rules should also be able to see the category labels on the outermost brackets of a word, which provide information needed for lexical insertion. This parallels Hayes's claim that a rule must be precompiled if it refers to very specific syntactic information. Our theories are very similar in their sorting criteria, and it will not always be easy to distinguish between their predictions.

A direct prediction of my model is that no strictly syntactic information can be referred to by P2 rules. P1 rules may access such information, though they need not. That is, just as not all lexical rules apply cyclically or refer to morphological structure, not all P1 rules must be limited to small syntactic domains (Turkish Stop Devoicing, discussed below, may be one such case). But there should be no P2 rule which refers to syntactic constituency. Such a rule would be a counterexample to Bracket Erasure. We can recognize P2 domains by their variable size and by the fact that they do not necessarily resemble any syntactic constituent. A P1 rule, on the other hand, can be blocked in predominantly syntactically

---

[1]It may be that for some languages, these head-adjunct junctures actually favor phonological interaction while head-complement junctures do not. (See Chen 1987c and Chen (this volume)).

[2]A similar proposal is made in Mohanan 1986.

[3]Other information might, of course, become available, such as organization into prosodic domains. Rules sensitive to prosodic categories could thus apply cyclically, but this time the nested bracketings would be those supplied by the prosodic hierarchy. McHugh (this volume) argues for such a case in Chaga.

defined contexts, even in the absence of pre-boundary lengthening, pausing or beginning of a new intonation contour between the words that fail to interact. I am not aware of any clear cases where rules which otherwise exhibit clusters of P2 characteristics nonetheless refer to syntax (i.e., are restricted to phonological phrases). As we shall see when we look at the English Rhythm Rule, however, the application of the theory is not so clear in the real world as it might be in our thought experiments.

1.2   Ingradience and Structure-preservation

Lexical rules are neutralizing, or 'structure-preserving'—they do not create allophonic variants. As a corollary, they must be ingradient, producing an output that could be an underlying segment or sequence, and referring only to such outputs. The postlexical application of the Akan vowel harmony rule (Clements 1981, Kiparsky 1985b) operates along a cline, creating slightly more harmonized allophones as distance from the determinant decreases. The distance is stated in number of syllables, but perhaps further investigation would show an even more gradient effect, depending for instance on the length of the intervening syllables, as we shall shortly see has been suggested for the English Rhythm Rule. Kiparsky 1985b has proposed that some postlexical rules may be gradient while all lexical rules apply in an all-or-nothing, binary fashion. Other sorts of behavior should also label a rule as gradient. For instance, the prototypical P2 rule of Turkish Continuant Devoicing (section 3), devoices /r/'s and voiced fricatives about halfway through the segment. Since lexical rules are structure- preserving, such half-and-half, partially altered foci could never be underlying segments. Any rule producing them must be postlexical, preferably operating at the P2 stratum.

The English Rhythm Rule's increased likelihood of application as some ideal structural description is reached (see Hayes 1984, and section 2 below) also appears gradient, but it might simply be an optional, variable rule; perhaps even lexical rules can show this characteristic. Labov's work has certainly shown that many rules can have complex phonological, morphological, and sociological factors governing their frequency of application, and it is by no means clear that such complex behavior cannot also characterize P1 and clearly lexical rules.

However, Hayes also suggests that the Rhythm Rule and related rhythmic phenomena may be dependent on actual physical time or some idealized version of it. Since time is not a phonological category, reference to it suggests that a rule is gradient and, *ex hypothesi*, belongs to the P2 stratum.

1.3   Rate-sensitivity versus Style-sensitivity

This distinction was introduced by Hasegawa 1979 in a discussion of some Japanese postlexical rules. Hasegawa objected to Zwicky's 1972 conflation

of fast and casual speech, for in Japanese, distinctions between registers
are sharply drawn and independent of rate. The rate-sensitive rules she
discussed correspond to our P2 rules, while the style-sensitive ones cover
both lexicalized allomorphy and P1 rules. The association of certain
postlexical rules with particular styles has not been much investigated,
and I do not know if register-dependence is in fact a typical characteristic
of P1 rules. Certainly, many, like the Modern Greek rules of section 4,
lend a casual air to the discourse, but others, like the Rhythm Rule, seem
quite style-neutral.

1.4   Lexical Exceptions and Lexicalizability

Because the lexicon is the repository of exceptional information, lexical
rules can access this marking. I propose that the information may be
kept through the P1 stratum, since several postlexical rules with lexical
exceptions have been noted. The Rhythm Rule and Turkish Stop Devoicing are two such rules; another is Yoruba Contraction (Bangboṣe 1965).
There is also a postlexical parallel to lexical exceptions, namely the failure
of a rule to generalize across X-bar categories, referring instead to category labels or to more idiosyncratic syntactic relationships as in Chizigula
(Kenstowicz and Kisseberth, this volume) and Modern Greek.

Another well-known property of lexical rules is that their outputs are
possible words and can be lexicalized, i.e., reinterpreted as words which
have undergone no rules. We shall see that the English Rhythm Rule,
which is clearly postlexical, may also have contributed words to the lexicon.

1.5   Strict Cycle Effects

Lexical rules apply only in derived environments, that is, environments
created by the addition of new morphology or the application of another
phonological rule at the current cycle. We shall see that Turkish Stop
Devoicing exhibits this same effect.

1.6   Pause-sensitivity

Mohanan 1982, 1986 proposed that pause insertion takes place postlexically and thus that lexical rules are not blocked by pause. The suggestion
is extended in Kaisse 1985, where I proposed that pause insertion occurs
between levels P1 and P2. Indeed, many P1 rules are insensitive to pause
(for instance, the Modern Greek vowel deletion rules discussed below)
but Maes 1988 has shown that pause insertion is more likely a test for
whether a rule creates or depends upon linked structures than for whether
it belongs to the P1 or P2 stratum. Maes notes that pause insertion is
not identical to creation of intonational phrases; any rule sensitive to the
latter clearly belongs in stratum P2.

1.7   Availability to Versification

Kiparsky 1985a proposes that a language's poetic meters may refer only to categories that play a role in its lexical phonology. Thus Chinese, which has lexical tones, can and does have meters based on tone, but English, whose tones are assigned postlexically as intonation, cannot. If Kiparsky's claim extends to the output of rules as well, postlexically derived stress configurations should not be accessible to rules of versification. We shall see in section 3, however, that the output of the Rhythm Rule is indeed usable in scansion, suggesting that the P1 rules share yet another lexical characteristic.

1.8   Ordering

Finally, the Lexical Phonology model makes the strong prediction that no rule requiring word-external information, or otherwise clearly diagnosed as postlexical, may precede a word-bounded rule. Within the lexicon, the ordering prediction is weakened in some versions (see, e.g., Halle and Mohanan 1985), but we generally expect that the most lexicalized rules will apply before the least lexicalized. Similarly, the P1/P2 theory would be strongest if it insisted that all P1 rules must precede all P2 rules. Precompilation theory is to be preferred in this matter, for it is more falsifiable. It makes the surprising but apparently correct prediction that precompiled rules may precede classical lexical rules; it also predicts that no precompiled rule may follow a postlexical rule. I will raise a few potential ordering problems both for precompilation theory and my theory in the following sections. I do not think we should throw in the towel on the ordering prediction, but there are cases where it will be particularly difficult for precompilation to explain the ordering of rules.

2   Test Run I: the English Rhythm Rule

The English rhythmic adjustment which reverses the prominences of secondary stresses in phrases like *Mississippi delta* and *complex fraction* shows many P1 characteristics. In Kaisse 1987, I show that the rule is seriously laden with exceptions. Words like *complex* and *abstract*, where two adjacent syllables form the focus of Iambic Reversal, are in fact relatively unusual, and dozens of phonologically and morphologically comparable words do not allow reversal of the prominences. A few examples of exceptions to the Rhythm Rule are *exact, benign, superb, abstemious,* and *grotesque.* The Rhythm Rule's output is also available to rules of versification, but I will not burden the reader again with the entire limerick that illustrates this point. One line, which scans only if the Rhythm Rule has applied to *Tennessee,* reads

(1) A Tennessee drummer named Bette

In addition, the output of the Rhythm Rule may be lexicalized. The adjective *abstract,* "referring to art that is not representational" (Kiparsky 1982b:144) presumably comes from such lexicalization, and to this we may add the initially stressed variant of *abject* (cf. *abject poverty*) and perhaps the marginally initially stressed *Romance* (from *Romance languages?*).

A fourth lexical characteristic of the Rhythm Rule is its sensitivity to nested compound and syntactic bracketing, as shown in the contrast between the phrases 'one-thirteen **Jay** Street' and 'Bill's **thirteen clothes** pins.' It would take too much space here to illustrate these derivations and the others which Kiparsky 1979, Prince 1983, Hayes 1984, and Kaisse 1987 adduce, but I believe it is generally accepted that the Rhythm Rule applies first to the innermost constituents supplied by the morphology, then to progressively larger ones, as defined directly or indirectly by the syntax.

As far as structure preservation goes, a fairly simplistic approach yields a comfortable result: both the input and output stress patterns are possible lexical stress configurations, as witnessed by the lexicalization of *abstract* or the existence of pairs like *Mississippi* vs. *Abernathy.* But to my ear the Rhythm Rule often involves not a stress shift but the suppression of the High pitch accent on the offending syllable. A second complication involves the fact that there are no exceptions to the Rhythm Rule when a stressless syllable intervenes between a word's stressed syllables: no words like *Japanese, anaphoric,* or *Minnesota* fail to undergo reversal of prominences. I had hoped that this absence of exceptions correlated with the non-neutralizing character of Iambic Reversal on such words, since normally English words with a syllable following the last stressed syllable place the main stress on that last foot. I still think there is something to this idea, but B. Hayes and W. Leben have convinced me that the existence of words with final vocalized sonorants like *Abernathy* and *alabaster* make the argument tenuous at best.

Thus far, the Rhythm Rule is still behaving quite tractably as a P1 rule. However, things become more complicated when we turn to the subject of gradience. Hayes 1984 observes that the Rhythm Rule is increasingly more likely to apply the closer together the clashing syllables come, presenting the paradigm in (2):

(2)   Tennessee abbreviations   (adjustment least likely)
      Tennessee legislation
      Tennessee connections   ⇕
      Tennessee relatives   (adjustment most likely)

It is not clear whether propensity to apply based on approximation to a target structure is truly gradient or not—what we are counting are phonological entities, namely syllables. But Hayes also suggests in an appendix that the spacing requirement of eurhythmy counts not syllables but actual time. The likelihood of applying the Rhythm Rule increases from (3a) to (3b) because the length of the initial syllable of the second word decreases.[4] Time is not a notion we want phonological rules, particularly those of P1, to refer to directly.

(3) a. Korbel champagne

b. Korbel tequila

Thus, the Rhythm Rule may refer to non-binary contrasts. Hayes provides several other suggestive examples, including ones indicating that (allophonic) lengthening of a syllable competes with the Rhythm Rule in creating eurhythmy. He tentatively concludes that the so-called Rhythm Rule and the other rhythmic adjustments which he discusses 'co-conspire' with phonetic length adjustment to create eurhythmic grids.

Hayes does not argue that lengthening must actually be ordered before the kinds of rhythmic adjustment he is treating by means of beat addition or movement; rather, all the rules are options which may be chosen to achieve the eurhythmic target. Thus we are not faced here with a case where a rule which shows primarily P1 characteristics (the Rhythm Rule) must be ordered after a rule with mainly P2 characteristics. However, in the next section we shall be confronted with an ordering problem of exactly this sort. For now, we may conclude that the Rhythm Rule is essentially a P1 rule, though its classification is complicated by its strong relation to timing, intonation, duration and eurhythmy, and by its optionality and variability, phenomena which I do not pretend to understand.

3   Test Run II: Turkish Final Devoicing

Turkish has a neutralization rule which devoices stops and affricates syllable-finally. The rule must be postlexical, because stops and affricates can optionally fail to devoice if the following word begins with a vowel, as shown in (4b).

(4) a. šarap, šarabɨ, šaraplar   'wine' (nom. sg., acc. sg., nom. pl.)

b. šarap aldɨ *or* šarab aldɨ   'he bought wine'

c. šarap verdi (*šarab verdi)   'he gave wine'

---

[4]There are no experimental data, to my knowledge, which bear on Hayes's intuition of gradient application. Silverman and Pierrehumbert (forthcoming), who investigated lengthening and pitch peak movement in clashes where the structural description of the Rhythm Rule is not present, found that while prenuclear pitch peaks shift farther leftward within a syllable if the clashing syllable is fewer syllables away, this gradience is not found in the related operation of lengthening. Lengthening is sensitive only to the presence or absence of clash, not to the number of syllables separating the accents. One might speculate that the Rhythm Rule is a grammaticized instantiation of the tendency for pitch peaks to move leftward, away from clashing peaks, an instantiation which moves the peak leftward an entire foot. Perhaps the Rhythm Rule has preserved the syllable-counting quality of its phonetic ancestor.

Turkish also devoices /r/, /v/, /z/ and, for some speakers, /l/ before pause—that is, in something resembling utterance-final position.[5] This Continuant Devoicing is a prototypical postlexical (P2) rule, for it cares nothing for lexical or syntactic information. It applies in an environment of variable length: in (5c), where the liquid is final in its clause but not final in the sentence, devoicing normally occurs, but can be inhibited by a rapid delivery with no perceived pause between the clauses. (ŗ represents devoicing.)

(5) a. ahɨŗ   'stable'

b. ahɨr sattɨ (*ahɨŗ)   'he bought a stable'

c. ačɨlɨnja   ahir,   ičeri   girebiliriz
   when-opens stable,   inside   we-can-go

Example (5b) illustrates that the syllabification of the /r/ into a coda and its position before a voiceless obstruent do not induce devoicing. The /r/ in that example would be devoiced only if the speaker paused between object and verb.

Continuant Devoicing has several other purely postlexical (P2) characteristics: it is, to my knowledge, automatic—there are no words that ever fail to undergo it, and it is a noticeable component of a Turkish accent in English. As noted in section 1.2, it not only produces segments that do not happen to occur lexically in Turkish (like voiceless [r]), it produces segments that could not be underlying in any language, such as fricatives that are devoiced halfway through.

Stop Devoicing presents a clear contrast to Continuant Devoicing in almost every regard, and indeed these two Turkish rules provide an excellent (though, as we shall see, not a perfect) illustration of the segregation of characteristics I would hope to find between P1 and P2 rules. The most noticeably lexical effect presented by Stop Devoicing is the existence of dozens, perhaps hundreds, of exceptions—borrowed but often old and well-integrated words which, at least for some speakers in some speech styles, have unalternating voiced stops.

(6)   ofsayd,   ofsaydɨ,   ofsaydlar   'offside'
      Serhad,   Serhaddɨ,   Serhadlar   'Serhad' (a name)
      diftong,   diftongu,   diftonglar   'diphthong'

Unlike Continuant Devoicing, which operates in all styles of speech, from the most to the least formal, Stop Devoicing tends to lose its exceptions, but only in informal, unguarded speech.

Stop Devoicing shows the lexical phenomenon of apparent exceptions in underived forms, i.e., strict cycle effects, as illustrated below:

---

[5]Turkish devoicing is discussed at some length in Kaisse 1986. My analysis here differs in a few respects from the earlier one, and has benefitted from discussion with M. Dobrovolsky and K. Rice.

(7)   abla   'older sister'
      dobra dobra   'forthrightly'
      üǰra   'far'

Again, there are at least dozens of words like this, many of native origin. Yet neither the exceptions nor the strict cycle effects permit Stop Devoicing to be construed as lexical. If a stop were devoiced lexically, it would then be impossible to know later whether it had underlyingly been voiced, and could reemerge as voiced before a word-initial following vowel.

Two characteristics of Stop Devoicing do not pan out as we might have hoped. For one thing, I am unable to discover any clear cases of syntactic environments in which Devoicing must occur. Not only object-verb, but also subject-verb pairs can show the kind of interword resyllabification that bleeds devoicing; even placing one of the words in a conjunct has no effect. (In all the cases in (8), a devoiced stop is also possible, of course.)

(8)   šarab aldɨ   'he took wine'
      šarab akɨyor   'wine is pouring'
      bira ve šarab akɨyor 'beer and wine are pouring'

We cannot test the environment between complements of a verb because all complements which do not have a protective case suffix after the stem-final consonant must occur immediately before the verb. However, extra syntactic environments can be created by 'leaking' constituents past the normally sentence-final verb. In (9), the imperative form of 'go,' normally [git], can reappear with its underlyingly voiced consonant (cf. *gid-iyor*) if the leaked word begins with a vowel. The glosses attempt to convey the marked reading such leaking produces.

(9)   sen bir gid Adanaya   'just go to Adana, would you?'
      gid okumaya   'go in order to read'
      alda gid ananɨ   'take your mother and go away'
      take-and go mother

In the last example, *ananɨ* is the object not of 'go' but of the first verb, yet Devoicing can be prevented. The only case my informant and I could discover where Devoicing seemed nearly obligatory was when a coordinate structure was leaked past the verb. However, such cases are so unnatural in their implicatures that the informant could not judge whether the strangeness of the sentence came from the voicing of the consonant.

(10) ??gid   eve   ve   čifliye
       go   house-to   and   farm-to

We must conclude that Stop Devoicing respects no significant syntactic conditions. It resembles those lexical rules which do not refer to morphological information. The absence of syntactic conditions is not incompatible with my theory, but neither does it lend support.

Actually, it is not too surprising that Stop Devoicing shows no syntactic effects, for it must follow the postlexical and exceptionless liaison rule
which resyllabifies a single word final consonant into the empty onset of
the next word.

(11) Resyllabification (postlexical, optional)

Locating Stop Devoicing after Resyllabification poses a genuine ordering problem, albeit a less than astonishing one, for syllabification rules
have often been observed to reapply whenever their structural descriptions
are met.[6] To my knowledge, Resyllabification has no P1 characteristics—
it is the sort of natural, automatic P2 rule which recurs in near-identical
form in many languages. Several people have suggested ways out of this
difficulty. Hayes (this volume) proposes that Stop Devoicing can also be
treated as an exceptionless postlexical rule by the following expedient: the
lexicon contains nonalternating voiceless stops ([−voice]), non-alternating
voiced stops ([+voice]), and alternating stops ([0voice]). A postlexical rule
making onsets voiced and codas voiceless applies only to stops unspecified
for voicing. This ternary-feature solution obscures the fact that the voicing alternation is nonautomatic. One must see whether there are opaque
[+voice] stops in any lexical entries to determine this. We cannot readily
distinguish between a truly automatic rule like Continuant Devoicing and
a nonautomatic one. Furthermore, Hayes's solution treats the many native Turkish words with morpheme-internal voiced stops (the examples in
(7)) as exceptional in the same unsystematic way as the borrowed words
in (6) . Yet the former, to my knowledge, show no tendency to 'regularize'
with voiceless variants, nor is there alternation within or among speakers.   M. Dobrovolsky (personal communication) has suggested splitting
up the devoicing rule into a lexical rule which applies only before another
syllable and a separate postlexical rule applying in the final position of
final syllables. This solves the strict cycle problem but is of no help with

---

[6]That Resyllabification is postlexical and interacts with the phonology is recon-
firmed by the fact that the rule distributing palatal(ized) and velar(ized) consonants,
argued by Clements and Sezer 1982 to be dependent on lexically assigned syllabification, actually depends on the backness of the tautosyllabic vowel after words are
strung together (k' indicates a palatal):

(a)   ok   'arrow'
      ok atɨyor   'he is throwing an arrow'
      ok' istiyor 'he wants an arrow'

(b)   yük'   'load'
      yük alɨyor   'he is taking a load'
      yük' istiyor 'he wants a load'

Thanks to E. Selkirk for suggesting that I look at this phenomenon.

the forms in (6): the exception-laden postlexical rule would still follow Resyllabification. Finally, Rice (this volume) proposes that the word-final consonants optionally remain extrametrical throughout the lexical derivation, and thus may fail to devoice. Devoicing is lexical, therefore, but cannot see the extrametrical consonants, which reappear when they are syllabified into word-initial onsets. This tack seems promising, but must wait for careful evaluation until we have a greater understanding of when and how extraprosodicity can turn off. I am grateful to these linguists for attempting solutions to the vexing problem of properly characterizing Turkish Devoicing. Languages like English and Turkish which have undergone striking changes in their lexicons through the additions of thousands of borrowed words can no doubt be expected to trouble phonologists for some time.

4   Modern Greek Vowel Deletion

A set of three rules in modern Athenian Greek deletes a word-final vowel when the next word begins with vowel. Which rule applies is dependent on a complex set of syntactic conditions. Their statement in Kaisse 1977a, 1977b might be improved upon, but they nonetheless are very clear candidates for P1 status and, because they mention category labels in addition to syntactic relationships, for precompilation in Hayes's theory.

The unfortunate fact is that all the vowel deletions are fairly recoverable because the deleted vowel leaves its trace on the preceding consonant before it is deleted. This trace is usually an allophonic one, though it may also be a neutralization—deleted round vowels leave allophonically rounded consonants, deleted front vowels leave palatalized consonants, some of which do not occur in underlying representations. The only neutralization occurs when the voiced velar fricative becomes [y] before a front vowel. (In the following examples, I mark the site of the deleted vowel with an apostrophe.)

(12) a. to   aloγo   aγapay→ aloγ^{w}o aγapay → aloγ^w' aγapay
         the   horse   loves

   b. efevγe   olotaxos   → efevye olotaxos → efevy' olotaxos
         he-left   at-full-speed

There are also surface contradictions of the palatalization rule which go in the opposite direction, where a non-palatal consonant appears before a front vowel.

(13)   ta   aloγa   exun   → ta aloγ' exun
          the   horses   have

These examples strongly suggest that a set of rather idiosyncratic, neutralizing P1 or precompiled rules must follow and counter-bleed or counter-feed a set of allophonic rules of rounding and palatalization. A careful analysis could conceivably turn up syntactic conditions even on rounding and palatalization, but I would be surprised if this turned out to be the case.

Condoravdi (this volume), which I saw as this article went to press, is a notable improvement over the somewhat piecemeal listing of syntactic environments given in Kaisse (1977a,b). Condoravdi argues that there is a set of prosodic categories derived from the notions of X^{head} and X^{max} which allow a prosodic statement of our three rules. In defense of my earlier analysis, I should add that my informant's idiolect was less tractable than Condoravdi's to generalization in broad syntactic/prosodic terms because my informant applied different rules in V-PP combinations than in V-Adv strings. In any case, Condoravdi's analysis, if extendable to the problematic idiolect of my informant, rescues the precompilation theory by removing the Greek rules from the lexicon. It does not markedly improve matters for our theory of segregated postlexical strata, however. Since Condoravdi's rules apply within or between phonological phrases or the new minimal phrase which she coins for the Greek prosodic hierarchy, we would still expect those rules to show P1 characteristics and thus to apply before the allophonic palatalization and rounding rules.

Another alternative has been suggested to me by S. Hargus. Rather than seeing the vowel deletions and the consonant assimilations as two separate processes, we can regard them as a single process whereby the place features of a vowel are spread onto the preceding consonant, while the vowel's timing slot is deleted:

(14)   C   V
     ┌----------‡
     [place]   [place]

Intuitively this captures quite closely what is going on: the vowel no longer takes up any time, and its syllable is eliminated. But speakers report that they 'feel like' they are producing the vowel—because, presumably, it is being absorbed into preceding consonant. The only potential problem with this solution is that the spread of vowel features takes place whether or not the vowel is deleted, so that a separate, redundant rule spreading the features of non-deleted vowels would also be required.

I do not think that the ordering problem is soluble within Hayes's precompilation theory. Hargus's solution will not work within the lexicon because allophonic feature spreading cannot occur there. And we would have to dismantle the lexicon and the theory of Lexical Phonology quite thoroughly in order to sandwich postlexical allophonic rules in before the operation of a precompiled rule. Within my theory, if Hargus's solution proves unworkable or if other ordering problems cannot be disposed of, it may be necessary to grant that rule ordering is not predictable, i.e., that there may be P1 rules or blocks of P1 rules which follow P2 rules. In just the same way, if we are to believe Halle and Mohanan 1985, blocks of noncyclic rules may be sandwiched before cyclic rules in the lexicon. This is not a happy conclusion, as it weakens the predictions of the model, but it still allows us to recognize a suite of characteristics which distinguish two types of postlexical rules.

8

Focusing on Phonological Phrases in Chicheŵa
JONNI M. KANERVA

THE PHONOLOGY OF A language has multiple layers of patterns and rules that affect the ultimate phonological form of an utterance. From segment to word to phrase and beyond, each level of structure not only contains the forms of its parts but also adapts their combination to that level's own patterns of form. The theory of Prosodic Phonology is being developed as an explicit model of these levels, their interrelationships, and their interactions with other linguistic subsystems (e.g., Selkirk 1978, 1980a, 1986; Nespor and Vogel 1982, 1986; Vogel 1984; and Hayes 1989). Research has focused largely on two of these levels: the intonational phrase (IP) and the phonological phrase. It is generally found that the IP is a broad constituent, often taking in an entire clause or more; its patterns of formation show high variability with respect to syntactic constituent structure and are sensitive to factors from semantics and discourse. The phonological phrase, on the other hand, is markedly smaller and is tightly coupled to the syntax. The evidence I present from Chicheŵa[1] phrasal phonology paints a different picture. Much of the

I would like to thank Dr. S. Mchombo, my Chicheŵa teacher and consultant, for his patience and invaluable help. I am also grateful to J. Baart, J. Bresnan, C. Condoravdi, P. Kiparsky, W. Leben, and many others for their helpful comments and discussion of this work.

The material in this paper is drawn from my ongoing study of Chicheŵa phonology in my forthcoming dissertation, for which I wish to acknowledge the financial and institutional support provided by CSLI, a Mellon Dissertation Year Grant, and NSF Grant No. BNS-8609642.

[1]Chicheŵa is a Bantu language spoken in East Central Africa. It is the official language of Malawi and has speakers in neighboring regions of Mozambique, Tanzania,

variability normally attributed to the IP occurs in Chicheŵa at the next level down. Prosodic constituents at this level are medium-sized and, for a given syntactic structure, may be formed into several alternate groupings. This indeterminacy goes well beyond that allowed for phonological phrases; it is resolved, furthermore, by taking into account the semantically and pragmatically motivated feature focus. I conclude that the results from Chicheŵa indicate (a) the need to test systematically across languages for the influence of focus on the formation of prosodic domains and (b) the possibility of a previously unrecognized level in the Prosodic Hierarchy, the Focal Phrase, occurring between the phonological phrase and the IP.

1   Identifying Phonological Phrases

Prosodic Phonology posits a hierarchy of levels, in which prosodic constituents at each level are exhaustively spanned by prosodic subconstituents at the next level down (whence the alternative name for the theory: the Prosodic Hierarchy). According to current theory, an utterance (U) divides into one or more IPs, each of which divides into one or more phonological phrases, and so on down. My strategy for identifying phonological phrases in Chicheŵa, therefore, is to identify first IPs and then find their daughter constituents: phonological phrases.

1.1   Intonational Phrases

Three phenomena in Chicheŵa provide evidence for IP constituency. First, Chicheŵa has lexically distinctive tone (High vs. Low), yet the final syllable of an IP never bears it. There, instead, one finds one of a set of intonational contours: high rising, mid level, and low falling.[2] These can be regarded as intonational boundary tones—High, Mid, and Low—on par with Low Tone Insertion in Slave IPs (Rice 1987).

Second, each IP is the domain of tonal catathesis.[3] It is common in tone languages that a sequence of High tones will be roughly level in pitch, but a High tone following a Low tone will have lower pitch than those High tones preceding the Low. This pattern holds for Chicheŵa, except that

---

and Zambia. The linguistic data of this study represent solely the speech of Dr. Mchombo, a practicing linguist fluent in both Chicheŵa and English. Dr. Mchombo was raised in Nkhotakota, Malaŵi, and describes his speech as central Malaŵi dialect. All data were gathered in interview or tape recording sessions.

What appears to be another dialect of Chicheŵa is analyzed in Mtenje 1986. Mtenje formulates versions of a few of the phrasal rules to be discussed herein, but his analysis primarily deals with lexical rather than phrasal phenomena. I have been unable to check his analysis against another speaker's data in the same dialect.

[2]The low falling contour, for example, drops to the speaker's pitch baseline, or even beyond into irregular voicing or voicelessness.

[3]I adopt this term from Poser 1984 for the same reason as he does: to avoid the standard but potentially ambiguous term downdrift.

an IP boundary, even with no pause present, breaks the catathesis chain: the first High tone of an IP usually is markedly higher than the last High tone of the preceding IP (unless that IP is short and has not moved down much in pitch from its own initial High).

Third, there is considerable lengthening of the final two syllables of an IP.[4] Lengthening of similar magnitude does not regularly occur elsewhere.

Do the Chicheŵa IPs thus determined show the constituency predicted for them by the theory? According to Nespor and Vogel 1986:189, the basic cross-linguistic rule of IP formation is the following:

(1) An I [= IP] domain may consist of

a. all the φs [= phonological phrases] in a string that is not structurally attached to the sentence tree at the level of s-structure, or

b. any remaining sequence of adjacent φs in a root sentence.

Part (a) of this rule is meant to include "parenthetical expressions, nonrestrictive relative clauses, tag questions, vocatives, expletives, and certain other moved elements" (p. 188). IPs formed by (1) are then subject to IP restructuring, whereby an IP may variably be broken down into smaller IPs as a function of length, rate of speech, style, and contrastive prominence.

I have checked many of the possibilities for Chicheŵa and have found that vocatives, parentheticals, nonrestrictive relative clauses, tag questions, root sentences in conjunction, and topics regularly form their own IPs. The match so far is excellent. Within these IPs, moreover, there is variable phrasing that resembles Nespor and Vogel's IP restructuring. Here is the problem, however. This next level of phrasing shows none of the three phenomena that distinguished the IP; instead, it is marked by its own cluster of phonological rules. It must therefore be a separate prosodic level below the IP.

1.2   Below Intonational Phrases

The prosodic level below the IP, in current theory, is the phonological phrase. Chicheŵa phrases at this level, which I will *tentatively* assume is the phonological phrase, are picked out as the domain of four rules:[5]

---

[4]The final syllable may, nevertheless, be relatively short when followed by a pause, much as if it and the pause were sharing time.

[5]Phonological rules can reveal their dependence on prosodic structure in several ways. The most fundamental of these is for a rule to apply only when its entire structural description lies within a single prosodic constituent (i.e., domain) of prescribed type. A second way may be viewed as a special case of the first: the rule additionally requires one of the domain edges in its structural description. Rules of these two types occur in Chicheŵa phonological phrases, and are called, by Selkirk 1980a:111, domain span and domain limit rules, respectively. Other rule types exist in general (e.g., domain juncture) but, since unattested in Chicheŵa, will not be discussed here.

(2) (Penultimate) Lengthening   domain limit
     (Tone) Retraction   limit
     Nonfinal Doubling   span
     Prehigh Doubling   span

Lengthening lengthens vowels in the penultimate syllable of each phonological phrase.[6] By Retraction, on the other hand, the tone of the final syllable in the phonological phrase shifts onto the second mora of the long penultimate syllable.[7] Example (3) (from Bresnan and Kanerva 1989) illustrates the alternations that Lengthening and Retraction together induce.[8]

(3) mteengo   'price'   mtengo uuwu   'this price'
     mleéndo   'visitor'   mlendó uuyu   'this visitor'
     mtéengo   'tree'   mténgó uuwu   'this tree'
     nkhúlúúlu   'cicada'   nkhúlúlú iiyi 'this cicada'

The second High-toned syllable of *mténgó uuwu* 'this tree' is not underlying but arises by Nonfinal Doubling. This rule spreads a singly linked High tone to the following syllable as long as that syllable is not in the domain-final (disyllabic) foot. Nonfinal Doubling is illustrated further in (4) (from Bresnan and Kanerva 1989), in which each phonological phrase contains one singly linked underlying High tone.

(4) dókótaala   'doctor'   dókótala uuyu   'this doctor'
     mtsíkaana   'girl'   mtsíkána uuyu   'this girl'
     chigawéenga 'terrorist'   chigawéngá iichi 'this terrorist'
     mnyamaáta   'boy'   mnyamatá uuyu   'this boy'

Doubling fails to occur only in *chigawéenga*, *mnyamaáta*, and *mnyamatá uuyu*. These are precisely the cases in which the recipient syllable would be in the domain-final foot.

Finally, Prehigh Doubling spreads a singly linked High tone to the following syllable as long as it is not the last High tone of the phonological phrase. The cases that distinguish Prehigh Doubling from Nonfinal Doubling involve a High tone spreading onto the domain-final foot (from Bresnan and Kanerva 1989):[9]

---

[6]Since the penultimate syllable of an IP is also the penultimate syllable of some phonological phrase, the extra length found there may be viewed as the cumulative result of lengthening at both levels.

[7]For a phonological phrase that lies at the end of an IP, Retraction thus has the perhaps noncoincidental effect of freeing up the final syllable for the intonational boundary tones discussed previously.

[8]All data are presented in standard Chicheŵa orthography, with the additional transcription of tone and length. High tones are marked by an acute accent (´); surface Low tones, which are profitably analyzed as underlyingly absent (with a few exceptions, e.g., fn. 11), are unmarked. Long vowels are transcribed as a sequence of identical vowels. Unless otherwise noted, the data are in citation form, which includes the effects of postlexical rules.

[9]The two Doubling rules also appear to differ in case the High tone would spread across a word boundary. Prehigh Doubling is nearly exceptionless, especially when

(5) njoovu   'elephant'   yá, wá   'Associative Marker'
     mwaána   'child'   ndí   'and, with'

     njovu yá mwáána   'elephant of child'
     njovu ndí mwáána   'elephant and child'
     mwaná wá njoovu   'child of elephant'
     mwaná ndí njoovu   'child and elephant'

Lexically, the second (final) syllable of *mwaána* 'child' bears a High tone. This High tone triggers doubling onto the domain-penultimate syllable in the forms for 'elephant of child' and 'elephant and child.' The forms for 'child of elephant' and 'child and elephant' lack the High tone trigger, hence no doubling occurs. Lengthening and Retraction apply to give these phrases their final shape.

The four Chicheŵa phonological phrase rules are stated formally below:

(6) a. Lengthening: $\emptyset \to V \; / \; \underline{\quad} \; \sigma \;$)

     b. Retraction: σ   σ)
                       ⟍ ͙ ⟋
                          T

     c. Nonfinal Doubling: F   F
                                  |
                               σ   σ
                               ⌊ ͏⟋
                               H

     d. Prehigh Doubling: σ   σ
                             ⌊ ͏⟋
                             H   H

Two individual utterances are discussed below as a summary for this section. These illustrate IPs, phonological phrases, and the rules that identify them.[10]

(7) (Zipáatso) | (zikupsyá páng'ónópang'óono).
     'The fruit is ripening gradually.'

          Lexical forms: zipátso   'fruit'
                           zikupsyá   'is ripening'
                           pang'ónopang'óno   'gradually, slowly'

---

the trigger High is close the to the spreading High. In contrast, Nonfinal Doubling often fails to spread a High across a word boundary even though inside a phonological phrase. Further research is needed to determine the nature of this variation.

[10]From here on, additional phrasing information will be transcribed: phonological phrases will be enclosed in parentheses, and IPs will be separated by a vertical bar. Intonational details will not be transcribed, but some may be inferred from the discussion of IP characteristics above and from the location of the IP boundaries.

The first IP in (7) shows lengthening, and its final syllable bears a mid level contour. There is catathesis in the second IP, but neither catathesis nor pause between the first and second IP. The phonological phrase boundary in (7) is indicated by the penultimate syllable of *zipáatso,* which shows both Lengthening and Retraction. That the utterance forms *zikupsyá* and *páng'ónópang'óono* phrase together is shown by the application of Prehigh Doubling, which has spread the High tone at the end of *zikupsyá* onto the first syllable of *páng'ónó'pang'óono* (cf. the respective lexical forms).

(8) (Anapátsá mwaána) (njiínga) | (ósatí mfúumu).
'They gave the child the bicycle, not the chief.'

Lexical forms: anapátsa   '(they) gave'
              mwaná   'child'
              njingá   'bicycle'
              ósatí[11]   'not'
              mfúmu   'chief'

The first IP in (8) ends in a low falling contour and shows lengthening; in particular, the IP-penultimate syllable in *njiínga* is noticeably longer than the penultimate syllable in *mwaána,* which is lengthened only at the phonological phrase level. Catathesis occurs twice in the first IP, not only within the first phonological phrase but also between it and the second phonological phrase. No catathesis, however, occurs between the IPs. In fact, the High tones of the second IP are all higher pitched than those in *njiínga* and even *mwaána.* At the phonological phrase level, the two High tones in *anapátsá* arise by the application of Prehigh Doubling, with the High tone trigger located in the following word *mwaána;* hence, the two words must lie in the same phonological phrase (as indicated also by the absence of Lengthening and Retraction in *anapátsá*). The phonological phrase break between *mwaána* and *njiínga* prevents the High tone of the former from spreading onto the latter, and all phonological phrase boundaries are marked again by Lengthening and Retraction.

2   Predicting Phonological Phrase Formation

Phonological phrases are thus identifiable; are they predictable, though? A variety of algorithms, some language-specific and some purportedly universal, have been proposed to derive phonological phrase constituency from syntactic constituency. A sample of these proposals is presented below:

---

[11]The word *ósaáti* (citation form) appears to be a lexical exception to the postlexical rule of Prehigh Doubling (which would otherwise make its middle syllable High). Alternatively, it can be analyzed as having an underlying Low tone, as a few other Chicheŵa morphemes appear to have.

(9) Nespor and Vogel 1982:228–229, universal

Join into a ϕ [phonological phrase] any lexical head (X) with all items on its non recursive side within the maximal projection and with any other non lexical items on the same side (e.g. prepositions, complementizers, conjunctions, copulas ...).

(10) Nespor and Vogel 1982:230, Optional ϕ restructuring

A non branching ϕ which is the first complement of X on its recursive side loses its label and is joined to the ϕ containing x [sic] under a new node labelled ϕ'.

(11) McHugh 1986:156, Chaga (Bantu)

Proceeding from left to right, parse the syntactic string into P-PHRASES [phonological phrases], where:

a P-PHRASE is a maximal string of words in which, if the string contains more than one word, each word P-GOVERNS the next.

X P-GOVERNS Y iff

(i) X is the head of X^{max}, and
(ii) X^{max} dominates Y.

(12) Selkirk 1986:385, universal

The idea is that a unit of phonological structure, a derived domain, will have as its terminal string the stretch of the surface syntactic structure that is demarcated by the right of left ends of selected constituents, as [below]:

a. $_\alpha$[..., where ... contains no $_\alpha$[
b. ...]$_\alpha$, where ... contains no]$_\alpha$

The general claim I am making here is that α will be drawn from the set of categories defined in X-bar theory, and that α indicates only a level (or type) in the X-bar hierarchy.

(13) Chen 1987c:131, Xiamen (Chinese)

TG [Tone Group] formation (final version) Mark the right edge of every XP with #, except where XP is an adjunct c-commanding its head. [# is a notational device to indicate TG edges. p. 113]

The VP is a good place to test the appropriateness of these algorithms for Chicheŵa phonological phrases. The Chicheŵa VP, as analyzed by Bresnan and Mchombo 1987:745, has the following basic phrase structure:

(14)   VP →   V   (NP)   (NP)   PP*
       ↑=↓   (↑ OBJ) = ↓   (↑ OBJ2) = ↓   (↑ OBL) = ↓

Example (15) is a sufficiently complex VP; it contains a verb, a direct object, and an instrumental oblique.[12]

(15) A-namenya nyumba ndi mwala.
'pro-hit the house with a rock.'

Assuming that the prepositional phrase *ndí mwáála* is either a phonological word or a clitic group (i.e., indivisible at the phonological phrase level), there are in principle four phrasing possibilities for this VP:

(16)   a. (Anaményá nyumbá ndí mwáála).

       b. (Anaményá nyuúmba) (ndí mwáála).

       c. (Anaméenya) (nyumbá ndí mwáála).

       d. (Anaméenya) (nyuúmba) (ndí mwáála).

The algorithms of Nespor and Vogel (with phonological phrase restructuring), McHugh, Selkirk [right end, α = XP], and Chen predict that the object will phrase with the verb, as in (16b); those of Nespor and Vogel without restructuring and Selkirk [left end, α = XP] predict that the object will phrase apart from the verb, as in (16d). Collectively, the algorithms are correct in allowing (16b) and (16d). They all fail, however, to allow for (16a), which is also attested.

Chicheŵa phonological phrase formation, exemplified in (16), thus raises what I will call the indeterminacy problem: a given syntactic structure can correspond to more than one phonological phrase grouping. Unlike phonological phrase generations in other languages, no deterministic syntax-driven phonological phrasing rule can apparently exist for Chicheŵa.

3   Focus as the Deciding Factor

The indeterminacy problem also occurs in English sentence accent. One cannot predict, from the syntactic constituent structure alone, where the main sentence accent (or primary stress) will fall. The following are just some of the possibilities for an English sentence corresponding to (16) above:[13]

(17)   a. He hit the house with a *rock*.

---

[12]It is also a complete sentence, since the subject marker *a-* can be an incorporated pronominal subject (Bresnan and Mchombo 1987).

[13]In these examples and the other English examples to come, the location of the main sentence accent will be marked by the italicized word.

b. He hit the *house* with a rock.

c. He *hit* the house with a rock.

d. *He* hit the house with a rock.

3.1 Semantic Characteristics of Focus

In generative studies, a notion of focus has repeatedly been called on to account for accent placement (e.g., Chomsky 1971, Jackendoff 1972, Culicover and Rochemont 1983, Gussenhoven 1984, Selkirk 1984, and Rochemont 1986). Roughly, focus corresponds to the pragmatic distinction between new and given information. A more precise and workable conception comes from the semantic studies of Jackendoff 1972 and (with some differences) Rooth 1985. Focus, in their analyses, is formally treated as a syntactic marker "which can be associated with any node in the surface structure" (Jackendoff 1972:240). This augmentation of syntactic structure, termed focus structure (Selkirk 1984:200), receives both semantic and phonological interpretation. The meaning of a sentence containing focus involves a specific range of alternatives, which collectively indicate the presupposition (or old information) of the sentence.[14] The location of focus indicates what semantic material is taken to vary with respect to a constant skeleton provided by the nonfocus material. The semantic value of the focus then selects which of these structured alternatives are pertinent. For example, the two sentences

(18) a. He hit the house with a *rock*.

b. He hit the *house* with a rock.

involve different sets of alternatives (indicated informally):

(19) a. $A = \{ x \mid$ He hit the house with $x \}$

b. $B = \{ x \mid$ He hit x with a rock $\}$

The respective assertions are of the nature[15]

(20) a. $|$a rock$|$ is an element of A.

b. $|$the house$|$ is an element of B.

I thus restrict my attention to contrast-like focus. Other kinds of focus have been noted, for instance presentational focus (Culicover and Rochemont 1983), but will not be treated here.

---

[14] Jackendoff and Rooth differ somewhat in the formal semantic objects they take to be the alternatives. For expository ease, I will follow Jackendoff in generally discussing sets of individuals rather than sets of relations containing a variable individual. Rooth 1985:17 mentions that his and Jackendoff's sets encode the same information and can essentially be translated back and forth.

[15] The expression $|x|$ means the semantic value (e.g., referent) of x.

As indicated above, focus indicates that structured alternatives are under consideration or are otherwise relevant to the discourse (Jackendoff 1972:246, Rooth 1985:13). On this basis one can understand how the three tests below all pertain to the same notion of focus:

(21) a. Question-answer pairs

b. Association with focus

c. Selectively contrastive adjuncts

Question-answer pairs are heavily used in the studies of English sentence accent cited at the beginning of this section. The rationale underlying this test is that a 'natural' response to a question should have the same presupposition as the question, that is, the question and answer should have equivalent focus structures (Chomsky 1971:199, Jackendoff 1972:230). Rooth 1985:13 expresses the same notion more incisively: "a question introduces a set of alternatives into a discourse," and the function of focus in the answer is "to signal that alternatives of [the same] form are indeed under consideration." (Also, one might add, the answer indicates which of the alternatives are true or relevant.) Thus, the following questions can be paired with those in (17), and the questioned element is taken to be focused in the corresponding answer:

(22) a. What did he hit the house with?

b. What did he hit with a rock?

c. What did he do to the house with a rock?

d. Who hit the house with a rock?

Association with focus, as termed by Jackendoff 1972, concerns the semantic interaction between focus structure and certain words such as *only* and *even*. Jackendoff gives examples like the following (p. 248):

(23) *John* even gave his daughter a new bicycle.   [= (6.89)]
John even gave his *daughter* a new bicycle.
John even gave *his* daughter a new bicycle.
John even gave his daughter a *new* bicycle.
John even gave his daughter a new *bicycle*.
John even *gave* his daughter a new bicycle.

The meaning of these sentences is clearly related to the structured alternatives provided by their focus structures. In the second sentence, for example, the sense (or presupposition) is that, of all the people to whom John may have given new bicycles, his daughter is the least likely; yet she, too, was given one by him. Indeed, Rooth's 1985 semantic analysis of this phenomenon makes explicit formal use of the focus-derived alternatives.

Selectively contrastive adjuncts is the term I give to constructions like the following:

(24) a. He hit the house with a *rock*, not a *stick*.

  b. He hit the *house* with a rock, not the *tree*.

  c. He *hit* the house with a rock, he didn't *carve* on it (with the rock).

  d. *He* hit the house with a rock, not *me*.

Again, structured alternatives are relevant. The value of the focus in the main clause is asserted, and the alternative in which the adjunct focus replaces that value is specifically negated.

Because there is a principled notion of focus, the tests for focus assignment are not arbitrary, and further tests could be derived if needed. The three focus tests presented above, however, will be more than sufficient for their upcoming task.

3.2 Phonological Consequences of Focus

In the English accent examples above, the syntactic focus marker has a straightforward phonological consequence: it directly locates the sentence accent. The full relationship is actually not quite that simple (e.g., Rochemont 1986), yet it is beyond doubt that focus is systematically involved in the location of English sentence accent. In Chicheŵa, as will now be shown, focus again resolves an apparent indeterminacy problem, this time in phonological phrase formation.

Chicheŵa phonological phrase grouping was tested on the set of VPs in (25), which cover a range of syntactic types. The ditransitive predicate of (25a) is nonderived, whereas that of (25b) is a derived causative. The obliques in (25c-e) differ in their thematic roles: they are recipient, instrumental, and locative, respectively. VPs (25f-h) involve passivized predicates, and (25i) has a simple intransitive predicate.[16]

(25) a. [V OBJ OBJ2]
     Anapátsa mwaná zóováuala.
     'He gave the child clothes.'

  b. [V OBJ OBJ2]
     Anadyétsa nyaní nsómba.
     'They fed the baboon fish.'

  c. [V OBJ OBL]
     Anapéreka mphátso kwá mfúmu.
     'They gave a gift to the chief.'

---

[16]The examples in (25) are shown with their lexical tones and vowel length. Their postlexical form depends, naturally, on which phrasing alternative is taken.

d. [V OBJ OBL]
Anaménya nyumbá ndí mwalá.
'He hit the house with a rock.'

e. [V OBJ OBL]
Anapéza galú kudámbo.
'She found the dog in the swamp.'

f. [V OBJ2 OBL]
Anadyétsedwá nsómba ndí Mavúto.
'They were fed fish by Mavuto.'

g. [V OBJ2]
Anadyétsedwá nsómba.
'They were fed fish.'

h. [V OBL]
Analúmidwá ndí njúchi.
'They were stung by bees.'

i. [V OBL]
Anagóna mnyumbá yá Mavúto.
'They slept in Mavuto's house.'

Cutting across the factor of syntactic types is that of focus assignment, which can be varied systematically for a given VP. In the next group of examples, the two VPs (25d) and (25i) will be examined in this way by means of question-answer pairs.[17]

(26) a. (**VP**)
[What did he do?]
(Anaményá nyumbá ndí mwáála).
'He hit the house with a rock.'

b. (V OBJ **OBL**)
[What did he hit the house with?]
(Anaményá nyumbá ndí mwáála).

c. (V **OBJ**) (OBL)
[What did he hit with the rock?]
(Anaményá nyuúmba) (ndí mwáála).

d. (**V**) (OBJ) (OBL)
[What did he do to the house with the rock?]
(Anaméenya) (nyuúmba) (ndí mwáála).

---

[17]In all the focus-phrasing examples, the Chicheŵa sentence will be preceded by a schematic representation of its focus structure and phrasing and by the question that set the context, if one was used. Focus is indicated in the schematic by bold typeface.

(27) a. (**VP**)
[What did they do?]
(Anagóná mnyumbá yá Mávúuto).
'They slept in Mavuto's house.'

b. (V **OBL**)
[Where did they sleep?]
(Anagóná mnyumbá yá Mávúuto).

c. (**V**) (OBL)
[What did they do in Mavuto's house?]
(Anagóona) (mnyumbá yá Mávúuto).

To test the whole VP as nonfocus, one can include a phrasal subject and have it be the focus of the question. The VP, being already present in the question, is thereby nonfocus in the answer:

(28) a. (**SUBJ**) (VP)
[Who hit the house with the rock?]
(Mwaána) (anaményá nyumbá ndí mwáála).
'The child hit the house with the rock.'

b. (**SUBJ**) (VP)
[Who slept in Mavuto's house?]
(Aána) (anagóná mnyumbá yá Mávúuto).
'The children slept in Mavuto's house.'

The phrasing pattern that emerges is:

(29) If there is focus inside the VP, (a) a domain starts at the verb and ends at the focused constituent; (b) any following nonfocus constituents each form their own domain. (c) Otherwise, the VP forms a single domain.

Clause (b) above may be demonstrated rather dramatically:

(30) a. (V **OBJ**) (OBL) (TEMP)
[Just what did he hit with the rock yesterday?]
(Anaményá nyuúmba) (ndí mwáála) (dzuulo).
'He hit the house with the rock yesterday.'

b. (**V**) (OBJ) (OBL) (TEMP)
[Just what did he do to the house with the rock yesterday?]
(Anaméenya) (nyuúmba) (ndí mwáála) (dzuulo).

The phrasing generalization in (29) holds, in fact, for all of the VPs in (25). Therefore, within the VP, phrasing is largely indifferent to the syntax and depends, instead, on focus.[18]

The phrasing-focus relationship is replicated by data from the other two focus tests: association with focus and contrastive adjuncts.[19] Some examples:

(31) a. (ngo-V **OBL**)
(Anaangógóná ḿnyumbá yá Mávúuto).
'They only slept in *Mavuto*'s house.'

b. (**ngo-V**) (OBL)
(Anaángogóona) (mnyumbá yá Mávúuto).
'They only *slept* in Mavuto's house.'

(32) a. (V **OBL**)
(Anagóná mnyumbá yá Mávúuto), | (ósatí pákhoomo).
'They slept in Mavuto's house, not outside.'

b. (**V**) (OBL)
(Anagóona) (mnyumbá yá Mávúuto), | (ósatí ánavíina).
'They slept in Mavuto's house, not danced.'

One can even combine the two tests:

(33) a. (ngo-V **OBL**)
(Anaangógóná ḿnyumbá yá Mávúuto), | (ósatí pákhoomo).
'They only slept in Mavuto's house, not outside.'

b. (**ngo-V**) (OBL)
(Anaángogóona) (mnyumbá yá Mávúuto), | (ósatí ánavíina).
'They only slept in Mavuto's house, not danced.'

Although focus plays such a strong role in determining phonological phrasing, one nonetheless needs syntactic information too. In particular, the right edge of a VP appears to form an absolute boundary to phonological phrase formation. Bresnan and Mchombo 1987:746 show that subject and topic NPs are freely orderable with respect to the VP; hence, the VP can be followed by a subject or a topic. Even with favorable focus placement, however, neither kind of post-VP constituent can phrase together with the VP preceding it. Consider first a nonfocus VP followed by a focus subject:

---

[18]In Bresnan and Kanerva 1989, it was claimed that a verb and its primary object obligatorily phrase together. This pattern had emerged because focus was not considered in gathering the data. Even with the focus tests, however, the primary object is harder to split off from the verb than other VP elements. Perhaps this is due to its tighter semantic composition with the verb.

[19]The Chicheŵa equivalent to English *only* is a verbal prefix *-ngo-*. Interestingly, this morpheme shows two different tonal patterns, according to whether the verb or some other VP constituent is focused and thereby associated semantically with *-ngo-* (Sam Mchombo, personal communication).

Chicheŵa *ósaáti* is like English *not*, yet it can also have the less abrupt sense of *but not*.

(34) a. **(VP) (SUBJ)**
(Anaményá nyumbá ndí mwáála) (mwaána), | (ósatí ṁleenje).
'hit the house with a rock, the child, not the hunter.'

b. **(VP) (SUBJ)**
(Anagóná mnyumbá yá Mávúuto) (mwaána), | (ósatí ṁleenje).
'slept in Mavuto's house, the child, not the hunter.'

Even if the focus subject directly follows the nonfocus verb, they still do not phrase together:

(35) **(V) (SUBJ)**
(Anavíina) (amáayi), | (ósatí ábaambo).
'danced, the women, not the men.'

These examples contrast with all of those above (e.g., (26b), (27b), (31a), etc.) in which a nonfocus verb phrases together with the focus constituent following it *inside* the VP.

There is a similar contrast in the phrasing of nonfocus material that follows a focused subject. As shown in (28), a VP in this position will form a single phonological phrase. Compare, then, what occurs with a post-VP topic NP that links anaphorically to the incorporated object pronoun (object marker) in the verb:[20]

(36) a. **(SUBJ) (VP) (TOP)**
[Who hit the house with the rock?]
(Mwaána) (ana-í-ményá ndí mwáála) (nyuúmba).
'The child hit it with a rock, the house.'

b. **(SUBJ) (VP) (TOP)**
[Who found the dog at the swamp?]
(Mwaána) (ana-ṁ-pézá kúdáambo) (gaálu)
'The child found it at the swamp, the dog.'

As above, even if the topic NP immediately follows the verb, the two do not phrase together:

(37) a. **(SUBJ) (V) (TOP)**
[Who hit the house?]
(Mwaána) (ana-í-méénya) (nyuúmba).
'The child hit it, the house.'

b. **(SUBJ) (V) (TOP)**
[Who found the dog?]
(Mwaána) (ana-ṁ-pééza) (gaálu)
'The child found it, the dog.'

Therefore, focus and constituent structure both must be taken into account to predict phonological phrasing in Chicheŵa.

---

[20]The interaction of object markers and topics with tonal retraction was first noted by Bresnan and Mchombo 1987:745.

4   Conclusion

A level in Prosodic Phonology may be identified by its relative position in the prosodic hierarchy, by a level-specific cluster of phonological properties, and by its principles of construction. In this paper, Chicheŵa IPs were first identified by all three means: as subconstituents of U, by their phonological characteristics, and by the universal rule of IP construction. Phonological phrases were then identified hierarchically, as subconstituents of IP. The construction properties of these putative phonological phrases, however, do not fit in the cluster of phonological phrase algorithms noted by various authors (e.g., Hayes 1989 and Nespor and Vogel 1986) for a diverse and growing sample of languages (e.g., Chaga, Chimwiini, English, Ewe, French, Italian, Japanese, and Xiamen Chinese). Chicheŵa phonological phrases are strongly dependent on focus, and are generally larger and more variable with respect to the syntax than what is reported for phonological phrases in these other languages. How can this disparity be resolved?

On one hand, the disparity might not even be genuine. If more specific and systematic attention were paid to focus as a factor in phrasing across languages, it could well be found that phonological phrasing is not, for instance, as tightly bound to the syntax as previous studies would suggest. This possibility is supported already by proposing phonological phrase algorithms for Hausa (Inkelas 1988) and Korean (Cho (this volume)), which contain key clauses referring to intonational emphasis and focus, respectively.

On the other hand, the Chicheŵa domains could represent a truly distinct pattern of prosodic organization. I propose that, if the cluster of phonological phrase algorithms does hold up under scrutiny of focus, then the Chicheŵa domains instantiate a previously unrecognized level of prosodic structure, intermediate between phonological phrases and IPs. In light of the dominant role played by focus, a suggestive name for this level would be Focal Phrase (FP). The FP, as part of the universal prosodic hierarchy, should be identifiable cross-linguistically. A good place to look might be in the phenomenon of IP restructuring in Italian and English (Nespor and Vogel 1982, 1986). Unlike their phonological phrase restructuring, which optionally accretes material to a rule-formed phonological phrase, Nespor and Vogel's IP restructuring optionally splits up a rule-formed IP. If these split IPs were actually FPs, one might be able to excise the unusual restructuring rule from the theory (P. Kiparsky, personal communication). Another candidate is Hungarian, for which Vogel and Kenesei 1987 provide a provocative study of the interaction of phonological constituency with focus, semantic scope, and semantic operator status. They note that the IP level "appears to delimit a domain which is too broad for the rules in question" (p. 253); the phonological phrase, on the other hand, is clearly too small and lacks the necessary flexibility besides. In the end, they settle for treating their phrase as an IP with a language-specific phrasing rule; their rule, interestingly enough, resembles Chichewa FP formation, (29), more than universal IP formation, (1). If this prosodic constituent in Hungarian were determined to be an FP, it would strengthen the connection between FP formation and particular semantic factors. Finally, several of the Chichewa patterns—especially the phrasing rule in (29)—were prefigured by Byarushengo, Hyman, and Tenenbaum's 1976 study of tone in Haya, another Bantu language. Their analysis predates Prosodic Phonology and is phrased in terms of "assertion" rather than focus, but it is clearly germane to Prosodic Phonology and quite likely to Focal Phrases in particular.

The proposal to add a level to the prosodic hierarchy may cause concern. Will Prosodic Phonology fall victim to a cancerous proliferation of prosodic levels? I envision two alternatives regarding this possibility: (a) as research progresses, clusters of prosodic phenomena (expressed theoretically as prosodic levels) will settle into a stable and discrete, although possibly fine-grained, hierarchy; or (b) further distinctions will continue to arise and thereby smear the hierarchy into a continuum. Either outcome would be significant, and the way to find out which is by trying to make each posited level as theoretically (and empirically) meaningful as possible. As long as a new level improves the accuracy, clarity, and consistency of other levels, and is itself well-defined, it should be seriously considered.

9

Chizigula Tonology: the Word and Beyond

MICHAEL KENSTOWICZ AND CHARLES KISSEBERTH

CHIZIGULA IS A BANTU language spoken on the coast of Tanzania just below the border with Kenya.[1] This paper reports some of the results of our study of the tone of the language, with special attention to the phrasal tonology. See Kisseberth (in preparation) for a more detailed and more comprehensive account of Chizigula tonology.

The study of phrasal phonology in general, and the phrasal phonology of Bantu languages in particular, has flourished in recent years. There are a number of reasons for this. Perhaps the most important reason is that in phrasal phonology one can be fairly confident that the alternations observed are the product of rules rather than a matter of memorization. Since the alternations that occur in phrasal phonology appear in connection with (in principle) novel combinations of words that instantiate syntactic principles, there is no way in which 'memorization' of surface forms can be involved (one cannot 'memorize' novel phrases that one constructs on the basis of one's syntactic knowledge of a language). Thus there can be no doubt that such alternations are properly to be analyzed in terms of phrasal phonology rather than being treated as arbitrary aspects of the lexicon.

It per haps should be noted that the same conclusion extends to at least part of the word-level phonology in Bantu. Because of the complex agglutinative structure of the Bantu verb, it is possible, for essentially

---

[1]More precisely, Chizigula is G31 in Guthrie's 1967 classification of the Bantu language family. We wish to thank our principal language consultants, Z. Mochiwa and A. Kishe, for the patience, dedication, insightfulness, and enthusiasm with which they helped us to uncover the system underlying the surface of Chizigula tonal pattern.

any verb, to construct paradigms consisting of (hundreds of) thousands of items. The fact that the Bantu speaker can automatically produce any member of this set of forms and assign it a consistent tonal shape suggests that these representations are being computed by the grammar rather than merely being drawn from a list. There are simply too many forms to make memorization a meaningful alternative. The interaction of this complex verbal system with the syntax makes the necessity for a rule-based approach even more overwhelming.

At the present time there are, to our knowledge, no studies that delimit which phonological processes can have a phrasal domain. Perhaps all processes could conceivably have phrasal domains. Nevertheless, it seems fair to say that certain features (e.g., accent, tone, vowel length, syllabification-related phenomena) are more commonly found operating at the phrasal level. The Bantu languages, being for the most part tone languages, are prime candidates for exhibiting phrasal domains. But Bantu languages are not just tone languages; they are tone languages of a particular type—namely, languages where High tones are 'mobile.' High tones 'spread,' perhaps even 'shift,' and in any case often surface on syllables other than those with which they are underlyingly associated. As languages of this type (as opposed, for example, to Chinese and other such languages where tones are more stable, largely remaining on the syllable where they 'start off'), Bantu languages are likely to exhibit alternations at the phrasal level.

The Bantu languages are also fertile ground for comparative study. Several hundred 'languages' (as well as many 'dialects' of these languages) have developed as Bantu speakers diffused over a vast geographic area in the past two and a half millenia. Enough time has elapsed to permit significant tonal differences to evolve. But the time depth is not so great as to obscure the basic underlying unity of these languages. Through the study of the Bantu languages we may hope to obtain a good sense of the range of structural variation that is possible and the factors that tend to be significantly rather than merely accidentally connected to these changes. Also, linguistic research has progressed to the point where the answers to the questions we are asking often require the felicitous cooccurrence of several features. With such a large pool of linguistic systems to draw from, questions that can be posed but not answered in one system can sometimes be answered by looking at another, similar system.

In addition to these general factors, several more specific reasons make the study of Chizigula tonology important—particularly at the phrasal level. First, in a surprising number of cases, the tonal structure of a given word in Chizigula reveals itself only when the word is placed in a particular phrasal context. Many words whose isolation forms take the same tonal shape diverge dramatically when embedded in a phrase. It is only by studying its phrasal behavior that the tonal structure of any given word can be accurately assessed. (As we shall see, a full understanding of a word's phrasal behavior often requires representations of considerable abstractness.) Second, at least three separate tonal rules pervade the phrasal phonology of Chizigula. Virtually any utterance of the language illustrates these rules, and no special contexts are needed to observe their operation. Since these rules are separate processes, the question arises as to what extent their domains coincide.

The paper is organized into three parts. In the first we sketch the basic tonal features of the Chizigula word. We then introduce the major tonal alternations that arise when the word is placed in a phrasal context. These two sections lay the groundwork for our discussion of the phonological phrasing in the final part of the paper. Chizigula tonal alternations are quite complex. In this paper we outline an analysis which seems to us to hold considerable promise. But we readily admit that there are aspects of the tonology which we do not yet understand well and that other interpretations of our data are certainly possible. Kisseberth (in preparation) will attempt to provide a thorough description of the language so that the process of linguistic restatement (one of the most time-honored traditions of phonological study) will be facilitated.

1 Part One

As in most Bantu languages, the simplest place to enter the tonal system of Chizigula is through the infinitive. The Chizigula infinitive consists of a prefix *ku-*, the root, and a final vowel suffix *-a*. We shall refer to the root plus final vowel suffix as the stem. As in most other Bantu languages, verbs subdivide into two tonal classes—a High-toned class and a toneless class. The toneless class in most Bantu languages is straightforwardly described: none of the syllables of the stem manifests a High-toned syllable. Chizigula is no exception. The High class of verbs in Bantu is more complex. In some languages this class is characterized by a High tone only on the initial syllable of the stem. In other languages, the High tone that associates to the first syllable also spreads onto subsequent syllables. In yet other languages, after spreading onto other syllables, the High tone disassociates from the syllable that was in some sense its point of origin. In Chizigula, the High tone surfaces on the root's final syllable. The initial syllable of the root, and the syllables (if any) intervening between that syllable and the final syllable, appear toneless, as the forms in (1) illustrate. (The acute accents marks High tone; Low tone is unmarked.)

(1) a.   ku-lagaz-a   'to drop'
          ku-damany-a   'to do'
          ku-songoloz-a   'to avoid'

     b.   ku-lombéz-a   'to ask'
          ku-bindilíz-a   'to finish'
          ku-hangalasány-a   'to carry many things at once'

Penultimate position in the word, rather than final position in the root, more accurately describes where the High tone falls. Chizigula verbs may be freely extended by suffixes that mark changes in the verb's argument structure (e.g., benefactive, reciprocal, causative). In an extended verb drawn from the High-toned class, the tone appears to shift from the stem to the extensional suffix. If there is more than a single extension, the High appears on the rightmost one.

(2) ku-damany-a   'to do'   ku-lombéz-a   'to ask'
     ku-damany-iz-a   'to do for'   ku-lombez-éz-a   'to ask for'
     ku-damany-iz-an-a   'to do for   ku-lombez-ez-án-a   'to ask for
         each other'   each other'

This migration of tones towards the right edge of the word is found in a number of other Bantu languages (e.g., Kisseberth 1984, Goldsmith et al. 1986) as well.

A natural conclusion is that the penultimate syllable in Chizigula is accented. The penult is, after all, one of the most frequent locations for accent in the world's languages. In fact, some of the neighboring Bantu languages (e.g., Swahili) that have lost tonal distinctions emerge with a penultimate stress. Finally, attraction of tones to accented syllables represents a distinct kind of tonal association found in many intonation systems (cf. Liberman 1975). However, we hasten to add that we are using the term 'accent' here in an abstract, phonological sense. The Chizigula penult does not display the normal cues for stress—it does not have increased duration (except in phrase-final position), nor is it necessarily raised in pitch. Rather, its prominence is manifested phonologically by attracting a tone from the left.[2] To be more precise, we shall assume that Chizigula has the accent rule summarized in (3a) and the tonal association principle stated in (3b).

(3)   a. assign a binary left-headed metrical foot at the right word edge

     b. shift a High tone rightwards to the accented syllable

Attraction of tone to the penult can take place over great distances (by phonological standards) in Chizigula. A number of prefixes contribute a High tone to the verb. When combined with a toneless root, this prefixal tone systematically surfaces on the penult, as we illustrated in (4). In (4a) we cite the present tense inflection for the verb *ku-gulus-a* 'to chase.' The inflectional element is a fusion of the present tense marker -*a*- and the preceding subject prefix. The third person subject prefixes *a*- 'he,

---

[2](See Goldsmith 1987a for a recent discussion of the role of tone and accent in Bantu.) The Chizigula penult also attracts the tones of intonation contours. For example, the toneless stems of (1a) are realized with a sharp drop in pitch on the penult in prepausal position. If this pitch drop reflects an extra low 'boundary' tone, then the fact that the drop begins on the penult makes sense under our analysis, since this boundary tone would be attracted to the accented syllable.

she' and *wa-* 'they' consistently impose a High tone on the verb, whereas first and second person subject prefixes do not. The High contributed by the third person subject prefix does not surface on the prefix itself, but rather appears on the penult syllable. In (4b) we see this prefixal High tone realized at greater and greater distances from the prefix where it originates, but always on the penult syllable of the word.

(4) a. ku-gulus-a   'to chase'
      n-a-gulus-a   [ni-a   'I am chasing'
      w-a-gulus-a   [u-a   'you (sg.) are chasing'
      a-gulús-a   [á-a   'he, she is chasing'
      ch-a-gulus-a [chi-a   'we are chasing'
      mw-a-gulus-a [mu-a   'you (pl.) are chasing'
      w-a-gulús-a   [wá-a   'they are chasing'

    b. ku-songoloz-a   'to avoid'
       n-a-songoloz-a   'I am avoiding'
       a-songolóz-a   'he is avoiding'
       ku-hugus-a   'to shell'
       ku-hugusahugus-a   'to shell' repeatedly'
       n-a-hugusahugus-a   'I shell repeatedly'
       a-hugusahugúsa   'he shells repeatedly'

    c. High-Tone Extension Rule

```
                *
  *  * * * * [* *]
  a [hugusahugusa]
      ------------
  H
```

This sort of 'action-at-a-distance' is the most striking feature of the tonal system of the language. The metrical grid sketched in (4c) and the association of the High prefixal tone with the accented syllable illustrates the intended analysis.

When a high-toned prefix combines with a High-toned verb stem, what surfaces is a sequence of High-toned syllables that starts at the beginning of the stem, followed by a Low and then by the penult High. The data in (5) illustrate this down-up-down-up patterning for verb stems of varying length.

(5) infin. ku-bindilíza   ku-lulungánya   ku-hangalasánya
    1 sg.   na-bindilíza   na-lulungánya   na-hangalasánya
    3 sg.   a-bíndilíza   a-lúlungánya   a-hángálasánya
            'finish'   'take advantage of'   'carry many things
                                                 at once'

infin.	ku-hangalasanyíza	ku-hangalasanyizíza
1 sg.	na-hangalasanyíza	na-hangalasanyizíza
3 sg.	a-hángálásanyíza	a-hángálásányizíza
	'carry many things for'	'carry many things for (intensively)'

We may describe these data by saying that the lexical High of the root associates to the accented penult, while the prefixal High associates with the initial syllable of the stem to yield a representation like that in (6a). The intervening sequence of toneless syllables is then filled in by a rule spreading High tone to the right. We state this rule in (6b). (The circle denotes an unlinked tone-bearing unit) (TBU).

(6) a.   a [hangalasanyiza]

      H   H

   b. High Tone Spread   V   Ⓥ

                                  L

                                  H

   c. a [hangalasanyiza]

        H   H

In Chizigula, as in a number of other Bantu languages (e.g., members of the Sotho language cluster—Sesotho, Setswana, Northern Sotho[3]), a High does not spread onto a TBU that itself precedes a High tone-bearing unit. There are, of course, a variety of ways of obtaining this result—e.g., we might stipulate that Highs do not spread in this environment, or we might allow the High to spread and then invoke a delinking operation to counteract the results of such an unrestricted spreading, or we might introduce by rule a Low tone to serve as a 'buffer' between the spreading High and the following High, and so forth. (The first two analyses assume that all TBUs which fail to associate with a High tone are assigned a Low tone by default.) Whichever sort of analysis we choose, it will represent an implementation of what is commonly known as the Obligatory Contour Principle, i.e., the principle that prevents adjacent TBUs from being linked to adjacent identical tones (Leben 1978, McCarthy 1986). This OCP effect explains the Low tone on the antepenultimate syllable of *a-hángálásanyíza*.

High tone also fails to spread onto the final syllable of the words in (5); this is a pausal effect. As soon as these words are embedded in a phrase, the High-Tone Spread Rule (6b) applies, and the last syllable of the word is realized with a High tone (see Part 3). One way to account

---

[3]We refer here to work on these languages presently being carried out by C. Kisseberth in conjunction with B. Koali, S. Mmusi, M. Molotsane, and W. Monareng.

for the failure of a High to spread onto a phrase-final vowel would be to mark such vowels as extratonal. As such, they are not part of the domain in which a rule such as High Tone Spread operates. A Low tone would ultimately be assigned to the final syllable by default. A second type of analysis would postulate that a pausal Low tone is assigned to the final syllable. The presence of the Low tone on the final syllable would prevent preceding High tone from spreading onto that syllable (since High spreads only onto toneless syllables).

A natural question to ask at this point is how the association of the prefixal High to the stem-initial syllable in (5) takes place. One approach would be to try to somehow directly associate the High contributed by a subject prefix to the first stem TBU. This could be done by marking the initial TBU (i.e., the TBU resulting from the coalescence of the subject prefix and the present tense marker /a/) as extratonal. In that case, general one-to-one, left-to-right linking conventions will associate the High contributed by the extratonal subject prefix to the first TBU in the stem.

A second approach would not mark the first syllable of the verb as extratonal, but would rather allow the general association convention to link the High contributed by the subject prefix to the initial syllable of the verb. What would then be required would be a rule shifting the High from that initial syllable to the stem-initial TBU.

No independent evidence has been found to motivate treating the initial syllable as extratonal. Furthermore, under certain circumstances it is actually possible for the High tone of the subject prefix to surface on the initial syllable of the verb and not to shift to the stem.[4] Consequently, we will pursue here the line of analysis where the High is first associated to the initial syllable of the word and only later shifted to the first stem TBU. There appear to be two basic options for achieving this shift to the stem. The first option is one suggested in Kenstowicz 1987, where the apparent shift was attributed to the presence of accent on the first stem TBU. In other words, it was assumed that if a High in a prefix could not link to the penult accent (because the penult was already linked to a High), then the prefixal High would instead link to the accent on the initial stem TBU. This interpretation may well be correct, and we will see in Part 3 that there is independent evidence at the phrasal level for attraction to stem-initial position.

However, the association of the prefixal High to the stem-initial tone-bearing unit could also be seen as arising ultimately from a rule that shifts a High one syllable rightward. Quite a few Bantu languages displace their High tones one syllable to the right. Downing 1988 has discovered convincing evidence for such an analysis in Kijita; similar evidence can be

---

[4]When a High verb stem has the syllabic structure -cvvcv- (the successive vowels appear to belong to separate syllables, impressionistically), a prefixal High remains anchored to the prefix. (Presumably the failure of Shift here is an instance of an OCP constraint holding on successively syllabic rhymes.) Thus we find examples such as *á-kaúl-a* '(s)he is looking.'

cited for Silozi.[5] Consequently, we might propose a rule such as (7), applying before High Tone Spread, which shifts a High one TBU to the right. We shall argue later that this rule would help explain some otherwise mysterious features of Chizigula.

(7)   V   V
      ‡⟋⟋´
      H

We have suggested two accounts of how the High tone of the subject prefix ends up on the first stem TBU. Both explanations have some independent motivation. It may simply be that two separate explanations both predict the same shift. In what follows, we will assume that it is High Tone Shift (7) that is responsible for the appearance of the subject High on the first stem vowel.

The behavior of disyllabic High-toned roots is quite important to the analysis of Chizigula tone. Such roots show a consistent downstep (marked by an exclamation point) between the prefixal High that associates to the first stem vowel, and the root High.

(8) a.   ku-lombéza   ku-tabána   ku-fundíka
          na-lombéza   na-tabána   na-fundíka
          a-lómb'éza   a-táb'ána   a-fúnd'íka
          'ask'   'weave a spell' 'tie a knot'

     b.   a [lombeza]
            | |
            H   H

     c.   a [lombeza]
          ‡⟋´‡⟋´
          H   H

Under the analysis where a High tone associates first to the leftmost TBU in the domain, then shifts one TBU to the right, and finally undergoes attraction to the head of a following foot, we will have the following

---

[5]This statement is based on our interpretation of the tonal data for Silozi presented in Gowlett 1967. A more detailed look at the Silozi system will be contained in the comparative study of Sotho tone referred to in footnote 3. It should be pointed out, however, that shifts such as those found in Kijita and Silozi can generally be treated as a two-step operation whereby a High spreads one TBU to the right and then delinks from its original location. In the Chizigula case, it is possible to argue that the 'spread' aspect of the shift under discussion is not the same as the more general High Tone Spread rule operative in the language. In particular, we have seen that a High does not spread onto a TBU when the next TBU has a High anchored to it. But a High does shift from the third person subject prefix onto the first stem vowel even when that vowel is followed by a High TBU (cf. *a-lómb'éz-a* discussed below). Thus, we conclude that if the appearance of a High on the first stem vowel is to be attributed to a High tone shift rule, that rule does not involve the kind of spreading that we have subsumed under the label High Tone Spread.

analysis of the data in (8). The root High will associate to the first stem TBU (assuming that the stem is the relevant domain for the root High tone). The prefixal High tone will associate to the prefix, yielding the form in (8b). Finally, High Tone Shift moves both of these High tones one TBU to the right, yielding (8c). The root High is now associated with the penult; attraction to the accented syllable is vacuous. We assume that downstep is the superficial reflex of a rule inserting a buffering low tone between the two adjacent Highs (clearly, a repair strategy to prevent a surface OCP violation).[6]

The analysis we have just sketched thus postulates a three-step association of the rightmost High tone in Chizugula. First, the left-to-right association convention assigns High to the initial syllable in its domain. The High Tone Shift Rule (7) then moves it to the following syllable. Finally, High is attracted to the accented penult. Though this solution may appear roundabout, evidence exists for each of the individual steps.

Initial association of a High tone to the leftmost TBU in the relevant domain helps us to better understand the tonal dissimilation that occurs when an object prefix is added to the verb. In Chizigula, plural human object prefixes such as *wa-* 'them' contribute a High tone while singular *ni-* 'me' and *ku-* 'you' do not. This point is evident in the contrast between *na-ku-gulusa* 'I am chasing you' versus *na-wa-gulúsa* 'I am chasing them' in the paradigms of (9).

(9) ku-gulusa   'to chase'
     na-ku-gulusa   'I am chasing you'
     na-wa-gulúsa   'I am chasing them'
     a-ni-gulúsa   'he is chasing me'
     a-ku-gulúsa   'he is chasing you'
     a-wá-gulúsa   'he is chasing them'

     ku-lombéza   'to ask'
     na-ku-lombéza   'I am asking you'
     na-wa-lombéza   'I am asking them'
     a-ní-lombéza   'he is asking me'
     a-kú-lombéza   'he is asking you'
     a-wá-lombéza   'he is asking them'

When a third person prefix such as *wa-* combines with a High-toned root, we expect two High tones. But in fact only a single High emerges. There is no contrast between *wa-* and *ku-* (cf. *na-wa-lombéza* vs. *na-ku-lombéza*). We may account for this fact by appealing to Meeussen's Rule—a dissimilation process found in a number of Bantu languages that eliminates one of two successive High tones (Goldsmith 1984). Since the rightmost

---

[6]Notice that if we must resort to such a rule of Buffer Low Insertion here, there is some plausibility for resorting to this same rule to explain the failure of a High to spread onto TBU that is itself followed by a High TBU (cf. the data in (5) above and the discussion of these data). In other words, we could insert a Low in front of any High TBU, to buffer that TBU from a preceding High.

High tone is displaced to the penult in Chizigula, we cannot at this point tell which High tone deletes and which emerges at the penult. (We shall argue later that it is in fact the tone of the object that deletes.) Note that Meeussen's Rule applies in Chizigula regardless of the length of the verb stem: *na-wa-lulungánya* 'I am taking advantage of them,' *na-wa-hangalasanyíza* 'I am carrying many things for them.' If it is proper to construe Meeussen's Rule as an OCP effect barring adjacent high tones, then application of the rule in *na-wa-lulungánya* makes sense if the high tone of the root is first assigned to the root-initial syllable and only later shifted to the accented vowel. As (10) shows, on this assumption the high tones of the root and the object prefix occupy successive TBUs; application of Meeussen's dissimilation rule follows from this configuration.

(10)   [na [wa [lulunganya]]]
              | |
              H   H

We now turn to the major analytic puzzle that has arisen in our study of the Chizigula verb: the behavior of monosyllabic roots. The paradigms in (11) show that monosyllabic roots fall into two distinct tonal categories, just like the polysyllabic ones examined hitherto.

(11)   ku-guh-a   'to take'   ku-fis-a   'to hide'
        ku-guh-il-a   'to take for'   ku-fis-íz-a   'to hide for'
        ku-guh-il-an-a 'to take for   ku-fis-iz-án-a   'to hide for
                        one another'   one another'

        ku-lim-a   'to cultivate'   ku-toz-a   'to hold'
        ku-lim-il-a   'to cultivate   ku-toz-éz-a   'to hold for'
                        for'

        ku-lond-a   'to look for'   ku-on-a   'to see'
        ku-lond-an-a   'to look for   ku-on-án-a   'to see one
                        one another'   another'

The extended forms show that the roots [fis], [toz], and [on] belong to the High-toned class. The problem is to explain why the unaugmented forms are not *ku-físa, *ku-tóza, *ku-óna. In other words, the opposition between the High-toned and the toneless roots is systematically neutralized in unextended monosyllabic roots. Before turning to a possible explanation of this fact, let us look at two additional pieces of evidence which show that *ku-fisa, ku-toza,* and *ku-ona* do in fact have a latent High tone.

First, as the data in (12) illustrate, these roots activate Meeussen's rule when they combine with a High-toned object prefix. In *na-wa-gúh-a* the High tone of the object prefix appears on the penult of the following toneless root [guh] 'take.' But when the root belongs to the High-toned class, both the object High and the root High are missing: *na-wa-fis-a*.

(12)   ku-guh-a   'to take'   ku-fis-a   'to hide'
       na-guh-a   'I take'   na-fis-a   'I hide'
       na-ku-guh-a   'I take you'   na-ku-fis-a   'I hide you'
       na-wa-gúh-a   'I take them'   na-wa-fis-a   'I hide them'

This contrast is explained if the postulated latent High of [fis] is available to initiate Meeussen's Rule. It also suggests that Meeussen's Rule eliminates the High tone of the preceding object. If the root High were deleted we would be unable to explain the contrast between *na-wa-gúh-a* and *na-wa-fis-a*.

Second, the roots [guh] and [fis] also contrast when combined with a High-toned subject prefix. As the paradigms of (13) demonstrate, the latter exhibits a sharp falling tone on its penult in this context in contrast to the simple High tone of the former.

(13)   inf.   ku-guh-a   ku-lim-a   ku-fis-a   ku-toz-a
       1 sg.   na-guh-a   na-lim-a   na-fis-a   na-toz-a
       3 sg.   a-gúh-a   a-lím-a   a-fîs-a   a-tôz-a
               'take'   'cultivate' 'hide'   'hold'

This contrast between the simple High of *a-gúh-a* and the fall of *a-fîs-a* is phonetically quite striking. Its phonological explanation poses a real challenge. A possible account runs as follows. We saw earlier that a buffer low tone is inserted between adjacent Highs to trigger the downstep in *a-lómb'éza*. On the assumption that the falling tone of *a-fîs-a* reflects a HL combination, we can attempt to assimilate the otherwise mysterious falling tone in *a-fîs-a* and *a-tôz-a* to the buffer Low phenomenon. But this implies that *a-fîs-a* does in fact contain a latent High.

The most dramatic evidence for the latent High of *ku-fis-a* will emerge in the phrasal tonology. Before taking up this point, let us sketch a possible account of the data considered so far. We propose that the latent High reflects two properties that we have attributed to Chizigula. The first is that a high tone associates to the root-initial syllable and then shifts one syllable to the right. The second is that a disyllabic metrical foot is assigned at the right edge of the word. Consider the derivations of *ku-fis-a* and *a-fîs-a* under these assumptions. The initial representations in (14) show the result of initial tone association. In the next step, the High tone shifts one syllable to the right. The construction of a binary left-headed metrical foot at the end of the word follows. Rightward attraction of High to the accented penult is inapplicable in the derivation of *ku-fis-a*, and vacuous for *a-fîs-a*, a buffer Low tone is then inserted between the adjacent Highs to produce a falling tone in *a-fîs-a*. (Note that the buffer Low is associated to the TBU immediately to the left of the second High.)

(14)   ku-fisa   ku-fisa   ku-fisa   ku-fisa
       | → | → | →
       H   H   H   H

We may derive the surface forms by postulating a rule to delink a final High tone. This rule states an essentially exceptionless generalization over the surface forms of Chizigula—phrase-final vowels associated with a High tone are systematically absent.[7] This delinking may have a metrical motivation. Our earlier discussion emphasized the role played by the head of the foot in attracting High tone from the left. But metrical phonology has also taught us that the foot has a recessive position which tends to repel prominence. We suggest that it is the metrically recessive character of the final syllable that motivates a delinking of the final High tone.

In (15) we summarize the details of our analysis:

(15) a. left-to-right tonal association

   b. Meeussen's rule for the object plus verb complex

   c. shift of High tone one syllable to the right

   d. assignment of a binary left-headed metrical foot at the right word edge

   e. possible assignment of a binary left-headed metrical foot at stem-initial position[8]

   f. rightward attraction of tone to the head of the metrical foot

   g. insertion of a buffer Low between adjacent Highs

   h. rightward spread of High tone to toneless syllables

   i. delinking of a High tone from a metrically weak position

   j. assignment of default Low tone

---

[7] A word-final vowel may be linked to a High tone in phrase-medial position. However, even in this environment, a High linked to a word-final syllable will in fact stay linked only if there is no available TBU for it to be attracted to. These points are discussed in Part Three.

[8] If there is a stem accent, it will have to be subordinated in some fashion to the penult accent, since High is attracted to the penult syllable (as long as that syllable is not already linked to a High) rather than to the stem-initial syllable. A High is attracted to the stem syllable only in the event it cannot shift to the penult.

2 Part Two

Three tonal processes pervade the phrasal phonology of Chizigula. All three correspond to processes we have observed operating at the word level; we will note where necessary any questions regarding the complete identification of the word-level and phrase-level manifestations of these processes. We shall refer to the processes in question as High Tone Anchoring (15f) High Tone Spread (15h) and Low Buffering (15g).

We will first illustrate the application of these three processes in phrases consisting of a verb plus following object. We will use this context not only to demonstrate the existence of these three processes at the phrasal level, but also to show how the phrase level data support the earlier classification of monosyllabic verb stems into two types (i.e., stems like [guh] 'take' versus stems like [fis] 'hide'). The data in (16) provide the first set of relevant data. In (16a,b) the object noun *ma-tunguja* 'tomatoes' is shown following various verbal words based on the roots [guh] and [fis]. (16c,d) illustrate some other nouns and verbs whose tonal structure is parallel to that in (a) and (b), respectively.

(16) a. ku-guha ma-tunguja   'to take tomatoes'
          na-guha ma-tunguja   'I am taking tomatoes'
          a-gúhá má-túnguja   'he is taking tomatoes'

      b. ku-fisa ma-tungúja   'to hide tomatoes'
          na-fisa ma-tungúja   'I am hiding tomatoes'
          a-fis-a ma-tungúja   'he is hiding tomatoes'

      c. n-a-ongól-á tándángovi   'I am hunting a (sp.) animal'
                                   (cf. tandangovi)
          a-gúh-á mí-zégázega   'he is taking a pole on his shoulders'
                                   (cf. m-zegazega)
          a-gúh-á lápúlapu   '(s)he is taking a sisal dish-rag'
          a-gúh-á má-lápúlapu   '(s)he is taking a sisal dish-rag'
                                   (cf. lapulapu 'sisal dish-rag,'
                                   ma-lapulapu 'sisal dishrags')

      d. n-a-on-a ma-tandangóvi   'I see some (sp.) animals'
          n-a-on-a mi-zegazéga   'I see a pole'
          n-a-on-a ma-lapulápu   'I see sisal dish-rags'

In the examples involving the stem [guh] we see that *matunguja* is pronounced all-Low when it follows a verbal word which lacks High tones (e.g., *kuguha* and *naguha*). However, when *matunguja* follows a verb with a fixed High on its penult (e.g., *agúha*), we see that the High on the penult of the verb spreads rightward as far as the antepenultimate syllable of the noun object. These data then clearly indicate the applicability of High Tone Spread at the phrasal level.

Of course, we have not yet clearly established the tonal structure of *matunguja* and the other nouns of its type in (16). The basis for determining the tonal structure of a noun will evolve in the discussion below. For the present, let us simply assume that *matunguja* et alia fall into the toneless class of nouns. Given this assumption, and given the formulation of High Tone Spread as a rule extending a High rightward onto toneless syllables, then the data in (16) are consistent with the view that exactly the same rule of High Tone Spread is operative at the word and the phrasal levels. The only real issue is the following: why does the spreading of the High tone rightward stop at the antepenultimate TBU? We would like to suggest that the reason for this is that High Tone Spread may not spread a High tone onto the head of a metrical foot.

The data in (16b), based on the root [fis], provide evidence for the analysis proposed in Part One where a High was claimed to be part of the underlying structure of this root. At the phrasal level, this High is actually manifested. In particular, in (16b) the floating High tone we postulated in the verb anchors to the penultimate TBU of the following noun. These data justify the phrase-level rule of High Tone Anchoring. Furthermore, they suggest that anchoring is subject to the principle postulated in Part One, namely that High is attracted to the head of a foot.

The essential issue regarding the identification of High Tone Anchoring and the rightward attraction of a High to the head of a metrical foot is the following: at the word level, High tone is attracted to (a tonally unoccupied) head. There is no need to distinguish Highs that are anchored already from those that are not. (In our analysis, we have assumed that all of the Highs are anchored through left-to-right tone association.) At the phrasal level, however, it is necessary to distinguish between Highs anchored to the penult (e.g., *úha*), and Highs that would be anchored to the final TBU but in phrase-final position float (e.g., *nafísa*). Only the latter relocate to the head of a foot in the following noun. Fixed High tones, by contrast, remain on the verb and spread rightward. One way to capture this distinction is to say that High Tone Anchoring does not move a High away from the head of a foot. Such a constraint would properly delimit those Highs which are affected at the phrasal level, and it would not cause any complications for the word-level application of the rule.

So far we have seen the application of (a) High Tone Spread and (b) High Tone Anchoring on the phrasal domain of a verb and object noun. The former case arises when the verb has a fixed High on its penult; the latter case arises in verbs with final High (which floats in phrase-final position). So far we have considered only the case where the verb is followed by a toneless noun such as *matunguja*. Before we can continue further with this discussion, it is necessary to take a more detailed look at the tonal structure of two other word classes—nouns and adjectives.

While verb stems fall into just two tonal classes, regardless of length, in most Bantu languages, nouns and adjectives are typically more complex. For example, in Venda, a noun with two syllables in the stem can have any one of four tone patterns (LL, LH, HL, HH), while a noun with three syllables in the stem can have any one of eight possible tone patterns (LLL, LLH, LHL, LHH, etc.).[9] Chizigula reflects this more complex state of affairs—but only at an abstract level. At the phonetic surface, the isolation form of a disyllabic nominal stem exhibits just two tonal types: toneless versus penultimate High tone. In (17) are shown disyllabic nouns and adjectives.

(17) m-toho   'pestle'   tana   'good'
      simba   'lion'   kulu   'big'
      nyumba   'house'   tali   'tall'
      m-phémba   'maize cobs'   dódo   'small'

Let us consider nouns first. While on the surface only two types occur, the High Tone Anchoring process illuminates a further three-way split among the toneless subtype. The latent high of *n-a-ona* 'I see' diagnoses two of these subtypes in (18a): *simba* 'lion' surfaces with a fall, while *m-toho* 'pestle' and *nyumba* 'house' surface with a plain High. But as we see in (18b), *m-toho* and *nyumba* differ in their effect on a following adjective such as *tana* 'good.' *Nyumba* donates a latent High Tone while *m-toho* does not.

(18) a. na-ona m-tóho   'I see a pestle'
          na-ona sîmba   'I see a lion'
          na-ona nyúmba   'I see a house'
          na-oná m-ph'émba   'I see maize cobs'

      b. m-toho m-tana   'a good pestle'
          simba n-thána   'a good lion'
          nyumba n-thána   'a good house'
          m-phémbá n-th'ána   'good maize cobs'

Let us tentatively suggest some conclusions to be drawn from (18). It seems clear that *m-toho* must be toneless. It has no surface High and it does not donate a High tone to a following word, as it would be expected to do if it had a latent High in its structure. When *m-toho* follows a word with an unassociated High, that High anchors to the penult TBU of *m-toho*. This is of course simply the consequence of High Tone Anchoring. It is also clear that *simba* and *nyumba* must both have High tones in their structure, since they both donate a High to a following word. Furthermore, it seems that their High tone must not be associated with the penult TBU of the noun, since if it were there would be no way for High Tone Anchoring to link it to the following adjective. (Recall that only High tones in metrically weak syllables are able to reassociate to the head of a foot to the right.) What their underlying difference is must still be sorted out. Finally, it is clear that *mphémba* has a fixed High tone on

---

[9]See Cassimjee 1986 for a detailed autosegmental analysis of Venda tonology.

its penult TBU. The fact that *mphémba* donates a High to a following adjective (*-tana*, in (18b)) shows that *mphémba* must also end in a latent High.[10]

Adjectives also fall into four tonal classes, as (19) documents.

(19) a.   nyumba n-thána   'a good house'
           nyumba n-khûlu   'a big house'
           nyumba n-tháli   'a tall house'
           nyumbá n-dódo   'a small house'

      b.   tana vidala   'very good'
           kulu vidâla   'very big'
           tali vidâla   'very tall'
           dódó vidâla   'very small'

It is clear that *tana* is entirely parallel to *-toho*, *kulu* is parallel to *simba*, *tali* is parallel to *nyumba*, and *dódo* is parallel to *-pémba*.

Let us now consider in a little more detail what underlying representations should be postulated for these items so that their behavior with respect to High Tone Anchoring can be accounted for. Assuming that the grammar distinguishes two underlying tones (High vs. toneless/Low) and allows just one tone per syllable, there are four possible tonal types ('Low' is understood to mean toneless in an analysis where Low tones are assigned by default): LL, LH, HL, and HH. *-toho* and *-tana* clearly belong to the LL category while *-pemba* and *-dodo* seem best regarded as HH. (One of these High's surfaces on the noun itself, while the other delinks; more on this below.) *Simba, nyumba, kulu,* and *tali* each have a latent High tone; but how can they be differentiated among themselves? In particular, why do *simba* and *kulu* anchor a preceding latent High as a fall, while *nyumba* and *tali* do not? We suggest that at the point where High Tone Anchoring applies, the former have a final linked High tone while the latter have a simple floating High.

(20)   simba   nyumba
           |
      H   H   H   H

The floating High links to the penultimate TBU of the noun in each case. The resulting sequence of two High tones triggers the Low Buffering rule, which inserts a Low between the two Highs. (We have not of course yet built the entire case for assuming that Low Buffering applies phrasally— but convincing evidence (in addition to the present data) will be developed below.) In all of the cases noted at the word level, the buffering Low hooked up to the syllable in front of the second High in the sequence. No

---

[10] Actually, the pronunciation *mphémbá nth' ána* is just one of two possible pronunciations. In the other pronunciation, *mphémbá nthana*, the High on the penult of the noun spreads rightward, but no additional High tone appears on the following adjective. We will not pursue in any detail here the analysis of this alternative pronunciation.

evidence was available as to where the buffering Low would hook up if the second High was not associated.

In the case of *simba*, above, the buffering Low associates to the left of the second High (anchored to the final vowel), yielding a falling tone on the penult TBU of *simba*. In the case of *nyumba*, the second High is not anchored. Therefore, no principle forces the Low to anchor to the penult syllable. In fact, since the penult syllable is linked and the ultimate syllable is unlinked, one would expect the Low to anchor to that final syllable and this is exactly what it does.[11]

How can we account for the fact that at the point where High Tone Anchoring operates, *simba* has a High associated with its final syllable and *nyumba* does not? We suggest the following scenario. Suppose that in underlying representation, *simba* has a High associated with its first syllable, and *nyumba* has a High associated with its second syllable. (Incidentally, this analysis is in accordance with the historical tonal pattern.) If we then posit a rule that shifts High tones one syllable to the right, the High on the initial syllable of *simba* will shift to the final syllable, while the High on the final syllable of *nyumba* will shift off of the word entirely, and be left floating.[12]

The postulation of a rule shifting High tone one syllable to the right not only accounts for (a) the shift of High from a subject prefix (coalesced with the tense/aspect marker in the present tense forms cited earlier) to the first syllable of a following stem, but also for the contrast between *simba* and *nyumba* in position after a floating High.

We have now proposed the essential outlines of an analysis of three classes of disyllabic noun and adjective stems. In one class, the stem is toneless. In another class, a High is associated with the first stem TBU. This High shifts to the final syllable and then undergoes Final Delinking. The third class has a High associated with its final TBU; when this High shifts rightwards, it is set floating.

A few comments are in order concerning the fourth class. This class, we have claimed, has two High tones. The second of the two High tones will naturally shift rightwards, ending up floating. But what about the first High tone? Shouldn't it shift from the first stem position to the following TBU? If it did, it would, of course, naturally undergo Final

---

[11]It should be noted that if *nyumba* were not itself phrase-final, the buffering Low would not necessarily anchor onto the noun at all; rather, its surface location would be immediately in front of the first High tone in the following word (that High tone would itself be the result of the anchoring of the latent High of *nyumba*).

[12]This analysis assumes a formulation of the High Tone Shift rule, given originally as (7), where there need not be a following TBU for the shift to take place. That is, a rule such as (7′) is invoked:

(7′)   H
       ǂ- - -ᵥ
       x (x)

(7′) is to be understood as saying that High delinks in all cases, and relinks to a following TBU if one exists.

Delinking and the word would be pronounced all-Low on the surface. This is incorrect. The High on the first stem TBU must not shift. We thus propose that a High tone does not shift from the head of a foot when followed by a High on the following (metrically weak) syllable.[13] Thus, given a representation such as

(21)   mphemba
       | |
       H   H

the first High will not be able to shift onto the final TBU. The second High will, however, be able to shift off of the final syllable. Notice that in this analysis, the second High is floating, and thus the Low introduced by Low Buffering will link not to the penult of the word but rather to the final TBU.

The four types of disyllabic noun and adjective stems discussed above do not constitute an exhaustive survey of the stem structure of Chizigula nouns and adjectives. Additional complexities arise when the stem is trisyllabic or longer.[14] Nevertheless, the above discussion provides an adequate backdrop against which to carry out a description of the phrasal operation of High Tone Spread, High Tone Anchoring, and Low Buffering.

In (16) above we illustrated the juxtaposition of a verb and a toneless noun. In (22) we illustrate the juxtaposition of a verb and a following noun with a fixed High in its tonal structure.

---

[13]A High does shift from the head of a metrical foot when no High follows on the next syllable—recall the discussion earlier of disyllabic High roots like [fis]. Notice that the failure of a High to undergo High Tone Shift when anchored to the head of a foot is parallel to the failure of Highs on heads to undergo High Tone Anchoring (as discussed above). There is some independent evidence for blocking High Tone Shift from affecting a High located on the penult when another High follows. This evidence comes from verb roots that consist simply of a consonant or consonant cluster. All such roots in Chizigula are High. For example the first person present tense, of 'eat,' a-dy-a, is toneless on the surface. (The High of the root /dy/ associates to the syllable dya by the convention associating the first tone in a domain to the first TBU in the domain, and High Tone Shift then moves the High off the word entirely.) In the third person present tense form, by contrast, we find á-dy-a. The High of the prefix does not shift. Note furthermore that the High of the prefix, being penultimate, is in metrically strong position.

[14]Perhaps the most interesting trisyllabic forms are nouns like lutamwâsi which have a falling tone, in their isolation form, on the penult. This phonetic representation obviously suggests an underlying representation with two High tones. Presumably, these High tones would have to be located on the first and the second TBUs of the stem (since noun class prefixes in Chizigula, as in many Bantu languages, can be argued to be toneless). In order to generate the correct surface form, it would be necessary to permit both of these High tones to shift (onto the penult and final TBU respectively). The buffer Low tone would then be introduced, forming a falling tone on the penult TBU. Finally, the High associated with the final TBU would delink by virtue of being in a metrically weak (phrase-final) position. Notice that in this analysis of lu-tamwâsi, the High on the initial stem syllable is able to shift even though there is a following High. This contrasts with the mphémba case, where a High on the penult accented syllable cannot shift when followed by a High.

(22) n-a-on-a tófáli   'I see a brick'
                             (cf. tofáli 'brick')
      n-a-on-a káb'úli   'I see a grave'
                             (cf. kabúli 'grave')
      n-a-on-a ma-tóf'áli   'I see bricks'
                             (cf. ma-tofáli 'bricks')

From these data we see that if the penultimate TBU is occupied by a
High tone, if the stem is trisyllabic and if the first stem TBU is toneless,
then the floating High of the verb anchors to the first stem TBU.

The data in (23) illustrate the case where the first stem TBU is unavailable for anchoring, since it is also the penultimate syllable and bears
a fixed High tone.

(23) n-a-on-a má-k'úli   'I see some dogs'
      n-a-fis-a má-t'ági   'I am hiding eggs'
      n-a-kom-a má-k'úwi   'I am killing some turtles'
      n-a-on-á k'úli   'I see a dog'
      n-a-fis-á t'ági   'I am hiding an egg'
      n-a-kom-á k'úwi   'I am killing a turtle'

From these examples, we see that when the first stem syllable is unavailable, the High anchors to the prefix if there is one, and otherwise links to
the last vowel of the verb.

Another point needs to be observed. When High anchors to its designated point, a Low is introduced between it and the fixed High of the
noun (resulting in as downstep in (23)). For Low Buffering to account for
this, the rule must operate at the phrasal level, because it is not until the
phrasal level that the sequence of two High tones arises.

The anchoring hierarchy uncovered so far can be sketched out as follows: Anchor High to the head of a foot if it is not already associated
to High. If that fails, anchor High to the first stem TBU. If that fails,
anchor High as close to the first stem TBU as possible (i.e., to a prefix, if
there is one, otherwise to the final vowel of the word in which the floating
High originates).

At the word level we invoked two rules to achieve the association of
High tones. One rule attracted a High rightwards to the head of a metrical
foot. This is obviously the same as the first part of what we have called
the anchoring hierarchy. The second rule shifted High tone one syllable
to the right. If we assume that (a) Final Delinking operates only at the
end of a phrase, and that (b) High Tone Shift is a phrase-level as well as
a word-level rule, then the application of High Tone Shift will properly
account for the shifting of the High tone to the prefix of a noun when
the stem-initial TBU is unavailable.[15] There is, then, just one aspect of

---

[15]The failure of a High to shift from the last TBU of a word when the immediately
following TBU bears a High can be explained as a consequence of the general proposition that High shifts only onto a toneless TBU. That is, just as we have seen that

the Anchoring Hierarchy not accounted for by rules that we have already
motivated at the word-level: the anchoring of floating High to the stem-
initial TBU. Earlier we entertained the possibility of viewing the shift of
prefixal High to the verb stem as an instance of attraction of High tone
to the head of a foot. This required treating the initial stem syllable as
accented. The phrasal evidence now lends some support to this idea. If
the stem-initial syllable is accented, then the shift of the High from a
subject prefix to the verb stem has an ambiguous interpretation either as
an instance of High Tone Shift or as attraction to the head of a foot.

We have now provided a somewhat detailed look at the interaction
of a verb and following noun where that noun is either toneless or has a
fixed High tone in its structure. The remaining part of this section looks
in more detail at the case where a verb is followed by a word which has a
High tone underlyingly associated to its penult. This High tone of course
spreads onto the last TBU of the noun and delinks when that noun is
phrase-final. First consider the case where the verb has a fixed High as
its last tone.

(24)   a-gúl-á tonthe   '(s)he is buying a banana'
                               (cf. tonthe tána)
       a-gúh-á támbala   '(s)he is taking a rag'
                               (cf. tambala tána)
       a-gúh-á má-támbala   '(s)he is taking rags'

In (24) the High of the verb spreads onto metrically weak TBUs, stopping
when it encounters the noun's final foot (The latent High of the noun is
not manifested on the surface.)

When, as in (25), the verb has a floating High tone, that High anchors
to the head of the noun's final foot at the end of the noun (the High that
was originally on this syllable has meanwhile shifted to the final syllable).
A buffer Low tone is assigned to the penultimate TBU, producing a falling
tone.[16]

(25)   n-a-dy-a tônthe   'I am eating a banana'
       n-a-on-a tambâla   'I see a rag'

---

attraction to the head of a foot is blocked when the head is already linked to High, so
we can assume that High Tone Shift is likewise blocked when the next syllable is linked
to a High. There is evidence for this proposal from trisyllabic nouns such as *léndléle*
'loofah,' where we see that a High on the initial stem syllable cannot shift since it is
followed by a High on the penult (the latter fails to shift since it is itself followed by a
High on the final syllable, which delinks in phrase-final position).

[16]This pattern is somewhat more complex than it first appears. When a prefix is
added to a trisyllabic stem such as *tambala*, two pronunciations are actually available:
n-a-on-a má-támbala and *n-a-on-a ma-tambâla* ('I see rags'). The latter pronunciation
is in accordance with the data in (25), but the former pronunciation requires that
attraction to the head of a following foot be blocked. (The High of the verb simply
shifts one syllable to the right—i.e., to the prefix of the noun.) We will not discuss
this point further here.

In this section we have demonstrated that several tonal processes—High Tone Spread, High Tone Anchoring (including attraction to the head of a foot and High Tone Shift), and Low Buffering —operate at the phrase level as well as at the word level. In the next section we will investigate the domain of these rules in Chizigula.

3   Part Three

In an insightful study of phrasal phonology, Selkirk 1986 hypothesizes that the output of the syntactic component of a grammar (consisting presumably of an X-bar representation of the surface structure of a sentence) is broken down into a linear sequence of non-overlapping phrasal domains by a rule that places a phrase boundary at the beginning or end of a given X-bar level. Selkirk demonstrates how such an analysis accounts for the phrasing that was demonstrated in Kisseberth and Abasheikh 1974 to be required for the proper application of vowel lengthening and shortening processes in Chimwiini.

Given that Chizigula and Chimwiini are both Bantu languages, it is perhaps natural to expect that their prosodic domains might be governed by similar principles. The present section seeks to explore the extent to which these expectations are met.

In Chimwiini there is an obligatory phrasal break between the subject and main verb of a clause. This constraint operates not only at the level of the main clause, but also in subordinate clauses as well. While Chizigula permits the option of a prosodic break between a subject and a following verb, this break is by no means necessary. Below we illustrate a variety of possible pre-verbal structures.

Consider first the case of simple sentences consisting of a subject NP and a VP. When the subject NP ends in a floating High tone, two pronunciations are possible. Either the High anchors to the first TBU of the verb, or it does not anchor at all. In the latter case a prosodic break obtains between the subject and the verb. The two alternatives are depicted in (26) for each of three sentences. The (ii) examples exhibit a phrase break between subject and verb; the (i) examples do not.[17]

(26)   a.   i. wana w-á-sezíg-a   'the children are playing'
           ii. wana w-a-sezíg-a

       b.   i. wana w-á-g'úh-a   'the children are taking (s.t.)'
           ii. wana w-a-gúh-a

---

[17]In our data, a High from a pre-verbal noun always anchors onto the initial TBU of the verb and never displaces to the accent. The failure of displacement to accent occurs elsewhere. (When a noun has a definitizing pre-prefix appended to it, a preceding High cannot be attracted to its accented syllable. Instead, the High simply shifts onto the pre-prefix.)

c. i. wana wêngi w-á-sezíg-a   'many children are crying'
    ii. wana wêngi w-a-sezíg-a

If the verb has a High tone on its initial stem TBU, then the floating High
of the subject anchors to the last vowel of the subject when no prosodic
break follows. Otherwise, the floating High will simply fail to surface.

(27) a. i. waná w-'éz-a   'the children are coming'
          ii. wana w-éz-a

      b. i. wana wêngí w-'éz-a   'many children are coming'
          ii. wana wêngi w-éz-a

A second piece of evidence that the phrasal break between the subject
and the verb is not obligatory is that when there is a High tone on the
penult of the subject NP, that High may spread onto the final TBU of the
NP (and possibly into the verb, circumstances permitting). Of course,
in the event that the phrase break option is selected, an alternative pronunciation results in which the High does not spread. In (28), the (i)
examples lack the phrase break that separates noun and verb in the (ii)
examples:

(28) a. i. wandélé w-á-sezíg-a   'the girls are playing'
          ii. wandéle w-a-sezíg-a

      b. i. wandélé w-a-gúh-a   'the girls are taking (s.t.)'
          ii. wandéle w-a-gúh-a

      c. i. wandélé w-'éz-a   'the girls are coming'
          ii. wandéle w-éz-a

At present, we are not certain whether one of the two phrasing alternatives cited above should be regarded as the norm. In a number of
cases the norm seems to be no prosodic break between the subject and
the main verb. This is particularly true when the verb is in some sense
'dependent,' as in cases where *níyo* 'and then' immediately precedes:

(29) níyó 'ádya   'and then (s)he ate it'
                          (ádya '(s)he eats')
      níyó nálima   'and then I cultivated'
                          (nalima 'I am cultivating')
      níyó walíma   'and then they cultivated'
      níyó wálima   'and then you (sg.) cultivated'
      níyó wádamánya   'and then they cultivated'
      níyó wádámanya   'and then you (sg.) cultivated'
      níyó watêga   'and then they set traps'
      níyó nátega   'and then I set a trap'
      níyó nálombéza   'and then I asked for'
      níyó walómb'éza   'and then they asked for'

Notice first of all that there is no phrasal break between *níyo* and the verb. The High on the penult of *níyo* spreads rightward into the verb (it is stopped only by the need to have a buffer Low between it and a High in the verb, or by an accented penultimate syllable). If there were a phrasal break between *níyo* and the verb, the High on *níyo* would not be able to spread at all.

Interestingly, it appears that verbs in this construction can be 'deaccented.' By this we mean that the penult syllable of the verb can lose the power to halt spreading. This is illustrated in (30), where the (ii) examples contain the deaccented version of the verbs in the (i) examples:

(30) a. i. níyó nálima matunguja   'and then I cultivated tomatoes'
          ii. níyó nálímá mátúnguja
          (*matunguja* is a toneless noun)

      b. i. níyó nádámanya ndima   'and then I did work'
          ii. níyó nádámányá ndima
          (*ndima* is a noun with a floating High)

      c. i. níyó weza kuṇgwila   'and then you come to grab/catch him'
          ii. níyó wézá kúṇgwila

The deaccenting process seems to be limited to medial toneless words. We have not as yet studied the full range of deaccenting in Chizigula and will not discuss the matter further here.

Now consider the case where a subject noun intervenes between *níyo* and the verb.

(31) níyó wana wál'íma   'and then the children cultivated'
      níyó wana wádamánya   'and then the children did'
      níyó wávyele wál'íma   'and then women cultivated'
      níyó wandélé walíma   'and then girls cultivated'
      níyó wánthú wádamánya 'and then the people did'

In (31), there is no prosodic break between *níyo* and the subject, as shown by the fact that the High of *níyo* spreads onto the final syllable of that word. There is also no phrase break between the subject and the verb, as seen by the fact that the floating High of *wana* and *wavyele* anchor onto the verb (which in isolation is *walíma*), and by the fact that the fixed High of *wandéle* spreads onto the last syllable of the noun subject.

But this type of construction does permit a break between the subject and the verb, as shown in (32):

(32) níyó wanthu wadamánya   'and then people did'
      níyó wávyele walíma   'and then women cultivated'
      níyó wandéle walíma   'and then girls cultivated'

Next consider the case where *níyo* is ordered between the subject and the verb:

(33) a. wanthu níyó wádamánya   'and then the people did'

b. wana níyó wádamánya   'and then the children did'

The failure of the floating High of *wana* to surface in (33b) shows that there is a break between the subject and *níyo*; however, there is no break between *níyo* and the verb.

The word *níyo* is not alone in encouraging a break between the subject and the verb. The interrogative *kwa mbwâni* 'why' also illustrates the effect of non-subject preverbal elements on the phrasing of subject-verb sequences. The falling tone on *kwa mbwâni* indicates that this phrase has a floating High tone—which we expect to anchor onto a following word when no phrasal break intervenes. The following examples show that when *kwa mbwâni* immediately precedes a verb, there is no prosodic break: the floating High of *kwa mbwâni* anchors to the first TBU of the verb, and then spreads rightward.

(34)   kwa mbwâni w-á-gúluk-a   'why are you running?'
                               (cf. waguluka 'you are running')
       kwa mbwâni w-á-gulúk-a   'why are they running?'
                               (cf. wagulúka 'they are running')

When *kwa mbwâni* precedes the subject, we also find (in the normal case) no break between any of these elements. The data in (35) demonstrate this.

(35)   kwa mbwâni wavyêle wágulúka   'why are the women running?'
       kwa mbwâni wánd'élé wágulúka   'why are the girls running?'
       kwa mbwâni wánthú wágulúka   'why are the people running?'

Notice that in every case the floating High of *kwa mbwâni* surfaces on the following noun (converting *wavyele* to *wavyêle*, *wandélé* to *wánd' élé*, and *wanthu* to *wánthú*). This shows that *kwa mbwâni* is not separated from the subject noun prosodically. But notice also that the subject noun is not separated from the verb. The floating High of *wavyele* anchors onto the first TBU of the verb, the High tone on the penult of *wandéle* is able to spread onto the last vowel of that noun as well as into the verb, and the floating High tone that has anchored onto the noun *wanthu* in the last example is able to spread into the following verb.

Elements introducing subordinate clauses regularly seem to induce the lack of a phrasal break between the subject and verb of that clause. An example illustrating this point is *kwa víya* 'because.' First of all, consider the case where *kwa víya* immediately precedes the verb.

(36) a. kwa víyá n-á-guh-a   'because I am taking'

b. kwa víyá w-a-gúh-a   'because they are taking'

Here we see that there is no phrasal break between *kwa víya* and the following verb. In (36a), the High on the penult of *víya* spreads into the toneless verb word *naguha*. In (36b), the intrusion of the buffer Low prevents spreading into the verb *wagúha*. That there is no break, however, is shown by the fact that the High of *víya* is able to spread onto the final vowel of that word.

Next consider the case where a subject noun intervenes between *kwa víya* and the following verb.

(37) a. kwa víyá wanthu wadamánya   'because people are doing'

     b. kwa víyá wávyele wádamánya   'because women are doing'

The rightward spreading of High from *kwa víya* shows that there is no phrasal break between *kwa víya* and the following subject noun. There is also no phrasal break between the subject noun and the following verb (as shown by the fact that the floating High of *wavyele* anchors onto the following verb).

The preceding data show that while a subject noun in the main clause may be separated from the verb by a prosodic break, this is not necessary; furthermore, the presence of pre-verbal elements other than the subject favors the absence of a break between the subject and the verb.

In Chimwiini, adverbial elements in sentence initial position are prosodically separated from whatever follows them. The examples cited above involving phrases like *kwa mbwâni* and *kwa víya* illustrate that preverbal adverbials in Chizigula are not similarly structured. The time word *dyelo* 'today' can also be used to exemplify this point. *Dyelo* has a floating High tone (cf. *ni dyêlo* 'it is today).

(38) a. dyelo nálima   'today I cultivate'

     b. dyelo wánthú walíma   'today people cultivate'
       dyelo wánthu, walíma

     c. dyelo wavyêle wál'íma   'today women cultivate'
       dyelo wavyêle, walíma

     d. dyelo wánd'élé walíma   'today girls cultivate'
       dyelo wánd'éle, walíma

These examples illustrate (a) that the floating High of *dyelo* may anchor onto an immediately following verb or subject noun. That is, the adverb and following constituent are in the same phrase. Notice that the subject and following verb may be in the same prosodic phrase (as is normal, when the subject is preceded by a sentence-initial element—see above) or may be separated. There is also an alternative to the above, in which the adverb *dyelo* is prosodically separated from the following verb or subject. In that case, the floating High of *dyelo* does not surface.

Another significant feature of the Chimwiini prosodic system is that there is a prosodic break between the noun phrases in a double object construction. Chizigula differs in this respect, since the normal case is for no break to appear anywhere in a verb plus double object sequence. We will examine such constructions and show that for purposes of High Anchoring and High Tone Spread, there is no necessary prosodic break anywhere in the construction. For the sake of simplicity, we will consider just the case where both noun phrases consist of a single (head) noun.

We will examine first the case where the verb is toneless, so that it cannot affect the immediately following noun. The interaction between the first and the second noun in the double object construction is specified in detail in (39). (L= a toneless word, H= word with a High anchored to the penult, and H*=a word with a floating High tone.)

(39) a. first noun toneless

　　　nambikila wanthu nkhánde
　　　　L　　　L　　　H
　　　'I am cooking people food'

　　　nambikila wanthu nyama
　　　　L　　　L　　　L
　　　'I am cooking people meat'

　　　nambikila wanthu papayu
　　　　L　　　L　　　H*
　　　'I am cooking people papaya'

　　b. first noun has a floating High

　　　nambikila m̥vyelé nkh'ánde
　　　　L　　　H*　　　H
　　　'I am cooking the woman food'

　　　nambikila m̥vyele nyáma
　　　　L　　　H*　　　L
　　　'I am cooking the woman meat'

　　　nambikila m̥vyele papâyu
　　　　L　　　H*　　　H*
　　　'I am cooking the woman a papaya'

　　c. first noun has a High anchored to the penult

　　　nambikila m̥ndélé nkh'ánde
　　　　L　　　H　　　H
　　　'I am cooking the girl food'

　　　nambikila m̥ndélé nyama
　　　　L　　　H　　　L
　　　'I am cooking the girl meat'

nambikila m̧ndélé pápayu
  L   H   H*
'I am cooking the girl papaya'

Examination of these data reveals immediately that there is no prosodic break between the two nouns. In (39b) we see that the floating High of the first noun does not remain floating, but rather anchors on its own final syllable when *nkhánde* follows, or on the penultimate vowel of a following toneless word (i.e., *nyama*). (39c) demonstrates that *m̧vyele* is not domain-final. In (39), the High on the penult of *m̧ndéle* spreads onto the last vowel of this word in all cases, and onto the first vowel of the second noun when that vowel is eligible to receive it. This behavior demonstrates that there is no break between the first and the second noun since spreading is blocked in a domain-final word.

Next, let us consider the case where the verb contains a (fixed) High tone anchored, of course, to the penultimate TBU of the verb.

(40) a. first noun is toneless

ambikílá wanthu nkhánde
'(s)he is cooking people food'

ambikílá wanthu nyama
'(s)he is cooking people meat'

ambikílá wanthu papayu
'(s)he is cooking people papaya'

 b. first noun has a floating High tone

ambikílá wávyelé nkh'ánde
'(s)he is cooking the women food'

ambikílá wávyele nyáma
'(s)he is cooking the women meat'

ambikílá wávyele papâyu
'(s)he is cooking the women papaya'

 c. the first noun has a High anchored to the penult

ambikílá wandélé nkh'ánde
'(s)he is cooking the girls food'

ambikílá wandélé nyama
'(s)he is cooking the girls meat'

ambikílá wandélé pápayu
'(s)he is cooking the girls papaya'

In (40), the fact that the High tone on the penult of the verb spreads onto the final vowel establishes that the verb is not domain-final. The data in (40b) show that there is also no prosodic break between the first noun and the second noun, since the floating High of *wavyele* is able to anchor. The data in (40c) illustrate the same point; the penultimate High of *wandéle* is able to spread onto the final vowel of this word (and beyond, when circumstances permit).

Finally consider the case where a verb has a latent High and is followed by a double object construction.

(41) a. first noun is toneless

nenkha wánthú nkh'ánde
'I am giving people food'

nenkha wánthú nyama
'I am giving people meat'

nenkha wánthú pápayu
'I am giving people papaya'

b. first noun has a latent High tone

nenkha m̥vyêle nkh'ánde
'I am giving the woman food'

nenkha m̥vyêle nyáma
'I am giving the woman meat'

nenkha m̥vyêle papâyu
'I am giving the woman papaya'

c. first noun has a High anchored to the penult

nenkha wánd'élé nkh'ánde
'I am giving the girls food'

nenkha wánd'élé nyama
'I am giving the girls meat'

nenkha wánd'élé pápayu
'I am giving the girls papaya'

The data in (41) show that the floating High of the verb anchors, thus establishing that there is no break between the verb and the first noun. The data in (41a) show that when the floating High of the verb anchors onto the penult vowel of *wanthu*, it can then spread rightward onto the last vowel of this noun. Clearly, then, there is no break between the first and the second noun. The data in (41b) show that the floating High of the first noun anchors,[18] (41c) shows that a High on the penult of the first noun spreads onto the last vowel of that noun (and beyond, if circumstances permit), both establishing the absence of a prosodic break between the two nouns.

---

[18] Actually, in the case where the m̥vyele is followed by nkhánde, the floating High fails to anchor. Further work is required to determine whether this failure to anchor is obligatory and, if so, what principle accounts for it.

What we have seen is that Chizigula syntactic structure imposes fewer constraints on prosodic structure than does its sister Bantu language Chimwiini. There are cases where Chizigula evidences prosodic breaks akin to those in Chimwiini. For example, sentence-initial preposed object nominals evidence a phrasal break:

(42) matunguja, naguha   'tomatoes, I take'
      matambala, naguha   'rags, I take'
      wandéle, naguha   'girls, I take'

But it is not the case that reordering of elements in Chizigula generally requires breaks before and after the reordered elements. We have already seen that the reordering of the subject with a variety of pre-verbal elements generally entails the absence of a prosodic break (cf. the discussion of *níyo*, *kwa mbwâni*, *dyelo* above). Similarly, reordering of elements in post-verbal position allows the absence of prosodic breaks.

For example, when the post-verbal interrogative *zéze* 'how?' immediately follows a verb, there is no phrasal break between it and the verb.

(43) a. agóná z'éze   'how does she sleep?'

      b. wadyá z'éze   'how do you eat?'

In (43a), we see that the High on the penult of *agóna* '(s)he is sleeping' spreads onto the final vowel of the verb (which would not be possible if the verb were final in a prosodic domain). A Low tone is also inserted between the High of this verb and the High of *zéze* due to the phrasal application of the Low Buffer rule. In (43b) the floating High of *wadya* 'you are eating' anchors onto the final vowel of that verb, which would not be possible if the verb were domain-final.

When *zéze* follows a noun object, there is no phrasal break between the object and *zéze* nor between the verb and its object. This is shown in (44):

(44) akánthá nyama zéze   'how does she cut the meat?'
                            (*nyama* is a toneless noun)
      agúhá waná z'éze   'how does she take children?'
                            (*wana* has a latent High tone)
      agúlá nkh'ándé z'éze 'how does she buy food?'
                            (*nkhánde* has a High on the penult)

Reordering *zéze* between the verb and the object, does not affect the phrasing;

(45) akánthá z'ézé nyama   'how does she cut the meat?'
      agúhá z'ézé wana   'how does she take children?'
      agúlá z'ézé nkh'ánde   'how does she buy food?'

Thus while certain reorderings (e.g., preposing object nouns) entail phrasal breaks, most reorderings in Chizigula do not. The preceding data have shown that non-clausal elements in the verb phrase generally do not require any phrasal break. Clausal complements of verbs behave similarly. Consider a verb that governs a following subjunctive complement. The subjunctive form of the verb is characterized, generally speaking, by a fixed High tone on the penult syllable of the verb. Examples of this construction follow:

(46)   n-a-ung-a ní-l'ím-e   'I want to cultivate'
       n-a-ung-a ní-damány-e   'I want to do'
       n-a-ung-a ní-sáfalís-e   'I want to boil (s.t.)'

       n-a-ung-a ní-f'ís-e   'I want to hide'
       n-a-ung-a ní-lombéz-e   'I want to ask for'
       n-a-ung-a ní-hángálasány-a   'I want to carry many things'

The verb *n-a-ung-a* 'I want' has a floating High associated with it (the monosyllabic verb root [ung] is of the High type). The subjunctive verb that follows has a fixed High on its penult syllable. The floating High of the main verb anchors in every case onto the initial syllable (the subject prefix) of the subjunctive verb. This High spreads rightward onto toneless syllables. There is, of course, a buffer Low tone between this High and the High of the penultimate syllable.

These data require a certain amount of discussion with respect to our analysis. That the floating High of the verb anchors to the first TBU of the verb is, of course, accounted for by our rule of High Tone Shift. That is, the High that is associated to the final vowel of the verb (which would delink if that word were phrase-final) shifts rightward onto the first TBU of the verb. (We have already pointed out that attraction to the head of a foot does not apply between a pre-verbal noun and following verb.)

The fact that the High of the main verb docks onto the first vowel of the subjunctive verb demonstrates clearly that there can be no prosodic break between the main verb and its complement. The behavior of main verbs with a fixed High on the penult demonstrates the same point.

(47)   a-gámb-á wa-gúh-e   '(s)he says that they take'
       n-a-longél-á wá-damány-e   'I am saying that they do'
       n-a-longél-á wá-sáfalís-e   'I am saying that they boil (s.t.)'
       n-a-longél-á wa-fís-e   'I am saying that they hide'
       n-a-longél-á wa-lét-e   'I am saying that they bring'
       n-a-longél-á wá-lombéz-e   'I am saying that they ask for'
       n-a-longél-á wá-hángálasány-e   'I am saying that they carry
                                          many things'

The fixed High on the penult of the main verb clearly spreads rightward when a subjunctive verb follows; this spreading High tone does not treat the final syllable of the main verb as domain-final, but rather spreads across it into the subjunctive complement. There is, of course, always a buffer Low between the High of the main verb and the High on the penult of the subjunctive verb.

When the main verb and its subjunctive complement are separated by a nominal that is the subject of the subjunctive clause, there is no prosodic break between any of these elements.

(48) n-a-ung-a wá-nthú wa-gúh-e   'I want people to take'
      n-a-ung-a wá-nthú wá-damány-e   'I want people to do'
      n-a-ung-a wá-nthú wá-sáfalís-e   'I want people to boil (s.t.)'

In these examples the main verb has a floating High tone that docks onto the accented (penultimate) syllable of the following toneless noun, showing that there is no prosodic break between the verb and following noun. Once the floating High anchors to the accented syllable of the noun, it spreads rightward onto the final syllable of the noun and possibly into the subjunctive verb, where it is separated from the High of the penult by a buffer Low tone. Clearly, the ability of the penultimate High of the noun to spread rightward establishes that there is no prosodic break between the noun and the subjunctive verb.

The absence of a prosodic break in this environment is also supported by nouns other than toneless ones like *wa-nthu*. The following data illustrate nouns with a floating High in their structure.

(49) n-a-ung-a wa-vyêle wá-g|úh-e   'I want women to take'
      n-a-ung-a wa-vyêle wá-damány-e   'I want women to do'
      n-a-ung-a wa-vyêle wá-sáfalís-e   'I want women to boil (s.t.)'

In these examples, the floating High of the main verb anchors onto the noun *wa-vyele*, which itself has a floating High tone. The falling tone on the penultimate syllable of *wa-vyele* represents the expected reaction of the initial accented (High) syllable of a stem when preceded by a High tone. But the floating High of *wa-vyele* also docks onto the following subjunctive verb. Clearly, no prosodic breaks occur in these constructions.

It is not just a main verb and following subjunctive complement that exhibit the lack of a prosodic break. For instance, there is another sort of clause that is in some sense dependent on a preceding clause, though perhaps not to be considered a complement, and this also exhibits a lack of prosodic breaking. The construction we refer to is called the 'consecutive' in Bantu linguistic terminology.

(50) n-a-guh-a yuwe n-a-kong-a ku-m-tow-a
      I-take   stone I-begin   to-beat-him
      'I take a stone and begin to beat him.'

      n-a-guh-a nkhome n-á-kong-a ku-m-tow-a
      I-take   whip   I-begin   to-beat-him
      'I take a whip and begin to beat him.'

n-a-guh-a lénd'élé n-á-kong-a ku-m-hak-a
I-take   loofah I-begin   to-wash-him
'I take a loofah and begin to wash him.'

Here a contrast arises from the difference between a toneless noun *yuwe* 'stone' (cf. *yuwe tana*) and a noun with a floating High tone like *nkhome* 'whip' (cf. *ni nkhóme*, but *nkhome nthána*). In the former case the second finite verb in the consecutive construction, *nakonga,* is realized as in its underlying toneless form. In the latter case, however, the floating High of the object of the first finite verb in the consecutive construction links to the first syllable of *nakonga.* Clearly there is no prosodic break between the two clauses. This is supported by the example in (50), which shows that a High on the penult TBU of the object of the first verb in the construction spreads rightward into the second verb.

It is not of course the case that clausal boundaries are not connected with prosodic breaks. For example, when a dependent clause not functioning as an argument of the verb precedes a main clause, there is a prosodic break at the end of the dependent clause. In (51), for example, the latent High of *ku-dy-a* does not anchor to the verb *n-a-gon-a,* but instead simply undergoes Final Delinking.

(51) nízé nihézé kudya, nagona   'after I finished eating, I slept'

What we have seen in this section is that the prosodic structure of Chizigula is considerably less articulated than that of Chimwiini. In particular, within the clause there is very little evidence for prosodic breaks, though the subject-main verb juncture allows an optional break. Preposed objects and initial (non-argument) dependent clauses illustrate that the prosodic domain is smaller than the utterance.

In this paper we have examined in some detail a very remarkable tone system, notable for (a) the abstract relation between its underlying and surface forms, and for (b) the massive extent to which the rules operate across not just word boundaries, but also within phrasal domains that are considerably wider than those of sister languages such as Chimwiini. We have attempted to show that the relationship between the surface tone pattern and the underlying form is mediated by the presence of a left-headed binary foot at the right edge of the word. Furthermore, we have established that the same principles that operate at the word level operate at the phrase level. The operation of these principles in a significant array of syntactic contexts has been amply documented.

10

Tone and Syntax in Kiyaka

LUKOWA KIDIMA

THIS PAPER IS PART of a continuing investigation (Kidima 1987b (forthcoming)) of the tone system of Kiyaka, a Bantu language spoken in south central Zaïre and northern Angola. In earlier work (Kidima 1987b), I focused on the tonal and accentual processes, assuming that tone association rules are subject to phrasal conditions. Specifically, the study suggested that tone association rules apply within the boundaries of the phonological phrase. However, what is meant by 'phonological phrase' was not discussed in that investigation. The present paper addresses this issue.

The paper is divided into two major sections. Section 1 is a brief summary of the basics of Kiyaka tone, as analyzed in Kidima 1987b.[1] It covers major notions such as tone patterns and tone groups, tone donation, accent, and phrasing. Section 2 provides a definition of the phonological phrase in Kiyaka. Illustrative data are given involving different types of syntactic constituents. Finally, phrasing is examined with regard to the free word order of Kiyaka main clauses.

I would like to thank B. Hayes for critical comments, suggestions and discussions on earlier versions of this paper as well as for continuing support during the whole investigation of Kiyaka tone.

[1] For references on tone and accent in Bantu, see Clements and Goldsmith 1984, and the references cited there. Previous works on Kiyaka tone include van den Eynde 1968, Meeussen 1971, and Goldsmith 1987a. Both Kidima 1987b and Goldsmith 1987a use accent. However, there is a great conceptual difference in the meaning and the role of "accent" in these two papers. A complete review of the literature on Kiyaka is provided in Kidima (forthcoming).

1   Basics of Kiyaka Tone

1.1   Phonetic Tones and Accent

Kiyaka has three phonetic tones: a Raised High tone (R), a High tone (H), and a Low tone (L). The Raised High tone is indicated by the double stroke [″]; the High tone will be indicated by a single stroke [´]; the Low tone will not be marked.

In Kidima 1987b, these phonetic tones were analyzed as follows. Raised High is the realization of a High that surfaces on an accented vowel. Such a High is realized with a higher pitch than a regular High would have. The regular High tone is the result of a High realized on a non-accented vowel. Low tone means the absence of High tone and is thus supplied by default. That is, whether it links to an accented or to an unaccented syllable, a Low tone is phonetically the same.

Hyman 1978 argues that tone and accent coordination can be possible only if both tone and accent are phonemic in the language in question. In Kiyaka, the contrastive role of accent is restricted to CVVCV stems. One set of CVVCV stems receives accent on the first mora, while the second set exhibits accent on the second mora: CV́VCV versus CVV́CV. Kiyaka has pairs of lexical items that are distinguished only by the placement of the accent in the stem-initial syllable. In environments where the initial accent is not realized (i.e., not linked to a High tone), these pairs are always ambiguous. Thus for example, ndŏongo 'needle' and ndoŏngo 'palm wine' appear as distinct in some contexts but are identical (ndoongŏ) in others.

1.2   Tone Patterns

A characteristic of the tonal system of Kiyaka is that every stem, noun or verb, can surface with as many as four different tone patterns. For instance, in the following example, the noun *khoko* shows up as RL, LR, LL, and RR, respectively.

(1)   T1:   khŏko   '(it's) a chicken'
      T2:   khokŏ lădidi   'the chicken disappeared'
      T3:   khoko lădidi   'the chicken that disappeared'
      T4:   khŏkŏ lădidi   'it's a/the chicken that disappeared'

A verb stem can also exhibit four tone patterns, as illustrated by the stem *ladidi* in the example below.

(2)   T1:   beto tu-lădidi   'we who disappeared'
      T2:   betŏ tu-ladidĭ   'we disappeared'
      T3:   tu-ladidi beĕto   'we disappeared (instead of some other
                               people)'
      T4:   tu-lădídĭ ko   'we did not disappear'

Here we see that the verb has the following tones: LRLL, LLLR, LLLL, and LRHR.

1.3   Tone Donation

My analysis of the tone patterns is based on the notion of 'tone donation,' whereby one word contributes tone to another. Many words in Kiyaka have an underlying floating High. If one of these words is followed by another word, the floating High will surface on that following word. In the following examples, the High of *ndoongo* surfaces on the following possessive form, where it is realized phonetically as Raised.

(3)   [[ndoongo]   zaandi]]   ndoongo zǎandi   'his needles'

 [[H]   H]]

In the above example, tone donation is implemented by the rule of High Attraction, according to which a floating High is attracted rightward by the closest accent within the same phonological phrase.

(4)   High Attraction

Associate a floating High to the first unlinked, accented syllable to the right of its domain:

$$[\ [V_0 \, V \ldots]]$$

 [H[   ]]

(where ... can contain unaccented or unlinked accented tone-bearing units)

For the rule of High Attraction to apply, the presence of a floating High to the left of the stem is necessary. If a word has no floating High, no High will appear on the stem-initial syllable of the following word. Thus for instance, *zoba* and *heko* fail to induce a High on the stem-initial syllable of the following possessive in (5a) and (5b), respectively. The former is toneless, and the second has a prelinked (and therefore non-donatable) High on the last syllable. Finally, in (5c) the phrase *zoba zoba* 'real idiot,' which results from the reduplication of a toneless noun, contains no High at all.

(5)   a.   [[zoba] dyaandi]   zoba dyaandǐ   'his idiot'

  [[   ]   H]

  b.   [[hekó] dyaandi]   hekó dyaandi   'his tsetse'

  [[H]   H]

$$\overset{*\ *\quad *\ *}{c.\ [\ [zoba]\ [zoba]\ ]}\qquad zoba\ zoba\qquad \text{'the real idiot'}$$

$$[[\quad][\quad]]$$

Unless there is multiple tone donation within a phrase, Kiyaka subscribes to the principle of one High per phrase. Thus, in (5a), the High of *dyaandi* docks at the end of the phrase precisely because there is no tone already linked in the phrase. In (5b), however, a linked High exists, and causes the High of *dyaandi* to delete.

Normally, accent determines the landing site of the donated High. In the specific case of *ndoongo*, the landing site is the first mora in (6a) and the second in (6b).

(6) Accent determines landing site of donated High

$$\overset{*\qquad *}{a.\ [\ [ky\text{-}a\ [ndoongo]\ ]\ ]}\qquad kya\ nd\breve{o}ongo\quad \text{'of the needle'}$$

$$[[\quad H[\qquad H]\ ]$$

$$\overset{*\qquad *}{b.\ [\ [ky\text{-}a\ [ndoongo]\ ]}\qquad kya\ ndo\breve{o}ngo\quad \text{'of the palm wine'}$$

$$[[\quad H[\qquad H]\ ]$$

That accent determines the landing site of the donated High is further supported by the data in (7). These examples indicate that the donated High can skip over several syllables. The /-a/ of *kya*[2] is the donor morpheme:

(7) 1 syllable: ky-a   yĕko   'of separation'
                7-of   5-separation
    2 syllables: ky-a   ma-yĕko   'of separations'
                7-of   6-separation
    3 syllables: ky-a   ku ma-hăta   'of the villages'
                7-of   to 6-village
    4 syllables: ky-a   ku ba-mi-loŏngi 'of among teachers'
                7-of   to 2-4-teacher

We saw earlier that tone donation may fail because the preceding morpheme has no tone to contribute to the following word. But tone donation can also fail in case there is no word to receive the floating tone. Here again, the 'one High per phrase' principle is at work. Specifically, a floating High that cannot be donated will dock to the last vowel in the domain, provided that no High is already linked elsewhere in the phrase.

$$\overset{*\qquad *}{(8)\ a.\ [ndoongo]}\qquad ndoong\breve{o}\quad \text{'as for the needle, ...'}$$

$$[\qquad H]$$

---

[2]Numbers in glosses refer to Bantu noun classes.

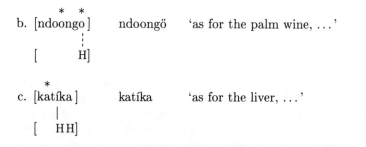

b. [ndoongo]   ndoongŏ   'as for the palm wine, ...'

   [H]

c. [katíka]   katíka   'as for the liver, ...'

   [HH]

In (8), we notice that the floating High docks to the last vowel of *ndoongo* in both (a) and (b). In (c) however, the presence of a linked High prevents the floating High from linking. It deletes, and the toneless vowels receive default Low tone.

Finally, note that accent determines whether the donated High will surface as Raised or High.

(9) a. [[ndoongo][yina]]   ndoongo yína   'that needle'

    [[H][H]]

   b. [[ndoongo] pe]   ndoongo pé   'the needle as well'

    [[H] H]

In both (9a) and (9b), *ndoongo* contributes a High to the following morpheme. In the first example, the donated High lands on an accented vowel and the result is a Raised High (R). In the second case, the High lands on an unaccented vowel (accents occur only on noun and verb stems in Kiyaka); the resulting tone is a regular High.

In summary then, the interaction of tonal specification, accent, and tone donation determine the surface tones in Kiyaka. Fuller documentation can be found in Kidima 1987b. For present purposes, the crucial point is that tone donation is phrase-bounded. I discuss this topic in the following subsection.

1.4   Phonological Phrases

Adjacency of two words does not guarantee that tone donation will take place between them, because tone donation occurs exclusively within a phonological phrase. The same sequence of words occurs in each of the examples below. However, tone donation is possible only in (10a).

(10) a. [[beto] [tusuumbidi]]   beto tusuŭmbidi
                                    'we who bought'

    [[H] [H]]$_\phi$

$$
\begin{array}{ccc}
* * & * & * \\
\end{array}
$$

b. [beto] [tusuumbidi]   bető tusuumbidí
    ⋮   ⋮   'we bought'

[H]$_\phi$[H]$_\phi$

Crucially, the two words form a phonological phrase in (10a) but not in (10b). Consequently, tone association yields different results in (10a) and (10b) even though the tonal specification is the same in both cases. In (10a), the High of *beto* will surface on the stem-initial syllable of the verb, whereas the High of the verb *tusuumbidi* deletes. In (10b), on the other hand, each High attaches to the end of its phrase since no High is linked in either of these phrases. High deletion does not occur in (10b).

The phonological phrase also plays a crucial role in accounting for the four tone patterns that were illustrated in (1) and (2). Specifically, these four tonal allomorphs can be derived correctly if we assume the following parameters: the position of the stem in the phrase (i.e. phrase-final or nonfinal), and whether or not the stem is preceded by a floating High. Compiling these four possibilities yields us the following tonal allomorphs:

(11) Four Tonal Allomorphs

T1:	Phrase-final, preceded by High	[H —]$_\phi$
T2:	Phrase-final, not preceded by High	[—]$_\phi$
T3:	Not phrase-final, not preceded by High	[— X]$_\phi$
T4:	Not phrase-final, preceded by High	[H — X]$_\phi$

The patterns illustrated schematically in (11) correspond exactly to the four examples seen earlier in (1), and repeated below:

(12) T1: khőko   '(It's) a chicken'
     T2: khokő lădidi 'the chicken disappeared'
     T3: khoko lădidi 'the chicken that disappeared'
     T4: khőkő lădidi 'It's a/the chicken that disappeared'

These forms have the following underlying representations.

$$
\begin{array}{cc}
* * & * * \quad * * \\
\end{array}
$$

(13) T1: [[khoko]]   T2: [[khoko]] [[ladidi]]

     [H[H]]$_\phi$ [[H]]$_\phi$[H[H]]$_\phi$

$$
\begin{array}{cc}
* * \quad * * & * * \quad * * \\
\end{array}
$$

     T3: [[khoko] [ladidi]]   T4: [[khoko] [[ladidi]]]

     [[H] [H]]$_\phi$ [H[H] [H[H]]]$_\phi$

Note first that the noun *khoko* has an underlying floating High. The stem receives the tone of a preceding copula (whose sole phonological content is a High) to yield T1 (*khőko*). T2 is arrived at by attaching the floating High of *khoko* to its final syllable; *khokő* constitutes a phrase on its own, and thus has no other word to donate its floating High to. In T3, *khoko* is all-Low because it donates its floating High to a following word (*ládidi*).

In T4, an additional rule applies. First, the noun stem receives a floating High from its left, while it sends its own floating High to the right. Then a rule of Plateauing (14) spreads the lefthand High rightward until all toneless moras are linked. Plateauing is triggered by the presence of two linked Highs that are separated by one or more toneless moras. The process is shown in (14).

(14) Plateauing: (phonological phrase bounded)

$$[\text{V} \quad \text{V}_0 \quad \text{V}]$$

$$[\text{H} \qquad \text{H}]_\phi$$

The example in (15) illustrates this process.

(15) T4:   [[khoko] [[ladidi]]]   Input

    [H[H] [H[H]]]$_\phi$

  [[khoko] [[ladidi]]]   High-Association

    [H[H] [H[H]]]$_\phi$

  [khoko ladidi]   High-Deletion

    [H   H   ]$_\phi$

  [khoko ladidi]   Plateauing

    [H   H   ]$_\phi$

  khókó ládidi   Output

As can be seen in the input to High Association in (15), tone donation creates the appropriate context for Plateauing. The floating High to the right is deleted because there is no word to donate it to. After Plateauing, any tone-bearing units not assigned a tone are made Low by a rule of default Low insertion.

In summary then, reference to the phonological phrase is crucial in accounting for the tonal phenomena in Kiyaka. Both tone donation and Plateauing are phonological phrase bounded. These two processes can be thus used for diagnosing phonological phrasing. The next question is, what is a phonological phrase? The second part of this paper addresses this issue.

2   The Phonological Phrase

In this section I examine the derivation of the phonological phrase, which I claim to be the domain of application of the tone rules discussed in the preceding section. The basic assumption is that tone rules apply to a phonological structure derived from the syntax by means of certain restructuring rules. For the syntactic account on which restructuring rules are based, I will assume the theory of Government and Binding in general, and an account of word order along the lines of work by Koopman 1984 and Kinyalolo 1987. Crucial will be the movement of the verb into INFL, as well as NP preposing and postposing.

2.1   Defining the Phonological Phrase

In Kiyaka, the basic element in a phonological phrase is the head, which can be a noun or a verb. Function words that are grammatically dependent on the head generally cliticize to the head and thus automatically form part of the same phonological phrase. As for non-clitic words, the correct generalization appears to be as follows: a phonological phrase is composed of the head and everything that falls under its maximal projection. This rule can be formulated as follows.

(16) Phonological Phrase Formation: Kiyaka

    a. In $[\ X^0 \ ... \ Y'' \ ... \ ]_{X''}$, where X^0 is the head of X'', X^0 and Y'' form a phonological phrase.

    b. Any lexical head that is not affected by (a) forms a phonological phrase.

The formulation in (16) comes close to the rule of phonological phrase construction proposed for Chimwi:ni by Hayes 1989. The major difference is that in Kiyaka, what can phrase with a head does not have to be its complement. We will see, for instance, that the subject, which is not a complement of the verb, can nevertheless phrase with the verb when both surface within the maximal projection of the verb.

To illustrate the definition in (16), consider an example containing a head noun modified by a demonstrative. The target forms are the following:

(17)   Khoko   wŭna
       chicken   that
       'that chicken'

The figure in (18) shows the internal structure of this constituent. Since *wuna* is within the maximal projection of the head *khoko*, the two are joined into a single phonological phrase (indicated by brackets in the output). Within this phrase, the leftmost High is donated to the initial syllable of the demonstrative. The second High deletes for two reasons:

(18)

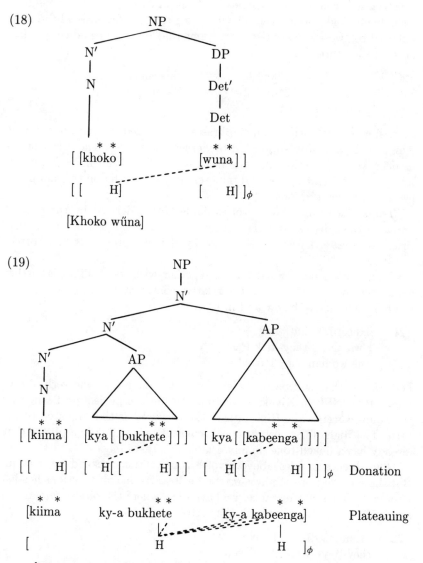

(19)

Donation

Plateauing

first, there is nothing to donate it to, and second, it cannot link within the phrase because of the pre-existing linked High. Finally, the toneless syllables get a default Low tone.

The phonological phrase definition in (18) also correctly predicts that constructions composed of the head and one or two complements will form a single phonological phrase. The following example features a head noun followed by two associative constructions that function as adjectives (see (19) for structure).[3]

(20) kiima   kya   bukhě̃tě̃   kyá   kábéě̃nga
     7-thing   7-of   14-beauty   7-of   12-red
     'a beautiful red thing'

In example (20) both modifier phrases are headed by the noun *kiima*. This is independently supported by agreement between the prefix of the associative construction and the head noun. The head noun *kiima* belongs to class 7 (prefix *ki-*) and imposes the same prefix on the modifying associative constructions.

The surface tonal pattern of example (20) is derived by the phrase-bounded rules discussed earlier: after tone donation and Plateauing take place, toneless syllables receive Low by default, producing the correct result.

That a head noun must phrase together with its modifier is further supported by the behavior of the relative construction, demonstrated by the reduced relative below and in (23):

(21)   nkheetó   bátǎdidi
       1-woman   they-look-Past
       'the woman they looked at'

For reasons that will become clear later, I assume that the verb always moves into INFL in Kiyaka, remaining within the projection headed by the noun *nkheeto*. The High tone of the prefix *ba-* is thus donated to the verb. The High of the verb deletes because it cannot link in a phrase that already has a linked tone; finally, Plateauing takes place.

The three examples above involve constructions headed by a noun. But the same pattern of phrasing can be observed in constructions headed by a verb. Thus, for instance, we have (22), where the object remains in situ and phrases together with the verb.

(22)   basuǔmbídǐ   khǒko
       they-buy-Past   1-chicken
       'they bought a *chicken* (instead of something else)'

---

[3]In this structure, AP refers to the associative phrase, which is generally composed of the associative morpheme followed by a noun. The associative (*kya* in this example) always cliticizes to the following noun, although the agreement marker (class 7 *ki-*) is determined by the preceding noun. In this and following examples in this section, details concerning the syntax will be kept to a minimum for the sake of clarity. In most cases, only the relevant constituents will be given.

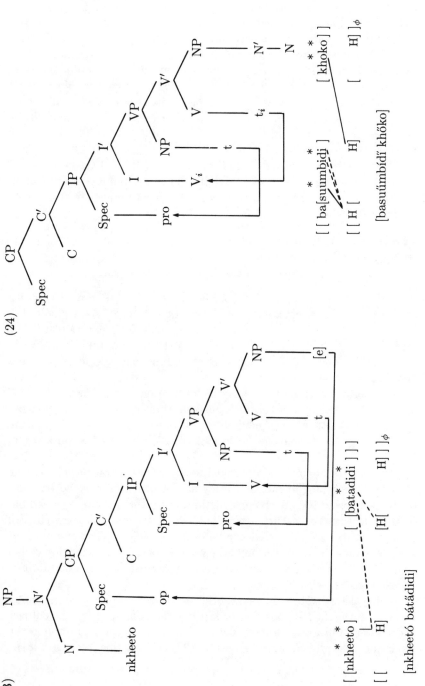

The phrasing for this clause is accounted for as shown in (24). Following Koopman 1984 and Kinyalolo 1987, I assume that the verb moves into INFL for morphological purposes: agreement and tense affixation. As will be shown later, this position accounts for Verb-Subject word order, which obtains whenever the subject remains in situ. In the particular case of (24), the object NP is in situ and thus within the projection of the verb. Consequently, the verb and the object NP are included within a single phonological phrase. As we would expect, the tone of the verbal prefix *ba-* is donated to the verb stem, which in turn gives its own tone to the object noun. The tone of the noun deletes, and Plateauing takes place between the two associated tones.

The phrasing illustrated by (24) is in no way limited to the verb and its object when the latter remains in situ. The verb and its subject can, in fact, phrase in the same way, provided the subject remains in situ, which is the case in (25) (see also 27).

(25) basuúmbídí̯   báána
      2-buy-Past   2-child
      'The *children* bought (instead of some other people)'

Here the verb moves into INFL while the subject NP remains in situ and thus within the maximal projection of the verb. As a result, the verb and its subject phrase together. The tone rules apply as usual: the initial accent of the subject noun attracts the floating tone of the verb. The floating tone of the subject deletes and all toneless moras receive a default Low.

It is this example that provides the motivation for verb movement into INFL in Kiyaka. In general, phonological phrasing joins heads together with material in the same maximal projection, and it is only by moving the verb into INFL that we can obtain shared phonological phrasing in this case.

It is important to point out that the two constructions headed by the verb have something in common: they have a special reading with regard to the postverbal NP. Both constructions carry the meaning 'instead of.' It appears that the occurrence of an NP in situ is marked in Kiyaka. In fact, we will see later that the subject and object NPs usually occur outside the maximal projection of the verb. In other words, the postverbal position of the subject or object NP does not necessarily mean that it must phrase together with its verb.

In Kiyaka as well as in many other languages, the subject normally surfaces in the TOPIC position or [Spec, CP]. Consequently, the subject and its verb phrase separately, because the two elements are not in the same maximal projection. The data in (26) confirm this (see also (28)).

(26) baaná   basuúmbidi
      2-child 2-buy-Past
      'the children bought (= as for the children, they bought)'

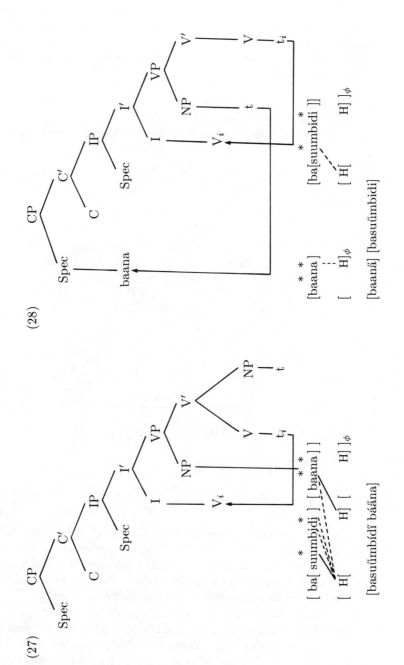

In this example, each constituent is a phonological phrase for the reasons mentioned above. *Baana* has a floating tone which will associate to the last syllable of the phrase, since no High is linked yet in the phrase; within the phrase containing the verb, the High of the prefix *ba-* is attracted by the leftmost accent.

The object, too, can surface preverbally and outside the projection headed by the verb:

(29)   khokŏ   ba-n-súumbidi
       1-chicken   they-it-buy-Past
       'they bought the chicken (=as for the chicken, they bought it)'

(30)

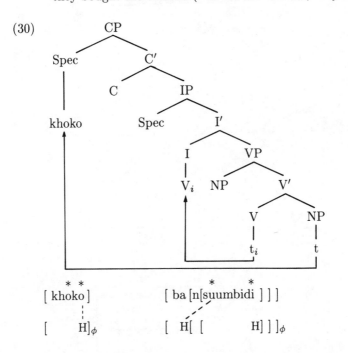

[khokŏ] [ba-n-súumbidi]

For this construction I assume that the object NP is in [Spec, CP]; the verb has as usual moved into INFL. It is also important to note that in cases where the object is preposed, object agreement obligatorily appears on the verb. This agreement is shown by the presence of a prefixed syllabic *n-* between the subject prefix *ba-* and the verb root *suumb-*.

This section has shown that a noun and its modifiers always phrase together. The verb also phrases together with whatever surfaces within the same maximal projection. When this condition is not met, the verb and its subject or object phrase separately. In addition, I have suggested that in Kiyaka, separate phrasing for the verb and its subject or object is the norm rather than the exception: the structures where the verb and subject or object phrase together involve an NP in situ, with a corresponding marked interpretation. Further motivation for this characterization is provided in the following discussion on the interaction between phrasing and word order.

2.2 Word Order and Phonological Phrasing

The preceding section has shown that NPs generally have a restricted internal word order. This explains why all constituents within an NP phrase together with the head noun. Apart from this case, word order in Kiyaka clauses can be said to be free. The different word orders, however, are associated with different possibilities for phonological phrasing. In this section I suggest that this results from the interaction between the rule of phrasing formulated in (16) above and a syntactic constraint that limits the number of full NPs within the projection headed by the main verb on surface.

I mentioned earlier that the subject and the object usually surface outside the maximal projection of the verb. In other words, the verb is the only constant element within its projection. This means that the verb generally phrases separately from other elements of a sentence. When it does phrase with other material, that material is limited to a single constituent. Thus for instance, the verb cannot phrase with its subject and object at the same time. (31) indicates that such a construction is not well-formed.

(31) *[baana   ba-suúmb-ídï   mǎdya]
       2-child   they-buy-Past   6-food
       'The children bought food'

To account for the ungrammaticality of (31), I assume that Kiyaka is subject to a syntactic constraint that limits the number of constituents within IP to two: the verb and one other. This constraint is formulated as follows.

(32) Single Argument Constraint

The maximal projection of the main verb may not contain more than one full NP on the surface.

In (33) the Single Argument Constraint fails to hold, and as a result the sentence is ungrammatical. As can be seen from the ungrammaticality of (33), the verb cannot phrase together with its subject and object. In fact, the Single Argument Constraint should rule out all logical combinatorial possibilities in which the subject, the verb and the object phrase together, as shown in (34).

(33)

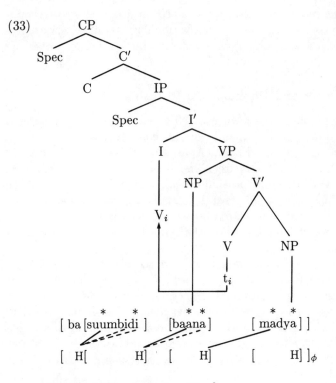

*[basuűmbídĭ báănă mădya]
they-buy-Past 2-child 6-food
'The children bought food'

(34) a. *[SVO]$_\phi$

b. *[SOV]$_\phi$

c. *[OVS]$_\phi$

d. *[OSV]$_\phi$

e. *[VOS]$_\phi$

f. *[VSO]$_\phi$

This prediction is borne out by the following ill-formed examples:

(35) a. *[baana   ba-suűmb-ídĭ   mădya]
           2-child   they-buy-Past   6-food
           'The children bought food'

b. *[baana mădyă básúűmbidi]

c. *[madya basuűmbídĭ báăna]

d. *[madya baáná básúúmbidi]

e. *[basuúmbídí mádyá báána]

f. *[basuúmbídí bááná mádya]

The motivation for the Single Argument Constraint is not known at present. However, this constraint has some important effects on the phrasing and word order of the language. To obtain a grammatical output from an underlying subject-verb-object structure, one of the following must take place:

(36) a. Move either the subject or the object into Spec of CP, adding agreement to the verb in the case of an object.

b. Postpose either the subject or the object, Chomsky-adjoining it to CP and optionally adding object agreement to the verb.

c. Both of the above.

In complying with (36a,b), one must control the relative position of the other argument. To this end, we will consider first the preposing or postposing of one argument while the second remains in situ. Given the definition of the phonological phrase in (16), the prediction is that whatever argument remains within the projection of the verb will phrase with the verb; the preposed or postposed argument makes up a phrase on its own. Following is the list of possible well-formed orders and phrasings.

(37) a. $[S]_\phi$ $[VO]_\phi$ [baaná]   [basuúmbídí   mádya]
                          2-child   they-buy-Past 6-food
                          'the children bought *food*'

b. $[O]_\phi$ $[VS]_\phi$ [madyá]   [basuúmbídí   má báána]
                          6-food   they-buy-Past-it 2-child
                          'the food, the *children* bought it'

c. $[VO]_\phi$ $[S]_\phi$ [basuúmbídí   mádya]   [baaná]
                          they-buy-Past   6-food   2-child
                          'They bought food, the children'

d. $[VS]_\phi$ $[O]_\phi$ [basuúmbídí   má báána]   [madyá]
                          they-buy-Past-it 2-child   6-food
                          'The *children* bought it, the food'

The syntax and phonological phrasing of each of these constructions are discussed below.

Argument Preposing

Subject preposing has already been illustrated by (28). The example below additionally indicates the preposed subject and the object in situ, as in (37a).

(38)

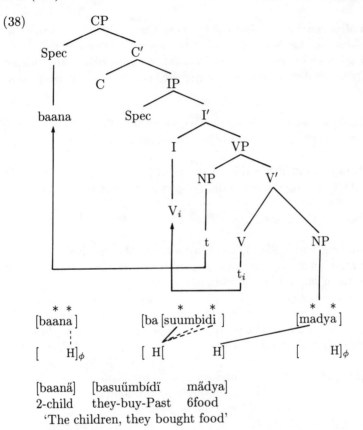

[baanǎ]   [basuǔmbídǐ   mǎdya]
2-child   they-buy-Past   6food
'The children, they bought food'

In this construction, only the subject is moved out of the projection headed by the verb. It thus phrases separately. The verb and the object phrase together because the latter remains in situ and thus within the maximal projection of the verb. Since the subject *baana* phrases separately, its floating High will link to its last syllable—the final syllable of the phrase. In the same way, the verb receives the High of the prefix *ba-*, while giving its own tone to the object *madya*. The tone of the latter deletes. Note, finally, that because it is in situ, the object does not induce agreement on the verb.

Object preposing was illustrated in (29). As we saw, preposing an object requires that the latter induce agreement on the verb. Thus in (29) we find the the nasal object-marking prefix *n'*- between the subject prefix *ba-* and the verb stem *suumb-*. Note, however, that the preposed object need not always be coreferenced by a prefix, as was the case in

(21). In the following example, which represents (37b), object agreement is expressed instead by *ma*, an enclitic on the verb.[4]

(39)

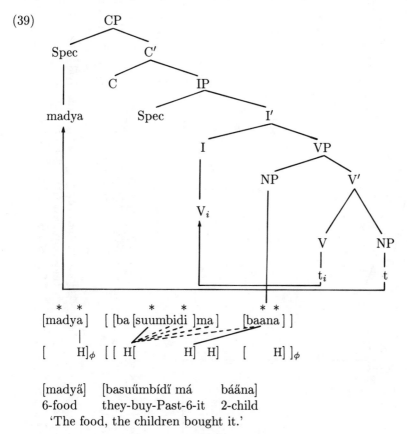

[madyá]   [basuúmbídíí má   báána]
6-food   they-buy-Past-6-it   2-child
'The food, the children bought it.'

We see that in this example, the subject remains in situ and therefore phrases with the verb. As expected, the object makes up a phrase on its own. Tone donation takes place between the verb and the subject; *madya* surfaces with its own High.

Argument Postposing

Argument postposing can also be used in order to make a sentence comply with the constraint in (32). A postposed argument will be Chomsky-adjoined to CP, thus phrasing separately from the verb. In (40) the subject is postposed, as in (37c); the object remains in situ and therefore phrases with the verb. Note that the in situ object does not agree with the verb. With the exception of the postverbal occurrence of the subject,

---

[4]The object agreement marker is a prefix if the corresponding noun is class 1 or 2; otherwise, it is an enclitic. *Madya* is class 6. More details about object agreement in Kiyaka can be found in Kidima 1987a.

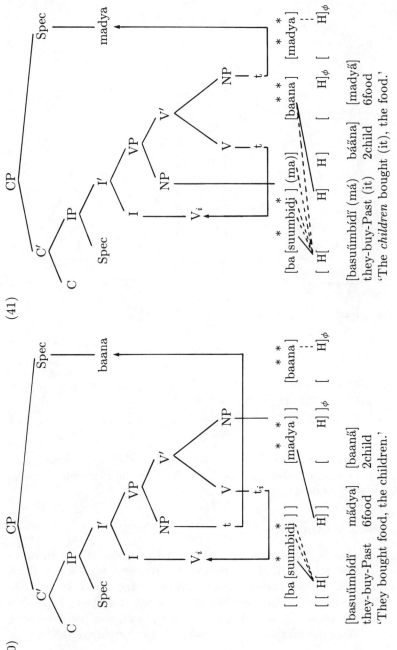

(40)

[[ba [suumbidi]] [mádya] [baaná]
   they-buy-Past   6food 2child
'They bought food, the children.'

(41)

[ba [suumbidi] (ma)] [basuúmbídí (má) báána] [mádyá]
they-buy-Past (it)   2child   6food
'The *children* bought (it), the food.'

everything else in this structure is identical to (28): the phrasing, and consequently the tonal behavior, match exactly.

Unlike object preposing, object postposing does not require agreement with the verb. Again, the subject is kept in situ in example (41). Since the verb and the subject phrase together, tone donation will take place between them as usual. The object *madya* phrases separately and receives its own High on the phrase-final syllable.

Argument Preposing and Postposing

When both argument preposing and postposing take place, as in (36c), both NPs surface outside of the projection of the verb, which is the only constituent to surface within the VP projection. The ultimate result is that each constituent phrases separately. If we provide appropriate object agreement in each case, then all possible permutations are grammatical.

(42) a. $[S]_\phi$ $[V]_\phi$ $[O]_\phi$ [baanä]   [basuǘmbídï (má)]   [madyä]
2-child   they-buy-Past-it   6-food
'the children bought the food'
(=the children bought it, the food)

b. $[S]_\phi$ $[O]_\phi$ $[V]_\phi$ [baanä] [mädya] [basuǘmbídï má]

c. $[V]_\phi$ $[O]_\phi$ $[S]_\phi$ [basuǘmbídï (má)] [madyä] [baäna]

d. $[V]_\phi$ $[S]_\phi$ $[O]_\phi$ [basuǘmbídï (má)] [baäna] [madyä]

e. $[O]_\phi$ $[V]_\phi$ $[S]_\phi$ [madyä] [basuǘmbídï má] [baanä]

f. $[O]_\phi$ $[S]_\phi$ $[V]_\phi$ [mädya] [baanä] [basuǘmbídï má]

For illustrative purposes, the derivation for $[O]_\phi$ $[V]_\phi$ $[S]_\phi$ (42e) is in (43). The additional orders (42b,c,d,f) obtain when both the subject and object occur on the same side of the verb. This is made possible by just Chomsky-adjoining one of the constituents to CP on the same side of the verb. Finally, let us note that structures such as example (43) suggest that the position [Spec, CP] does not have a strict ordering: we find Spec on the left of CP as [Spec, CP] or the right of CP as [CP, Spec].

In summary, argument preposing and postposing accounts for the fact that only the verb always surfaces in IP. In turn, the rule of phonological phrasing formulated in (16) guarantees that constituents which do not surface under the maximal projection of the verb will not phrase together with it.

(43)

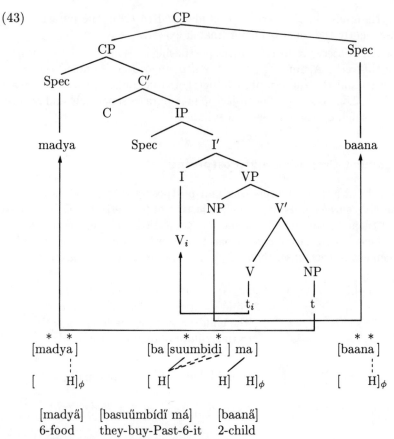

[madyă]   [basuŭmbídíˊ má]   [baaně]
6-food   they-buy-Past-6-it   2-child
'The food, the children bought it'

3   Conclusion

In this paper, I have examined the formation of the phonological phrase, which is the domain of tone rules in Kiyaka. Specifically, I have discussed the role that syntax plays in defining this domain. The phonological phrase is defined using the notions of head and maximal projection. Moreover, the phrasing of postverbal subjects indicates that what falls into a maximal projection does not have to be a complement of the head.

In addition, I have attempted to account for the phonological phrasing associated with free word order in Kiyaka main clauses. To this effect, I have suggested that Kiyaka has a constraint that forces NPs in excess of one to move out of the IP. As a result, the verb phrases together with at most one constituent, namely the one that remains in situ. Other constituents generally surface outside the projection of the verb, either as [Spec, CP] (with preposing) or Chomsky-adjoined to CP (with postposing).

11

The Phrasal Cycle in Kivunjo Chaga Tonology
Brian D. McHugh

In *The Sound Pattern of English* (SPE), Chomsky and Halle 1968 maintained that all phonological rules may apply cyclically, and that cyclicity of phonological rules reflects the nested bracketing structure, both morphological and syntactic, of the strings to which those rules apply. However, the organization of the grammar assumed in SPE did not force cyclicity on phonological rules. The structure-building component (syntax and morphology) interacted with the phonological component only once in the derivation: its final output served as the input to the phonology. Thus it is equally conceivable that in such a framework phonological rules should fail to refer to bracketing entirely, or that they should refer to bracketing information in a noncyclic fashion.

The theory of Lexical Phonology (Kiparsky 1982b, Mohanan 1982) has brought a partial remedy to the lack of a principled account for cyclicity by proposing that cyclicity correlates with the type of domain in which a rule applies. In this theory only word-level, or lexical, phonological rules are cyclic. Their cyclicity follows from the structure of the lexicon, in which morphological rules are interleaved with phonological rules, as shown in (1). The prediction made by Lexical Phonology is that only through such interaction between a structure-building component and the phonology can phonological rules refer to structure and apply to nested structures in a cyclic manner.

By that criterion, then, Lexical Phonology predicts that sentence-level, or postlexical rules will neither refer to syntactic structure nor apply cyclically to syntactic trees. This is because phrase structure rules are fundamentally different from word-formation rules in nature. While word-

(1)

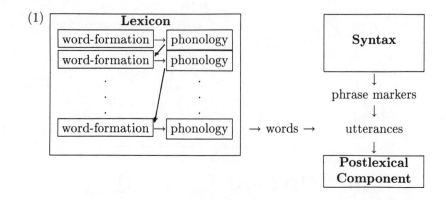

formation rules are additive, creating structure from the inside out, phrase structure rules are elaborative, filling structure in from the top down, as illustrated in (2) below. Thus, while in the lexicon a cycle of phonological rules applies each time new phonological material is added to the representation, in the syntax insertion of phonological material (i.e., lexical insertion) does not take place until the end of the derivation, at which point the entire utterance is already present, and no further material will be added. Therefore, since phonological material is added to the syntactic string only once, there can be no justification for sentence-level cyclicity or reference to hierarchical structure.

(2)   Word formation   Phrase structure elaboration

[root]   [   ]s
[[root]affix]   [[   ]NP[   ]VP]s
[[[root]affix]affix] [[   ]NP[[   ]V[   ]NP]VP]s
                      [[[   ]N]NP[[   ]V[[   ]N]NP]VP]s
                      [[[John]N]NP[[saw]V[[Bill]N]NP]VP]s

Unfortunately, Kiparsky and Mohanan's claim that the sentence-level phonology does not refer to syntactic structure is too strong. The large and growing literature on phonology-syntax interaction has yielded overwhelming evidence that certain sentence-level phonological rules in fact do refer to syntactic structure. In addition, it has been claimed that sentence-level rules may be cyclic (Selkirk 1984; Kaisse 1985; Chen 1986a, 1987c). The emerging consensus appears to be that Kiparsky and Mohanan's postlexical component actually comprises two distinct classes of rules, which I will call phrase-level (p-level) and utterance-level (u-level). P-level rules are sensitive to syntactic structure and, as I will argue here, also apply cyclically. U-level rules, on the other hand, conform to the predictions of Lexical Phonology by not referring to syntactic bracketing and not applying cyclically. Since their domain is the entire utterance, we may assume that u-level rules will apply after p-level rules.

One theory which has been proposed to describe and predict the behavior of p-level rules is the Prosodic Hierarchy (Selkirk 1980a, 1986;
Nespor and Vogel 1982, 1986; Hayes 1989). The central insight of Prosodic Hierarchy theory is that phrasal rules do not refer directly to syntactic structure, but rather to a modified 'prosodic' structure derived by
rule from syntactic trees. Modification of syntactic structure is necessary
since prosodic domains are often not coextensive with syntactic phrases
(Selkirk 1980a; Nespor and Vogel 1982, 1986; Hayes 1989; McHugh 1987).
In (3) I cite the parameterized algorithm used in which Nespor and Vogel
1986 to define the phonological phrase cross-linguistically.

(3) *Phonological Phrase Formation*

I. ϕ *domain*

The domain of ϕ consists of a C [clitic group] which contains a
lexical head (X) and all C's on its nonrecursive side up to the C
that contains another head outside of the maximal projection
of X.

II. ϕ *construction*

Join into an n-ary branching ϕ all C's included in a string
delimited by the definition of the domain of ϕ.

III. ϕ *relative prominence*

In languages whose syntactic trees are right branching, the
rightmost node of ϕ is labelled *s*; in languages whose syntactic
trees are left branching, the leftmost node of ϕ is labelled *s*.
All sister nodes of *s* are labelled *w*.

ϕ *Restructuring (optional/obligatory/absent)*

A nonbranching ϕ which is the first complement of X on its recursive
side is joined into the ϕ that contains X2.

Prosodic domains are arranged in a hierarchy, so that rules applying to
smaller domains precede rules applying to larger domains:

(4) word
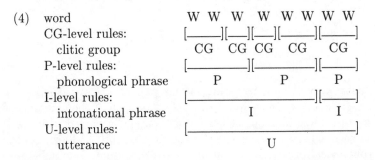

In this framework, rules which apply within prosodic domains are
level-specific, not cyclic. However, if the same inventory of rules were

to apply at each level, we could motivate a phrasal cycle by proposing that phonological rules be interleaved with prosodic domain construction rules:

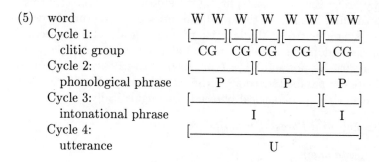

(5) word   W W W   W W W W W
     Cycle 1:   [_____][__][__][_____][_____]
     clitic group   CG   CG CG   CG   CG
     Cycle 2:   [_____][_____][____]
     phonological phrase   P   P   P
     Cycle 3:   [_____][_____]
     intonational phrase   I   I
     Cycle 4:   [_____]
     utterance   U

This would in effect yield a 'compounding-style' cycle, analogous to morphological compounding. In compounds, each component is a lexical stem or word, which may undergo rules on its own cycle before being compounded. Thus the entire word undergoes rules on every cycle, as shown in (6). Likewise, in a compounding-style phrasal cycle the entire utterance would undergo rules on each cycle, as shown in (7).

(6) Compounding-style cycle in lexical phonology:

$$[[\sigma \, \sigma]_w \, [\sigma \, \sigma]_w]_w$$

     Cycle 1: $\longleftarrow$ $\longleftarrow$
                 rules   rules

     Cycle 2: $\longleftarrow\!\!\!\!\!\longrightarrow$
                     rules

(7) Compounding-style cycle in phrasal phonology (e.g., prosodic hierarchy plus cyclicity; SPE):

$$[[w \, w]_p \, [w \, w]_p]_u$$

     Cycle 1: $\longleftarrow$ $\longleftarrow$
                 rules   rules

     Cycle 2: $\longleftarrow\!\!\!\!\!\longrightarrow$
                     rules

The data we will be considering in this paper, however, suggest an 'affixation-style' cycle. In such a cycle, only a portion of the utterance is parsed into prosodic domains at first, and then newly parsed material is added on each successive cyclic level, as illustrated in (9). This parallels the morphological process of affixation, in which a stem alone undergoes rules on the first cycle, while affixes do not undergo rules until the cycle on which they are added to their bases, as in (8).

(8) Affixation-style cycle in lexical phonology:

$$[[\sigma\ \sigma]_w\ [\sigma\ \sigma]_w]_w$$

Cycle 1: $\longleftarrow$
rules

Cycle 2: $\longleftarrow\!\!-\!\!-\!\!-\!\!\longrightarrow$
rules

(9) Affixation-style cycle in phrasal phonology (e.g., Chaga):

$$[[w\ w]_p^{\,}\ [w\ w]_p]_u$$

Cycle 1: $\longleftarrow$
rules

Cycle 2: $\longleftarrow\!\!-\!\!-\!\!-\!\!\longrightarrow$
rules

The algorithm by which syntactic structures are parsed into phonological phrases in Kivunjo Chaga appears in (10). As Kivunjo is an almost exclusively right-branching language, part I of Nespor and Vogel's definition of the phonological phrase (3) is largely irrelevant. The restructuring provision of (3), however, is obligatory for Kivunjo.

(10) Kivunjo Chaga Phonological Phrase Formation (proceeds from left to right)

For each pair of consecutive words X and Y,

    a. if X is the head of the syntactic phrase that dominates Y, then X and Y form part of a single phonological phrase;

    b. otherwise they are phrased separately.

The effect of this parsing algorithm is that maximally binary right-branching structures which satisfy a simple head government criterion constitute phonological phrases. As stated in (10), the phonological phrase formation rule proceeds iteratively from left to right, examining in turn each pair of words in the utterance. The interleaving of phonological rules with each step in this parsing process, then, derives cyclicity for p-level rules. In (11) I present a model of the organization of the sentence-level phonology. This proposal is not incompatible with Lexical Phonology, but rather enriches it by applying the principles underlying it to another component of the phonology. It adds no complication to the theory since it is based on the simple assumption that a cycle of phonological rules applies every time new structure is created out of or added to old structure. The u-level component is non-cyclic not by stipulation, but by the fact that its domain is the maximal one, namely the entire utterance.

(11)

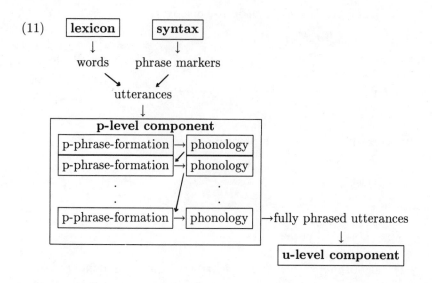

The structure given in (11) above will give rise to an affixation-style cyclic derivation such as that shown in (12) below:

(12)

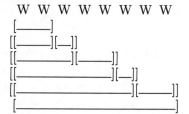

$$
\begin{array}{l}
\text{W W W W W W W W} \\
\text{[\_\_\_\_\_]} \\
\text{[[\_\_\_\_\_][\_]]} \\
\text{p(honological-phrase)-level [[_____][\_\_\_\_]]} \\
\text{[[_____][\_]]} \\
\text{[[_____][\_\_\_\_]]} \\
\text{u(tterance)-level [_____]}
\end{array}
$$

In (13) I tabulate the claims made by the theories and proposals discussed above with regard to phonological cyclicity and reference to structure:

(13)

	word-level	sentence-level	
		p(hrase)-level	u(tterance)-level
SPE		structure-sensitive cyclic	
Lexical Phonology	structure-sensitive cyclic	structure-insensitive noncyclic	
Prosodic Hierarchy		structure-sensitive noncyclic	structure-insensitive
Phrasal Cycle	structure-sensitive cyclic	structure-sensitive cyclic	structure-insensitive noncyclic

1   The Tonology of Kivunjo Chaga

(Ki)Chaga is a Bantu language or group of closely related languages spoken on the lower slopes of Western, Southern and Eastern Kilimanjaro in Northern Tanzania. Kivunjo is the Chaga dialect or language spoken in Vunjo district, the South Central portion of the region.

Like other varieties of Chaga, and like most languages of the area, Kivunjo has lexical tone. It displays a considerable tonal variety on the surface, as can be seen from example (14).

(14) Tone symbols:

    ´=high (H)   ″=superhigh (S)   ˆ=falling (HL)   ˇ=rising (LH)
    ˋ=low (L)   ꞌ=downstep (!)   ⌢=falling (SL)

These tones can all be derived from a simple underlying inventory of High (H) and Low (L) through the application of a number of p-level and u-level rules, some of which will be the focus of the argument for cyclicity presented below.

1.1   Tone Shift

A prerequisite for studying any aspect of Kivunjo tone is a discussion of its rule of Tone Shift, a process in which every syllable's underlying tone surfaces one syllable late. Example (15) illustrates the application of Tone Shift within words.

(15) Tone Shift within a word:

    a. Low object prefix m̀-: stem-initial syllable surfaces Low

        m̀-sètsĕ

        / / /\

        L*L*   L   H

        her/him-amuse   'amuse him/her!'

    b. High object prefix lu-: stem-initial syllable surfaces High

        lù-sétsĕ

        / / /\

        L*H*   L   H

        us-amuse   'amuse us!'

Example (16) below demonstrates that Tone Shift applies not only within words, but also across word boundaries.

(16) Tone Shift across a word boundary:

    a. Low-final noun: adjective's initial syllable surfaces Low

        mbùrú   ngììû

        / / ⟋ /\

        L H *L*   L H L

        goat   black 'a black goat'

b. High-final noun: adjective's initial syllable surfaces High

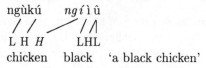

ngùkú   ng í ì û

L H *H*   LHL

chicken black 'a black chicken'

In both cases, the utterance-final syllable's underlying tone, having nowhere else to go, remains linked to the final syllable, forming a contour with the penultimate syllable's underlying tone, which has been shifted to the final syllable. In (15), we see the verb stem's Low tone combining with the imperative suffix's High to form a rising tone, while in (16) the HL lexical stem tones of the adjective form a falling tone on the last syllable. Below, in (17), the last two tones of the utterance are identical, and so a level tone results.

(17) Tone shift in high-toned verb: High tone combines with imperative High tone on final syllable to form High

a. Low object prefix

 m̀-kàpé

LL   *H H*

him/her-hit 'hit her/him!'

b. High object prefix

lù-kápé

LH   *H H*

us-hit 'hit us!'

It should be noted here that the utterance-final 'surface' tones given above and throughout this paper are abstracted away from the effects of intonational boundary tones. These tones, Low for statements and High for questions, when distinct from the last word's own final tone, combine with the last word's tone to form contours, and in so doing may trigger various u-level rules. Generally, though, the systematic surface forms I give here are attested on the surface in one or the other intonational context, if not both.

1.2   Phonological Phrasing

All p-level rules in Kivunjo are triggered directly or indirectly by proximity to a phonological phrase boundary. For the data under consideration here, only the ends of phonological phrases are relevant. Thus the pattern produced by phonological phrasing is one of alternation between a word's phonological phrase internal form, in which its underlying tones show up unaltered (though one syllable later due to Tone Shift), and its p-phrase-final form, in which the various phrasally triggered tone rules may apply.

Combining this alternation with that between utterance-final position, in which the last two tones form a contour on the last syllable, and utterance internal position, in which a word's last tone shifts to the following word's first syllable, yields a three-way paradigm, shown across the top of (18) below. (The fourth possible combination, p-phrase-internal but utterance-final, is logically impossible since the phonological phrase is a subdomain of the utterance.) This three-way phrasing paradigm in turn interacts with the two-way sandhi paradigm for the tone which a word's initial syllable receives from the preceding word, producing a minimum of six distinct sandhi variants (and often more, due to the effects of other feature-changing rules) for each word. This is is tabulated in (18).

(18)

	utterance-internal		utterance-final
	p-phrase-internal	p-phrase-final	
	'p-internal'	'junctural'	'u-final'
post-L	...mbùrú ò...$]_p$...$]_u$	...mbúrű$]_p$ [ő...$]_p]_u$	...mbùrû$]_p]_u$
post-H	...mbúrú ò...$]_p$...$]_u$	...mbúrű$]_p$ [ő...$]_p]_u$	...mbúrû$]_p]_u$

Tone Shift applies exceptionlessly and is oblivious to syntactic or morphological structure. For this reason I assume it to be a late, u-level rule that applies after the p-level component, and hence after the rules that form the basis of the argument for cyclicity in section 4. I will therefore state all p-level rules in terms of pre-Tone Shift representations.

1.3   Underspecification

Despite the fully specified representation of tone used for illustrative purposes in (15)-(17), there is evidence that tone is underspecified in Kivunjo underlying representations. What this means, following Kiparsky 1982b and Pulleyblank 1983, is that only High, the marked feature for a binary tone system, may be specified in lexical entries. Under this analysis, then, 'Low-toned' syllables are in fact toneless underlyingly, as illustrated in (19). I use a lower-case sigma (σ) to designate a syllable.

(19) Underspecification

$$\begin{array}{l} \sigma \\ | \\ H \end{array} = \text{High-toned syllable} \qquad ⓢ = \text{'Low-toned' syllable}$$

Throughout the lexical and p-level components of the phonology, tone rules continue to apply to underspecified forms. Syllables which remain toneless by the end of the p-level are then supplied with the unmarked tone feature Low by a default rule, given in (20).

(20) Default ⓢ$\rightarrow \sigma$ (applies after various spreading rules)

$$\begin{array}{l} | \\ L \end{array}$$

In (20) I adopt Pulleyblank's convention of circling a syllable to indicate that it bears no tone.

At the u-level, following the application of Default, rules may refer to specified Low tone. It is here that we may assume Tone Shift to apply, shifting fully specified representations such as those given in (15)-(17).

1.4   Accent

Several facts of Kivunjo tonology indicate the presence of accent in addition to tone. The Kivunjo accent is unlike that of more typical accentual languages in that it has no overt phonetic manifestation. Rather, it serves an organizational function, along with phonological phrasing. All p-level tone rules are directly or indirectly triggered by accent. In effect, accent and proximity to a phonological phrase boundary are necessary but by themselves insufficient to trigger p-level tone sandhi. Their combined effect, through the application of these tone sandhi rules, is to give p-phrase-peripheral accented syllables higher tones than their unaccented or p-internal tonal counterparts.

Accent is assigned in the morphology by a typologically ordinary rule, given in (21), which accents the penultimate syllable of a 'lexical' stem:

(21) Accent Rule: Assign accent to a lexical stem, choosing the penult if possible.

Stem = lexical root (N, V, A) + derivational suffixes

A lexical stem comprises a lexical root plus any derivational suffixes, but usually not including any prefixes. If a lexical stem consists of just one syllable, that syllable receives accent, even though there is no penult. This is not unusual: monosyllabic content words are likewise stressed in other languages with penultimate, antepenultimate, or second-syllable stress, e.g., English, Latin, Indonesian, Lakhota, and Polish. With the addition of prefixes to stems, the distinction between monosyllabic and polysyllabic stems gives rise to one between word-final and word-penultimate accent. In addition, some stem classes are lexical exceptions to the Accent Rule, producing a third option: no accent.

(22) *Three accent types*

a. Word-penultimate accent: words with stems of two or more syllables

b. Word-final accent: words with monosyllabic stems, or whose final two syllables have coalesced lexically (e.g., passive suffix -*o*)

c. No accent: function words, ethnonyms and other restricted lexical classes

2 P-level Tone Sandhi

The combination of the three accent types with the tone classes that are relevant to p-level rules produces a fifteen-member paradigm. I illustrate this paradigm with a keyword for each tone-accent combination, shown in its unshifted, underspecified underlying form, in (23). In cases where the keyword has more syllables than the two or three needed to exemplify a tone class, I mark tone only on the relevant syllables, and parenthesize the extraneous syllables. Asterisks mark the position of accent. As it is not in the scope of this paper to cover the entire paradigm in detail, I will focus on the three items enclosed in boxes: *leeri* 'money,' *mburu* 'goat,' and *Ndelya-ngo* 'one who takes heart.' The sandhi variants of these three words will largely suffice to support the argument for cyclicity.

(23) Tone-accent paradigm: underlying representations before Tone Shift

	penultimate accent	*final accent*	*no accent*
...LLL	* m-sulri 'nobleman'	* m-ki-pfi 'big (ugly) wasp'	m-caka 'Chaga person'
...HLL	* leeri | H 'money'	* (Nde)-wikio | H 'Blessed One' (woman's name)	(mu)-olrombo | H 'person from Rombo'
...HL	* mburu | H 'goat'	* (Nde)-mino | H 'Despised One' (man's name)	(m-ki)woso | H 'person from Kibosho'
...LH	* numba | H 'house'	* u-ku | H 'piece of firewood'	(m)-sia | H 'person from Siha'
...HH	* nguku | | H H 'chicken'	* (Nde-)lya-ngo | | H H 'One who Takes Heart' (man's name)	(m-m)riti | | HH 'person from Mriti'

If we then combine this fifteen-member tone-accent paradigm with the three-way phrasing distinction from (18) above, the result is a 45-member tone sandhi paradigm such as that given in examples (24)-(26) below.

In p-internal position, as shown in (24), each keyword's underlying tones emerge without modification other than that produced by Tone Shift. Thus it is possible to ascertain a word's underlying tone pattern directly by looking at the surface tones on its non-initial syllables and on the following word's initial syllable (represented by σ) in p-internal context. As in (23), I mark only a word's last two or three tones, as determined by the word's tone class, in the examples below.

(24) P-internal tone-accent paradigm

	penultimate accent	*final accent*	*no accent*
...LLL	m-sùlrì ò	m-kì-pfì ò	m-caka ò
...HLL	leérì ò	Nde-wikíò ò	mu-olrómbò ò
...HL	mburú ò	Nde-minó ò	m-kiwosó ò
...LH	numbà ó	u-kù ó	m-sià ó
...HH	ngukú ó	Nde-lya-ngó ó	m-mrití ó

Note that the three accent types are indistinguishable from one another in p-internal position. It is only in p-final position that accentual distinctions emerge, as a result of feature-changing rules sensitive to both accent and p-boundaries. Examples (25) and (26) below display the sandhi variants for our fifteen keywords in the two types of p-final context: u-final and junctural. I have emphasized in boldface type those items which undergo feature-changing p-level rules. As mentioned above, the u-final forms given in (25) are systematic surface forms obtained after the effects of intonational boundary tones have been factored out. In the junctural paradigm in (26), I mark the tones borne by the following LLH word *ukou* 'yesterday' to illustrate the extent of a rightward spreading rule which applies in certain members of the paradigm.

(25) U-final tone-accent paradigm

	penultimate accent	*final accent*	*no accent*
...LLL	**m-ˈsúlrî**	**m-ˈkí-pfî**	m-càkà
...HLL	leĕrî	**Nde-wikíˈó**	mu-olrómbò
...HL	mburû	Nde-minô	m-kiwosô
...LH	numbă	u-kŭ	m-siă
...HH	ngukú	Nde-lya-ngó	m-mrití

Observe that in u-final position only one of the three boxed-in forms, *leeri*, undergoes a feature change. By comparing the tones of *leeri* in (25) with its tones in (24), we see that the word's underlying HLL has been replaced with SSL. This would seem to be the result of rules which raise *leeri*'s pretonic High to Superhigh and spread the resultant Superhigh one syllable rightward. The High tone's pretonic position appears to be significant, as the High tones of *leeri*'s final-accented and unaccented counterparts fail to raise.

(26) Junctural tone-accent paradigm: verb + direct object + adverb

e.g., [*Ngilewona* __]$_p$ [*ukou*]$_p$ 'I saw (a) __ yesterday'

penultimate accent

...LLL	m-'sŭlrĭ]$_p$	[ŭkŏŭ
...HLL	leĕrĭ]$_p$	[ùkòŭ
...HL	mburŭ]$_p$	[ŭkòŭ
...LH	numbà]$_p$	[úkòŭ
...HH	ngukú]$_p$	[úkòŭ

final accent

...LLL	m-'kĭ-pfĭ]$_p$	[ŭkŏŭ
...HLL	Nde-wikĭ'ŏ]$_p$	[ŭkŏŭ
...HL	Nde-minŏ]$_p$	[ŭkòŭ
...LH	u-kù]$_p$	[ŭkŏŭ
...HH	Nde-lya-ngó]$_p$	[ŭkŏŭ

no accent

...LLL	m-càkà]$_p$	[ùkòŭ
...HLL	mu-olrómbò]$_p$	[ùkòŭ
...HL	m-kiwosó]$_p$	[ùkòŭ
...LH	m-sià]$_p$	[úkòŭ
...HH	m-mrití]$_p$	[úkòŭ

In junctural context, shown in (26), *leeri* undergoes the same change (only this time its last tone shifts to the following syllable rather than forming a contour with the penultimate tone). Thus we can consider the rules responsible for raising and spreading in *leeri* to be triggered at the end of any phonological phrase.

The other two boxed-in items, *mburu* and *Ndelya-ngo*, change their features only in junctural position. In the first case the HL of *mburu*, followed by the initial Low of *ukou*, is replaced by SS, just as in *leeri* the sequence HLL becomes SSL. Likewise, the final High of *Ndelya-ngo* plus the first two Low tones of *ukou* yield SSL juncturally. It therefore appears that the same basic process of raising and spreading which applies to *leeri* also affects *mburu* and *Ndelya-ngo*. However, while *leeri* undergoes raising and spreading in both p-final contexts, *mburu* and *Ndelya-ngo* raise and spread their final High only in junctural position. Also, while the High of *leeri* is attached to the pretonic antepenult, the High tones which raise in *mburu* and *Ndelya-ngo* are attached directly to an accented penultimate or final syllable. These differences in conditioning environment make it necessary to posit two separate raising rules.

The first of these rules I call Junctural Raising, because it applies only at the juncture between two phonological phrases, as shown in (27).

(27) Junctural Raising
$$\begin{array}{c} * \\ \sigma \\ | \end{array}$$

H → S /—]$_p$[

Junctural Raising's phonological environment is simple: it applies to the last High in the phonological phrase, provided that High is attached to an accented syllable. Looking back at the paradigm in (26), we see that Junctural Raising applies to the final-accented LH and HH words *uku* and *Ndelya-ngo*, and to penultimate-accented *mburu*. It correctly fails to apply to the High tones of the unaccented HL, LH, and HH keywords *mkiwoso, msia* and *mmriti* because, though p-final, they are not accented. It likewise overlooks the final High tones of the penultimate-accented LH and HH words *numba* and *nguku* because, though p-final, they are not attached to accented syllables.

However, as stated, Junctural Raising should not be expected to raise the pretonic phrase-final High of the final-accented HL keyword *Ndemino*, and yet it does, as can be seen from the data in (26). We know that Junctural Raising is responsible rather than the rule that raises the pretonic High of *leeri* because the High of *Ndemino* raises only in junctural context, while the High of *leeri* is raised in u-final position as well. Thus, in order to bring *Ndemino* into conformity with the structural description of Junctural Raising, we need a rule of Accent Retraction, which feeds Junctural Raising by moving an accent from a toneless syllable leftward onto the immediately preceding syllable if that syllable bears High tone. Accent Retraction appears in (28):

(28) Accent Retraction

Accent Retraction will also have the effect of shifting the penultimate accent of *leeri* to its antepenult. As a result, the rule that raises the High of *leeri* will apply to an accented High rather than to a pretonic one. This is desirable in that it allows us to generalize that only tones themselves attached to accented syllables may raise in Kivunjo, a fact that is borne out by other accentual phenomena in the language (see McHugh (forthcoming)). The other consequence of the retraction of accent onto the antepenult of *leeri* is that the rule raising its High must identify its target not by pretonic position, but by attachment to the antepenultimate syllable. I therefore call the rule Antepenultimate Raising, and formulate it in (29) below. Antepenultimate Raising still cannot be collapsed into a single rule with Junctural Raising, however, because of its more liberal phrasing context: it may apply at the end of any phonological phrase, regardless of whether that phonological phrase is u-final or not. We will see in the next section that the difference in phrasing requirements between the two rules is essential to the argument for cyclicity.

(29) Antepenultimate Raising

$$\mathrm{H} \rightarrow \mathrm{S} \ / \ \underline{\quad} \ \left. \begin{array}{c} * \\ \sigma \ \widehat{\sigma} \widehat{\sigma} \\ | \\ \end{array} \right]_p$$

Raising of High to Superhigh is only one part of what happens to the three keywords under consideration here. The other part is the spreading of the Superhigh one syllable rightward. As there appear to be no differences in spreading behavior among the three examples, spreading can be accomplished by a single rule of Superhigh Spread, given in (30). Since phrasing effects have been built into the raising rules, Superhigh Spread need not refer to a p-boundary.

(30) Superhigh Spread $\quad \begin{array}{ccc} * \\ \sigma & \sigma & \widehat{\sigma} \\ \llcorner \cdots \mathord{\nearrow} \\ \mathrm{S} \end{array}$

In the simplest case, Superhigh Spread will apply if two toneless syllables follow the Superhigh. This is true of *leeri* in u-final and junctural position, and of *mburu* and *Ndelya-ngo* in junctural position when followed by a LLH word such as *ukou*. This can be seen in the derivations given in Table 1. In each of the derivations in Table 1, Superhigh Spread applies to a Superhigh followed by two toneless syllables. As formulated above in (30), though, Superhigh Spread requires only that the second syllable following the original Superhigh tone be toneless. It places no restrictions on the tone of the immediately following syllable. Thus Superhigh Spread is blocked by a High two syllables away, as can be seen below in (31a), but not by a High on the immediately following syllable, as in (31b).

(31) *Ngiwonyi* —]$_p$ [*ulalu*]$_p$ 'I see (a) — now'

(a)   (b)

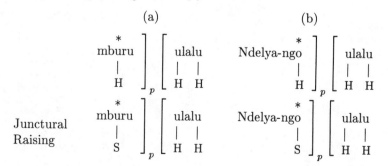

Table 1

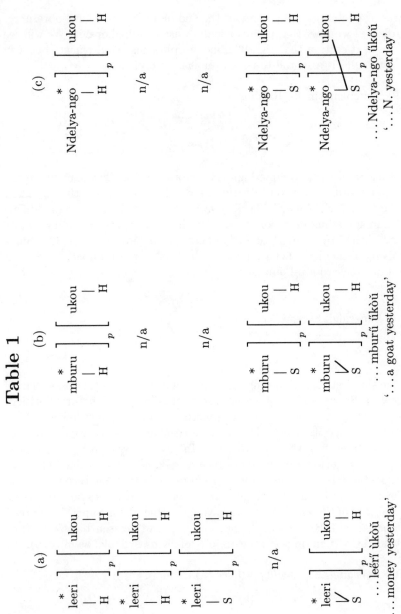

	(a)	(b)	(c)
Underlying Representations	leeri ⌐ ukou ⌐ *—H —H ⌐ _p	mburu ⌐ ukou ⌐ *—H —H ⌐ _p	Ndelya-ngo ⌐ ukou ⌐ *—H —H ⌐ _p
Accent Retraction	leeri ⌐ ukou ⌐ *—H —H ⌐ _p	n/a	n/a
Antepenultimate Raising	leeri ⌐ ukou ⌐ *—S —H ⌐ _p	n/a	n/a
Junctural Raising	n/a	mburu ⌐ ukou ⌐ *—S —H ⌐ _p	Ndelya-ngo ⌐ ukou ⌐ *—S —H ⌐ _p
Superhigh Spread	leeri ⌐ ukou ⌐ *—S —H ⌐ _p	mburu ⌐ ukou ⌐ *—S —H ⌐ _p	Ndelya-ngo ⌐ ukou ⌐ *—S —H ⌐ _p
Tone Shift	...leérí úkòú '...money yesterday'	...mburú úkòú '...a goat yesterday'	...Ndelya-ngo úkőú '...N. yesterday'

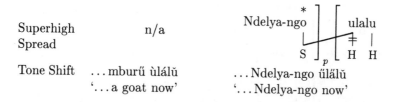

| Superhigh | n/a |
| Spread | |

Tone Shift   ... mburǔ ùlálǔ   ... Ndelya-ngo ǔlálǔ
'... a goat now'   '... Ndelya-ngo now'

This failure to be blocked by an immediately following High tone will play an important role in the discussion which follows.

3   Affixation-style Cyclicity in Chaga

Because of the difference in phrasing context between the two Raising rules, and the indifference of Superhigh Spread to the tonal specification of the syllable immediately following the Superhigh, it is possible to set up a tonal configuration in which adjacent accented High syllables compete to raise and spread. In such a configuration, shown in (32), a sequence of two toneless syllables must follow the two accented High-toned syllables so that either of the High tones, if raised, has an opportunity to spread. For ease of reference, I will call this the Rival High Configuration.

$$(32)\ \text{Rival High Configuration}\quad \overset{*}{\sigma}\ \ \overset{*}{\sigma}\ \ \textcircled{\sigma}\ \textcircled{\sigma}$$
$$\qquad\qquad\qquad\qquad\qquad\quad\ \ |\quad\ |$$
$$\qquad\qquad\qquad\qquad\qquad\ \ H_1\ \ H_2$$

By varying the phrasing of this configuration, we will be able to identify the role phrasing plays in predicting (a) which accented High will raise, and (b) which resultant Superhigh will spread (in the event both raise). The role of phrasing in determining the result will then shed light on the question of cyclicity.

H_1 in (32) can raise only by Junctural Raising when attached to the p-final syllable, because only a High which is the last High in the phonological phrase may raise. Consequently all relevant phrasings of the Rival High Configuration must place a juncture between the two High tones. H_2, on the other hand, can raise in three different ways, depending on its position in its phonological phrase. In (33a) below, it is attached to the p-phrase-antepenultimate syllable and raises by Antepenultimate Raising; in (33b) it is linked to the penult and raises by Junctural Raising; finally, in (33c) it is attached to the final and only syllable of a monosyllabic phonological phrase and raises by Junctural Raising.

$$(33)\ \text{a.}\quad \left.\begin{matrix}\overset{*}{\sigma}\\ |\\ H_1\end{matrix}\right]_p\ \left.\begin{matrix}\overset{*}{\sigma}\ \ \textcircled{\sigma}\ \textcircled{\sigma}\\ |\\ H_2\end{matrix}\right]_p$$

b. $\left[\begin{array}{c}* \\ \sigma \\ | \\ H_1\end{array}\right]_p \left[\begin{array}{cc}* \\ \sigma & \textcircled{σ} \\ | \\ H_2\end{array}\right]_p \left[\begin{array}{c}\textcircled{σ}\end{array}\right.$

c. $\left[\begin{array}{c}* \\ \sigma \\ | \\ H_1\end{array}\right]_p \left[\begin{array}{c}* \\ \sigma \\ | \\ H_2\end{array}\right]_p \left[\begin{array}{cc}\textcircled{σ} & \textcircled{σ}\end{array}\right.$

A three-phrase utterance is needed to create the structures in (32). This can be done by adding an indirect object to the "verb + direct object + adverb" sentence frame used to build two-phrase utterances in (26). The indirect object, which intervenes between the verb and the direct object, will supply H_1, and need not vary. It should have an accented High-toned final syllable, which is available in the HH final-accented keyword *Ndelya-ngo*. To achieve the different phrasing possibilities for H_2, the direct object following *Ndelya-ngo* must vary between a HLL penultimate-accented word such as *leeri*, a HL penultimate-accented word such as *mburu*, and a High accented monosyllable such as *ngu* 'firewood.' For the third phrase in the construction we may continue to use the adverb *ukou*, which has enough toneless syllables to allow for the environment of Superhigh Spread in each case. Thus the configurations in (32) will be exemplified by the sentence frame and three options given in (34):

(34) *Ngileenenga Ndelya-ngo* _____ *ukou*
                        leeri
                        mburu
                        ngu

    'I gave Ndelya-ngo _____ yesterday'
                    'money'
                    'a goat'
                    'firewood'

With an affixation-style cycle, the derivation of this construction will proceed as in (35):

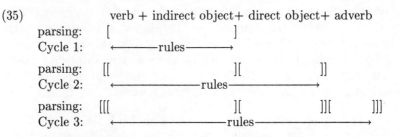

(35)   verb + indirect object+ direct object+ adverb
    parsing: [   ]
    Cycle 1:   ⟵——————rules——————⟶

    parsing: [[   ][   ]]
    Cycle 2:   ⟵—————————rules—————————⟶

    parsing: [[[   ][   ][   ]]]
    Cycle 3:   ⟵————————————rules————————————⟶

When we examine the outcome of each phrasing option, the rightmost extent of Superhigh compared with a fixed reference point will tell us which tone has raised and spread. If H_1 raises and spreads first, it will delink H_2, preventing H_2 from itself raising or, if already raised, from spreading. As a result the underlying HHLL will surface as SSLL (shifted one syllable rightward by Tone Shift). If, on the other hand, H_2 raises and spreads first, it will prevent H_1 from spreading (assuming H_1 raises) by placing a tone on the second syllable following H_1, thereby violating the structural description of Superhigh Spread. Thus if H_2 spreads, underlying HHLL will derive SSSL on the surface.

Since in each case H_1 is the final High of *Ndelya-ngo*, that tone may serve as our fixed reference point. After Tone Shift it will surface on the first syllable following *Ndelya-ngo* so that in effect we can tell which High has spread by observing the number of Superhigh-toned syllables that follow *Ndelya-ngo*. If two Superhigh-toned syllables follow, we know that H_1 has spread at the expense of H_2. If, however, three Superhigh-toned syllables follow *Ndelya-ngo*, H_2 must have spread, bleeding application of Superhigh Spread to H_1. In Table 2 I provide affixation-style cyclic derivations of the three possible phrasings of the configuration. For simplicity I omit the verb. In all three derivations, no relevant rules apply on the first cycle, which has as its domain only the first phonological phrase: the verb and its indirect object *Ndelya-ngo*. The accented final High of *Ndelya-ngo* cannot raise on the first cycle because the only raising rule whose structural description it meets is Junctural Raising, yet Junctural Raising needs to see more than just a phonological phrase boundary following the High. On Cycle 1 the second phonological phrase has not yet been parsed, and so Junctural Raising cannot tell yet whether the p-boundary following *Ndelya-ngo* is junctural or u-final. Junctural Raising must therefore wait until the second cycle to apply to H_1.

On Cycle 2, the action begins. In Case A, Accent Retraction, which does not crucially refer to phrasing of any kind, shifts the penultimate accent of *leeri* to its antepenult, feeding Antepenultimate Raising. Antepenultimate Raising may apply to H_2 on this cycle because its structural description refers only to a single right-hand phonological phrase boundary, which is present at this stage. Junctural Raising, now eligible to raise H_1, also applies. The two Raising rules are not crucially ordered with respect to each other, but both must precede Superhigh Spread to feed it. Thus Superhigh Spread, when it finally applies, finds two potential targets: S_2, followed by two toneless syllables, clearly meets the rule's structural description. S_1, followed first by S_2 and then by a toneless syllable, also meets the structural description of Superhigh Spread as formulated in (30). As Superhigh Spread cannot apply to both, it must choose between the two tones. In the surface form of Case A there are three Superhigh syllables following *Ndelya-ngo*, which indicates that Superhigh Spread has chosen S_2. One possible reason for this might be that Superhigh Spread iterates from right to left, and so selects the rightmost target meeting its structural description. Alternatively, Superhigh Spread might be blocked by an immediately following Superhigh, even though it

Table 2

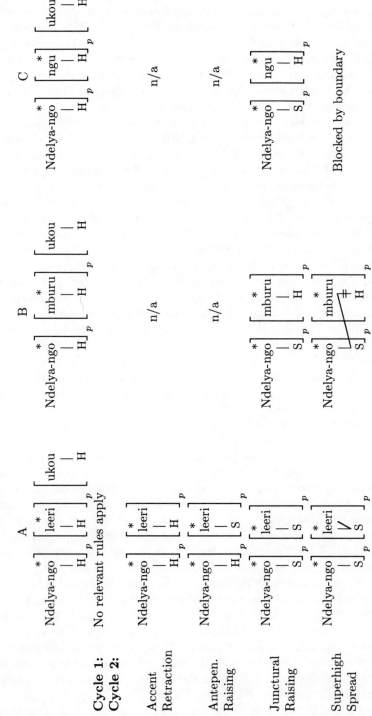

Cycle 3:

Column 1

$$\text{Ndelya-ngo} \left[\begin{array}{c} * \\ - \\ S \end{array} \right]_p \left[\begin{array}{c} * \\ \text{leeri} \\ \vee \\ S \end{array} \right]_p \left[\begin{array}{c} \text{ukou} \\ - \\ H \end{array} \right]_p$$

Rule	
Accent Retraction	n/a
Antepen. Raising	n/a
Junctural Raising	n/a
Superhigh Spread	n/a

U-Level:

Tone Shift — Ndelya-ngo lééri úkoũ
'...N. money yesterday'

Column 2

$$\text{Ndelya-ngo} \left[\begin{array}{c} * \\ - \\ S \end{array} \right]_p \left[\begin{array}{c} * \\ \text{mburu} \\ \diagdown \\ S \, H \end{array} \right]_p \left[\begin{array}{c} \text{ukou} \\ - \\ H \end{array} \right]_p$$

Rule	
Accent Retraction	n/a
Antepen. Raising	n/a
Junctural Raising	bled by S spread on Cycle 2
Superhigh Spread	n/a

U-Level:

Tone Shift — Ndelya-ngo mbũrũ úkoũ
'...N. a goat yesterday'

Column 3

$$\text{Ndelya-ngo} \left[\begin{array}{c} * \\ - \\ S \end{array} \right]_p \left[\begin{array}{c} * \\ \text{ngu} \\ - \\ H \end{array} \right]_p \left[\begin{array}{c} \text{ukou} \\ - \\ H \end{array} \right]_p$$

Accent Retraction — n/a

Antepen. Raising — n/a

$$\text{Ndelya-ngo} \left[\begin{array}{c} * \\ - \\ S \end{array} \right]_p \left[\begin{array}{c} * \\ \text{ngu} \\ - \\ S \end{array} \right]_p \left[\begin{array}{c} \text{ukou} \\ - \\ H \end{array} \right]_p$$

Junctural Raising

$$\text{Ndelya-ngo} \left[\begin{array}{c} * \\ - \\ S \end{array} \right]_p \left[\begin{array}{c} * \\ \text{ngu} \\ \diagup \\ S \end{array} \right]_p \left[\begin{array}{c} \text{ukou} \\ - \\ H \end{array} \right]_p$$

Superhigh Spread

U-Level:

Tone Shift — Ndelya-ngo ngũ úkoũ
'...N. firewood yesterday'

is not blocked by a High in that position. Regardless of the reason, this example shows that in the absence of other factors eliminating one tone or the other, when Superhigh Spread must choose between two adjacent Superhigh tones it selects the second.

By the end of Cycle 2, the derivation of Case A is complete, and the concatenation of the third phonological phrase adds no information crucial to deciding the outcome of the competition between S_1 and S_2. Since both raising rules apply in the same cycle, this example does not present any cyclic rule orderings. Rather, it serves as a control for the other two derivations by showing that the unmarked outcome of the Rival High Configuration is for S_2 to spread, producing a sequence of three Superhigh syllables after *Ndelya-ngo* on the surface.

In Case B, Accent Retraction and Antepenultimate Raising are inapplicable, so the only raising which takes place on Cycle 2 is that of H_1 by Junctural Raising. H_2 may not undergo Junctural Raising until Cycle 3 for the same reason H_1 must wait until Cycle 2 to undergo the rule: the phrasal juncture needed for H_2 to raise will not be visible until the third cycle. In the meantime, however, H_2 is no barrier to the spreading of the now-raised S_1. In spreading, S_1 causes H_2 to delink by a condition allowing only one tone per non-final syllable in Kivunjo. By the time the phrasing environment for Junctural Raising finally appears on the third cycle, it is too late: H_2 is no longer linked to an accented syllable and so can neither raise nor spread. As a result only two Superhigh syllables follow *Ndelya-ngo* in the surface form of Case B.

This cyclic analysis of Case B accomplishes the desired effect of allowing Junctural Raising to apply once in Cycle 2, feeding Superhigh Spread on the same cycle, which in turn bleeds a reapplication of Junctural Raising on Cycle 3. This ordering constitutes an A-B-A ordering paradox, incompatible with the standard assumption that rules are extrinsically ordered and may apply at only one stage in the derivation. Such ordering paradoxes are typically adduced as evidence for cyclicity when it can be shown that (a) there is a correlation with a change in structure and (b) neither of the crucial orderings between the two rules can be replaced by some noncyclic effect. The cyclic derivations in Table 1 certainly show a correlation with structural change; we must now consider noncyclic approaches to deriving the same forms.

In the case at hand, it would not help to try to eliminate the feeding relationship between Junctural Raising and Superhigh Spread, since this could only be done by collapsing the two rules into one. Even were we to surmount the notational problems this would create, we would still be left with the question of how to ensure that in Case B, Junctural Raising applies to H_1 first, in effect bleeding its own application to H_2. This will be addressed below.

The other crucial ordering in the paradox is the bleeding relationship between Superhigh Spread on Cycle 2 and Junctural Raising on Cycle 3. In order to eliminate this link, it would be necessary to transform it into a blocking relationship between successive iterations of either Superhigh Spread or Junctural Raising at the same point in the derivation. Two such scenarios come to mind, both involving iterativity, a time-honored device for allowing repetitive application of a rule without violating extrinsic ordering.

First, we could allow both H_1 and H_2 to raise by Junctural Raising, and have the blocking take place between subsequent iterations of Superhigh Spread. However, in order to allow S_1 to spread and thereby bleed spreading of S_2, we must assume that Superhigh Spread is not blocked by the presence of another Superhigh on the immediately following syllable. Yet recall that in the discussion of why S_2 spreads in Case A, one proposed reason was precisely the opposite, namely that Superhigh Spread is in fact blocked by an immediately following Superhigh. To reconcile our noncyclic analyses of both Case A and Case B, we would have to abandon the Superhigh blocking analysis of Case A in favor of its alternative, namely that Superhigh Spread chooses S_2 in Case A because it iterates from right to left and finds S_2 first. However, in Case B the direction in which Superhigh Spread iterates must be left to right in order for S_1 to raise first. Thus to render these two analyses compatible we would have to make directionality of iteration contingent on whether a certain rule had applied: right to left just in case Antepenultimate Raising has applied to the same or overlapping structure; otherwise left to right. Making direction of iteration a function of whether another rule has applied in the derivation seems an undesirable increase in the grammar's power, and one which has no empirical support beyond the present case.

The other scenario would be to make Junctural Raising a non-iterative, or self-blocking rule which scans from left to right for an environment meeting its structural description, picking the leftmost potential target, which in this case would be H_1. The rule's noniterativity would effectively prevent it from then applying to H_2. This analysis is easily falsifiable with data in which Junctural Raising in fact does apply twice to overlapping structures. Such data can be found in Case C.

In Case C, just as in Case B, H_1 raises by Junctural Raising on Cycle 2, while H_2 must wait until Cycle 3. This time, however, Superhigh Spread cannot apply on Cycle 2 to S_1 because there is only one syllable following it in the domain of Cycle 2. Superhigh Spread needs to refer to the second syllable following the Superhigh, which, although toneless, will not be available until Cycle 3. Thus on Cycle 2 Superhigh Spread is in effect bled by the placement of the p-juncture. On Cycle 3, before Superhigh Spread has a chance to reapply, H_2 raises by Junctural Raising, whose phrasing requirement is now met. When Superhigh Spread finally applies, it faces the same situation as it does in Cycle 2 of Case A: it must choose between two potential targets. Here, just as in Case A, Superhigh Spread selects S_2. As discussed above for Case A, this could mean either that Superhigh Spread iterates from right to left, or that Superhigh Spread is blocked from spreading onto another S syllable.

The derivation of Case C constitutes a counterexample to the noncyclic analysis of Case B in which one application of Junctural Raising blocks its own subsequent reapplications to overlapping environments. Here, both H_1 and H_2 have raised by Junctural Raising. To reconcile Case B with Case C, it would be necessary to invent an ad hoc condition stating that, perhaps, the presence of a monosyllabic phonological phrase disables Junctural Raising's self-blocking feature.

The other noncyclic analysis proposed for Case B would require Superhigh Spread to choose the rightmost structure satisfying its structural description if Antepenultimate Raising had applied, and otherwise the leftmost. To accommodate the data from Case C, this condition would have to be further modified, since here it would need to require Superhigh Spread to apply to the rightmost target even though Antepenultimate Raising had not applied. Thus our final proposal would be that Superhigh Spread iterates from left to right unless (a) Antepenultimate Raising had applied, or (b) one of the targets was a monosyllabic phonological phrase. To render such an approach a bit more plausible, we could recast it in terms of a hierarchy of configurations to which Superhigh Spread would preferentially attempt to apply. Yet this would be tantamount to building such information into the structural description of the rule, a regression to the era of disjunctive ordering in stress rule statements.

(36) Superhigh Spread with disjunctively ordered phrasing conditions (where the absence of phrase boundaries marked between syllables is construed to positively indicate their absence in cases (a) and (b))

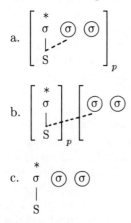

Unlike the stress rules of SPE, however, the disjunctive parts of (36) would be impossible to collapse into a single formula using parentheses.

The contortions we must resort to in order to account for the data in Table 1 without reference to cyclicity render untenable any attempts to eliminate the crucial orderings in the A-B-A ordering paradox found in Case B. In effect, any noncyclic analysis of the Rival High Configuration must explain, without being able to temporarily eliminate the third phonological phrase from the domain of rule application, why Superhigh Spread's choice of target depends on the number of syllables in the second cyclic domain. A cyclic analysis, on the other hand, allows us to examine progressively larger domains according to a straightforward, syntactically motivated parsing procedure, and to correlate those nested domains with the orderings of uncomplicated raising and spreading rules.

4   Types of Cyclicity

Thus far I have argued that an affixation-style cyclic analysis of the facts is preferable to a noncyclic analysis. It still remains to be shown, however, why a compounding-style cycle would not work. The crucial order in which rules must be allowed access to phrases in Table 2 is between the second and the third: in Cases B and C, Junctural Raising and Superhigh Spread must be limited at first by the end of the second cyclic domain, and only after applying there be allowed to reapply through to the third cyclic domain. However, the data in Table 2 do not crucially require the first and second phonological phrases to be so ordered—only that they be combined with each other, so that Junctural Raising can apply to H_1 first in Case B, before the third phonological phrase is added to the derivation. Thus a hybrid cycle, such as (36), which combines aspects of the compounding-style and affixation-style cycles, could also derive the right tone patterns, provided the second phonological phrase is added to the first before the third is added to the second.

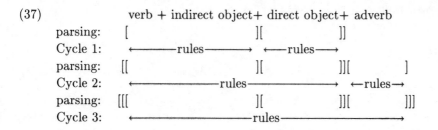

(37)   verb + indirect object+ direct object+ adverb

Other cycles, such as the strict compounding-style cycle (38), or a hybrid cycle (39) in which the second two phonological phrases are combined first, fail.

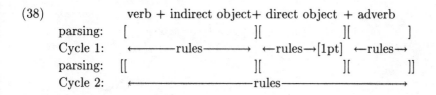

(38)   verb + indirect object+ direct object + adverb

(39)   verb + indirect object+ direct object+ adverb

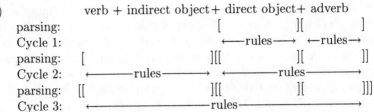

What remains, then, is to examine additional cyclic data from Kivunjo to see whether a crucial ordering can be established between the first and second phonological phrases. If one can be found, we have a basis for choosing the strict affixation-style cycle over the hybrid cycle displayed in (37).

5   Conclusion

In this paper I have distinguished two separate levels of postlexical, or sentence-level, phonological rules: the p-level, which makes use of phonological phrasing derived by rule from syntactic structure, and the u-level, which is structure-insensitive. I have argued that phrasal cyclicity represents a natural extension of the principles governing Lexical Phonology to p-level phonology: just as lexical rules are interleaved with morphological processes, so are p-level rules interleaved with phonological phrase formation processes. I have also drawn a distinction between two types of cyclicity: affixation-style and compounding-style. The data I have presented from Kivunjo Chaga provides empirical support for the claim of p-level cyclicity, and requires either an affixation-style cycle or a modified compounding-style cycle.

12

On the Separation of Prosodic and Rhythmic Phonology
MARINA NESPOR

ONE OF THE MOST hotly debated issues in the syntax-phonology connection is whether phonology has direct access to syntax or whether phonological structure mediates between the two components. In the last ten years, the shared belief of the different parties of this dispute is that the domain within which external sandhi rules apply is not isomorphic with syntactic constituents. According to the direct access to syntax approach, phonological rules 'read' their domain of application from the syntactic tree in one of three ways: by referring either to left or to right branches (Napoli and Nespor 1979 and Clements 1978, respectively), by calculating the structural distance between two words in terms of the number of nodes that separate them (Rotenberg 1978), or by determining whether the relation of c-command holds between the nodes that dominate the two words in question (Kaisse 1985).

According to the indirect access to syntax approach, structure-building rules intervene between surface syntactic structure and the application of phonological rules. Opinions vary, however, as to the nature of this structure. According to the prosodic phonology approach, this level of representation is a constituent structure tree (see, among others, Selkirk

Unfortunately, I was not able to attend the Stanford workshop on the Phonology-Syntax Connection. Different parts of this paper were read at the University of Essex as one of a series of lectures on the Logical Problem of Language Acquisition (March 1988) and in the GLOW 1988 Phonology Workshop in Budapest. I thank the participants of both meetings for their comments.

1978, 1980a; Nespor and Vogel 1982, 1986; Booij 1985; Hayes 1989).

According to the rhythmic structure approach, two levels of representation mediate between syntax and phonology. The first is intonated surface structure, on which the second—the metrical grid—is built (Selkirk
1984). The grid is a hierarchical structure not analyzed into constituents
(Liberman and Prince 1977, Prince 1983). It is to this structure that both
external sandhi rules and rhythmic rules make reference.

My view is that both prosodic structure and the metrical grid are
significant levels of representation:[1] prosodic structure mediates between
syntax and the prosodic component of postlexical phonology, and the
grid mediates between prosodic phonology and the phonology of rhythm.
External sandhi rules (as well as internal ones, for that matter) apply
on a hierarchy organized into constituents, while rhythmic rules apply
on a hierarchy that contains only a sequence of more or less prominent
periodicities. According to this view, the interface between syntax and
phonology is limited to prosodic phonology; in the case of rhythmic phonology one can hardly speak of reference to syntax at all.

This paper is divided into two parts. The first part is dedicated to
the prosody-to-rhythm mapping, and to the rhythmic component of phonology. While the general lines of Nespor and Vogel's 1989 proposal for
rhythmic phonology will be assumed in section 1, one modification will
be proposed in section 2 that makes the rhythmic component even more
general across languages. In the second part of this paper (section 3), I
will argue for an interpretation of the relation between *raddoppiamento
sintattico* and the rules of rhythm in Tuscan Italian that is made possible
only in a grammar that separates prosodic and rhythmic phonology in
the way described in sections 1 and 2 (see also Nespor 1988a).

1   The Rhythmic Component of Phonology

The rhythmic component of phonology, in the proposal of Nespor and Vogel 1989,[2] allows the definition of an arhythmic sequence to vary somewhat
across languages, while positing universal rules to take care of eliminating
the different arhythmies. The definition of an arhythmic configuration,
in particular, depends on whether or not a language is syllable-timed.
That is, in Nespor and Vogel 1989 (N&V from here on) it is proposed
that languages are not to be classified as syllable-timed or stress-timed
(as proposed in Pike 1945 and Abercrombie 1967, among others), but

---

[1] The relevance of both trees and grid is in agreement with the original proposal of
Liberman 1975 and Liberman and Prince 1977 (see also Hayes 1984).

[2] See also Nespor 1988b and Nespor and Vogel 1988. In this paper, I will most often
refer to Nespor and Vogel 1989, since it is, of the three papers, the most comprehensive
about the rhythmic component of phonology whose general lines will be assumed here.
Nespor 1988b (in Greek) contains the original proposal about the rhythmic phonology
of Greek, and Nespor and Vogel 1988 contains an account of rhythm in 'syllable-timed'
languages.

rather that all languages are, to some extent, stress-timed. Some have a tendency to syllable-timing in addition.

After briefly outlining, in this section, the organization of the rhythmic subcomponent of phonology, I will propose in the next section that there is no distinction in the rhythmic subcomponents of the two types of languages. The machine-gun versus morse-code distinction first mentioned by Arthur Lloyd James to illustrate the difference in sound between Spanish and English (Lloyd 1940) is thus not one of rhythm. It must be accounted for in some other subcomponent of phonology.

Rhythm is represented, as already mentioned, in terms of the grid, which is constructed on the basis of information contained in the prosodic tree.[3] That is, each syllable is assigned one position, marked by an x on the first grid level. Subsequently, the DTE (designated terminal element) of each higher prosodic category (excluding, for reasons I will not go into here, the clitic group), is assigned one additional x on a separate grid level. (1) contains an example of a prosodic tree and its corresponding grid.

(1)

```
                                    x     PU (phonological utterance)
      x                             x     IP  (intonational phrase)
      x           x                 x     PP  (phonological phrase)
 x    x    x    x                   x     PW (phonological word)
 x    x    x    x             x     x     F   (foot)
 x x  x x  x x   x  x  x   x  x x  x S    (syllable)
 Come vedi, vado spesso da Benedetto.     'As you see, I often go
                                           to Benedetto.'
```

Grid configurations produced in this way are not always well-formed. In particular, there are cases in which words get strung together in such a way that some prominences are too close together, and others too far apart. These two situations are commonly known as stress clashes and stress lapses, respectively (see, among others, Selkirk 1984). When either of these arhythmic configurations arises, one of three rhythm rules applies to eliminate it, producing a more rhythmic string. Within N&V's

---

[3]The particular version of prosodic theory that I will assume is that in Nespor and Vogel 1986.

proposal, a crucial difference obtains between minimal clash and stronger clashes, and different remedies are shown to apply in the two cases. The type of configuration determines the remedy.

Minimal clash is defined as the lowest-level configuration in which two adjacent prominences disturb the sense of rhythmic alternation. The relevant level is determined by a parameter. For example, N&V define the minimal clash for Standard Northern Italian as two adjacent prominences at the third level in the grid, as illustrated in (2).

(2) Minimal clash in Northern Italian.

<pre>
        xx
        xx
        xx
   ... pp ...
</pre>

For Athenian Greek, by contrast, the minimal level of clash is the second level in the grid, as shown in (3) (Nespor 1988b).

(3) Minimal clash in Athenian Greek.

<pre>
        xx
        xx
   ... pp ...
</pre>

Let us now consider lapses, which are defined as three contiguous unstressed grid positions (Selkirk 1984). What counts as unstressed depends on the definition of minimal clash; only those levels below the level of the minimal clash are relevant for determining lapses. An apparent lapse configuration at any higher level will not be considered arhythmic. Thus, for a language such as Italian, where the minimal clash is defined at the third level, the only possible lapses are those in (4). For Greek, where the clash is defined at the second level, only the configuration in (4b) is considered a lapse.

(4) a.   x   x   x
       ....x.........x.........x......

    b. ....x x x.......

Two of the rules that eliminate the arhythmic configurations we have seen so far are Beat Deletion and Beat Insertion, given in (5) and (6), respectively. Both apply in order to eliminate different types of stress clashes. Beat Deletion applies in the case of minimal clashes, and Beat Insertion in the case of stronger clashes.

(5) Beat Deletion

Delete an x at the level at which the minimal clash is defined.

(6) Beat Insertion

Insert an x at the lowest grid level between two clashing positions if the first is more prominent than the level at which the minimal clash is defined.

The application of Beat Deletion and Beat Insertion in Italian is exemplified in (7) and (8), respectively. The bold x in (7) is the one that undergoes Beat Deletion, while x in (8) represents the position introduced by Beat Insertion.

(7)   x
    x x
    x x
    x x
sarà fatto al più presto
'(it)will be done as soon as possible'

(8)   x   x
      x   x
      x   x
      x **x** x
questa città cresce a vista d'occhio
'this city grows very rapidly'

The last rule of the rhythmic component, Beat Addition, given in (9) and exemplified in (10), adds a beat to eliminate a stress lapse. It applies independently of whether that lapse has been created by concatenation a particular sequence of words or by the application of Beat Deletion. The roman numerals indicate the height of the grid column.

(9) Beat Addition

In a configuration defined as a lapse, add an x.

Condition on Beat Addition: Beat Addition may not create a clash.

(10) tele*fona se glielo* scriverai prima di....
    2 4 1 1 1 1 1   2 1 4   → 2 4 1 1 2 1 1 2 1 4
    'call if you will write it to him before...'

In (10), Beat Addition adds a prominence on *se*, thus eliminating the lapse of 5 syllables at level 1 in the grid.[4]

One of the innovations of this theory of rhythm with respect with previous theories (see, among others, Liberman 1975, Liberman and Prince 1977, Prince 1983, Hayes 1984, Selkirk 1984) is that there is no rule of movement: results that are obtained by movement in other theories derive in the present theory from the two independently needed rules of Beat Deletion and Beat Addition. That is, the presence of a clash does not require that an *x* in the grid is moved somewhere else. Deletion of an *x* is sufficient to eliminate a clash. Only if this deletion creates a lapse is a prominence added somewhere else.

A second point, particularly important for the present discussion, is that Beat Deletion is not restricted to any one domain of application. Recall that for the Rhythm Rule (also known as Stress Retraction, or Iambic Reversal), it was necessary to specify that it is bound to the phonological phrase (Selkirk 1978, Nespor and Vogel 1982, 1986, Hayes 1989). However, since Beat Deletion may apply only at the minimal clash level (for Italian, level 3), it will never remove the leftmost of two clashing prominences across phonological phrases, since in that case the leftmost prominence would have at least four *x*'s in the grid. There is thus no need to stipulate the domain of application of Beat Deletion. Beat Deletion makes no direct reference to the prosodic hierarchy; it sees only the grid.

languages does not necessarily imply that the physical correlates of the rules are the same. Thus, for example, Beat Insertion may be physically realized either as word-final syllable lengthening or as pause in Italian, while the additional possibility of a jump in pitch is available in Greek.

2   Isochrony

Determination of the height of the prominences which constitute the minimal clash in a given language is not the only parameter in N&V's system. A second parameter delimits two types of isochrony; it distinguishes languages that are syllable-timed from ones that are not, and consists of the definition of adjacent positions in the grid. N&V propose that syllable-timed languages differ from others in that in syllable-timed languages, in order to be adjacent, two positions must correspond to adjacent syllables at the linguistic level, while in languages that are not syllable-timed, two positions can be considered adjacent even when the syllables to which they correspond are separated by another syllable.[5]

---

[4]There is a certain amount of variation as to where precisely Beat Addition applies. For a discussion of the mechanisms that govern this variation (as well as, to a lesser extent, that of Beat Deletion) see N&V.

[5]It is well known that rhythmic adjustments take place in English even if the offending prominences are not strictly adjacent. For different analyses of the phenomenon see, among others, Hayes 1984 and Selkirk 1984.

The latter configuration is shown in (11) and exemplified in (12).

(11) Minimal clash definition in American English:

```
x       x
x       x
x  (x)  x
p       p
```

(12) a. Tennessee legislature
213 4121 → 312 4121 (or, if no lapse is created, 212 4121)

  b. Mississippi legislature
2131 4121 → 3121 4121 (or, if no lapse is created, 2121 4121)

As observed in Hayes 1984:70, however, the syllable intervening between the clashing prominences must be short in order for rhythmic readjustment to take place. Thus, while words with a short final syllable (e.g., *Mississippi*) are likely to undergo readjustment, words with phonetically long final syllables (e.g., *Adirondack* or *Massapequod*) are not, as may be seen in (13).

(13) Adirondack legislature
2131 4121 → no change

These facts present a problem for a theory such as the one assumed here, in which rhythm rules see only positions in the grid and thus do not have access to the linguistic content of a string. A rule whose structural description is a configuration described in terms of x's in the grid cannot distinguish between short and long syllables.

As a solution to this problem, I would like to propose, contra N&V, that the fact that a clash avoidance rule applies in English even when a syllable intervenes between the clashing prominences is *not* due to a different definition of minimal stress clash. Rather, it is accounted for by a special readjustment in the mapping from the prosodic hierarchy onto the grid. The rules which accomplish this mapping do, in fact, have access to both the prosodic structure and the grid.

The mapping component for English thus contains a principle according to which a 'very short' syllable at the end of a word is optionally not assigned a position in the grid, i.e., it is 'extrarhythmic.' The arhythmicity of 'short' syllables is established by Position Deletion, an optional rule that applies to either word-final or word-initial positions if they are occupied by a short syllable:[6]

---

[6]Something like Position Deletion also turns up word-internally. Kiparsky 1977 mentions two rules which optionally delete a syllable position word-internally, preserving the associated phonetic material. These are the Victory Rule, according to which an unstressed vowel is deleted word-internally before a sonorant followed by an unstressed vowel, and the Resolution Rule, which permits a VCV sequence to count as a single metrical position in the poetry of Chaucer and Shakespeare.

(14) Position Deletion[7]

Delete an x at the first level of the grid if it corresponds to a 'short' syllable at the edge of a word.

Position Deletion is thus the fourth rule of the rhythmic component: two rules either lower or raise an existing grid column (Beat Deletion and Beat Addition, respectively), and two rules either delete or insert a grid position (Position Deletion and Beat Insertion, respectively). Although Position Deletion is in some sense the counterpart of Beat Insertion, it has a different status from the other three rules: it is a readjustment rule of the prosody-to-grid mapping. Of the four rules, Position Deletion is the only one with access to information about the phonetic content of a position.

This proposal is reminiscent of a situation that is well-known in poetic metrics; under certain conditions, two adjacent syllables in a verse may count as one single position in the grid, to account for what is commonly known as the phenomenon of sinaloepha.

It should be observed that under the present proposal, the minimal clash definition in English, a language that is not syllable-timed, is identical to that proposed for Italian, a syllable-timed language. If the morsecode versus machine-gun distinction is not one of rhythm but of syllable types, as well as other nonrhythmic phonological characteristics, as proposed by Dauer 1983 on phonetic grounds, then the fact that the rhythmic subcomponent of the two groups of languages looks the same is a desirable result.[8]

If the rhythmic components of the two language types are the same, we must then ask why English has Position Deletion while syllable-timed languages do not. A close examination of data from standard Italian as spoken in Milan shows that, in fact, a readjustment rule like Position Deletion is necessary for Italian as well. As we have noted, adjacency is generally required of those syllables constituting a clash in Italian. However, the clash avoidance rule of Beat Deletion, which is usually triggered by minimal clashes, also applies in precisely those cases where a syllable consisting of only one vowel intervenes in between the clashing prominences. Examples of this are given in (15), where the underlined positions are the ones that have undergone Position Deletion.[9]

Position Deletion may thus be more general than is proposed above, in the sense of not needing a condition on which portion of the word may undergo the rule. In English the set of syllables which count as short word-internally may also be more restricted than what counts as short word-finally. I leave this for future research.

[7] Actually, the most appropriate name for this rule is Beat Deletion, since it describes an operation that is the opposite of Beat Insertion. This name is already used, however, for a rule that deletes an x from the top of a grid column. The latter rule would be more aptly termed Beat Subtraction, to parallel Beat Addition. For the time being, however, I will maintain the existing terminology, in order to avoid confusion.

[8] This conclusion diverges from Selkirk 1984, in which the distinction between stress timing and syllable timing is represented in the grid.

[9] As was mentioned for English, in Italian it is also possible that Position Deletion

(15) a. ventidue orsi   'twenty-two bears'
213$\underline{1}$ 41 → 312$\underline{1}$ 41 (or, if no lapse is created, 212$\underline{1}$ 41)

b. ventitre aerei   'twenty-three airplanes'
213 $\underline{1}$411 → 312 $\underline{1}$411 (or, if no lapse is created, 212 $\underline{1}$411)

It should be observed that in Italian, as in English, Position Deletion is exclusively a rhythmic rule. The syllable corresponding to the deleted position is still present in the *prosodic* hierarchy, as seen from the fact that prosodic rules that crucially refer to a final, stressed syllable will not apply to a word whose penultimate syllable is stressed and whose final syllable, which consists of a vowel, is unstressed (hence subject to Position Deletion in the rhythmic phonology). One such case occurs with *raddoppiamento sintattico* (RS). RS is a rule of certain varieties of Italian which applies across a sequence of two words ($w_1 w_2$) to lengthen the initial consonant of w_2. The rule applies only if w_1 ends in a stressed vowel and if w_2 starts with a consonant other than the initial *s* of a consonant cluster (see, among others, Pratelli 1970, Vogel 1977, Chierchia 1986). The application of RS is exemplified in (16a). (16b) shows that RS fails to apply when a short syllable intervenes between the rightmost stressed vowel of w_1 and the initial consonant of w_2.

(16) a. ventitré barche → ventitré [b:]arche

b. ventidúe barche → ventidúe [b]arche (∗ventidúe [b:]arche)

The example in (16b) contrasts with (17), a form found in certain dialects of Italian, where the final syllable of *ventidue* (i.e., *e*) is deleted. In this case, RS does apply.

(17) ventidú barche → ventidú [b:]arche

We turn now to the problem of how to define the notion of short syllable. Though I do not have a solution at the moment, I would like to suggest that what counts as short and long depends on the variety of syllable types available in a given language.[10] Thus in Italian, a language with a restricted number of syllable types, only a syllable containing exactly one vowel is considered short. On the other hand, in English, a language with a large variety of syllable types, a CV syllable also counts as short.

---

may apply word-internally. In words with an internal unstressed syllable containing only one vowel, such as *Mauro, feudo* 'feud,' the short syllable may or may not count for syllabification. Thus both *Mauro* and *feudo* can have either two or three syllables. I leave the investigation of this word-internal phenomenon for future research.

[10]Kaye, Lowenstamm, and Vergnaud (forthcoming) propose a theory in which syllable structure is defined in universal grammar rather than varying across languages. The present proposal is not incompatible with such a theory, since what is relevant in the distinction between so-called syllable-timed and stress-timed languages is that in the former, two vowels are separated by a restricted number of consonants, while in the latter, a large number of consonants may intervene between two vowels in surface structure.

We may now draw the conclusion that the rhythmic component of phonology is the same for syllable-timed and for stress-timed languages; it is characterized by an aspiration towards maximal rhythmic alternation (see, among others, Sweet 1913, Dell 1984, Selkirk 1984). This is in keeping with the results of phonetic experiments carried out by, among others, Dauer 1983, Borzone de Manrique and Signorini 1983, and den Os 1988. All of these studies show that the distinction between syllable-timed and stress-timed languages is not one of rhythm, since no distinction in timing exists between the two groups of languages. The present proposal is thus the phonological counterpart of these phonetic discoveries. The only parametric value remaining in the rhythmic component is the definition of how high in the grid the minimal clash is defined in a given language; that is, at which level of the grid the need for alternation is the strongest. This parameter is independent of the property of syllable-timing. The one example we have seen of variation along this parameter involves Italian and Greek, both syllable-timed languages.

One reason why the inclination towards alternating stress has often been overlooked in syllable-timed languages may be that most machine-gun languages have fixed stress. In these cases, therefore, the occurrence of stress clashes is limited to languages with word-initial or word-final stress, and, in particular, to instances where a stressed monosyllabic word is adjacent to the stressed end of another word.

A close look at languages of the machine-gun type which *lack* fixed stress reveals the existence of clash avoidance rules similar to those of English. As we said above, both Italian and Greek need rules such as Beat Deletion and Beat Insertion in order to avoid clashes. In addition, even in languages with fixed stress, in those cases in which clashes arise they are eliminated. Although I presently lack a detailed analysis of Turkish rhythm, the examples in (18) show that even in this fixed-stress language, rhythmic adjustments do apply to eliminate clashes:

(18) Turkish.

    a. híc bír habér → híc bir habér 'no news'

    b. bír mektúp vár → bír mektúp X vár 'there is a letter'

The example in (18a), showing destressing of *bír* indicates that Beat Deletion has applied. (18b), where a small pause is inserted in between *mektúp* and *vár*, suggests the application of Beat Insertion.[11]

3 Tuscan Italian

In the second part of the paper, I will show that by locating prosodic phonology at the interface between phonology and syntax, and by rep-

---

[11]Since the Turkish data at my disposal are incomplete, I do not claim that these are the only rhythmic adjustments that are available to eliminate arhythmic configurations. Further research is needed to decide whether this is the case.

resenting rhythmic phonology in a distinct structure which results from mapping prosodic structure onto rhythmic structure, we gain insight into the interaction between RS and the rhythm rules of Tuscan Italian.

Nespor and Vogel 1979 observe that in the case of a stress clash, the rule of Stress Retraction applies in Northern Italian to eliminate the clashing configuration. Examples of the application of this rule are given in (19), where 'á' indicates primary stress and 'à' indicates secondary stress.

(19) a. metá tórta → mèta tórta 'half cake'

b. sará cótto → sàra cótto 'it will be cooked'

Within the rhythmic subcomponent of phonology outlined above, this phenomenon is analyzed as Beat Deletion followed (possibly) by Beat Addition. The presence of the minimal clash triggers Beat Deletion, realized physically as destressing. In the case that a lapse is created, Beat Addition applies to add a prominence elsewhere, eliminating the lapse.

Nespor and Vogel 1979 observe, in addition, that in the cases in (19), the Tuscan varieties of Italian exhibit RS instead of Stress Retraction (although the presence of a stress clash is not a necessary condition for the application of RS). This is shown in (20):

(20) a. metá tórta → metà [t:]órta

b. sará cótto → sarà [k:]ótto

They propose that the reason for the absence of the rhythm rule in these varieties is that RS, by lengthening the initial consonant of w_2, introduces sufficient phonological distance between the two stresses so that they are no longer perceived as clashing. Within a theory of phonology such as the one proposed here, however, prosodic rules apply on trees, and rhythmic rules apply on the grid. It is therefore impossible for the rules of rhythm to have access to any segmental information of a string, including consonant length. As it stands, the proposal of Nespor and Vogel 1979 is inexpressible in the framework presented here. In order for the effect of RS to be visible to the rules of rhythm, RS must apply to the grid. For instance, it might introduce an extra position to eliminate the clash. The extra x would introduce enough distance to render the originally clashing prominences no longer adjacent, so that they do not constitute a clash in the representation of rhythm. This solution is in fact proposed in Yip 1988.

Several arguments, can be brought against this solution, however. First, RS, a prosodic rule, would have to have power normally unavailable to prosodic rules, namely the ability to alter grid configurations. Though prosodic rules may change the grid configuration indirectly, they never do so directly. For example, a prosodic rule that deletes a syllable has the indirect effect of eliminating one position from the grid, since a grid position represents the time span corresponding to a single syllable.[12] An example of such a rule is the vowel deletion rule of Italian, shown applying in (21).

(21) farán béne ← faranno bene   '(they)'ll do well'

That an x has been deleted from the final syllable of *faranno* can be seen from the fact that the primary stress of *farán* clashes with the primary stress of *béne*.

Prosodic rules that do not alter the number of syllables of a string never have the power attributed to RS in the proposal of Yip 1988: that of directly changing the grid. Giving RS this power would in addition make it a nonlocal rule, in the sense that it would operate on two different structures (the prosodic tree and the rhythmic grid), another undesirable consequence.

The second argument against having RS insert a position in the grid is that since each grid position stands for a time unit, such a proposal predicts that a long consonant stretching across two words will be longer than a long consonant contained within a single word. However, this difference is not significant in Italian. On the contrary, measurements reported in Korzen 1980 of word-internal long consonants and of long consonants generated by RS reveal that they are equally long. In support of this finding, Korzen 1986 shows that native speakers find ambiguous minimal pairs of the type reported in (22), where the first member of each pair contains a word-internal long consonant and the second member a consonant lengthened by RS.

(22) a.   abbraccia / ha braccia   '(he) hugs / (he) has arms'
     b.   abbisogno / ha bisogno   'need (*noun*) / (he) needs'
     c.   accasa   / a casa   '(he) goes home / at home'

A third undesirable consequence of construing RS as the addition of a grid position is the incorrect prediction that the lengthening of the consonant will be the same whether there is a clash or not. However, an experimental study reported in Marotta 1986 reveals that the RS consonant is actually much longer in the context of a clash. That is, if w_2 bears its primary stress on the initial syllable, the consonant is longer than it otherwise would be. To show this, Marotta considers these three types of sentences:

a. sentences in which the context of application of RS is met and where the main stresses of w_1 and w_2 give rise to a clash

b. sentences in which the context of application of RS is met but no arhythmic configuration is created

---

[12]Exceptions to this are silent demibeats, whose physical realization might be a pause (Selkirk 1984, Nespor and Vogel 1989).

c. sentences where the phonological conditions for RS are met (i.e., w_1 ends with a stressed vowel and w_2 begins with a consonant other than the initial s of a consonant cluster) but where w_1 and w_2 do not meet the configurational requirements necessary for RS to apply (see Nespor and Vogel 1982, 1986).

Examples of these sentences are given in (23a,b,c), respectively.

(23) a. Ho visto città *píccole* in Olanda.
      '(I) have seen small cities in Holland.'

  b. Ho visto città *pulíte* in Olanda.
     '(I) have seen clean cities in Holland.'

  c. Ho visto città *davvero* pulite in Olanda.
     '(I) have seen really clean cities in Holland.'

Measurements of the initial consonant of w_2, italicized in the above examples, reveal that while no lengthening takes place at all in cases such as (c), the initial consonant of w_2 is lengthened both in cases of the (a) and of the (b) type. It is lengthened significantly more in (a), where there is a stress clash.

The fourth argument against treating RS as a grid position insertion rule is that the insertion of an X by RS should be able to create a lapse in environments such as that in (24), where the bold 1 represents the grid position putatively inserted by RS.

(24) a. Perché te lo chiedi?
      2 3 **1** 1 1 6
      'Why do you wonder about it?'

  b. Perché glielo dici sotto voce?
     2 3 **1** 1 1 4 1 3 1 6 1
     'Why do you say it to him with such a soft voice?'

The stress readjustment expected in such a case would be the addition of an x in the grid to *te* in (24a) and to *glie* in (24b), resulting in secondary stress on these clitics. However, the fact is that no stress readjustment takes place in these cases. This must be taken as an indication that there is no lapse in the first place, i.e., that no position was ever inserted by RS.

These four arguments essentially preclude the possibility that RS changes the grid configuration. We must thus account for the data of Tuscan Italian in a different way, and I propose to do so within the phonological system presented in this paper, which separates prosodic and rhythmic phonology. My proposal is that RS is a strictly prosodic rule, whose application is blind to the (non)existence of a stress clash. What makes cases of stress clash special is that in exactly these cases, we find the further application of a rhythm rule. The data reported in

Marotta indicate that the particular rule which applies in these cases is Beat Insertion; that is, the extra lengthening of the initial consonant of w_2 is just one more physical correlate of Beat Insertion. In particular, when RS has applied and made the initial consonant of w_2 ambisyllabic (Vogel 1977), the only possible physical realization of Beat Insertion is to make the consonant even longer.

Beat Insertion is, however, not the only remedy for minimal clashes in the context of RS, according to my data.[13] An alternative remedy is Beat Deletion, as shown in the following example, where the final syllable of *sarà* may be destressed.[14]

                       3 4
(25) La mia bici sará vécchia, ma funziona bene.
      → either 2 4 or 3 X 4 (with X=extra lengthening of C)
      'My bike may be old, but it works well.'

Up till now, we have seen how the rhythm rules apply in Tuscan Italian in the case of minimal clashes whose second word undergoes RS. If this proposal is on the right track, the same rhythmic adjustments that apply in the case of RS must also be present in cases of minimal stress clashes that are not in an RS context. For example, we expect to find such adjustments when w_2 starts with a vowel, or with a consonant cluster in which the first consonant is *s*. My Pisa data show that this is indeed the case; where w_2 starts with a cluster beginning with *s*, as in the cases in which w_2 starts with a vowel, either Beat Deletion or Beat Insertion applies, as exemplified in (26).

                    3 4
(26) a. Quel monte sará árso circa un anno fa.
          → either 2 4 or 3 X 4
          'That mountain must have burned about a year ago.'

                    3   4
      b. Ora di sera saró stánca anch'io.
          → either 2 4 or 3 X 4
          'By evening I will be tired as well.'

Beat Insertion has the physical correlate either of a pause or of length-

---

[13]The present analysis is based on a corpus of data consisting of tape recordings of six speakers of the variety of standard Italian spoken in Pisa. The recordings have been transcribed by two trained linguists, working without the aid of machines.

[14]One may ask why no rhythmic adjustment was observed in the context of RS in Nespor and Vogel 1979. The reason, I believe, is that the rule posited there to avoid a clash was not destressing but Stress Retraction. Since the appearance of a stress in an unstressed position is more easily perceived in Italian than is destressing, it was on the basis of that phonetic feature that the analysis was formulated. Most of the examples given there, however, do not have a new stress at all, since no lapse is created by Beat Deletion. Posting a rule of movement rather then two separate rules (deletion and addition) may have obscured the presence of destressing in certain cases.

ening of the last syllable of w_1.[15] Beat Deletion, instead, is realized as destressing.

If we now consider clashes stronger than the minimal one, we can see that in all segmental contexts, Beat Insertion, as predicted, is the only remedy. It applies when w_2 starts with a vowel, with an *s*-initial consonant cluster, or with a single consonant, as illustrated in (27a,b,c), respectively.

(27) a. Come sempre, scriverá X órride poesie.
'As always, (he)'ll write horrible poems.'

b. In questa cittá X stóna un monumento cosí grande.
'In this town, such a big monument is out of place.'

c. Come sempre, si lamenterá X sénza nessuna ragione.
'As always, (he) will complain for no reason.'

The fact that Beat Insertion applies to remedy clashes higher than the minimal clash is predicted in N&V. For minimal clashes, however, only Beat Deletion is predicted in syllable-timed languages. This follows from a clash elimination principle which establishes that material dominated by a grid column higher than that at which the clash is defined is strengthened, whereas material dominated by a grid column of the level at which the minimal clash is defined is weakened.

By contrast, in languages that are not syllable-timed, N&V predict the possibility that minimal clashes are eliminated either by Beat Deletion or by Beat Insertion. From the data we have just seen of Tuscan Italian, a syllable-timed language, we may thus conclude that the availability of two rhythm rules to solve minimal clashes is just one more characteristic of the rhythm component, blurring the line between syllable-timed and non-syllable-timed languages. Since the definition of adjacency of two prominences involved in a clash, and the availability of either one or two mechanisms to solve minimal clashes, are the only parameters according to which languages that are syllable-timed differ from languages that are not (according to N&V's proposal, whose general lines I have assumed), and since Italian and English have been shown not to differ for either, I must conclude that the rhythmic component is the same for the two types of languages. Again, the machine-gun versus morse-code distinction must be accounted for in a subcomponent of the phonology other than the rhythmic one.

4 Conclusions

According to the general framework of phonology assumed in this paper, rules of rhythm apply on the grid. They are not at the interface with

---

[15]Lengthening of the last syllable of w_1 before a word starting with an *s* cluster has also been noted in Nespor and Vogel 1979.

syntax, since it is prosodic—not rhythmic—structure which mediates between syntax and the phonology of rhythm. Prominences represented on the grid reflect (indirectly) the DTEs of prosodic structure, whose constituents are not isomorphic to the syntactic ones. Rhythm thus functions independently of the syntactic structure of a given language.

Separating the phonology of rhythm from prosodic phonology permits the rhythmic component to be viewed as uniform across languages: no distinction needs to be drawn between syllable-timed and stress-timed languages. On the basis of an analysis of Tuscan Italian, I have shown that by having prosodic rules and rhythm rules apply on different structures, a number of complex phenomena obtain a straightforward account.

Finally, I would like to mention that when the phenomena usually described by the prosodic rule of Stress Retraction are instead dealt with in the rhythmic component, we achieve welcome results for the typology of fast speech rules proposed in Nespor 1987. According to this proposal, the prosodic rules whose domain of application enlarges in fast speech correspond to the highest prosodic levels, namely either the intonational phrase or the phonological utterance. Hayes 1984 has pointed out that Stress Retraction in English, a rule confined to the phonological phrase, has a domain of application that broadens in fast speech. If Stress Retraction is indeed a prosodic rule, this observation thus poses a problem for the typology of fast speech rules just mentioned. Within the present framework, however, this observation is not problematic, as the facts mentioned by Hayes can be accounted for in the rhythmic component—for example, by some mechanism of fast speech phonology, of the type proposed for Polish in Rubach and Booij 1985, that flattens certain grid columns in fast speech. What is a clash at levels higher than the minimal one at normal rates of speech might become a minimal clash at higher rates. Beat Deletion would thus apply in fast speech to prominences that would not be in the context of application of the rule at slower rates. I leave the investigation of the influence of the rate of speech on Beat Deletion in English for future research.

13

Syntax, Lexical Rules and Postlexical Rules in Kimatuumbi

DAVID ODDEN

KIMATUUMBI PRESENTS TWO PROBLEMS in syntax-phonology interaction. First, some rules are conditioned by syntax in a way that prosodic structures cannot satisfactorily explain. Second, a number of inter-word rules, which we expect to be postlexical, actually must be lexical. This conclusion requires modifications of claims made in the theory of Lexical Phonology (Kiparsky 1982b, Mohanan 1982) concerning the distinction between lexical and postlexical rules.

1 Syntactically Conditioned Rules

First we will consider rules which refer to syntactic bracketing. (These are discussed at length in Odden 1987, to which the reader is referred for further details.) The relevant rules are Shortening, Phrasal Tone Insertion, Initial Tone Insertion, and Lengthening. Shortening applies to the head of a phrase, i.e., X in X′. Phrasal Tone Insertion takes as its conditioning environment the syntactic seam between two X″ daughters of an X″ phrase. Initial Tone Insertion is blocked from applying across]s but does apply across [s. Finally, Lengthening applies only to members of the same S.

1.1 Shortening

The data in (1) show application of Shortening to a head when followed by a modifier within NP.

(1) kįkóloombe   'cleaning shell'
     kįkólombe chaángu   'my cleaning shell'
     lукaámba   'string'
     lукambá lwalúpuwáanįįké   'string which broke'

The noun must be followed by a modifier in the NP to be shortened. If it is followed by some adjacent verb, or a noun in a different NP, Shortening will not apply.

(2) a. [kįkóloombé]$_{NP}$ [chaapúwaanįįke]$_{VP}$
         shell   broken
         'The shell is broken'

     b. [naampéį [kįkóloombe]$_{NP}$ [Mambóondo]$_{NP}$]$_{VP}$
         I-him-gave shell   Mamboondo
         'I gave Mamboondo the shell'

One might conclude that long vowels shorten if followed by another word in the same phrase. In fact, however, within NP, only a vowel in the head noun of the phrase shortens. Non-nouns, including adjectives such as *kįkeéle* 'red' and determiners such as *cheéne* 'the' or *chootį* 'all,' are not subject to Shortening.

(3) a. [kįkólombe kįkeéle chaángu]$_{NP}$
         shell   red   mine
         'my red shell'
         *kįkólombe kįkelé chaángu

     b. [įkólombe cheéne yanaanchįmá]$_{NP}$
         shells   the   many
         'the many shells'
         *įkólombe chené yanaanchįmá

     c. [makálala gootį gaángu]$_{NP}$
         bird nets all   my
         'all of my bird nets'
         *makálala gotį gaángu

Mere presence in an NP is not sufficient to condition Shortening.

Turning to other phrases, (4) shows that Shortening applies to a verb followed by a range of complements, such as an NP, a headless relative clause, or a purpose clause.

(4) naa-kálaangįte   'I fried'
    naa-kálangįte chóolyá   'I fried food'
    naan-kálangįle yóopáta eéla   'I fried for him to get money'
    naan-kálangįle ywaápalá kálaanga   'I fried for the one who
                                         wants to fry'

As predicted, when the verb is in a subordinate clause (italicized below) and the following word is in a higher sentence, Shortening does not apply, since the next word is not in the VP immediately dominating the verb.

(5) a. [naampéį [[[ywaá-*kaátįte*]VP]S]NP [eéla]NP]VP
       I gave   Rel-cut   money
       'I gave money to the one who cut'

   b. [naayúwįne [[*aakálaanga*]VP]S lįįso]VP
      I-heard   he'll fry   yesterday
      'Yesterday I heard that he will fry'

Shortening can apply to a possessive pronoun, which may also be a phrasal head. When a possessive pronoun is followed by a noun complement, the vowel of the pronoun is shortened.

(6) a. [[kįkólombe]N [chaáke]PP]NP
       'his cleaning shell'

   b. [[kįkólombe]N [chaké Mambóondo]PP]NP
      'Mamboondo's cleaning shell'

Adjectives in Kimatuumbi do not generally constitute the head of a phrase with a modifier . To render 'the very red cleaning shell,' one selects the verb *kéelya* 'to be red,' which may be modified by the adverb *sáána*, giving *kįkólombe chakįkeélįįle sáána* 'the cleaning shell which is very red.'
However, certain adjectives are reduplicated in their plural form:

(7) ngalawá ngeéle   'red dhow'
    ngalawá ngelé ngeéle   'red dhows'

The repetition of the adjective in (7) constitutes an example of an adjective serving as the head of a phrase and followed by a word in its phrase. The vowel of the head is shortened, as predicted.
Shortening thus applies to the head of the phrase, a context which can be concisely represented, assuming an X′ theory of syntax, as follows:

(8) Shortening

$$\overset{\sigma}{\overset{\big|}{\diagup\!\!\!\diagdown}}$$
V   V / [[—]x Y]x′   (Y contains phonetic material)

1.2   Phrasal Tone Insertion

A second rule referring to syntactic bracketing is Phrasal Tone Insertion (PTI). PTI places High tone on the final word in an X″ phrase, when that phrase is followed by an X″ phrase and both are dominated by another X″ phrase—in short, between phrasal daughters of a maximal projection. In (9), PTI locates a High on the word preceding the left VP bracket. We may assume that PTI inserts a floating High tone, which is mapped by an independent tone docking rule to the phrase-final vowel.[1]

(9) Mambóondo   'Mamboondo'
     [Mamboondó]$_{NP}$ [aawį̃le]$_{VP}$ 'Mamboondo died'

     kįyógoyo   'bird (type)'
     [kįyógoyó]$_{NP}$ [chaatį́tuumbuká]$_{VP}$ 'the bird has fallen'

High tone shows up on the last word of the phrase preceding the VP even if it is in a subordinate clause, as illustrated by mpyyngá in (10):

(10) [myndy [[ywaanáampeį̃   mpyyngá]$_{VP}$]$_S$]$_{NP}$ [waabúuį]$_{VP}$
      person   REL-I-him-gave rice   he-left
      'The person I gave rice left'

PTI must both be sensitive to syntactic structure, to determine if High will be inserted, and at the same time fairly blind to syntactic structure—as it is not sensitive to the nature of right brackets intervening between the vowel which actually receives the High tone, and the following phrase. Thus, PTI applies *whenever* a phrasal node immediately precedes VP. The presence of a verb is irrelevant for the rule; as shown in (11), PTI applies to the subject NP before a predicative adjective:

(11) a. [Mamboondóo]$_{NP}$ [[nnaáso]$_{AP}$]$_{VP}$
          M   tall
          'Mamboondo is tall'

      b. [mpyyngá]$_{NP}$ [[waangú]$_{PP}$]$_{VP}$
          rice   mine
          'The rice is mine'

PTI also applies to a subject NP which is separated from the verb by a complementizer, such as kįla 'whenever' or keénda, maná 'if.'

(12) Mamboondó kįla paáįsá   'whenever Mamboondo comes'
      Mamboondó keénda akáteléka   'if Mamboondo is cooking'
      Mamboondó maná atelį̃ké   'if Mamboondo had cooked'

---

[1]Some nouns, such as *Mambóondo* and *mpýýnga*, are lexically toneless, but are assigned High tone on the second vowel of the word in case they are utterance-final, by a rule discussed in Odden 1987. Other nouns, such as *kįyógoyo*, have a lexical High tone which remains in all contexts in the utterance.

Not just the subject NP, but also preposed objects or preverbal adverbs will acquire High tone in this manner. Example (13) shows PTI applying to each member of a series of preverbal phrases.

(13) [Mamboondó]_NP [naammwéenį]_VP
'I saw Mamboondo'

[iįjymá]_AdvP [Mamboondó]_NP [aayíiį]_VP
'On Friday Mamboondo went'

[iįjymá]_AdvP [kįyógoyó]_NP [Mamboondó]_NP [naampéį lį́]_VP
'I did not give Mamboondo a kiyogoyo on Friday'

An embedded VP will not trigger High insertion on a preceding daughter of the matrix clause, as shown in (14a,b):

(14) a. [ngwasa [Mamboondó [aatį́tuumbuká]_VP]_S]_VP
I-think   M.   he-fell
*ngwasá Mamboondó aatį́tuumbuká
'I think that Mamboondo fell'

b. [naamwénį Mamboondo [[[panáapangįté kaásį]_VP]_S]_AP]_VP
I-him-saw M.   when-I-did   work
*naamwénį Mamboondó panáapangįté kaásį
'I saw Mamboondo when I worked'

By this criterion the NP *Mamboondo* receives High in (14a) since it stands within the same S as the VP, but PTI is blocked from applying to *Mamboondo* in (14b) since an S boundary separates it from the VP.

PTI does not require a VP node for its application. The rule also applies when two sentences are conjoined.

(15) a. [maná naantumbįlé Mamboondó]_S [ndywae kyynnwáaya]_S
if   I-him-fell   M.   I-would him-nurse
'If I had fallen on Mamboondo, I would have nursed him'

b. [panáakalangįtée ñamá]_S [Mamboondó akalangae
when-I-fry   meat   M.   he-frying-past

kįndoólo]_S
sweet potato
'When I was frying meat, Mamboondo was frying a sweet potato'

c. [aatwétįį mpyyngá]_S [noobúuka]_S
he-took rice   and-left
'He took rice and then left'

Other cases of PTI support the maximal projection hypothesis. When NPs are conjoined, the first conjunct undergoes PTI.

(16) mpʉʉngá na kịndoólo   'rice and sweet potato'
      ñamá aʉ́ʉ nkaáte   'meat or rice'

Thus another PTI environment where VP nodes are irrelevant is in conjoined expressions, which have the structure $[[\ldots]_{N''} conj[\ldots]_{N''}]_{N''}$.

PTI also applies to the last word of a VP followed by the adverbs *píta* 'very' and *kwaálị* 'perhaps.' A number of phonological and syntactic tests show that these adverbs are sisters of the VP. For example, they may not intervene between the verb and its object, and they do not trigger Shortening on the verb.

(17) a. [nịịmpéendịịlé]$_{VP}$ [píta]$_{AP}$
          *nịịmpendịle píta
          'I really like him'

      b. [nịịmpendị kịtúumbilí]$_{VP}$ [píta]$_{AP}$
          *nịịmpendịlé píta kịtúumbili
          'I really like the monkey'

      c. [aakálaangá]$_{VP}$ [kwaálị]$_{AP}$
          *aakálangá kwaálị
          'perhaps he will fry'

The data seen so far might suggest that the rule applies between two X″ nodes, both dominated by a third phrasal node (X′ or X″). However, this incorrectly predicts that NP before NP in VP undergoes PTI.

(18) [naampéị lị́ [Mamboondo]$_{NP}$ [kịwikilyo]$_{NP}$ [ịịyma]$_{AP}$]$_{VP}$
      I-him-gave neg M.   cover   Friday
      'I didn't give Mamboondo a cover on Friday'
      *naampéị lị́ Mamboondó kịwikilyó ịịyma

There is an additional case where two phrasal nodes may appear inside a phrasal node without triggering PTI, namely, inside of NP, between an AP and a relative clause or possessive.

(19) a. [mwaanaa [ntepéengaʉ]$_{AP}$ [waángu]$_{PP}$]$_{NP}$
          child   wet   mine
          'my wet child'

      b. [mʉndʉʉ [ntepéengaʉ]$_{AP}$ [[ywaálịịlé]$_{VP}$]$_S$]$_{AP}$
          man   wet   REL-eat
          'the wet man who ate'

Example (19) shows that PTI fails to apply between two phrasal nodes when the node immediately dominating them also dominates a lexical head. Assuming that phrases dominating lexical heads are X′ nodes and that phrases dominating X′ nodes are X″ nodes, PTI can thus be formulated as (20).

(20) Phrasal Tone Insertion

$$\emptyset \Rightarrow H/[[\ldots \underline{\quad}]_{Y''}[\ldots]_{Z''}]_{X''}$$

1.3 Initial Tone Insertion

A third rule, Initial Tone Insertion (ITI), is sensitive to very specific syntactic information—it may not apply across]s, although it can cross [s. ITI assigns High to the first mora of a set of morphemes such as *cha-* 'of' or *na-* 'with,' when, as a first approximation, the preceding word has no High tones (the relevant morpheme is italicized).

(21) kịndoló *cha-*Mambóondo   'sweet potato of Mamboondo'
      mpụnga *wá-*Mambóondo   'rice of Mamboondo'
      mabígiị *ga-*bíli   'two beer brewing areas'
      mịtomondo *yị́-*bili   'two ntomoondo trees'

The restrictions on the triggering element pose an interesting problem. As shown in (22), a noun with High anywhere in the stem will block ITI. However, High tones in nominal prefixes do not affect the applicability of ITI.

(22) kị-wikilyo *gánị*   'what type cover'
      kị-túmbili *ganị*   'what type monkey'
      kị́-n'oombe *gánị*   'what type cows'
      kị́-nungungungu *bábili*   'two porcupines'

A verb triggers ITI if it has no stem High, or if the only High is on the first stem vowel.

(23) nị-kụpya *nálụpaáwa*   'I'm stirring with a ladle'
      naa-yíị *kị́soóko*   'I went to the market'
      naatị́-eendá *kụsoóko*   'I went to the market'
      ụnị-telékị *nakịkálaango*   'you should cook for me with the frying pan'

ITI applies in most configurations of words, irrespective of their syntactic relation. Both 'close' and 'distant' syntactic relations are possible between determinant and focus of ITI.

(24) [naammwénị [*pá*luúsi]PP]VP
'I saw him at the well'

[naammụ́lịge [Kịwịịyo]NP [*ná* mboópo]PP]VP
'I killed Kiwiiyo with a machete'

[nịtwetị [kịwikilyo *á*chi]NP]VP
'I took this cover'

However, ITI will not apply if the lefthand word is in an embedded clause and the focal morpheme (*na*) is in the higher clause.

(25) naammúlį̂ge [mųndų [[ywaátwetį̂į̂ ñama]$_{VP}$]$_S$]$_{NP}$
I-him-killed   person   REL-took meat

[*na* mboópo]$_{PP}$
with machete
'With a machete I killed the man who took the meat'
∗naammúlį̂ge [mųndų [[ywaátwetį̂į̂ ñama]$_{VP}$]$_S$ [*ná* mboópo]$_{PP}$

It might seem that ITI applies only to words in the same minimal S. However, when the determinant is in a higher clause and the focus is in a subordinate clause, ITI applies down into the embedded clause, as shown below:

(26) a. [naammwénį̂ [*ká*-apangá   kaásį̂]$_S$]$_{VP}$
         I-him-saw   when-he-do work
         'I saw him when he was working'

      b. [nyaamį̂nį̂ [*cháangú* chaaóbį̂te]$_S$]$_{VP}$
         I-expect   mine   it-lost
         'I expect mine is lost'

The generalization is that ITI applies across a lefthand S-bracket, but not across a righthand S-bracket. While Shortening and PTI are conditioned by the general relational nature (X′ and X″) of syntactic constituent structure, ITI is subject to a different syntactic constraint: it may not cross a righthand S-bracket.

(27) Initial Tone Insertion

$\emptyset \Rightarrow$ H/[$_{stem}$(H)X___   (X contains no]$_S$ brackets)

1.4 Lengthening

This last rule lengthens a vowel before a noun stem containing exactly two moras, and applies only to members of the same minimal S. Lengthening is illustrated in (28), where various object nouns follow the verb, as well as another object noun.

(28) aatwét*į̂į̂* ñáma   'he took meat'
      naammwén*į̂į̂* píli   'I saw a puff adder'
      naammúlįg*ee* mbaká   'I killed a cat'
      naampéį̂ Mamboond*oo* chúpa 'I gave Mamboondo a bottle'

Trisyllabic stems and disyllabic stems with long vowels do not cause lengthening, nor do bimoraic verbs and adjectives.

(29) naammwén*į̂* ñoóme   'I saw a cat'   ∗naammwénį̂į̂ ñoóme
      naatwét*į̂* ngalawá   'I took a canoe'   ∗naatwétį̂į̂ ngalawá
      ngalaw*á* ngulú   'large canoe'   ∗ngalawáa ngulú
      mbal*a* téma   'I want to chop'   ∗mbalaa téma

Lengthening also applies to the Level 3 locative prefixes *pa-*, *mụ-*, *kụ* and the copular prefix *nga-* 'it is,' but not to noun class prefixes (e.g., *kị-*), which, as we will shortly see, are added at Level 2.

(30) p*aa*-chụpa   'at the bottle'
     ng*aa*-mbaká   'it is a cat'
     k*ị*-líbe   'thing (Cl. 7)'   *kịị-líbe

Example (31) shows that Lengthening is blocked when the determinant and focus belong to different minimal S's.

(31) [nịyụwịne [mbaká aawị̣le]s]vp
     I-heard   cat   died
     *nịyụwịnee mbaká aawị̣le
     'I heard that the cat died'

We may conclude that, like ITI, Lengthening is blocked by S brackets.

(32) Lengthening

$$\mu \rightarrow \mu\mu / \_\_\, X[\mu\mu \quad]_\omega \qquad \text{(X contains neither]s, nor [s,}$$
$$\qquad\qquad\; [\text{noun}] \qquad\qquad \text{nor any segments)}$$

2   Lexical and Postlexical Rules

If the model of grammar proposed in Lexical Phonology is correct, the sandhi rules of the preceding section must be part of the postlexical phonology. This follows from the assumption that syntax is ordered between lexical and postlexical phonology.

Since the two phonological modules share many fundamental properties (the condition against crossing lines, a theory of phonological features and feature geometry, etc.), it is important to show that at least some differences exist between them. If lexical and postlexical phonology have no detectable differences, then the claim that there are two phonological modules is unsupported, and Occam's Razor demands elimination of the distinction.

Pulleyblank 1986 summarizes a number of properties which distinguish the modules (see also Kiparsky 1982b, 1985b; Mohanan 1982, 1986). For example, lexical rules may be sensitive to morphological or lexical properties, may apply cyclically, and cannot see the output of syntax, while postlexical rules are insensitive to morphological or lexical properties, and do not apply cyclically. However, work by Kaisse 1985 and others casts doubt on the proposition that this list of properties is correct, since some apparently postlexical rules have exceptions, are sensitive to morphological conditions, or apply cyclically. Kaisse proposes that the postlexical component should be divided into two subparts, P1 and P2, where P2 has the usual properties of postlexical phonology and P1 has the properties of lexical phonology, plus access to the output of syntax. The division of postlexical phonology into two components means that the sole property distinguishing lexical and postlexical phonology is access to the output of syntax. The remaining properties merely distinguish subcomponents of postlexical phonology.

This section shows that the standard model of Lexical Phonology is wrong in its treatment of lexical and postlexical rules. The rules discussed in the previous section must be ordered before lexical rules, and have other properties typical of lexical rules, arguing that they are lexical rules. Access to syntactic structure is not, therefore, a sufficient condition for consigning a rule to the postlexical component. The alternative proposed here, the Lexical Sandhi (LS) Theory, is that syntactic structures are in place throughout phonology and that lexical and postlexical rules have access to these structures. Application between words is not diagnostic of the lexical-postlexical distinction. Instead, sensitivity to nonphonological information, such as lexical properties, morphological structure, or labelled syntactic structure, constitute grounds for assigning a rule to the lexicon. The remaining traditional criteria for distinguishing lexical and postlexical rules are retained. Postlexical phonology contains only rules which are blind to nonphonological structures.

If lexical rules can see surrounding syntactic structure, we must ask what information from other words is available to lexical rules. It is assumed here that lexical rules see only the 'lexical form' of surrounding words, where lexical form is the shape a word takes after the application of obligatory lexical rules not conditioned by syntax. (This is necessary to resolve an ordering paradox caused by Shortening and Lengthening, both of which are lexical rules requiring access to information derived by syntax.) It will also be shown that morphological structure of neighboring words must be available to lexical rules.

Level 1 morphology in Kimatuumbi is concerned with stem formation, stems being composed of a root, extensions and the final vowel suffix. In Level 2, verbs add object markers, tense-aspect prefixes, and subject prefixes; nouns add noun class prefixes. Level 3 also contributes certain nominal prefixes, such as the locative prefixes ky- or pa-.

(33)   Level 3   Level 2   Level 1

$$
\left[\begin{array}{l} \text{pa} \\ \text{loc} \end{array} \left[\begin{array}{l} \text{k\i} \\ N \; Cl \end{array} \left[\begin{array}{ll} \text{tyatyaak-\i k-\i y} & \text{o} \\ \textit{root appl-caus} & FV \end{array} \right] \right] \right]
$$
'at the plastering tool'

We now turn to the interaction between sandhi rules and other lexical rules.

2.1   Glide Formation

The Glide Formation rule affects prevocalic y and $\i$. The noun prefixes $l\i$- (Cl. 5), $l y$- (Cl. 11), $k\i$- (Cl. 7) and $\i$- (Cl. 8) and the locative prefixes ky-

and *mʋ-* have underlying high vowels. If the following noun morpheme is vowel-initial, the prefix vowel desyllabifies, lengthening the following vowel.

(34) mị-kaáte   'loaves'   my-oótó   'fires'
     lị-kʋn'ʋ́ʋ́nda   'filtered beer'   ly-oowá   'beehive'
     kị-kálaango   'frying pan'   ky-ʋʋ́lá   'frog'
     mʋ-kịkálaango   'in the frying   mw-ịịkálaango   'in the frying
                        pan'   pans'
     kʋ-sʋʋ́le   'to school'   kw-ịịsíwá   'to the islands'

By contrast, when the stems in (34) are preceded by no prefix or by /a/, their initial vowel is phonetically short.

(35) ma-otó   'large fires'   ị-síwa   'islands'
     ka-ʋ́lá   'small frog'   ị-kálaango   'frying pans'
     ma-owá   'beehives'

Stems with underlying long vowels are given in (36), illustrating that compensatory lengthening has no detectable effect on long vowels.

(36) mw-eémbe   'mango tree'   eémbe   'mango fruit'
     my-eémbe   'mango trees'   ka-eémbe   'small mango tree'
     lw-áanjʋ́   'firewood piece'   aanjʋ́   'firewood'
     ky-ʋ́ʋndó   'knot'   ma-ʋ́ʋndó   'large knots'

Other morphological combinations yield environments for Glide Formation. The vowels of verbal *tʋ-* and *nị-* glide before a V-initial object prefix or the tense prefix -*a-*. When the applied suffix -*ị-* precedes the reciprocal -*an-*, it becomes a glide, -*an-* being compensatorily lengthened.

(37) tw-aa-túumbwịịke   'we fell'   /tʋ-a-túumbu-ị-k-e/
     ny-ʋʋ-twéetị   'I took it (Cl. 3)'   /nị-ʋ-twéetị/
     télek-y-aan-a   'to cut for each other'   /télek-ị-an-a/

A further condition on Glide Formation is that a high vowel does not desyllabify if it is long. The fact that vowel length may derive from application of Glide Formation itself indicates that the rule iterates from left to right.

(38) mʋʋ-até   'in the banana hands'
     (cf. *mwaanjʋ́*   'in the firewood' from /mʋ-aanjʋ́/)

     mwịịʋté   'you should pull them (Cl. 9)' (from /mʋ-ị-ʋté/)
     (cf. *bayʋʋté*   'they should pull them (Cl. 9)' (from /ba-ị-ʋté/))

If the prevocalic high vowel is not in the first syllable, Glide Formation is optional. The object prefixes *tʋ-* 'us,' *nị-* 'me' and *kị-* 'it (Cl. 7)' may remain syllabic before another vowel when preceded by the infinitive prefix *kʋ-* or the subject prefix *a-* 'he'; or the high vowel may undergo Glide Formation. Thus two variants are possible, as shown below:

(39) kʉ-nɪ-áandɪka   'to write me'   kʉ-ny-áandɪka
     kʉ-tʉ-ákya   'to hunt for us'   kʉ-tw-aákya
     aa-lʉ-ásɪɪme   'he borrowed it (11)'   aa-lw-aásɪɪme

There is also a tonal condition on the rule: a vowel with High tone does not glide before a long vowel, although it will before a short vowel. The locative prefix, mʉ-, illustrates this condition:

(40) nɪɪbwenɪ mʉ́-aanjʉ́   'I saw it in the firewood'
     *nɪɪbwenɪ mwáanjʉ́

     nɪɪbwenɪ mw-ɪ̣́-kálaango   'I saw it in the frying pans'
     /nɪɪbwenɪ mʉ́-ɪ-kálaango/

The tone and length conditions on the rule are formalized below with angled brackets, lacking a better expression:

(41) ⟨σ⟩ₐ   ⟨H⟩_b   ⟨optional⟩ₐ
       |
       V   V ⟨]_σ⟩_b
       ‡   Glide Formation (revised)
     [+high]

We now turn to the lexical status of Glide Formation. The most compelling argument for lexicality is that the rule is cyclic.

When Glide Formation is applicable at multiple points in a string as in (38), it applies left to right; underlying mʉ-ɪ-ʉté becomes mwɪɪ̣ʉté. In this case the vowels involved are both added at Level 2. Now consider (42), where a Level 3 locative prefix precedes a Level 2 vowel initial noun class prefix, which is itself followed by a stem vowel.

(42) [mʉ [ɪ-úlá]]   →   mʉyuúlá   'in the frogs'
     [kʉ [ɪ-aáɪ]]   →   kʉyaáɪ   'to the cooking pots'

This phonological structure is analogous to that of the example in (38), yet in (42) the *second* vowel of the sequence glides. The problem is to explain the contrast between /mʉ-ɪ-ʉté/, which becomes mwɪɪ̣ʉté, and /mʉ-ɪ-úlá/, which becomes mʉyuúlá. The relevant distinction, I submit, is the difference in morphological structure.

In mʉ-ɪ-ʉté, the vowel sequence is encountered on the same level, and Glide Formation applies to the first of the vowels. This is not the case for mʉyuúlá. At Level 2, where the class prefix is attached to the stem, Glide Formation applies to the only prevocalic high vowel at that level, giving yuúlá. At the next level, a prefix is added to yuúlá, but Glide Formation can no longer apply; mʉ- is not prevocalic.

(43) a. mʉ-ɪ-ʉte   Output of L2 morphology
        mwɪɪ̣ʉte   Glide Formation

b. į-úlá   Output of L2 morphology
   yuúla   Glide Formation
   mųyuúlá   Output of L3 morphology
   N/A   Glide Formation

If Glide Formation were truly postlexical, it would be blind to the difference between Level 2 and Level 3, and all vowel sequences would incorrectly be treated alike.

Another argument for the cyclicity of Glide Formation comes from the optionality of the rule when the vowel is preceded by any syllable, as in (39). Given this, the data in (44) are problematic, since the prefixes *lų*- and *kį*- must undergo the rule. The crucial difference between (44) and (39) is that (39) involves prefix sequences at the same level, whereas (44) involves prefixes at different levels.

(44) *[pa [lų-áanjų́]] → (oblig)   palwáanjų́   'at the firewood'
     *[mų [kį-átį́]] → (oblig)   mųkyaátį́   'on the family farm'

The cyclicity of Glide Formation explains the contrast between *palwáanjų́* and *aalųáandįįke*, which alternates with *aalwáandįįke*. When a prefix is preceded by another syllable at its own level, as in *aalųáandįįke*, application of Glide Formation to *lų*- is optional. In *palwáanjų́*, where gliding is obligatory, the prefix *lų*- is added at Level 2. It is not preceded by any syllable at that level. Glide Formation must apply, since the condition licensing optionality in the rule is missing. At Level 3 a locative prefix is added to the noun, but Glide Formation has already applied obligatorily on the earlier level.

2.2 Rule Interaction

Now consider the interaction between Shortening and lexical rules. Shortening must precede Glide Formation, since Shortening does not apply to long vowels created by Glide Formation, as in (45). A more accurate generalization is that Shortening does not apply to the output of Glide Formation at Levels 2 or 3.

(45) mų-aké lį́   →   mwaaké lį́
     'you should not hunt'   *mwaké lį́

     kį-andaangyo chaángu →   kyaandangyo cháangú
     'my forest farm'   *kyandangyo cháangú

This is the first manifestation of the problem; the lexical rule of Glide Formation follows the sandhi rule of Shortening. In LS theory, these facts can be explained by assigning Shortening to the lexical component. It is important to note that this ordering argument involves the application of Glide Formation at Levels 2 and 3. Glide Formation also applies, at Level 1, to the combination of the applied suffix -*į*- and the reciprocal suffix -*an*- in (46).

(46) ák-a   'to net-hunt'
     ák-an-a   'to net-hunt each other'
     ák-y-aan-a   'to net-hunt for each other' (/ak-i-an-a/)

Long vowels created by Glide Formation at Level 1 shorten in (47), in contrast to long vowels created at Levels 2 and 3. Glide Formation applies on two levels in underlying tu-ak-i-an-a ituúmbili; at Level 1, to the stem-internal sequence ia, and at Level 2 to the prefix-plus-stem sequence ua. As shown by surface twaakyana ituúmbili, the long vowel derived by Glide Formation at Level 1 shortens, but the long vowel derived by Glide Formation at Level 2 does not.

(47) /tu-ak-i-an-a ituúmbili/   →   twaakyana ituúmbili
     'we net-hunt monkeys for each other'

     /tu-a-mámaanduile ñuúmba/   →   twaamámandwile ñuúmba
     'we plastered a house'

Thus, Level 1 Glide Formation feeds Shortening, but Level 2 Glide Formation counterfeeds Shortening. The paradox evaporates if Shortening is assigned to the lexical phonology, is ordered after Glide Formation, and applies only at Level 1.

(48) ak-i-an-a ituúmbili   Output of Level 1 morphology
     akyaana ituúmbili   Glide Formation
     akyana ituúmbili   Shortening
     tu-akyana ituúmbili   Output of Level 2 morphology
     twaakyana ituúmbili   Glide Formation

Initial Tone Insertion, which assigns High to certain morphemes if the preceding word has no High, must be lexical as well. A High in the stem of the preceding word blocks ITI, but a High in the prefix of the preceding word does not.

(49) niná+kalaanga pámwoóto lí   'I haven't yet fried at the fire'
     kí+n'ombe bályu   'those cows'

ITI is sensitive to lexical information, namely the class of elements undergoing the rule. Finally, the rule takes syntax as part of its conditioning. In LS theory, the rule must therefore be lexical. Facts of ordering finish the proof. Recall that a High-toned vowel cannot glide before a long vowel. Now consider (50), where the prefix ku-, one of the morphemes undergoing ITI, precedes a long vowel.

(50) utilí kuaanjú → utilí kwaanjú   'you should run to the firewood'
     utilí kuaanjú → utilí kúaanjú   'you ran to the firewood'

The High assigned to ku- by ITI determines whether Glide Formation can apply before a long vowel—if the prefix takes a High tone, then it cannot glide. ITI precedes the lexical rule of Glide Formation, so ITI must also be lexical.

The constraint on information available in the lexicon from other words allows rules access to the lexical form of surrounding words. This predicts that in a sequence of words XY, no lexical rule applying to word X has access to the result of sandhi rules, such as Shortening, applying to Y. A striking demonstration of this claim comes from the interaction between Shortening and Lengthening.

Lengthening lengthens a vowel before a noun stem which contains two moras. Verbs and adjectives do not trigger Lengthening, which suggests that the rule is lexical. It is also sensitive to the level of prefixes, failing to apply to Level 2 prefixes. The rule is partially triggered by syntax, and has lexical exceptions.

(51) nga-ndy̨sí   'they are batches of yarn'
     twaammy̨lįge yaní   'we killed a monkey'
     aatwétį sįlá   'he took the weapon'

The interaction of Lengthening and Glide Formation completes the proof that Lengthening is lexical. The relevant structures involve bimoraic noun stems which are vowel-initial, and are preceded by a prefix with a high vowel.

(52) /my̨-até/   →   my̨y̨até   'in the banana hand'   (*mwaaté)
     /ky̨-ígo/   →   ky̨y̨ígo   'to the kidney'   (*kwįígo)
     /ky̨-úbi/   →   ky̨y̨úbi   'to the leopard'   (*kwuúbi)

Lengthening must precede Glide Formation. The prefix, which could undergo either rule, in fact lengthens, thereby blocking Glide Formation. Since Lengthening precedes Glide Formation and Glide Formation is lexical, Lengthening is lexical.

Now consider Lengthening and sandhi rules. LS theory correctly predicts that Lengthening does not bleed itself by lengthening one vowel and destroying the environment for reapplication of the rule, since LS rules have access only to the lexical form of neighboring words.

(53) naampéįį mbakáa píli
     'I gave the cat a puff adder'

     Mamboondóo chy̨páa mby̨yá baapéya lį́
     'Grandma will never give Mamboondo the bottle'

Lengthening applies to each word in a sequence of words followed by a bimoraic noun stem. Applying Lengthening to *mbaká* gives a trimoraic noun, a structure which could not trigger Lengthening in *naampéį*. As a lexical sandhi rule, Lengthening has no access to the changed moraic structure of the following word.

What about Lengthening and Shortening? Since Lengthening is in Level 3 and Shortening is in Level 1, Shortening cannot apply to long vowels derived by Lengthening. However, Shortening could create the structures which condition Lengthening. Yet as the data in (54) show, bimoraic structures created by Shortening do not lengthening the preceding vowel.

(54) apala mbopó yaángu   'he wants my machete'   /mboópo/
      *apalaa mbopó yaángu
      pambopó yaángu   'at my machete'
      *paambopó yaángu

Since Shortening creates the structure which triggers Lengthening and applies early, it should create new triggers for Lengthening. But since the lexical form of a word does not include the effect of Shortening, the lexical form of both *mbopó* and *mboópo* is *mboópo*, which does not trigger Lengthening.

While LS theory rejects one axiom of Lexical Phonology, it strengthens the theory in other ways, since the dichotomy between lexical and postlexical rules can be sharpened. This suggests reevaluation of cases where supposedly postlexical rules have exceptions, apply cyclically, or obey the Strict Cycle Condition. Such rules should in LS theory be lexical rules, since they are sensitive to nonphonological conditions.

2.3   Precompilation

Hayes (this volume), discussing similar problems, proposes a modification of phonological theory, namely precompilation theory, which accounts for the problems which LS theory handles. The theories are similar in empirical predictions, but certain considerations favor LS over precompilation theory. In precompilation theory, languages define sets of instantiation frames which may serve as the context for lexical phonological rules. Kimatuumbi Shortening is formulated as follows.

(55) $VV \rightarrow V \, / \, [\, \cdots \, \_\_ \, \cdots \,]_{[\text{Frame 1}]}$

Frame 1 is then defined as:

(56) Frame 1: $[\, \cdots [\, \_\_ \,]_X \, Y \,]_{X'} \; Y \neq \emptyset$

Two derivations are generated. The derivation where Frame 1 rules apply will generate the Frame 1 allomorph, and the other where these rules do not apply, generates the elsewhere form. Later, the appropriate allomorph is selected.

Frame definitions may include phonological information from neighboring words. Kimatuumbi Lengthening would apply in Frame 2:

(57) $V \rightarrow VV \, / \, \_\_ \,]_{[\text{Frame2}]}$

Frame 2 is defined as follows.

(58) Frame 2: $\_\_ \, X \, [\mu\mu]_{\text{noun stem}}$ (X does not cross S)

LS and precompilation theories are thus identical in the kind of information made available to lexical rules; the difference is that in precompilation theory, this information is only indirectly accessible.

The derivation of *naampéįį mbakáa píli* 'I gave the cat a puff adder' points out another similarity between the theories. (Details of the algorithm for lexical insertion are not given, so these interpretations are my own.) The input to phonological instantiation would be:

(59) [[[666]ᵥ [[42]ₙ]ₙₚ [[11]ₙ]ₙₚ]ᵥₚ]ₛ

where 666 is *naampéį* ∼ *naampéįį*, 42 is *mbaká* ∼ *mbakáa*, and 11 is *píli* ∼ *pílii*. We begin by inserting an allomorph of 666. To know which frame to select, we consult the phonological structure of the following word. But this information is not available, since lexical item 42 has not been inserted.

Now let us begin by inserting lexical item 11. It is not followed by anything, so *píli* is inserted. Word 42 is followed by a disyllabic noun stem, which defines Frame 2, so the variant *mbakáa* of 42 is inserted. Now 666 is followed by a trimoraic noun stem, which is inconsistent with Frame 2. Therefore the allomorph *naampéį* is inserted, yielding **naampéį mbakáa píli*.

A correct derivation requires that rules of instantiation scan the phonological structure of neighboring words prior to phonological instantiation of those words. We can constrain precompilation theory if we limit phonological instantiation to seeing phonological properties of the 'elsewhere' allomorph of neighboring words. This constraint is equivalent to the constraint in LS theory that only the lexical form is available to lexical sandhi rules.

Since precompilation theory emulates LS theory so well, the theories may be notational variants. Hayes cites two possible differences which argue for precompilation theory. First, in precompilation theory, no phonological rules have direct access to syntactic structures. Second, LS theory allows a cyclic rule to see information not morphologically part of that cycle.

The argument against direct access to syntax has force only if the precompilation reanalysis is not a notational translation of direct reference to syntax. Precompilation theory works if the rule is lexical, and thus precludes postlexical rules referring to syntax. However, the same constraint is imposed in LS theory. The second criticism provides an aesthetic argument against LS theory, but not an empirical argument. While LS theory allows direct access to material added on an 'outer cycle' (syntactic structures), precompilation allows access to the same information, mediated through frame definitions. Until a hypothetical example is constructed showing that one theory allows derivations which are impossible in the other theory on this point, the only possible comparisons are based on theoretical elegance.

A small difference between the theories is the set of criteria for assigning a rule to the lexical versus postlexical phonology. In LS theory, rules with lexical exceptions or morphological conditions must be lexical, but no such claim is made in precompilation theory. (However, Hayes does use lexical marking as evidence for the lexicality of certain rules.) An attempt at falsifying precompilation theory might proceed as follows. Suppose a sandhi rule has lexical and morphological conditions, but cannot be proven to be cyclic (a criterion held to necessitate assignment to the lexicon). With weak criteria for lexicality, the rule might be either lexical or postlexical. Suppose, further, that the rule spreads a feature between words. Such a rule could not be precompiled, thus could not be lexical: the supposed properties of precompiled rules thus become criterial in assigning a rule to postlexical phonology. (This problem actually does arise; see below.) If the criteria for assignment to lexical versus postlexical phonology are very strong, precompilation theory is more readily falsified, and more interesting. If the criteria are weak, precompilation theory is less falsifiable, and less interesting.

There are no knock-down arguments for LS versus precompilation theory. However, a number of technical problems tip the scales in favor of LS theory. The first problem is the computational complexity deriving from interactions of frame-triggered rules. Frames may overlap—for example, Kimatuumbi *káata ñáma* becomes *kátaa ñáma* 'to cut meat' by Shortening (F1) and Lengthening (F2).

(60)

	+F1,−F2	+F1,+F2	−F1,+F2	−F1,−F2	
	káta	káta	N/A	N/A	Shortening
	N/A	kátaa	káataa	N/A	Lengthening

The correct allomorph is the [+F1,+F2] allomorph. The derivation of each word in a language with one instantiation frame entails two parallel derivations. Having two instantiation frames entails four parallel derivations, and n frames entail 2^n derivations. LS theory requires only one derivation for each word.

Precompiled rules should not recognize contextual exceptions in surrounding words. The triggering word is not present in the lexical phonology, so exceptionality properties of the word are not visible. However, such exceptions do exist for Lengthening (see (51)).

Finally, precompilation theory has a hard time formalizing a rule spreading a feature from one word to another. The M-to-R rule of Clements 1978 may be a case. In Ewe, Mid tone becomes Raised between High tones, subject to syntactic conditions. Mid tone is [+hi,−up], Raised is [+hi,+up], and High is [−hi,+up]. The assimilatory nature of the rule is clear—Mid absorbs the surrounding upper register (it is immaterial to the argument whether the leftmost or the rightmost register feature spreads).

(61)   +up   −up   +up
       |
       +hi

The rule applies to /ātyíkē dzrágé/ and /ēkpé mēgbé/ to give *ātyíkē dzrágé*
and *ēkpé mēgbé* (which surface as *atyíkē dzrăgé* and *èkpē mēgbé*, by other
rules). Since a feature spreads from a neighboring word, the rule cannot
be precompiled, and thus ought not to be lexical. However, the rule has
lexical exceptions and is syntactically conditioned (Kaisse 1985, Clements
1978), suggesting that it is indeed lexical.

Another spreading rule which Hayes would probably consider to be
precompiled comes from Kipare, discussed in Odden 1985, 1986a and
Schlindwein 1985. The rule spreads High leftward when preceded by HL,
yielding downstep.

(62) kílá kahándi   → kílá ! káhándi   'each knife'
     vána vé!kírashínjiya → vá!ná vé!kírashínjiya   'the children were
                                                     sleeping'
     tetúfíníkíre shúve   → tetúfíníkí!ré shúve   'we didn't cover
                                                     the baboon'

Rule (63) accounts for the following alternations:

(63)   H   L   H
       ‡͑
       V

Various complications suggest that the rule is lexical. It will not apply
to the Low tone of a verb root if the preceding High tone is in the subject
prefix (64a). The High tone of the preposition *hé* cannot serve as the lefthand context for the rule (64b). The rule does not apply to the Low tone
of a subject prefix preceded and followed by High tones (64c). Finally,
the rule will not spread High tone from a subject prefix to a preceding
noun across a sentence bracket (64d). Furthermore, speakers apply the
rule in slow, syllable-by-syllable speech, suggesting that they are aware of
its effect (a similar argument has been used to support the lexicality of
Low Tone Raising in Hausa).

(64) a. ále nkhú!kú   'he should eat chicken'
     b. hé kisíma   'in the well'
     c. mghosí esí!kóma   'the man isn't killing'
     d. nemvóniye Gurísha ékíjenga nyumbá   'I saw Gurisha building
                                                 a house'

Whether these rules are taken to be lexical in precompilation theory,
hence precompiled, depends largely on the ultimate criteria for assigning
rules to lexical phonology. In LS theory, nonphonological information is
required, so they must be lexical.

14

Word-Internal Phrase
Boundary in Japanese
WILLIAM J. POSER

IN THE DIVERSITY OF views of how phrasal phonological rules refer
to morphosyntactic information, one of the few ideas that is common to
virtually all is that the domains of phrasal rules are necessarily no smaller
than the word. I present here what appears to be a solid counterexample
to this belief, namely a set of prefixes that are followed by a minor phrase
boundary, together with a brief discussion of the implications of this fact.

1 Properties of Japanese Minor Phrases

In order to appreciate the evidence of the following section, it is necessary
to have some understanding of the tonal system of Standard Japanese.
The smallest unit in Japanese to have a tonal pattern is the 'minor phrase.'
Each minor phrase has a basic tonal pattern which we may schematize as
'LH(L)'; that is to say, it begins Low, rises to High, and continues there,
until at some point it may fall again to a Low pitch.

The only lexically distinctive property is the location of the fall from
High to Low. This fall may occur on any syllable, or it may never occur
at all. The syllable after whose first mora the fall occurs is said to be
accented. If there is no fall, the word is said to be unaccented. A minor
phrase has at most one accent; if it is composed of more than one word,
as is often the case, then the leftmost lexical accent is realized, a process
which I will refer to as Accent Resolution.

I am grateful to Koichi Tateishi and Yo Matsumoto for discussion of these issues.
This research was supported in part by a grant from the System Development Foundation to the Center for the Study of Language and Information, Stanford University.

The non-distinctive initial rise is in principle always present, but its phonetic realization is variable. If the accent falls on the first syllable, there is no Low plateau but only a short rise at the beginning of the minor phrase, unless the minor phrase is preceded by another minor phrase, in which case the initial Low may be realized as a Low plateau at the end of the preceding minor phrase.[1]

2   Aoyagi Prefixes

The prefixes that are of interest to us, and their peculiar phonological properties, were first described by Aoyagi 1969, whence I will refer to them as Aoyagi prefixes. Representative examples of words formed with these prefixes are given in (1).[2] The pitch contour of the examples is shown schematically by the under- and over-lines.[3]

(1) Words Formed with Aoyagi Prefixes

Prefix	Gloss	Example	Gloss
móto	'former'	*mo̅todaiziN*	'former minister'
zéN	'former'	*ze̅Nsyusyoo*	'former Prime Minister'
hí	'un-'	*hi̅gooriteki*	'illogical'
kí	'your' (honorific/ formal)	*ki̅syokaN*	'your letter'
hóN	'this, the present'	*ho̅Nkaigi*	'this conference here'

The peculiarity of these words lies in the fact that they exhibit HLH or HLHL tone patterns, which are not possible for single minor phrases. In the first example, the fall from *mo* to *to* indicates the presence of an accent on the first syllable. Consequently, if we were dealing with a single minor phrase, we would expect everything thereafter to be Low. But in fact the pitch rises again and then falls, indicating the presence of a second accent on *dai,* as if Accent Resolution had failed to apply. The remaining examples are similar, only there is no second accent. The pitch falls on the accented syllables, e.g., *zeN* in the second example, but rather than

---

[1]Most of this description of Japanese pitch accent is well-known, though it is common to see the word rather than the minor phrase described as the unit possessed of a tone pattern. Most accounts claim that there is no initial Low tone if the accent falls on the first syllable or if the first syllable contains more than one sonorant mora. However, I have given evidence (Poser 1984) that in principle the initial Low is always present. See Pierrehumbert and Beckman 1986 for additional discussion of the status of the initial Low and its variable realization.

[2]The representation is approximately phonemic. An acute accent indicates the location of the underlying pitch accent.

[3]The rise that may occur at the beginning of an initial-accented word is not shown.

staying Low as expected, it rises again and remains High. Moreover, the fact that the pitch does not rise again on these examples until the second mora of the stem indicates the presence of the initial Low.

The prefixes illustrated by no means exhaust the list of Aoyagi Prefixes. A more extensive list is given in (2).

(2) A Partial List of Aoyagi Prefixes

Prefix	Gloss
boo	'a certain'
doo	'above-mentioned'
gen	'original'
han	'anti-'
han	'pan-'
hi	'un-'
hon	'the present'
ki	'your' (formal)
ko	'deceased'
moto	'former'
tai	'anti-'
tyoo	'ultra-'
zen	'former'
zen	'all'

The peculiar tone patterns of these prefixes are best explained on the assumption that they are followed by a minor phrase boundary. This immediately explains the possibility of there being two accents—the Accent Resolution rule is minor phrase-level and so will not apply. It also explains the presence of the Low region between the Highs in all of the examples—this is the minor phrase-initial Low.[4]

An alternative would be to attribute the peculiar tone patterns directly to the tonal properties of these prefixes, assuming that they are unusual in contributing a final Low tone which is realized at the boundary. But this would require lexical assignment of Low tone, which is otherwise unnecessary in Standard Japanese, and in any case would not explain the failure of Accent Reduction, an otherwise exceptionless rule, to apply.

In sum, the tone patterns induced by Aoyagi prefixes suggest that they belong to a different minor phrase from the stem to which they attach.

3 Aoyagi Prefixes are Prefixes

Although I have referred to these morphemes as prefixes, as do those who have previously discussed them (Aoyagi 1969, Kageyama 1982) and

---

[4]Kageyama 1982 contains a brief discussion of these prefixes in which he independently suggests that these prefixes are followed by a minor phrase boundary. Thanks to Yo Matsumoto for drawing my attention to Kageyama's discussion.

Japanese dictionaries, we must entertain the possibility that this characterization is incorrect and that they are really independent words, in which case the fact that they are followed by a minor phrase boundary will hardly be surprising. Although to my knowledge no evidence that these actually are prefixes has ever been given, there is good reason to believe that this characterization is correct.

Much of the time when we try to argue that something is part of a word we appeal to phonological criteria—does it trigger or undergo a word-level rule? I know of no double-edged tests for lexical status in Japanese, but there are a number of single-edged tests, such as induction of accent on a following morpheme, triggering of voicing assimilation, or triggering of *rendaku*, the voicing of the initial obstruent of the second member of a compound. The Aoyagi prefixes pass none of these tests, but since they are single-edged this does not constitute evidence against their being prefixes.

Indeed, failure to undergo word-level phonological rules is exactly what we should expect given the presence of a minor phrase boundary. If it is correct that minor phrases are composed of phonological words, then processes that are restricted to phonological words should not apply across a minor phrase boundary.[5]

However, there are a variety of other grounds for believing that Aoyagi prefixes are indeed lexically attached. The first is that they are inseparable from the following stem, unlike other pre-nominal modifiers.

Consider, for example, the words *kidaigaku* 'your university' and *motodaiziN* 'former minister,' each of which contains an Aoyagi prefix. As example (3) shows, the adjective *yuumei* 'famous' cannot intervene between the prefix *ki* and *daigaku*. Similarly, as examples (4) and (5) show, neither *yuumei* nor the adjective *erai* 'distinguished' can intervene between the prefix *moto* and the *daiziN*.

(3)*ki   yuumei na   daigaku
   your famous copula university
   'your famous university'

(4)*moto yuumei na   daizin
   former famous copula minister
   'a formerly famous minister'

(5)*moto erai   daizin
   former distinguished minister
   'a formerly distinguished minister'

These examples illustrate the larger generalization that no independent word can intervene between an Aoyagi prefix and the stem to which

---

[5]Of course, phonological rules that are lexical in the sense of Lexical Phonology (Kiparsky 1982a; Mohanan 1982, 1986 may still apply to the extent that they are not restricted to phonological words.

it attaches. In this the Aoyagi prefixes contrast with other nominal modifiers. For example, we can insert the adjective *yuumei* between the determiner *sono* 'that' and the following noun in the noun phrase *sono daigaku* 'that university,' yielding (6).

(6) sono yuumei na   daigaku
    that famous copula university
    'that famous university'

Similarly, consider the scope of the modifier over the following material. Independent words can have either narrow scope, in which they modify only the immediately following word, or wide scope, in which they modify the whole following NP. In (7), for example, *sono* 'that' can have scope either over the immediately following noun *uma* 'horse,' or over the whole NP of which *uma* is a modifier. But in the structurally similar (8) the Aoyagi prefix *moto* can have only narrow scope—it cannot modify the entire following NP.

(7) sono uma no   kubiwa
    that horse GEN collar
    'the collar of that horse (narrow scope)'
    'that horse collar (wide scope)'

(8) moto   daiziN   no   komoN
    former minister GEN adviser
    'adviser to the former minister (narrow scope)'
    *'former adviser to the minister (wide scope)'

The same is true when the following NP is a conjunction. In (9) the relative clause *tosi-o totta* 'aged' (literally, 'has passed years') may be construed either with the immediately following noun or with the whole conjunct. But in (10), which is identical but for the substitution of the Aoyagi prefix *moto* for *tosi-o totta,* only the narrow scope reading is possible.

(9) tosi-o-totta syuusyoo   to   daitooryoo
    aged   Prime-Minister and President
    'the aged Prime Minister and the President (narrow scope)'
    'the aged Prime Minister and President (wide scope)'

(10) moto syuusyoo   to   daitooryoo
     former Prime-Minister and President
     'the former Prime Minister and the President (narrow scope)'
     *'the former Prime Minister and President (wide scope)'

Thus, Aoyagi prefixes do not behave like independent words with respect to either separability or semantic scope.

If Aoyagi prefixes are not prefixes, what are they? They must be nominal modifiers of some sort, but as we have seen, they do not behave like other nominal modifiers with respect to such properties as separability and semantic scope. Moreover, they are morphologically peculiar in that they lack the inflection that nearly all other nominal modifiers have. The verbs of relative clauses are inflected for tense, as in (11). The same is true of conjugated adjectives, as in (12). Nominal adjectives must be followed by the copula, which itself is inflected for tense, as in (13). True nouns must be followed by the genetive marker *no*, as in (14).

(11) mi-ta   daizin
     see-past cabinet-minister
     'the cabinet minister (I) saw.'

(12) erai   daizin
     distinguished cabinet-minister
     'a distinguished cabinet-minister'

(13) hen   na   daizin
     strange copula cabinet-minister
     'a strange cabinet-minister'

(14) nagoya no   daizin
     Nagoya GEN cabinet-minister
     'the cabinet-minister from Nagoya'

The only Japanese nominal modifiers that are invariant are those that we may refer to as determiners, listed in (15).

(15) Japanese Determiners

Determiner	Gloss
kono	'this'
sono	'that (near you)'
ano	'that (away from us both)'
dono	'what'
konna	'this sort of'
sonna	'that (near you) sort of'
anna	'that (away from us both) sort of'
donna	'what sort of'
aru	'certain'

But this seems an unlikely category for morphemes with the semantics of the Aoyagi prefixes, and in any case we have seen that they behave differently from the determiners with respect to separability and semantic scope. In sum, if the Aoyagi prefixes are not prefixes they must be independent words, but they do not fit neatly into any morphological or syntactic category.

In addition to these syntactic properties, Aoyagi prefixes exhibit one other typically lexical property. The Japanese lexicon contains two major strata, native morphemes, known as *yamato-kotoba* and morphemes borrowed from Chinese, known as *kango*.[6] To a large extent Sino-Japanese morphemes combine only with other Sino-Japanese morphemes and native morphemes combine only with native morphemes. As we might expect, since lexical stratum is a lexical property, such combinatorial restrictions hold only inside of words; there are no such constraints on syntactic combinations of words.

Almost all Aoyagi prefixes belong to the Sino-Japanese stratum (*moto* is the only exception known to me) and to a very large extent they attach only to other Sino-Japanese morphemes. There are some exceptions to this, e.g., the prefix *haN* 'anti-,' which can be attached to names of any origin, as in *haN-tyomusuki* 'anti-Chomsky,' but most of them obey these restrictions. Since such combinatorial restrictions apply only within lexical words and involve lexical information, the fact that Aoyagi prefixes are subject to them argues that they are lexically attached.

It is difficult to find conclusive evidence of lexicality, but the Aoyagi prefixes behave like prefixes with respect to separability and semantic scope, fit into no syntactic category, and exhibit lexical combinatorial restrictions. This, combined with the fact that except for their phonology there is not a shred of evidence against treating them as prefixes, suggests that the traditional characterization as prefixes is correct, and that we are faced with a legitimate example of a word-internal phrase boundary.

4   Implications

The existence of the Aoyagi prefixes is surprising because we generally assume that the domains of phrasal rules are necessarily larger than words, because phrases are made up of words. But this is true only in a theory in which there is a single hierarchy of constituents.

One of the innovations of the metrical theory is the notion that there is a phonological constituent structure parallel to and distinct from the morphosyntactic constituent structure. Most of the work on the prosodic hierarchy has dealt with supra-word-level constituency, but there has been some work extending phonological constituency down inside words. Booij and Rubach 1984, 1987 have appealed to phonological words that may be morphosyntactic word-internal, and Inkelas 1989a has recently proposed a further extension, in which there are two completely parallel hierarchies. Viewed from this perspective we should not be surprised at the existence of word-internal phrase boundaries, for the words in question are morphosyntactic, whereas the phrases are prosodic, and there is no good reason to assume that the two hierarchies should be aligned. The properties of the Aoyagi prefixes may be readily described in terms of

---

[6]In addition, there are now many loans from languages other than Chinese, and so-called mimetic words, which though of native origin exhibit certain phonological peculiarities.

Inkelas's notion of dual prosodic and morphosyntactic subcategorization. Like other affixes, Aoyagi prefixes morphologically subcategorize a stem. Unlike other affixes, they prosodically subcategorize a minor phrase.

The existence of word-internal minor phrase boundaries also bears on the controversial question of whether phonological rules refer directly to syntactic structure, as proposed by Kaisse 1985 among others, or whether post-lexical rules refer only to a hierarchy of phonological phrases, as advocated by Selkirk 1978 and Nespor and Vogel 1986, among others, with reference to syntax possible only indirectly as a result of the influence of syntax on phonological phrasing.

It is difficult to find real differences between these two general approaches, though there are of course many differences between particular instantiations of them. There seems to be no difference in principle between the direct and indirect theories as far as how individual rules may parse the utterance. Any constraint that we might impose on direct reference to syntactic structure could equally well be formulated as a constraint on the mapping between syntactic structure and prosodic structure, and conversely.

A clearer difference is that under the indirect reference hypothesis the various phrasal rules must all parse the utterance in the same way,[7] whereas the direct reference hypothesis imposes no such constraint. Consider, for example, a direct reference theory in which there are no constraints on the parse and the corresponding indirect reference theory in which there are no constraints on the phrasing algorithm. Now add the constraint to the indirect reference theory that there be only one level of phrasing. This does not constrain the class of phrasal rules at all—any single rule could be formulated just as it might be without this constraint. But it requires that all phrasal rules use the same parse. We could, for example, parse an SOV sentence [SO][V] or [S][OV], but we could not have a language in which one rule used the former parse and another rule the latter parse. In this way the indirect reference hypothesis constrains the class of languages even though it does not constrain the class of rules.

The skeptic may reply that we are not playing fair—we have imposed a constraint on the indirect reference theory that we have not imposed on the direct reference theory. This is true, but the crucial point is that the direct reference theory provides no straightforward way of imposing a comparable constraint.[8] In our simple example it is not too difficult to find an equivalent constraint: we need only require that all phrasal rules parse the syntactic structure in the same way. But once we permit a richer phonological phrasing the problem becomes harder—we must not only limit the number of distinct parses to some fixed number, but they must also be hierarchically related. In sum, the indirect reference hypothesis

---

[7]More formally put, the constituents required by the phrasal rules must unify into a hierarchical structure.

[8]The same constraint, of course, cannot be imposed on the direct reference theory since *ex hypothesi* it has no notion of phonological phrase.

imposes what appears to be the right constraint in an extremely straightforward way, whereas it is more difficult to state this constraint under the direct reference hypothesis.

There is, however, a second way in which the two approaches differ. Even if we can constrain how individual rules parse the utterance equally well under either hypothesis, the indirect reference hypothesis allows us to impose tighter constraints on how information is used, since information to which the phrasing rules are permitted access need not be available directly to the phrasal phonological rules, and if it is not made available directly will be propagated to the phrasal rules only in a limited way.

The existence of the Aoyagi prefixes consequently provides an argument in favor of the indirect approach. Suppose that the application of post-lexical rules is governed directly by syntactic structure and that, therefore, there is no such entity as a minor phrase. Instead, post-lexical rules that in the indirect reference theory would be formulated as referring to minor phrases will refer directly to whatever information would be used in the indirect theory to parse the utterance into minor phrases. But since Aoyagi prefixes induce minor phrase boundaries word-internally, it would be necessary for post-lexical phonological rules to have access to the internal structure of words, including the identity of particular morphemes, since they must be able to distinguish the Aoyagi prefixes from other prefixes. This is of course a blatant violation of the generally sound hypothesis of Lexical Phonology (Kiparsky 1982a; Mohanan 1982, 1986) that post-lexical rules do not have access to the internal structure of words.

If the structure that governs the application of post-lexical rules is a phonological structure, distinct from syntactic structure, the behavior of the Aoyagi prefixes is not so problematic. That is, given a mechanism for constructing phonological phrases within the lexicon, post-lexical rules can refer to this information without being given unconstrained access to word-internal information.

5 Conclusion

Certain Japanese prefixes typically belong to a separate minor phrase from the stem to which they attach. Minor phrases typically contain more than one word and are domains of application of post-lexical rules, yet the evidence favors the traditional claim that these prefixes really are prefixes. It therefore appears to be possible for a prosodic phrase boundary to appear inside a lexical word. This fact provides an argument in favor of the indirect reference hypothesis, under which phrasal phonological rules refer to morphosyntactic structure only indirectly, via the prosodic structure. It also provides additional support for Inkelas's proposal that prosodic constituency exists in the lexicon and that morphemes can subcategorize for prosodic constituents as well as morphosyntactic constituents.

15

Predicting Rule Domains in the Phrasal Phonology

KEREN D. RICE

THE LITERATURE ON PHRASAL phonology has focused on the phrasal domains in which rules apply and how these domains are determined. (For instance, see Selkirk 1981a, 1984, 1986; Nespor and Vogel 1982, 1986; Hayes 1989; Kaisse 1985.) In this paper, I examine a different aspect of phrasal phonology, namely rule application and predicting domains of rule application. I propose that the principles of rule application that apply in the lexical phonology be extended to the postlexical phonology.

I begin with a discussion of and the principles that determine rule domains in the lexical component. I then turn to the postlexical component. The postlexical component, I assume, is composed of the levels of the prosodic hierarchy: phonological word, phonological phrase, intonational phrase, and utterance, as discussed in Selkirk 1981a, 1984, 1986; Nespor and Vogel 1982, 1986; Hayes 1984, and others.[1] I argue that rules of the phonological word and phonological phrase levels have properties traditionally assigned to lexical rules, and that rules of the intonational phrase and utterance levels have properties traditionally assigned to the postlexical phonology (see also Kaisse 1985). I suggest that for the phonology as a whole, it is only necessary to learn where a rule turns off; its actual domains of application are determined by the principles that have

I would like to express my thanks to Peter Avery for helpful discussion and comments on earlier drafts. Many participants at the Phonology-Syntax Connection workshop also influenced my thinking in the development of this paper.

[1]See the references in the text for arguments for (a) a prosodic hierarchy and (b) this particular structure for the prosodic hierarchy.

been argued to hold for the lexical component of the phonology.

I next examine and reanalyze some examples that appear to be problematic for this model. The first concerns the interaction between the syllabification of word-final consonants and rules such as word-final devoicing. The domain of a rule like word-final devoicing appears to be phrasal in cases where a voiced consonant remains before a vowel-initial word. Such rules are generally stated as applying on a postlexical level, for instance, the level of the phonological word. I argue that if the independently motivated principle of extraprosodicity is allowed to turn off at a stipulated level for a particular language, then a putative phrasal rule can be seen to obey the principles of the lexical phonology. The second problem concerns some of the domain span, domain limit, and domain juncture rules identified by Vogel 1984. I show that the mode of application of these rules is predicted by the proposed model.

1   Lexical Phonology

Within the model of Lexical Phonology, the phonology is divided into two components, the lexical phonology and the postlexical phonology. (See Kiparsky 1982a, 1985b; Mohanan 1986; Pulleyblank 1986; Kaisse 1985 and others.) This division is motivated by the different ways in which phonological rules apply in each component. These differences in rule application are summarized in (1), from Pulleyblank 1986:7.

(1) | **lexical rules** | **postlexical rules** |
|---|---|
| a. | may refer to word-internal structure | cannot refer to word-internal structure |
| b. | may not apply across words | may apply across words |
| c. | may be cyclic | may not be cyclic |
| d. | if cyclic, subject to strict cycle | noncyclic, hence across-the-board |
| e. | structure-preserving | need not be structure-preserving |
| f. | may have lexical exceptions | cannot have lexical exceptions |
| g. | must precede all postlexical rule applications | must follow all lexical rule applications |

In early Lexical Phonology, it was hypothesized that phonological rules were assigned to levels, either to a lexical level or to the postlexical level (e.g., Kiparsky 1982a). In more recent work on the lexical component, it has been argued that the phonology is better viewed as a unified block. Phonological rules are available from the outset of the phonology, with their actual application being governed by three interacting principles, the Strong Domain Hypothesis, the Strict Cycle Condition, and Structure Preservation. These principles are summarized in (2).

(2) Strong Domain Hypothesis (SDH): The grammar may stipulate merely where a rule ceases to apply. All rules are potentially applicable at the first level of the lexicon, and apply there provided only that the principles of the grammar permit it; at lower levels of the lexicon and in the postlexical phonology rules may be 'turned off' but no new ones may be added (Kiparsky 1984).

Strict Cycle Condition (SCC): If W is derived from a lexical entry W', where W' is nondistinct from XPAQY and distinct from XPBQY, then a rule A → B/ XP__QY cannot apply to W until the word level (Kiparsky 1985b:89).

Structure Preservation (SP): Nondistinctive features and structures cannot be introduced in the lexical phonology (after Kiparsky 1985b).

While the SDH states that rules are available until they turn off, preventing a rule from beginning application at any arbitrary point of the derivation, all rules do not in reality begin application at the first available domain. This, Kiparsky argues, is due to the interaction of the SCC and SP with the SDH.

2   Postlexical Phonology

Although 'postlexical phonology' encompasses word- and phrase- level phonology, the primary discussion in Lexical Phonology has centered on the word level.[2] Rule application has received sophisticated treatment in word-level phonology, as outlined above. In phrasal phonology, there has also been considerable focus on the domains in which postlexical rules apply and how those domains are determined (see Selkirk, Kaisse, Nespor and Vogel, Hayes, and others). The question of rule application is largely neglected, however, even in a model such as that of Kaisse 1985, which draws explicit parallels between the lexical and phrasal phonology. A typical rule of the postlexical phonology is generally simply assigned to the domain on which it applies. For instance, Kaisse 1986 identifies Turkish liquid devoicing as a rule of the utterance domain and Nespor and Vogel 1986 assign Italian syntactic doubling to the phonological phrase level. The conception of rule application at the level of connected speech is thus quite different from that at the level of word.

---

[2]See Kaisse 1985 for an exception to this statement. Kaisse treats rules of the phrasal phonology within a Lexical Phonology model, suggesting that just as the lexicon is divided into levels, so is the phrasal phonology. Her first level, P1 rules, consists of rules that are sensitive to sentence structure, specifically to the structural relationship between words in sentences; these rules have many of the characteristics of lexical rules that are shown in (1). Her second level, P2 rules, contains the rules that apply across-the-board, having characteristics of the postlexical rules in (1).

The principles available for predicting where and how rules apply at the word level have not been extended to the phrasal phonology, and rules of connected speech are simply marked for the domain they apply on.

I propose that the principles in (2) which determine domains of rule application in the lexical phonology are also relevant for the phrase-level phonology. In particular, the SDH predicts that rules will apply until they are turned off; this point can come at any level, lexical or phrasal.[3] SP delays the application of allophonic rules, or rules introducing nondistinctive features, until a nonderived level, the highest level of the prosodic hierarchy.

By considering rule application in the phrasal phonology to be governed by the same principles that govern word-level phonology, the phonology is unified. The phonology consists of a number of levels: lexical levels (determined by the language) and phrasal levels of phonological word, phonological phrase, intonational phrase, and utterance.[4] Levels below the utterance (or intonational phrase) have characteristics traditionally assigned to lexical rules, as outlined in (1). It is only rules of the highest domain, the utterance, that have characteristics generally thought of as postlexical: they are gradient; they can create novel segments, sequences, and syllable types; they do not have lexical exceptions. In addition, these are the rules that are sensitive to length of constituent and rate of speech; they are sensitive to location of focused elements and to pause (see Kaisse and Zwicky 1987). The characteristics of lexical rules thus extend far outside the lexicon, as do the principles determining application of the rules.

This model has advantages over the standard view of rule application in the postlexical phonology. It predicts that, subject to other constraints, any rule that applies postlexically can also apply lexically. It predicts that there will not be discontinuities in rule domains (see Mohanan's 1982 continuity of strata hypothesis). It requires learning about a rule only where it turns off, since its other properties are predictable from general principles of the grammar.

---

[3]My conception of the phrasal phonology may be somewhat different from that in the literature. In discussions of the prosodic hierarchy (e.g., the work of Selkirk, Hayes, Nespor and Vogel), phrasal prosodic domains are considered to be similar to the levels of foot and syllable. The levels such as syllable and foot are available everywhere (once the structure is assigned) while the other prosodic levels are, I claim, like lexical levels, ceasing to be available once they are left.

[4]There is disagreement in the literature about how many phrasal levels there are. Kaisse 1985 identifies two levels while Nespor and Vogel 1986 identify four, phonological word (clitic group), phonological phrase, intonational phrase, and utterance. As pointed out by Kaisse and Zwicky 1987, Kaisse's P1 rules are largely equivalent to Nespor and Vogel's phonological word and phonological phrase rules, while Kaisse's P2 rules are largely equivalent to Nespor and Vogel's intonational phrase and utterance level rules. I follow Kaisse, grouping together rules of the intonational phrase and utterance levels as they share properties; in particular, allophonic rules are available for application on these levels, but not before.

3   Extraprosodicity and Resyllabification

One potential problem for the proposed model comes from languages with rules affecting word-final consonants. For instance, in many languages word-final consonants devoice when the following word is consonant-initial, but fail to devoice when the following word is vowel-initial. Such cases have been treated by marking word-final devoicing as applying on a phrasal level, and ordering it after a rule of resyllabification which moves word-final consonants into an available onset position, bleeding word-final devoicing. In this section, I offer an alternative solution, one based on the proposal that word-final consonants that are possible onsets are extraprosodic.

Extraprosodicity renders a consonant or consonants invisible for purposes of the phonology. A consonant that is extraprosodic does not participate in syllabification (or other phonological rules); it becomes visible for syllabification and other rules only after extraprosodicity is turned off. According to Itô 1986 and Borowsky 1986, extraprosodicity turns off at the postlexical level, where the postlexical level is essentially the word level.

I propose that extraprosodicity is found universally and that it must be allowed to turn off at levels other than the word level.[5] In languages where extraprosodicity turns off at the word level, final consonants that are possible onsets are invisible until the word level. When extraprosodicity turns off, they become visible and must get syllabified. English is apparently such a language (see Nespor and Vogel 1986:64–65 for discussion). In languages where final consonants lose their extraprosodicity at the level of the phonological phrase, they are not visible until this level, and thus are not available for syllabification at earlier stages. If consonants can remain invisible until a stipulated level of the postlexical phonology, we can maintain the SDH. If, by contrast, extraprosodicity does not exist or must turn off at the word level postlexically, then the SDH, although tenable in the word-level phonology, must be abandoned for the phrasal phonology.

The assumption of extraprosodicity leads to a simplification of within-word syllabification. It is generally agreed that the CV syllable is unmarked, a within-morpheme sequence of VCV being syllabified universally as V.CV. In a theory without extraprosodicity, a morpheme of the shape CVC will be initially syllabified with the final consonant in the rhyme. If a vowel-initial suffix is added, the final consonant of the first morpheme must be delinked from rhyme position of the first syllable and resyllabified into onset position of the second syllable. Thus, two processes, syllabification and resyllabification, are required for filling onsets. Resyllabification is a structure-changing operation, one which destroys

---

[5]Itô 1986 argues that extraprosodicity is universally operative lexically and universally absent postlexically. Its availability at the (lexical) word level is, she suggests, subject to parametric variation.

syllable structure that has already been built. As discussed by Steriade 1988, syllabification rules generally operate in a structure-building way, not in a structure-changing way. Given this, it would be desirable to eliminate resyllabification from the inventory of putative cases of structure-changing rules.

Extraprosodicity allows between-morpheme cases of VC+V to be initially syllabified as V.CV, never as VC.V. If final consonants that are possible onsets are considered to be extraprosodic, then when syllabification of VC occurs, the final consonant is not visible and is not syllabified. When the suffix is added, extraprosodicity is lost since a segment can be extraprosodic only when on an edge. The consonant now syllabifies directly as an onset, giving the unmarked syllable structure. This is illustrated in (3), a Lardil example taken from Itô 1986. Extraprosodicity is marked by parentheses.

(3) ŋaluk-in 'story'

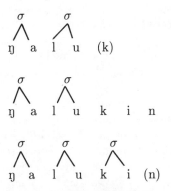

By using extraprosodicity at the word level, onsets can always be filled directly by syllabification. Onset consonants in cases such as (3) need not first be syllabified as rhymes and then resyllabified as onsets.

Many languages exhibit syllabification of a final consonant of one morpheme into the same syllable as an initial vowel of the following morpheme, both within words and between words. For between-word cases, the assumption has generally been made that word-final consonants are initially syllabified as rhymes and then resyllabified as onsets. This is made explicit in Nespor and Vogel 1986:68–69. The need for both syllabification and resyllabification is also implicit in the model of syllabification proposed by Itô 1986. While Itô accounts nicely for syllabification of the final consonant of a morpheme as an onset when the following morpheme within the word is vowel-initial, she proposes, as mentioned above, that extraprosodicity turns off at the word level. Prosodic licensing, the requirement that all units be linked to higher levels of structure, necessitates that once a consonant loses its extraprosodicity, it either be syllabified or lost by stray erasure. Thus, word-final consonants must be syllabified at the word level. By extension, in between-word cases, vowel-initial second words that have the final consonant of the preceding word filling onset position must have this consonant placed there by resyllabification.

I suggest that just as a distinction between syllabification and resyllabification is incorrect in the lexical phonology, it is also incorrect in the phrasal phonology; in other words, it is not the case that onsets are filled by syllabification at the word level but by resyllabification at higher levels of prosodic structure. This dichotomy arises only from the assumption that syllabification is complete at the word level. If this is not correct, and if segments can remain extraprosodic beyond the word level, then between-word syllabification is just like within-word syllabification. Extraprosodicity will still be blocked from turning off until at least the word level because of structure preservation, as argued by Itô. However, just exactly where it turns off is determined by the language.

I first look at a case from Turkish, analyzed within a Lexical Phonology framework by Kaisse 1986. Her analysis is problematic for a theory which assumes the SDH, prosodic licensing, and extraprosodicity. However, if extraprosodicity is allowed to turn off at a level later than the word, then a uniform analysis without resyllabification becomes available. I then look at similar cases in Slave (northern Athapaskan) and Cairene Arabic.[6]

3.1   Turkish

Kaisse 1986 discusses a Turkish process of syllable-final stop devoicing which, she suggests, has lexical and postlexical characteristics, but is best treated as a postlexical rule with lexical exceptions.

In Turkish, stops devoice syllable-finally, where syllable-final patterning is found both at word edge and word internally. Examples are given in (4).

(4) šarap, šaraplar (cf. šarap)   'wine' (nom. sg., nom. pl., acc. sg.)
     güč, güčler (cf. güjü)   'power' (nom. sg., nom. pl., acc. sg.)
     git, gitmek (cf. gider)   'go' (imp, inf, aor)

I assume that syllable-final devoicing is a delinking rule, as in (5), although the exact formulation is not relevant to this paper.

(5)   R
         |
         x
         |
         o   laryngeal
         ǂ
       [+voice]

---

[6]Nespor and Vogel 1986 suggest that French provides an argument for resyllabification, since a consonant must function as a rhyme to trigger a syllable-based rule but is actually syllabified as an onset. Space prohibits an analysis of the French facts here; briefly, I suggest that in French there is not resyllabification, but spreading to fill an empty onset.

A default rule applies, following delinking, to supply the unmarked value [−voice] to obstruents.

Syllable-final devoicing always applies within a word. However, it may fail to apply in connected speech when a consonant-final word is followed by a vowel-initial word.[7] This can be seen in the following examples, taken from Kaisse.

(6) šara*b* ald*ɨ*
     wine take
     'he took wine'

     bu šara*b* ak*ɨ*yor
     this wine pour
     'this wine is pouring'

     ren*g* anlamak
     color understand
     'to understand color'

     Arnavu*d* okuyor
     Albanian read
     'the Albanian is reading'

In the phrases in (6), the word following the stop in question is vowel-initial. When the following word is consonant-initial, devoicing is mandatory.

(7) šara*p* satt*ɨ*
     wine sold
     'he sold wine'

     šara*p* verdi
     wine gave
     'he gave wine'

As Kaisse points out, the existence of voiced stops in forms such as (6) cannot be regarded as intervocalic voicing since words such as those in (8) maintain a voiceless final consonant under all circumstances.

(8) top, toplar, topu 'ball' (nom. sg., nom. pl., acc. sg.)

     top ald*ɨ*
     ball took
     'he took a ball'

     *tob ald*ɨ*

---

[7]Kaisse 1986 notes that "not all speakers are able to inhibit devoicing before a vowel-initial word." The data discussed here come from the dialect that she identifies as the 'liaison dialect.' It might be noted that there is not total agreement on Kaisse's data. A native Turkish speaker with whom I consulted suggests that the stops in question are neither voiced nor resyllabified, but ambisyllabic, occurring in both the rhyme of the last syllable of the first word and the onset of the following apparently vowel-initial syllable. For this speaker's dialect, an analysis similar to the one suggested for French in note 6 might be proposed.

Kaisse offers the following analysis. She assumes that syllabification proceeds as outlined in (9).

(9) a. construct a syllable head over each V slot

b. attach at most one C as the onset of the syllable to its right

c. attach any remaining C's as codas to the syllable on the left

A word such as /šarab/ will be syllabified as in (10). Only the second syllable (the one relevant to the issue at hand), is shown.[8]

(10)   σ

r   a   b

In order to account for between-word cases, Kaisse assumes an optional rule of resyllabification, given in (11).

(11) Resyllabification

V   C   V

This rule she orders extrinsically before syllable-final stop devoicing. Kaisse remarks that since stops cannot be revoiced, devoicing cannot be allowed to apply lexically as a neutralization rule and continue to apply postlexically as well. Instead, she argues that devoicing must be marked as taking place at the postlexical level only, following resyllabification.

Implicit in Kaisse's analysis of Turkish devoicing is an abandonment of the SDH. If this hypothesis were incorporated into her solution, stop devoicing would apply to syllable-final stops at the word level. Given the SDH, the following representation for a word like [šarap] is predicted.

(12)   σ   σ

š   a   r   a   b

The final consonant must be syllabified, and final devoicing should apply since its structural description is met. This analysis thus forces a weakening in the theory of Lexical Phonology.

As well as weakening Lexical Phonology, Kaisse's analysis is problematic in requiring extrinsic ordering of resyllabification and stop devoicing. An achievement of nonlinear phonology and Lexical Phonology is that many cases formerly handled by rule ordering follow directly from representations and independent principles. While the effect of rule ordering persists, it is a result of higher level principles, rather than a stipulation in an individual grammar.

---

[8]Since internal syllable structure is not relevant to the issues discussed here, it will not be shown in the examples.

An analysis is possible consistent with the model proposed in section 2. By adopting extraprosodicity, the SDH can be maintained and extrinsic ordering eliminated. First consider a within-word case. Upon syllabification, a representative word has the representation in (13). The final consonant is extraprosodic, and thus not visible for syllabification.

(13)

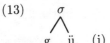

g   ü   (j)   syllabification, extraprosodicity

Affixation and syllabification yield the structure in (14). The consonant loses its extraprosodicity since it is no longer on an edge.

(14)

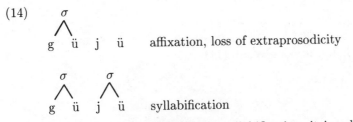

g   ü   j   ü   affixation, loss of extraprosodicity

g   ü   j   ü   syllabification

When the stop becomes available for syllabification, it is syllabified directly into the onset of the second syllable. At no point in the derivation is the structural description for stop devoicing met.

Between-word cases can be handled identically if extraprosodicity is allowed to remain beyond the word level. A derivation is shown in (15). The /b/ is extraprosodic at the word level, and thus not visible for syllabification. It becomes visible only when a word is placed after it, rendering it no longer on an edge. At this point, it must be syllabified.

(15)

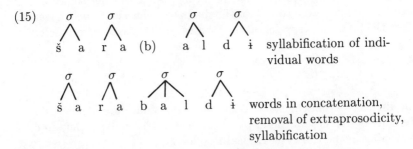

š   a   r   a   (b)   a   l   d   ɨ   syllabification of individual words

š   a   r   a   b   a   l   d   ɨ   words in concatenation, removal of extraprosodicity, syllabification

When the stop becomes available for syllabification, it is assigned directly to an onset. Again, the structural description for devoicing is never met during the derivation. Stop devoicing applies lexically whenever it can; with word-edge consonants it cannot apply until the consonant is syllabified, at a phrasal level.

Kaisse's analysis involves stipulating the domain of stop devoicing and a statement of rule ordering. The extraprosodicity analysis allows the maintenance of the SDH. What must be stipulated is where the rule stops applying. Extrinsic ordering of stop devoicing and resyllabification is not necessary since there is no resyllabification. Thus, by allowing extraprosodicity to shut off at a particular prosodic level, we achieve a more general analysis of Turkish.[9] Turkish no longer poses a problem for a model in which the lexical and postlexical phonology are unified.

3.2   Slave

A similar case to Turkish is found in Slave ([slevi]), an Athapaskan language of Canada. In Slave, syllable-final obstruents are neutralized to [h].[10]

(16)   ts'a*h*   -ts'a*dé*   'hat' (nonpossessed, possessed)
       mį*h*   -mį*lé*   'net'
       dzée*h*   -dzée*gé*   'gum'
       té*h*   -té*dhé*   'cane'

---

[9]Several interesting questions about Turkish arose in the course of discussion at the Phonology-Syntax Connection workshop.

(a) k-∅ alternations. As discussed by Sezer 1981, Clements and Keyser 1983 and others, underlying word-final /k/ deletes under certain circumstances. While /k/ deletes before a vowel-initial suffix, it remains before a vowel-initial word. The formulation of *k*-deletion is complex, and worthy of attention. I assume that it can be formalized and suggest that it turns off at the lexical word level. Word-final consonants do not meet the structural description of the rule since they are extraprosodic, and thus remain before a vowel-initial word.

(b) There are word-final geminates in Turkish. W. Poser pointed out that neither of the consonants of the geminate can be syllabified; if the first one were, one might expect final devoicing to always apply. This is not what happens. A notion of extraprosodicity in which both consonant positions of a geminate are invisible is needed. The structural description of syllable-final devoicing would then not be met until after affixation. At this point, the first half of the geminate would be in the rhyme and the second half in the onset if the affix is vowel-initial. The Linking Constraint (Hayes 1986) predicts that devoicing should not apply since the consonant is doubly linked, yielding a voiced geminate. Degemination occurs when the geminate is followed by a consonant; this can be followed by devoicing.

(c) The third issue is more complex. The maximal Turkish rhyme is binary branching. As discussed by Clements and Keyser 1983, there are several processes in Turkish which ensure that binarity is not violated. One is vowel shortening. It apparently applies within a word, suggesting that the final consonant is part of the rhyme as well as part of the onset. If this is the case, the extraprosodicity analysis might not be the best one. Rather, the analysis suggested for French, outlined in note 6, might be more appropriate. Under this analysis, there is not a phrasal distinction between voiced and voiceless consonants, with a voiceless consonant in a rhyme and a voiced consonant in an onset, but rather a difference between single consonants and geminates, with the single consonant occurring when the following word is consonant-initial and the geminate when it is vowel-initial. These data require further investigation.

[10]I use the practical orthography. A hook under a vowel represents nasalization; an acute accent is High tone. The following symbols require comment: dh=ð, ł=voiceless lateral fricative, l=voiced lateral fricative, e=[ɛ], ee=[e]. Note that laterals function as nonsonorants in Slave.

In the suffixed forms, the structural description for neutralization is not met since the consonant in question is in an onset. In the nonsuffixed forms, neutralization applies since the consonant is in the rhyme.

In addition to vowel-initial suffixes, Slave possesses vowel-initial clitics.[11]

Some are shown in (17).

(17)   égụh   'past'
       íle   'negative'
       e   'future'
       oli   'future'

When a consonant-final word precedes a vowel-initial clitic, neutralization fails to apply, as seen in (18).

(18)   ts'eʔáh   'one eats'
       ts'eʔál íle   'one does not eat'
       ts'eʔál oli   'one is going to eat'

When a consonant-final word precedes any other vowel-initial word, the consonant is neutralized to [h], as in (19).

(19) a.   ohʔáh   enịdhę
          1sg.opt.eat   3 want
          's/he wants to eat'
          cf. (18)

     b.   nénéh   adani
          3 is long   3 becomes
          'it is getting long'
          cf. nénédhi 'that is long (relative clause)'

     c.   dzéeh   elị
          gum   3 is
          'pink'
          cf. -dzéegé 'gum (possessed form)'

In a theory lacking extraprosodicity, where syllabification of all segments is required at the word level, neutralization will have to apply at the phonological phrase level. The stem-suffix and word-clitic combinations escape the rule because the consonant is in an onset when the phonological phrase is reached. In word-word sequences, the consonant is in a rhyme; thus meeting the structural description of the rule. The rule must be blocked from applying until the phonological phrase is reached; this can be done only by stipulating the phonological phrase as its domain.

Again, if we allow extraprosodicity to turn off at a stipulated level, we obtain an alternative treatment which conforms to the principles of

---

[11]See Rice (forthcoming a,b) for further discussion.

Lexical Phonology. Neutralization cannot apply to a form such as /ts'ad/ since the final consonant is extraprosodic and therefore invisible. When the suffix /-é/ is added, the consonant is no longer extraprosodic. However, the structural description for neutralization is still not met because the originally extraprosodic segment now forms an onset. A derivation of [-ts'adé] is shown in (20).[12]

(20)   ts'ad

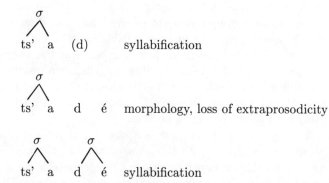

ts' a   (d)   syllabification

ts' a   d   é   morphology, loss of extraprosodicity

ts' a   d   é   syllabification

Assuming that words leave the word level with extraprosodic final consonants, then the clitic facts can also be accounted for in the same straightforward way. At the level of the phonological word, where stem and clitic are combined, the extraprosodic consonant becomes visible since it is no longer on an edge. It is then syllabified into the onset of the following syllable. Extraprosodicity shuts off in general at this point to ensure that at higher levels, final consonants are syllabified as rhymes and not as onsets (see (19)). Prosodic licensing places all now-visible word-final consonants in the rhyme, creating a structure that meets the structural description of neutralization.

3.3   Cairene Arabic

Broselow 1979, in a discussion of Cairene Arabic syllable structure, shows that syllabification takes place across words. Following Broselow, syllabification is indicated with '.' and emphatic sounds with capitals. (21a) and (21c) show that a word-final consonant syllabifies as the onset of a following vowel-initial word. (21b) is given for comparison with (21a).

(21) a.   FADDAl#ilwalad
          FAD.DA.lil.wa.lad
          'he preferred the boy'

---

[12]There are some consonant-initial suffixes in Slave as well. With these, the consonant must syllabify into the rhyme of the first syllable, and the structural description for neutralization is met.

b. (iddal)#FADDA#lilwalad
    FAD.DA.lil.wa.lad
    '(he gave) silver to the boy'

c. miš#ana
    mi.ša.na
    'not I'

In (21a) and (21c), if the final consonant of the first word is not syllabified until the word level, it can be syllabified directly as an onset postlexically. This analysis allows a simple account of emphasis. As discussed in Broselow and elsewhere, emphasis has the syllable as its domain. If the final consonant of /FADDAl/ in (21a) first syllabifies in the rhyme, it should be emphatic. It would have to lose its emphasis when resyllabified as onset of the following syllable. If it is syllabified directly as an onset, it is never within the domain of emphasis. Emphasis need not be undone, thus eliminating a structure-changing process.

Evidence from epenthesis in Cairene also suggests that extraprosodicity turns off at a phrasal level. As Broselow points out, the maximum number of consonants that can open or close a Cairene syllable is one, except in the case of syllable-final consonants at the edge of a phrase. When more than one consonant occurs at the beginning of a word, only the consonant closest to the vowel is directly syllabified. Epenthesis occurs so that other consonants may be prosodically licensed.[13] This is shown in (22).

(22) /kbiira/
      [kibiira]
      'big'

At the word edge, final consonant clusters are allowed, as illustrated in (23). While the core rhyme in Cairene is binary branching, adjunction at the word edge creates superheavy syllables.

(23) bint   'girl'
      katábt 'letter'

A closer examination of Cairene cross-word data shows that it is in fact not the word edge at which superheavy syllables are allowed, but in fact at the phrase edge. As the examples in (24) show, when a word with a superheavy syllable is non-phrase-final and followed by a consonant-initial word, epenthesis must take place. The epenthetic vowel is italicized.

(24) bint nabiiha → binti nabiiha   'an intelligent girl'

      katábt gawáab → katábti gawáab   'you (masc.) wrote a letter'

---

[13] Word-final adjunction of consonants is permissible.

As discussed in recent phonological literature (e.g., Itô 1986), epenthesis can be thought of as a syllable repair strategy motivated by the need for prosodic licensing. If the final consonants of the first words in the examples in (24) are licensed at the phrasal level, there is no reason for epenthesis to occur. However, if these consonants are extraprosodic until this level, then epenthesis will follow directly from the theory: once the consonants become visible through the loss of extraprosodicity, the unlicensed consonant cannot go into the rhyme without creating an illicit syllable. In order to license the consonant, epenthesis must take place.[14] A derivation of the first form in (24) is shown in (25).

(25) syllabification at word level

word concatenation, loss of extraprosodicity

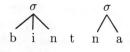

epenthesis

If the loss of extraprosodicity is held off in Cairene Arabic until the phrasal level, the domain of emphasis and the patterning of epenthesis are easily accounted for.

3.4   Summary

I have argued that the postlexical phonology is to be treated as an extension of the lexical phonology, where the SDH allows a rule to apply until it is turned off, and the SCC and SP determine when a rule will actually be able to apply. One set of potential counterexamples can be eliminated by allowing the point at which extraprosodicity turns off to be determined on a language-particular basis. This hypothesis allows the extension of the SDH to the phrasal phonology. In addition, it allows all syllabification into onsets to be direct, rather than by resyllabification.

4   Domain-sensitive Rules

Selkirk 1980a identifies three different types of domain-sensitive rules; domain span rules, domain limit rules, and domain juncture rules. Domain

---

[14]This analysis is implicit in Itô's treatment of Cairene: without discussion, she treats syllabification as occurring at the phrasal level in this language.

span rules apply across a particular domain (phonological word, phonological phrase, intonational phrase, utterance) without regard to the ways in which that domain may be subdivided into smaller domains. Domain juncture rules apply between domains, the phrasal equivalent of derived environment rules. Domain limit rules apply to one end of a particular domain.

Domain span rules appear to present a problem for the model proposed here since some apply just on phrasal domains. Domain limit rules are also potentially problematic in that some apply just at pauses, the edge of an intonational phrase or utterance. In the following sections, I examine these rules and show that they are not problematic; their properties are predictable from the principles of Lexical Phonology. I then look briefly at domain juncture rules to show that, to they extent that they even exist, they are also consistent with the proposed model.

4.1   Domain Span Rules

The domain span rules identified by Vogel 1984 include sandhi rules that apply across words, phonological phrases, intonational phrases, and utterances. This rule type is potentially problematic in that the intonational phrase and utterance rules appear to turn on, rather than turn off. I suggest that these rules do not need to be turned on; rather, SP predicts that they are unable to apply until a late level.

The rules given by Vogel that apply across intonational phrases and utterances are allophonic, introducing features not present in underlying representation.[15] For instance, English flapping is identified as a rule of the utterance domain, and Spanish spirantization as a rule of the intonational phrase domain. Examples of English flapping are given in (26).

(26) English flapping

water [ɾ]
right angle [ɾ]
Pat asked [ɾ]
Please wait. I'll be right back. ... wai[ɾ] I'll...

By contrast, the domain span rules that apply on smaller domains are not allophonic. Vogel includes Italian s-voicing, Sanskrit Ruki, Sanskrit Nati, and the American English Rhythm Rule in this set.

A careful reexamination of all domain span rules is beyond the scope of this paper. However, a significant generalization is that those rules which apply at the levels of word and phonological phrase are either neutralizing or structure-building, properties of lexical rules. Neutralizing rules such as Ruki and Nati are blocked from applying within morphemes by the SCC

---

[15] As discussed in note 2, Kaisse conflates the intonational and utterance levels into P2. These levels have similar properties in that they both refer to the highest sentential constituents, namely S″.

(see Kiparsky 1973), while structure-building rules escape the SCC and are allowed to apply in nonderived forms (see Kiparsky 1985b). Span rules at the word and phonological phrase levels share other properties with lexical rules: they do not introduce nondistinctive features, they may have lexical exceptions, and so forth. Span rules at the higher levels introduce nondistinctive and redundant features, properties traditionally assigned to postlexical rules. The span rules of the word and phonological phrase levels begin to apply immediately in the phonology and continue to apply until they turn off. Rules of the higher levels, while available throughout the derivation, are blocked from applying until the highest level because they are not structure preserving. It thus appears that domain span rules can be characterized as available throughout the derivation until they turn off.

4.2   Domain Limit Rules

Vogel 1984 identifies domain limit rules that apply at word edges and at pauses (intonational phrase, utterance). Rules that apply at pauses present a problem, since they again seem to need to turn on. I suggest, however, that the domain of pausal rules is predictable; since they introduce nondistinctive features, they are predicted by SP to apply only at the highest levels.

Word-edge rules identified by Vogel 1984 include vowel tensing in American English and depalatalization in Sanskrit. These rules are neutralizing and apply at the edge of every word. Consider, for example, American English vowel tensing, a rule which tenses word-final vowels. It applies at the edge of all words, taking effect when a word is the first member of a compound and when it stands on its own. This is illustrated in (27).[16,17]

(27) American English vowel tensing

city [i], cityhood [i], city street [i]

The final vowel of 'city' is word-final at some point in the derivations of all three words, and thus meets the structural description of tensing.

Domain limit rules that apply at pauses are of a different nature, introducing nondistinctive features. An example is Turkish liquid devoicing. Kaisse 1986 shows that this rule applies only to a liquid at the edge of an utterance. Kaisse's rule is given in (28), and some data from Kaisse follow in (29).

(28) Liquid devoicing

[+son, −nas] → [−voice] / __]$_{IP}$ (postlexical; at pause)

---

[16]See Halle and Mohanan 1985 for some different (and disagreeing) data.

[17]Tensing may be a foot-based rule rather than a word-based rule (Peter Avery, personal communication).

(29) ahïr̥   'stable'
      ahïrï   'of the stable'
      ahïrdan   'from the stable'
      ahïrlar   'stables'
      ahïraldï   'he bought a stable'
      ahïrsattï   'he sold a stable'
      ahïračïlïyo̥r̥ 'the stable is opening'

      ačilinjaahïr̥,   ičeri   girebiliriz
      when-opens stable,   inside we-can-go
      'when the stable opens, we can go in'

The SDH predicts that this rule should be available everywhere. Why, then, does it applies only before pause, in true utterance-final position?

Liquid devoicing is allophonic in Turkish. There are no underlying voicing contrasts between voiced and voiceless liquids, and the distribution of [voice] for liquids is predictable. SP prevents rules introducing predictable features from applying in derived environments.[18] If the phrasal phonology is considered to be governed by the same principles as the lexical phonology, there is only one place that allophonic rules can apply—they must be rules of the highest level, since only this level contains nonderived forms. The Turkish rule can thus be rewritten as the default rules in (30).

(30) [+sonorant] → [−voice] /__]
      [+sonorant] → [+voice]

No statement of domain is needed, as it is predictable from independent principles. In particular, SP will not allow the liquid devoicing rules to apply at an edge earlier in the phonology since they introduce nondistinctive structure. When SP does allow the rules in (30) to apply, on the intonational phrase level, the edge of the intonational phrase is the only visible edge.

Other domain limit rules can be treated in a similar fashion. Selkirk 1980a identifies Visarga in Sanskrit as a domain limit rule of the utterance domain; it applies as in (31).

(31) devas   →   devaḥ
      punar   →   punaḥ

The Visarga rule, as given by Selkirk, is shown in (32).[19]

---

[18]Given extraprosodicity, it may be possible for non-structure-preserving rules to 'apply' throughout the derivation as well. Note that with extraprosodicity, phrase-final liquids are not available until this point of the derivation. This in itself blocks liquid devoicing from taking effect —the liquids are not visible until extraprosodicity turns off. This possibility requires investigation.

[19][ḥ] is the pausal counterpart of /s/ and /r/ (and /r/ is the voiced counterpart of /s/; see Whitney 1889, section 118e and elsewhere). This rule is part of the more general syllable-final neutralization; since [ḥ] does not occur distinctively in Sanskrit, this part of the process is delayed until the utterance level.

(32) s, r → ḥ / [... __]ᵤ

Visarga is allophonic, creating a segment not present in the phonology. As a non-structure-preserving rule, it must be delayed until as late as possible, namely the utterance level. At this point, only utterance edges are visible.

Among domain limit rules, the level of phonological phrase is noticeably absent: no rule applies only to phonological phrase-final segments.[20] This is because a rule that turned off at the phonological phrase would have properties of a lexical rule, and its structural description would therefore be met at earlier levels. The rule should apply at these earlier levels, and would thus be a span rule that turned off at the phonological phrase level rather than a limit rule. Just as the SDH prevents a rule from restricting its domain to level 2 in the lexicon, it also prevents restriction of a rule to the phonological phrase. While a span rule that turns off at the phonological phrase will apply at all lower levels as well, a limit rule that applied just at phonological-phrase edge would have to be restricted to just this domain, violating the SDH. The model rightly predicts the absence of such rules.

4.3   Domain Juncture Rules

A number of rules are identified in the literature as domain juncture rules that apply on a phrasal domain. They include Sanskrit final voicing, Sanskrit stop to nasal, Mandarin third tone sandhi (Cheng 1987, and many others), Italian *raddoppiamento sintattico* (Nespor and Vogel 1982, 1986, and others), and Kimatuumbi vowel shortening (Cowper and Rice 1987).

I begin by illustrating a typical domain juncture rule and examining some of its properties. I then suggest that, while the properties of juncture rules can be accommodated in the proposed model, their existence is called into question by the SCC; such rules are generally reanalyzable as domain span rules.[21]

A typical domain juncture rule is Sanskrit final voicing (Selkirk 1980a, Vogel 1984, Kaisse 1985). The effect of this process is illustrated in (33).

(33)   sat-aha   → sadaha
        good day
        'good day' (compound)

        samyak   uktam   → samyag uktam
        correctly   spoken
        'correctly spoken' (phrase)

---

[20]One might think that in a language like Chimwiini, the rules that Selkirk 1986 identifies as stress and vowel shortening apply at the edge of a phonological phrase. However, these rules (and rules like Turkish stop devoicing) can be thought of as domain span rules which turn off at the level of the phonological phrase, rather than as domain limit rules.

[21]Many thanks to Paul Kiparsky for suggesting this idea to me.

parivrat   ayam   → parivrad ayam
mendicant   this
'this mendicant' (phrase)

tat   namas   → tad namas
that   homage
'that homage' (phrase)

Selkirk suggests that final voicing is a domain juncture rule applying on the utterance domain. She formalizes this rule as in (34).

(34) [−son] → [+voice] / $_U$(...$_W$(...—)$_{WW}$([+voice]...)$_W$...)$_U$

Final voicing is easily accommodated in the model proposed here: available at all levels, it applies between any two words in concatenation so long as the other conditions of the rule are met.

An observation one can make about 'phrasal' rules such as Sanskrit final voicing is that they apply not only between words within a phrase, but also between words within a compound.[22] Assuming the SCC, this observation receives no unified account if the rules in question are confined to some phrasal domain; the SCC makes word-internal structure unavailable at the phrasal level. Such a rule would have to be available at a lexical level to apply within compounds, and again at a phrasal level to apply between words, potentially creating discontinuous domains, which are disallowed by the SDH. If, as proposed here, rules are instead stated as turning off at the relevant prosodic level rather than as applying at that prosodic level, the parallel between compounds and between-word cases is predicted.[23]

Vogel 1984 identifies some rules as domain juncture rules applying between words within a phonological phrase, and others as applying between words within an utterance. In the latter case, the rule is available at the lexical word level to apply between the words of a compound, at the level of phonological phrase to apply between words within a phonological phrase, and at the level of the utterance. Vogel identifies no domain juncture rules as applying between phonological phrases on a higher domain

---

[22]Rules identified or formulated as domain juncture rules in the literature include Sanskrit final voicing, Mende consonant mutation (Cowper and Rice 1987 and elsewhere), Mandarin third tone sandhi (Cheng 1987, and many others), Kimatuumbi vowel shortening (Odden 1987), Turkish (Kaisse 1986), Ewe tone sandhi (Clements 1978), and Italian *raddoppiamento sintattico*. In all cases, these rules apply between words in compounds as well as between words in phrases.

[23]In some cases, different rules apply in compounds than apply between words. One example is the tone deletion rules of Shanghai Chinese, discussed by Selkirk and Shen (this volume). In compounds, there is spreading and deletion of noninitial lexical tones, while phrasally there is deletion and default Low insertion. This is not inconsistent with the account offered here. In Shanghai, it appears that spreading turns off at a lexical level. In the lexicon, where both spreading and default Low insertion are available, spreading takes precedence by the Elsewhere Condition. Default Low insertion need not be labelled as turning on at a phrasal level; independent principles predict that it cannot begin to apply until then.

or between intonational phrases on the utterance domain. We predict this gap: rules must be generally available for application, since they are active from the start of the phonology. A rule whose structural description is met at the phonological phrase level would also find its structural description met at the word level, and would have to apply there.

Domain juncture rules have characteristics similar to those of lexical rules.[24] They are often neutralizing; they do not introduce features not found in nonderived forms; they apply only in derived environments. The rules thus have exactly the properties predicted by the proposed model.[25]

While domain juncture rules can thus be accommodated, a close examination of some of these processes suggests that this rule type is actually unnecessary. Juncture rules appear to be superfluous, given appropriate syllabic representations and the SCC. Extraprosodicity allows strings formed at different levels of the phonology to have different syllabic structures (see discussion below). The SCC blocks rules from applying in nonderived environments; thus the fact that they apply only at juncture comes for free. I will reexamine some of the proposed domain juncture rules briefly, and show that they need not be analyzed as junctural, but reduce to span rules.

Consider Sanskrit final voicing (see (33)). As discussed above, this rule applies between words in both compounds and phrases. The rule voices a word-final obstruent before a word-initial voiced segment of any type. It fails to apply in affixation, as in (35).

(35) maru*t* + i → maru*ti*
      wind - locative

      va*c* + ya → va*c*ya
      speak - ger

      prañ*c* + ah → prañ*c*ah
      Easterner - nom pl

It is the failure of final voicing to apply in suffixation that suggests that it is a juncture rule, applying between but not within words. However, upon the introduction of richer representations that include syllable structure, then an alternative analysis emerges.

We look first at suffixation. Consistent with the discussion of extraprosodicity in section 3, the final consonant of a root is extraprosodic

---

[24]This is made explicit by Kaisse 1985, who identifies these properties as belonging to rules of P1. Rules that apply on P2 are not allowed access to any word-internal structure.

[25]Some of the rules proposed as domain juncture rules require careful analysis to see just what their properties are. One example of this is the tone raising rule found in Ewe. This rule applies between words in compounds and between words within a phrase. (See Clements 1978 for discussion.) It is unclear how the rule is best formulated; current formulations make it appear that it introduces a nondistinctive feature since it creates an extrahigh tone.

until the point of suffixation. On suffixation, this consonant is directly syllabified into the onset, as in (36).

(36)

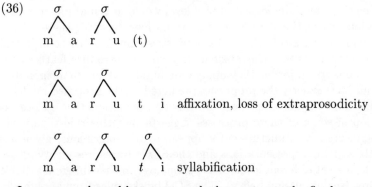

In compounds and between words, by contrast, the final consonant of the first morpheme will be syllabified leftward, assuming extraprosodicity is turned off at the word level.

(37) compounds (33)

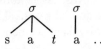

phrasal (33)

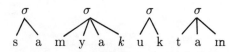

In syllable-final position, neutralization of laryngeal distinctions is found in Sanskrit (see Whitney 1889, sections 122, 141). This can be seen both within (38) and between (39) words.

(38) within word

bhodh-sya-ti → bhotsyati 'to know' (3rd sg. fut.)

(39) word-finally

agnimát for agnimáth, suhṛt for suhṛd, triṣṭúp for triṣṭúbh (Whitney, section 140)

A syllable-final consonant then assimilates in voice to the following segment. In (38) and (40a), the following segment is voiceless; in (40b,c,d), it is voiced.

(40) affixation

a. ad + si → atsi

b. cak + dhi → cagdhi

c. compounding – see (33)

d. phrasal concatenation – see (33)

What is called final voicing thus breaks down into two processes. First, laryngeal features are lost syllable-finally. Second, a rule of voicing assimilation spreads the feature [voice] onto a rhyme consonant. It fails to apply in some cases of affixation (34) because its structural description is not met: there is no rhyme consonant. When the rule's structural description is met, it does apply in affixation (40b), as well as in compounding (40c) and phrasal concatenation (40d).[26]

Other cases of domain juncture rules also yield to reanalysis. Consider, for instance, third tone sandhi in Mandarin (Cheng 1987), a rule which changes a third tone to a second tone when it falls before another third tone. This rule need not be restricted by stipulation to derived environments; the SCC prevents its application in nonderived environments anyway. The same is true of Kimatuumbi vowel shortening (Odden 1987), a rule that applies both within compounds and phrasally between words. Cowper and Rice 1987 state this rule as applying only between words; this can be guaranteed by the SCC, and the rule simply becomes a span rule which turns off at the level of the phonological phrase.[27]

Whether or not domain juncture rules exist, at least one prediction of the model is clear. Similar processes are expected in compounds and between words in a phrase. A rule might apply between words in a compound and not between words in a phrase, but no rule will apply between words in a phrase and not between words in a compound. (See also note 23.)

5   Summary

I have argued for a very restrictive model of the phonology, one in which both the lexical and the phrasal phonology are governed by identical principles. Extraprosodicity eliminates a potential class of counterexamples by guaranteeing invisibility of certain segments until higher levels of the phonology. Rules traditionally recognized as belonging to the phrasal phonology can now be seen as available throughout the lexical phonology, possibly marked to turn off at some level. Any level, lexical or phrasal, which is 'derived' in nature will show properties traditionally assigned to the lexical phonology, while only the highest levels, intonational

---

[26] A problem remains as to how spreading works; note that a feature such as [voice] is redundant for sonorants in Sanskrit, including the vowels. There is no apparent reason, given underspecification theory, why this feature should be able to spread. Sanskrit is more complex than indicated; for instance, while assimilation is generally regressive, there is some progressive assimilation as well (Whitney, section 160).

[27] See Odden (this volume), Hayes (this volume) for an alternative analysis.

phrase and utterance, exhibit characteristics normally attributed to the postlexical phonology.[28]

The rule types of domain span and domain limit are nonproblematic; the gaps in types of rules identified by Vogel are systematic.[29] Domain span rules are found at all levels, since a rule can be turned off at any level. Domain juncture rules probably do not exist. But if they do, they apply between words on any level but not exclusively between higher level constituents. Last, domain limit rules are found at word-edge and utterance-edge. Just these rule types and domains are predicted.

The predictions of this unified phonology model are clear and testable and will lead, I hope, to a clearer understanding of rule application in the phonology.

---

[28]In addition, one might expect to find morphemes that are added at postlexical phrasal levels as well as morphemes that are added at lexical levels, since much of the postlexical phonology is an extension of the lexical phonology. This appears to be the case; see Zec and Inkelas (this volume) for examples. Boundary tones can also be considered to be morphemes that are added at a phrasal level. See Hyman (this volume).

[29]Something more needs to be said about allophonic rules. Some allophonic rules might be thought to apply at levels smaller than that of the intonational phrase or utterance. If this is indeed the case, it presents a problem for the model proposed here, since this model delays all nonstructure preserving rules until the highest levels. Some allophonic rules appear to apply only within a word; an example is velarization of /l/ in English. However, this is a syllable-based rule, and since English syllabification is complete within the word (see Nespor and Vogel 1986:65), its structural description will thus never be met in between words. Some allophonic rules, particularly those which involve timing, are sensitive to position within a phrase. B. Hayes has pointed out to me that the vowel in *take Grey to London* is typically longer than the vowel in *take greater London*. Here again, syllabification may be a factor. These may also be rules that refer to grid structure. Once the structural properties of the various allophonic rules are understood, those that apparently must refer to domains smaller than the intonational phrase or utterance may no longer be problems.

16

Prosodic Domains in Shanghai Chinese

ELISABETH SELKIRK AND TONG SHEN

IN SHANGHAI CHINESE, AS in the other Chinese languages, tone is a lexical property of morphemes. Previous research has shown that in compounds all but the leftmost morpheme lose their lexical tone, and the lexical tones of that leftmost morpheme are associated in one-to-one fashion from left to right across the entire compound (Sherard 1972, Zee and Maddieson 1979, Yip 1980, Wright 1983). Recent research has also shown that the deletion and rightward association seen in compounds also apply to syntactically generated sequences of lexical items (N, A, or V) plus function word(s) (Jin 1986, Shen 1986). In further research we have found yet another type of tone deletion applying in phrasal contexts in Shanghai. A lexical item which follows a focused word may lose its own lexical tone, as long as it bears the appropriate structural relation to the preceding focused element. In this paper we examine the syntactic contexts in which tone deletion operates. It will be shown that an analysis in terms of prosodic structure domains defined in relation to syntactic structure (e.g., Selkirk 1984, 1986; Nespor and Vogel 1986) provides an exceedingly simple and revealing characterization of the distribution of the two sorts of phrasal tone deletion in a sentence. Unfortunately, limitations of space prevent us from considering in detail alternative analyses which give a central place to stress in accounting for the distribution of tone deletion in the sentence. We leave this for a longer work (in preparation). Our aim here is to present enough data to give a sense of the range of facts that any theory will have to account

Research reported on here was supported in part by NSF Grant BNS-86-17827.

for, and to provide an account within prosodic structure theory. The reader is also referred to Jin's 1986 valuable work, the only publication available in English which treats tone deletion as it applies in sentence contexts.

1   Tone and its Realization in Compounds

It is usual to distinguish five surface tones in Shanghai:

(1) | Tone A | Tone B | Tone C | Tone D | Tone E |
      |--------|--------|--------|--------|--------|
      | HL | MM' | LM' | H | LM |
      | sa | sa | 'za | saq | 'zaq |
      | sift | what | firewood | kill | stone |

Following Shen 1985 and Jin 1986 we will distinguish only three tones in underlying lexical representation:

(2) | Tone A | Tone B | Tone C | Tone D | Tone E |
      |--------|--------|--------|--------|--------|
      | HL | MH | LH | MH | LH |

These are the representations that appear in the text below. Details of the rules deriving (1) from (2) will not concern us here. What is relevant is that all the tones are contour tones, and that their distribution is identical in compounds and in restricted phrasal contexts.

Obligatory Tone Deletion removes lexical tones from all but the leftmost morpheme of a compound. That leftmost contour tone is distributed over the first and second elements of the compound, giving a level tone to each syllable (each syllable is a morpheme). Thus the disyllabic compounds in the third column of (3) are derived from the pairs of lexical items in the first two columns:

(3)   a. HL   MH   H L
         thi   tshi   thitshi
         'sky'   'air, gas' 'weather'

      b. MH   MH   M H
         hu   tshi   hutshi
         'fire'   'air, gas' 'anger'

      c. LH   MH   L H
         'bi   tshi   'bitshi
         'spleen' 'air, gas' 'temper'

      d. MH   MH   M H
         seq   tshi   seqtshi
         'wet'   'air, gas' 'athlete's foot'

In compounds of three syllables or more, the first two syllables bear the two level tones which make up the lexical contour tone of the initial morpheme. The remaining syllables are implemented phonetically with Low pitch, or as transition to Low pitch (following a High tone). We will represent all these later syllables with Low tone, supplied by a late rule, Default Tone Insertion.

It has been suggested that Obligatory Tone Deletion is crucially dependent on stress. Yip 1980 and Wright 1983 propose that in Shanghai compounds primary stress is assigned to the leftmost morpheme, and that the deletion of tone on subsequent morphemes is due to their relatively lesser stress. Yet native speaker intuition does not support the contention that the leftmost syllables in compounds are rhythmically more prominent. There is, moreover, neither vowel reduction nor shortening to support a stress difference among the syllables. So we will not assume that Obligatory Tone Deletion takes degree of stress as its crucial environment. An alternative is for the deletion rule to apply on a designated domain, deleting all but the leftmost lexical tone in that domain. We will offer a formulation of such a rule in Section 3.1.

The association of the second syllable with the second component of the first morpheme's tonal melody can be accomplished by the familiar left-to-right one-to-one association of autosegmental tonology (e.g., Clements and Ford 1979). We will assume that contour tones on a single syllable are not permitted in the lexical phonology. Thus, only the first tonal element will link on the first cycle; association of the second element takes place only after compounding, when a second syllable becomes available. The automatic one-to-one left-to-right association manifested in compounds will henceforth be referred to as LR Association. Following LR, Default Tone Insertion tonifies any remaining unlinked syllables. A derivation illustrating these three sequential operations on compounds is shown in (4):

(4)   MH HL   LH
       | | |
       sou-foN-dziN
       hand-wind-organ

       MH   Obligatory Tone Deletion
       |
       soufoNdziN

       M H   LR Association
       | ⋮
       soufoNdziN

       M H   L   Default Tone Insertion
       | | ⋮
       soufoNdziN
       'accordion'

2   A Few Basics of Shanghai Phrase Structure

Before we proceed with our examination of tone deletion in sentential contexts, a superficial review of the basic phrase structure of Shanghai Chinese is called for. In the basic word order of the sentence, a subject precedes its predicate. The head of the noun phrase is in strictly final position. Complement phrases preceding the head noun are followed by the subordinating particle 'geq. These include relative clauses, genitive NPs, NP and PP complements to the head, and AP modifiers. Determiner and quantifier elements usually appear at the left edge of NP. Verb phrases present a more mixed picture. The verb precedes the noun phrase direct object and the indirect object NP or dative PP. Moreover, sentential complements follow the verb. However, most prepositional phrases are normally found in preverbal position. A direct object supplied with a governing preposition may also appear preverbally, as may adverbs and other VP modifiers. Thus, the verb can appear in medial position in the VP, for example, following a PP and preceding an object NP. Finally, within PP, a preposition precedes its object.

With this basic picture of Shanghai word order in mind, let us now examine the contexts in the sentence where function words and lexical items may lose their tone.

3   Phrasal Tone Deletion I: Function Words

Jin 1986 and Shen 1986 point out that in certain phrasal contexts the sequence of a lexical item and following function word(s) has the same sort of tonal realization as a sequence of lexical items within a compound. The function word necessarily loses its tone (Obligatory Tone Deletion) and receives tone either from the preceding lexical item (LR Association), or via Default Tone Insertion:

(5)   V   ASP   Pro   Qprt

    LH   MH   LH   LH

    | | | |

    'mo   ku   'noN   'va

    LH   Obligatory Tone Deletion

    |

    'mo   ku   'noN   'va

    L   H   LR Association

    | ┊

    'mo   ku   'noN   'va

<pre>
   L   H   L   L   Default Tone Insertion
   | | ¦   ¦
  'mo   ku   'noN   'va
  scold   EXP   2sg   ?
</pre>

'(Has someone) scolded you?'

In (5) the verb is followed by three function words—an aspectual particle, a personal pronoun, and an interrogative particle. The latter three elements lose their own tone, the second verb tone associates to the rightmost vacant syllable, remaining syllables receive a default Low specification. In (6) are listed further examples where a sequence of lexical item plus function word(s) forms a single domain with respect to these tonal operations: such sequences are parenthesized. The tonal representation shown is the output of the three rules, meaning that the level tones associated with the first two syllables are the lexical (contour) tone of the first morpheme in the sequence.

(6) a. (V   Prt)
       L   H
      'jiN   leq
      'has won'

   b. (V   Pro)
       M   H
      taN   'noN
      'hit you'

   c. (V   Pro   Prt)
       M   H   L
      taN   'noN   leq
      'has hit you'

   d. (V)   (N   Prt)
      MH   L   H
      taN   'mo   leq
      'has hit the horse'

   e. (V   Pro)   (N)
       M   H   MH
      peq   'noN   tshe
      'give you vegetables'

   f. (V)   (N)   (N)
      MH   LH   MH
      peq   'mo   tshaw
      'give horses grass'

g. (V   Det +   Cl)
   M   H   L
   taN   'ljaN   tsi
   'hit several times'

h. (P)   (N)
   LH   LH
   'zaw   'mo
   'toward the horse'

i. (P   Pro)
   L   H
   'zaw   'noN
   'toward you'

We can think of the utterances of (6) as comprising a sequence of one or more domains of type x. Obligatory Tone Deletion applies on domain x, deleting all but the leftmost tonal contour. The lexical tones of the first morpheme of each domain x are realized within that x. If the domain contains more than one morpheme or word (i.e., more than one syllable) then the bipartite tonal melody will be distributed over the first two syllables by LR Association. If the domain consists of a single syllable, its melody is realized, as a contour tone, by Contour Tone Association. Our contention is that these tonological domains of type x correspond to prosodic constituents—in particular, to prosodic words (PW), part of the phonological representation of the sentence. What the examples in (6) make clear is that the tonological domains at issue are postlexical domains, made up of words concatenated by the rules of syntax. For example, the pronouns of the examples in (6) simply fill positions otherwise occupied by full noun phrases: V Pro N is an instance of a double object construction, as is V N N. Consider sentence-final particles. Their distinctive distributional property is their location in sentence-final position (probably as daughter to S). They group in domains of type x with whatever lexical item happens to immediately precede in surface structure, be it V (6a) or N (6d). These domains do not correspond to constituents in syntactic surface structure. For example, the N Prt sequence of (6d) is not a syntactic constituent, if we take the particle to be daughter to S and the N to be daughter to VP. More dramatic examples of the nonsyntactic character of the constituents corresponding to domains of type x will be discussed below.

We thus assume the domain of Obligatory Tone Deletion, LR Association, and Contour Tone Association to be the PW. Note that Contour Tone Association would produce incorrect results if it were to apply before the PW domain is formed: a contour tone would be produced on those verbs or nouns in (6) that are followed by function words, and would have to be undone on the PW domain. As for Obligatory Tone Deletion and LR Association, they have been said to apply on compounds. Yet there is no evidence that they apply cyclically within compounds, and the tonal patterns of compounds could just as well be derived assuming that, like other noncompound lexical items, a compound constitutes a PW on its own or in combination with following function words. Assuming a PW domain for these rules, we will give the following formulations:

(7) Obligatory Tone Deletion

$$(T_i T_j \ldots T_k \ldots)_{\text{PW}} \Rightarrow (T_i T_j \ldots \ldots)_{\text{PW}}$$

(8) LR Association

$$(T_i T_j \ldots)_{\text{PW}} \Rightarrow (T_i T_j \ldots)_{\text{PW}}$$
$$|\qquad\qquad\quad |\ \vdots$$
$$\sigma\sigma \ldots \qquad\quad \sigma\ \sigma \ldots$$

(9) Contour Tone Association

$$(\ldots T_i T_j)_{\text{PW}} \Rightarrow (\ldots T_i T_j)_{\text{PW}}$$
$$|\qquad\qquad\qquad \mathrel{\rlap{\,\diagdown}{\mathord{\downharpoonleft}}}$$
$$\sigma\qquad\qquad\qquad \sigma$$

3.1   Defining the Prosodic Word

Now we come to the question that is central to the concerns of this paper: How is the analysis of the sentence into prosodic words derived in Shanghai Chinese? In general, the problem is to characterize the relation between two sorts of hierarchical structure, autonomously defined: (surface) syntactic structure and prosodic structure. This relation, the syntax-phonology mapping, has been argued to be parameterizable, such that the grammars of individual languages may exploit a limited range of options in the syntax-phonology relation. We believe the following 'end-based' theory to be a promising articulation of the parameterized mapping within prosodic structure theory (see Selkirk 1986, Hale and Selkirk 1987, Chen 1987c, Selkirk and Tateishi 1988a, 1988b):

(10) The Syntax-Phonology Mapping

For each category C^n of the prosodic structure of a language there is a two-part parameter of the form

$$C^n: \{\text{Right/Left}; X^m\}$$

where X^m is a category type in the X-bar hierarchy.

A syntactic structure-prosodic structure pair satisfies the set of syntax-phonology parameters for a language iff the Right (or Left) end of each constituent of type X^m in syntactic structure coincides with the edge of constituent(s) of type C^n in prosodic structure.

A set of mapping parameters specifies the 'anchor points' at which syntactic structure and prosodic structure must coincide. The mapping does not fully characterize the prosodic structure of a sentence, however; it only constrains it, for prosodic structure is submitted to autonomous wellformedness principles, independent of the syntax. It has been hypothesized that a universal wellformedness constraint defines the general nature of prosodic structure (Selkirk 1981b, 1984; Hayes 1989; Nespor and Vogel 1986; but see Hyman, Katamba, and Walusimbi 1987):

(11) Prosodic Structure Wellformedness Constraint

The prosodic structure of a sentence must conform to the rule schema $C^n \rightarrow C^{(n-1)}*$.

According to (11), an utterance is exhaustively parsed into a hierarchy of constituent types C^n, C^{n-1}, etc. These are strictly layered, in that a constituent of type C^n dominates only constituents of lower types, i.e., C^{n-m}. And these constituents are organized into a wellformed tree or bracketing. (11) and a language-particular choice of parameterized syntax-phonology mapping rules together define the prosodic structure corresponding to a given surface syntactic structure. We will assume that the prosodic structure assigned to a sentence is the minimal structure consistent with the wellformedness constraint and the mapping rules.

In Shanghai, the left edge of a syntactic word belonging to the categories Noun, Verb, Adjective (= a 'lexical item') always coincides with the edge of a prosodic word. This means that Shanghai grammar has a syntax-phonology mapping rule with the parameter setting in (12):

(12) Shanghai Chinese Prosodic Word Rule:

Prosodic Word: {Left, Lex^0}

where Lex^0 stands for word belonging to the lexical categories N, V, A.

In accordance with (12), a PW will extend from the left edge of one lexical item to the left edge of the next, incorporating the function words that lie between. We see this in examples (6d-f) and below in (13)-(18). A mapping rule like (12) does not exhaustively characterize the location of PW edges in the prosodic structure of a sentence, however. For example, each edge of a sentence always coincides with the edge of a PW, regardless of whether or not the left edge of the syntactic category designated in the mapping rule is found there. The general wellformedness principle in (11) guarantees this result, as illustrated by the sentence-final PWs in (6). These extend from the left edge of a lexical item to the right edge of the utterance. The behavior of utterance-initial function words in Shanghai is also explained by the general prosodic wellformedness constraint. Note that in the isolation pronunciation of the PP in (6h), both the preposition and the noun constitute PWs on their own and bear contour tones. (12) only guarantees the placement of a PW at the left edge of the noun, but (11) requires that the whole sentence be parsed into PWs; hence the promotion of the preposition to PW status. Finally, note that parameter (12) will guarantee that compound structures are mapped into a single PW if we assume that it is the syntactic word, i.e., the Lex^0 which constitutes the interface between the phrase structure and word structure, which is identified in the mapping.

3.2   A Nontrivial Prediction of the End-Based Theory

One especially interesting feature of the general theory of the syntax-phonology mapping laid out in (10) is its extremely limited sensitivity to syntactic structure. For any particular level of prosodic structure, only the bracketing of the sentence into constituents of one particular X-bar type is relevant, and then only the left or right edge of such a constituent. No syntactic relations govern the mapping at all—neither dominance, nor sisterhood, nor c-command. Thus there is no guarantee that the words included in a prosodic constituent, such as PW, should bear any consistent syntactic relation to each other. In particular, a lexical item is not required to c-command its companion function words within a PW, nor is a function word required to c-command the lexical item within a PW. In this, our theory of the syntax-phonology mapping differs from that of Hayes 1989 or Nespor and Vogel 1986. For the prosodic constituent under consideration, which they refer to as the clitic group, and which we for mnemonic reasons are calling the PW, these authors suggest that the function word (read 'clitic') must c-command the lexical item with which it is grouped. In the examples considered up to now from Shanghai, this relation has indeed held. Additional evidence, however, shows that function words do not systematically c-command the lexical item that precedes them in a PW.

Examples (13) and (14) illustrate postverbal prepositional phrases whose prepositions obligatorily lose their own tone, acquiring the tone of a preceding verb by LR Association. This tonal evidence indicates that although the preposition does not c-command the verb, both belong to the same PW. The underlying tones and parentheses in (13b) indicate the hypothesized analysis into PWs, as generated by the end-based rule in (12).

(13) a.   V [P   [N]$_{NP}$]$_{PP}$

b.   (LH   LM)(LH   MH)
       | | | |
      'z   'laq 'zawNhe

     (LH   )(LH   )   Obligatory Tone Deletion
       | |
      'z   'laq 'zawNhe

(L   H)(L   H)   LR Association
 | ⋮ | ⋮
'z 'laq 'zawNhe
live at   Shanghai
'live in Shanghai'

The examples in (14) depict the three other prepositions that may appear postverbally in Shanghai sentences.

(14) a. (MH   MH)(LH HL) ⇒ (M   H)(L   H)
        tsou   taw 'noetsiN   tsou taw 'noetsiN
        'walk to Nanjing'

  b. (HL   MH)(MH HL) ⇒ (H   L)(M   H)
     fi   sjaN poqtsiN   fi sjaN poqtsiN
     'fly toward Beijing' (literary)

  c. (LH   LH)(HL MH) ⇒ (L   H)(H   L)
     'le 'z tsoNkoq   'le 'z tsoNkoq
     'come from China' (literary)

A similar situation with respect to PW formation obtains in (15), where a verb precedes a complementizer-initial sentential complement. The complementizer joins with the verb in a single PW.

(15) V   [Comp N   ...]_CP

   (MH   MH)(LH) ⇒ (M   H)(LH)
   tsjaw teq 'mo   tsjaw teq 'mo
   shout   horse 'shout (so loud) that the horses ...'

Note, moreover, that a personal pronoun embedded as a possessive in a postverbal noun phrase will also join the verb in a PW:

(16) V   [Pro   N]_NP

   (MH   LH)(LH MH) ⇒ (M   H)(L H)
   taN 'ngu 'njitsz   taN 'ngu 'njitsz
   hit 1sg son   'hit my son'

Other determiner or quantifier elements embedded in a branching noun phrase behave in similar fashion. (17) shows a sequence consisting of verb, indefinite quantifier, and classifier; the quantifier takes its tone from the verb, and the classifier receives default tone.

(17)   V [Q   + Cl N]_NP

  a. (MH MH   HL)(LH) ⇒ (M H   L)(LH)
     taw ?iq   pe 'zo   taw ?iq pe 'zo
     pour one/a cup tea   'pour a cup of tea'

  b. (LH LH   MH)(HL) ⇒ (L H   L)(HL)
     'ma ljaN   peN sz   'ma ljaN peN sz
     buy two/some book   'buy some books'

When embedded in similar contexts, indefinite determiners which double as wh-interrogative words may also lose their tone, taking on the second tone of the verb, as shown below.[1]

(18)   V [WH$_{indef}$ (Cl) N   ]$_{NP}$

a. (LH MH   )(MH) ⇒ (L   H) (MH   )
   'ma sa   pu   'ma sa   pu
   buy what/any   cloth   'buy any cloth'

b. (LH MH   MH)(HL) ⇒ (L   H L)(HL   )
   'ma tsi   po taw   'ma tsi po taw
   buy how many/some   knife   'buy some knives'

These examples show that preposition, personal pronoun, complementizer, indefinite determiner and classifier qualify as function words in Shanghai, insofar as they all undergo Obligatory Tone Deletion, acquiring tone by LR Association from a preceding lexical item or by Default Tone Insertion. They also show that the mapping from surface syntactic structure to prosodic structure is blind to the fact that these function words do not c-command the lexical items with which they form a PW.

Similar cases from other languages where a function word cliticizes to a word which is not its 'natural,' c-commanded host are cited in Klavans 1982, 1985. Klavans argues that particular function words may be simultaneously subcategorized for a syntactic host on one side and for a phonological host on the other. However, we believe that the data do not motivate such a theory. The grouping of function words with preceding non-c-commanded lexical items in Shanghai is, on our account, a simple consequence of (a) the end-based theory of the syntax-phonology mapping, (b) the choice of a left-edge parameter for PW in Shanghai, and (c) the particulars of Shanghai phrase structure. In other words, the radical 'rebracketing' of function words seen here is not a special fact about function word, or 'clitics.' Below we will see that this radical lack of isomorphy between phonological and syntactic constituency obtains at higher levels of phrasing in Shanghai as well. Our contention is that the examples cited in (13)-(18) follow naturally from the simple end-based mapping theory, and hence provide support for it.

3.3   Two Problematic 'Puzzles' for the Theory

Before the preceding examples can be viewed as supporting the end-based theory, however, a solution must be provided for two further sets of data. First, consider postverbal PPs embedded within an object NP, as in (19).

---

[1]Phrases like (18a) are used in yes-no questions or negative sentences such as 'Do you want to buy any cloth?' or 'I haven't bought any cloth.'

(19)   V [[P   [N   ]_{NP}]_{PP} Prt   N]_{NP}

a. (LH   )(LH)(LH   MH   LH)(LH MH)
⇒(LH)(LH)(L   H   L)(L H)
   'z   'laq 'zawNhe   'geq 'njitsz
   be   at   Shanghai   son
'be the son (who is) in Shanghai'

b. (MH   )(MH)(LH   HL   LH)(LH)
⇒(MH)(MH)(L   H   L)(LH)
   tsou   taw 'noetsiN   'geq 'lu
   walk to   Nanjing   way
'take the way (which leads) to Nanjing'

The prepositions in (19) retain their tone, in contrast to their behavior in (13) and (14). In (19) we must say that the prepositions are not in the same PW as the preceding verb, unlike those in (13) and (14). We will refer to the prepositions in (19) as 'strongly embedded' and those in (13) and (14) as 'weakly embedded.' Our analysis of the syntax-phonology mapping so far has no explanation for the difference in the two sorts of cases.

The second sort of problematic data involves noun phrase specifiers: not all determiners and quantifiers behave like those in (17) and (18). The quantifier morphemes translated as 'a' and 'some' in (17), can also obtain the numeral interpretations 'one' and 'two.' But when used as numerals they do not lose their tone. A verb preceding them is realized with a contour tone. Compare (20 a,b), where the numeral interpretation of the quantifiers is selected, with (17a,b), where they quantifiers are used indefinitely:

(20)   V   [Q   + Cl   N   ]_{NP}
a. (MH)(MH   HL)(LH) ⇒ (MH)(M   H   )(LH)
   taw   ?iq   pe   'zo   taw ?iq pe   'zo
   pour one/a   cup tea   'pour one cup of tea'
b. (LH)(LH   MH)(HL) ⇒ (LH)(L   H   )(HL)
   'ma   ljaN   peN sz   'ma ljaN peN sz
   buy   two/some   book   'buy two books'

In similar fashion, determiners like those in (18) which also are ambiguous between an indefinite and a wh-interrogative interpretation, do not lose their tone when used as wh-interrogatives. Compare (21a,b), which illustrates the wh-interrogative use of the determiners, with their behavior as indefinites in (18a,b):

(21)   V [WH_{inter}   (Cl) N   ]_{NP}

a. (LH)(MH   )   (MH)⇒(LH)(MH)(MH)
   'ma sa   pu   'ma sa   pu
   buy what/any   cloth 'What cloth ... buy?'

b. (LH)(MH   )(MH)(HL)⇒(LH)(M H)(HL)
   'ma tsi   po taw   'ma tsi po taw
   buy how many/some   knife 'How many knives... buy'

Undoubtedly related to this is the fact that demonstrative determiners never lose their tone in comparable circumstances.

The point, of these data is that while some NP determiners and quantifiers are treated as function words, forming a PW with what precedes, others behave more independently. We call the former 'strong' specifiers and the latter 'weak.'

We are now faced with two puzzles: (a) a difference between 'weakly' and 'strongly' embedded prepositions, and (b) a difference between 'weak' and 'strong' specifier elements within NP. In the following sections of this paper, we argue for a solution to these puzzles that leaves intact our simple end-based theory of the syntax-phonology mapping, preserving in particular the mapping rule proposed in (12) for PWs in Shanghai. We show that a higher level of prosodic structure, the major phrase, is motivated by other tonal phenomena of Shanghai, and we propose that the analysis of the sentence into a sequence of major phrases automatically forces, the up-to-now unexplained distribution of PWs seen in our two puzzles. This solution relies crucially on the notion that the prosodic well-formedness constraint in (11) plays an active role in the syntax-phonology mapping.

4   Phrasal Tone Deletion II: Lexical Items After Focus

Just as in a nontonal language like English, contrasting or emphasizing a word in Shanghai Chinese may render the fundamental frequency of that word more prominent. We use the term 'focus' to refer to this property of contrast or emphasis.

4.1   The Phonetics and Phonology of Focus

When a word is focused in Shanghai Chinese, the phonetic realization of its lexical tone employs a wider-than-normal pitch range. For example, the Low of the contour tone LH will be realized lower than normal, and the High higher. The pitch of neighboring words is also affected by the presence of focus. In particular, following a focus, the entire pitch register is lowered, and its range is considerably compressed. Within this lowered post-focus pitch range, one observes a contrast in tonal behavior that correlates with local differences in syntactic structure. In certain configurations, a post-focus word will be extremely reduced in pitch, and may even entirely lose its lexical tone, while in other configurations the pitch is less reduced, and lexical tone is maintained. It is this contrast in post-focus tonal behavior that concerns us in the present section.

Consider the contrasting pair of utterances in (22) and (23):

(22) a. [[[A]$_{AP}$ Prt   N   ]$_{NP}$ Prt   N   ]$_{NP}$

    b. (   )

    c. (LH   LM)(HL   LM)(MH)   Underlying
       'oN   'geq ho   'geq tsz

    d. (L   H)(H   L)(MH)   Normal
       'oN   'geq ho   'geq tsz

    e. (L   H)(L   L)(L)   Focused 1
       'oN   'geq ho   'geq tsz

    f. (L   H)(H   L)(L)   Focused 2
       'oN   'geq *ho*   'geq tsz
       red   flower's   seed
       'seeds of red flowers'

Example (22) contains a left-branching NP. The particle '*geq* is a subordinating particle required of all noun phrase complements, whether argument or modifier. The bracketing in the tonal tier is the PW bracketing, which groups '*geq* with what precedes. In all instances, '*geq* loses its own tone by Obligatory Tone Deletion, acquiring tone by LR Association from the preceding item. In normal speech, none of the lexical items loses its tone, as (22d) shows. But when the leftmost item in this same NP is focused, all following tones are deleted and replaced by default Low, as seen in (22e), where the focused word is italicized. (22f) demonstrates that when the middle lexical item in the NP is focused, the following, but not the preceding, item loses its tone.

The construction in (22) contrasts with that in (23). Here, the NP is right-branching: the initial AP modifies the head of the entire NP.

(23) a. [[A]$_{AP}$ Prt [[N   ]$_{NP}$ Prt   N   ]$_{NP}$]$_{NP}$

    b. (   )(   )

    c. (LH   LM)(HL   LM)(MH)   Underlying
       'oN   'geq ho   'geq tsz

    d. (L   H)(H   L)(MH)   Normal
       'oN   'geq ho   'geq tsz

e. (L   H)(H   L   )(MH)   Focused 1
   'oN   'geq ho   'geq tsz

f. (L   H)(H   L   )(L)   Focused 2
   'oN   'geq *ho*   'geq tsz
   red   flower's   seed
   'red seeds of flowers'

Corresponding to this syntactic difference is a difference in tonal behavior. As (23e) shows, when the adjective on the left is focused, neither of the following lexical items loses its tone. When the medial noun is focused, the rightmost noun may lose its tone, as shown in (23f). The bracketing in line (b) shows the indicated breakdown into domains of Post-Focus Tone Deletion.

Our hypothesis is that the difference in the tonal behavior of examples (22) and (23) is a consequence of a difference in prosodic structure. The (b) lines of (22) and (23) show the analysis into phonological phrasing which we attribute to these utterances. We will call these phrases major phrases (MaPs), for mnemonic reasons that will become clear below. The phonetic implementation of tone that is involved in determining pitch register thus relies on major phrasing: after a focus, material within the same MaP is realized within a radically lowered pitch register. At the beginning of a new MaP, the register is raised somewhat, though a preceding focus will still trigger a slight depression. This dependence of tonal implementation on phonological phrasing finds a precedent in the analysis of the implementation of tone in Japanese (Poser 1984, Beckman and Pierrehumbert 1986, Pierrehumbert and Beckman 1989, Selkirk and Tateishi 1988b). As for Post-Focus Tone Deletion, it remains moot whether it is a matter of phonetic implementation or of the phonology of the sentence. Since it seems to be distinct from pitch register manipulation, we assign it the status of a separate rule, whose domain is MaP:

(24) Post-Focus Tone Deletion (Optional)

$$T_i T_j \Rightarrow 0$$
$$|$$
$$(\ldots focus \ldots \sigma \ldots)_{\text{MaP}}$$

4.2   The Domain of Post-Focus Tone Deletion

A preliminary generalization concerning the distribution of tone deletion in the post-focus arena is that a lexical item following a focus loses its tone only if no left edge of a maximal projection separates it from the focus. An examination of tone deletion in utterances (22)-(23) shows that the generalization holds for these first examples. This generalization follows from a prosodic structure analysis under the assumption that MaP is the domain for Post-Focus Tone Deletion, as in (24), and that the left edge of a maximal projection in syntactic structure necessarily coincides with the edge(s) of MaP(s) in prosodic structure. The choice of the parameters 'Left' and 'X^{max}' in the syntax-phonology mapping of Shanghai guarantees the analysis into major phrases which the generalization reflects:

(25) The Shanghai Chinese Major Phrase Rule (provisional):

Major Phrase: { Left, X^{max} }

The general prosodic wellformedness principle in (11) guarantees MaP edges at the ends of the utterance. In what follows we will see that this prosodic structure analysis goes a long way towards providing the right characterization of the domain for Post-Focus Tone Deletion.

In combination with the particulars of Shanghai phrase structure, this end-based mapping theory yields some rather unexpected results. For instance, in (26), the preposition does not belong to the same MaP as its object NP:

(26) a. [[P   [N]$_{NP}$]$_{PP}$V   ]$_{VP}$

    b. (   )(   )

    c. (LH   )(MH)   (MH)   Underlying
       'zaw   he   tsou

    d. (LH   )(MH)   (MH)   Normal
       'zaw   he   tsou

    e. (LH   )(MH)   (L   )   Focused 1
       'zaw   *he*   tsou

    f. (LH   )(MH)   (MH)   Focused 2
       'zaw   he   tsou
       toward   sea   walk
       'walk toward the sea'

That the preposition and NP phrase separately is demonstrated by (26f), where even when the preposition is focused, the following noun still retains its lexical tone. On the other hand, that noun does cohabit a MaP with the following verb, of which it is not a complement. This is shown in (26e), where the focusing of the noun is accompanied by the deletion of the tone of the verb. In a parallel example, a postverbal noun which is a direct object of the verb is set off in a separate MaP, as (27) shows:

(27) a. [V   [N   ]$_{NP}$]$_{VP}$

    b. (   )(   )

    c. (MH)(LH   )   Underlying
       taN   'niN

d. (MH)(LH   )   Normal
    taN 'niN

e. (MH)(LH   )   Focused
    taN 'niN
    hit   people

An even more dramatic result of the end-based mapping is shown in the utterances of (28) and (29), which combine a preverbal PP and a postverbal NP. These examples show in no uncertain terms that the prosodic constituency corresponds to no proper analysis of the syntactic structure.

(28) a. [[P   [N   ]$_{NP}$]$_{PP}$[V   [N   ]$_{NP}$]$_{V'}$]$_{VP}$

      b. (   )(   )(   )

      c. (LH)(MHLH)   (MH)(LH   )   Underlying
          'laq ʔoqʻli   tshiq 'mi

      d. (LH)(M H)   (MH)(LH   )   Normal
          'laq ʔoqʻli   tshiq 'mi

      e. (LH)(M H)   (L   )(LH   )   Focused 1
          'laq *ʔoqʻli*   tshiq 'mi

      f. (LH)(M H)   (MH)(LH   )   Focused 2
          'laq ʔoqʻli   *tshiq* 'mi
          at   home   eat   noodle
          'eat noodles at home'

In (28e), focusing the preverbal noun triggers the deletion of the verb's lexical tone, indicating that that noun and the verb the same MaP. Note that the tone of the direct object noun remains intact, showing that in this construction as well as in (27) it is still in a separate MaP. In (28f), focusing the verb also also fails to induce tone loss on the following object noun, demonstrating the same point.

In (29) the NP object of the preverbal PP is complex, exhibiting the same right-branching internal structure as example (23). A MaP break falls in the middle of the highest preverbal NP, coinciding with the left edge of the embedded NP. The next left-edge-of-X^{max} to the right in (28) belongs to the postverbal NP. Hence the end-based mapping derives a MaP which extends from the middle of the NP object of the preverbal PP to the middle of V'. Note that focusing the preposition 'toward' or the adjective 'red' involves no deletion of following tones. Focusing of 'bird,' however, causes the deletion of tone on 'head' and 'open,' while focusing of 'head' also deletes the tone on 'open.' Neither these focusings nor focus on the verb will cause the deletion of tone from the object noun.

(29) a.

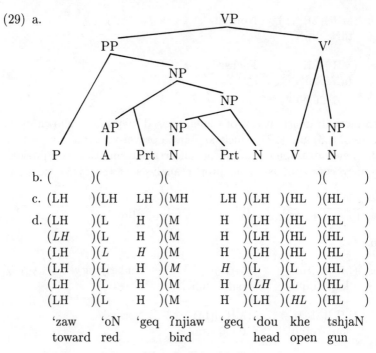

b. (   )(   )(   )(   )

c. (LH   )(LH   LH)(MH   LH)(LH)(HL)(HL   )

d. (LH   )(L   H)(M   H)(LH)(HL)(HL   )
   (*LH*   )(L   H)(M   H)(LH)(HL)(HL   )
   (LH   )(*L   H*)(M   H)(LH)(HL)(HL   )
   (LH   )(L   H)(*M   H*)(L)(L)(HL   )
   (LH   )(L   H)(M   H)(*LH*)(L)(HL   )
   (LH   )(L   H)(M   H)(LH)(*HL*)(HL   )

'zaw   'oN   'geq ʔnjiaw   'geq 'dou khe tshjaN
toward red   bird   head open gun
'shoot at the red head of the bird'

Another demonstration of the lack of isomorphy between syntactic and prosodic structure that this end-based theory is capable of producing in Shanghai is provided by (30) and (31). Example (30) is a subject relative. The predicate of the relative clause consists of a verb and following NP.

(30) a. [e [V   [N]NP]VP Prt   ]S′ N]NP

b.   (   )(   )(   )

c.   (MH)(LH   LH)(LH   )   Underlying
      tshiq 've   'geq 'niN

d.   (MH)(L   H   )(LH   )   Normal
      tshiq 've   'geq 'niN

e.   (MH)(L   H   )(L   )   Focused 1
      tshiq *'ve*   'geq 'niN

f.   (MH)(L   H   )(LH   )   Focused 2
      tshiq 've   'geq 'niN
      eat   rice   COMP people
      'people who eat rice'

As predicted by the mapping rule in (25), the object NP of the relative forms a MaP with the head noun. This is shown in (30e), where focusing the object noun causes the deletion of tone on the head noun. As expected, focusing of the relative verb has no such effect, as shown in (30f).

Example (31) depicts an object relative.

(31) a. [[[N   ]$_{NP}$ [V   e]$_{VP}$ Prt   ]$_{S'}$ N   ]$_{NP}$

b. (   ) (   )

c. (LH   ) (MH   LH   ) (MH   )   Underlying
    'mo   tshiq   'geq   tshaw

d. (LH   ) (M   H   ) (MH   )   Normal
    'mo   tshiq   'geq   tshaw

e. (LH   ) (M   H   ) (MH   )   Focused 1
    '*mo*   tshiq   'geq   tshaw

f. (LH   ) (M   H   ) (L   )   Focused 2
    'mo   *tshiq*   'geq   tshaw
    horse   eat   COMP   grass
    'grass which horses eat'

The subject NP is in a different MaP from the following verb, as shown by the preservation of tone on the verb in (31e) even when the subject NP is focused. This is just what we expect, given that the left edge of a VP will require induce a MaP break between the subject and any VP-internal material that follows. Note that in this example, the verb does join with the head noun of the matrix NP in a MaP. Example (31f) shows that focusing the verb causes tone loss on the head noun. (This example also shows that the trace of the object NP has no effect on the syntax-phonology mapping.)

Certain aspects of the examples reviewed here explain why the prosodic domain for Post-Focus Tone Deletion is set at the left edge of a maximal projection rather than at the edge of a branching constituent, or of a constituent of a lower level in the X$'$ hierarchy. NPs and VPs will always have a MaP boundary at their left edge, whether or not they are branching. By contrast, no MaP boundary ever occurs at the left edge of X$'$. The phrase structure of Shanghai generates configurations where the left edge of X$'$ does not coincide with the left edge of a maximal projection, namely V$'$. In this case no MaP edge is found at the left edge of V$'$ (28)-(29).

Observe that all instances of medial MaP boundaries in the examples above coincide with the left edge of maximal projections of the lexical categories N, A, and V; we refer to these projections as Lex^{max}.[2] Suppose we were to revise the parameter of the syntax-phonology mapping rule for MaP so that it made appeal to Lex^{max}:

---

[2]Nonmedial MaP edges, i.e., ones at the edges of the utterance, are required independently by prosodic wellformedness conditions, and so tell us nothing about the parameterized rules of the mapping.

(32) The Shanghai Chinese Major Phrase Rule:

$$\text{Major Phrase: } \{ \text{ Left, Lex}^{\text{max}} \}$$

For the data discussed in this section, both (32) and its predecessor in (25) derive exactly the same results. What might prompt a choice between the two? It is precisely the data of the two 'puzzles' mentioned earlier, as we will see.

We have a precedent for this appeal to the lexical/functional distinction in the PW mapping rule (12). Rule (12) requires that the left edge of a lexical word coincide with the edge of a PW, ignoring function word edges. Indeed, any theory which seeks a general account of the behavior of function word 'clitics' must appeal to the lexical/functional distinction. What is novel about (32) is that the distinction plays a role at a higher level in the hierarchy of syntactic categories. We think our 'puzzles' make a case for allowing theories of grammar to make such a distinction.

5   Modularity in the Mapping

At the end of Section 3, we outlined two 'puzzles' for the theory of the mapping of syntactic structure into prosodic words.

5.1   The Solution to Puzzle One

The first puzzle involved a difference in the tonal behavior of postverbal prepositions, which correlated with whether they were 'weakly' or 'strongly' embedded. (13), which is repeated here in modified form as (33), represents the weakly embedded case.

(33) a. V [P   [N   ]$_{\text{NP}}$]$_{\text{PP}}$
     b. (   )(   )
     c. (L   H   )(L   H   )
          'z   'laq   'zawNhe
          'live in Shanghai'

Example (19a), which we repeat here in modified form as (34), is representative of the strongly embedded case. The (c) lines in each of (33) and (34) depict phonetic tone.

(34) a. V [[P   N]$_{\text{PP}}$ Prt   N   ]$_{\text{NP}}$
     b. (   )(   )(   )
     c. (LH)(LH)(L   H   L   )(L   H   )
          'z   'laq   'zawNhe   'geq   'njitsz
          be   at   Shanghai   son
          'be the son (who is) in Shanghai'

In (33) the LH tone pattern of the preposition 'laq is obligatorily deleted, while in (34) it is preserved. We take this to mean that the verb and the following preposition form a single PW in (33), but belong to separate PWs in (34). The (c) lines depict the parsing of (33) and (34) into PWs. Note that the parsing in (34) goes counter to what the mapping rule in (12) would predict: herein lies the puzzle, which we aim to attribute to the major phrasing of the sentence.

If we assume that rule (32) properly characterizes the mapping of surface structure into MaP, then the MaP analysis of (33) and (34) is as given in the (b) lines. In (33b), no MaP edge occurs at the left edge of the PP, but one shows up at the left edge of the NP which is the object of the preposition. This is a consequence of the restriction of the MaP algorithm to lexical categories. In (34b), however, the preposition is preceded by a MaP boundary. Its presence here is to be attributed not to the left edge of the PP, but rather to the left edge of the NP that dominates it. Thus the crucial difference between strongly and weakly embedded function words may be construed as a difference in the MaP structure that mapping rule (32) imposes. Strongly embedded function words head a functional X^{max} which are embedded at the left of a lexical X^{max}, and are hence preceded by a MaP boundary.

Facts involving Post-Focus Tone Deletion support this MaP analysis of (34). When the verb is focused, the preposition retains its tone, as seen in (35).

(35) (LH)   (LH)   (L   H   L)   (L   H)
     'z   'laq   'zawNhe 'geq 'nji tsz
     'be the son (who is) in Shanghai'

This indicates that the preposition is not in the same MaP as the verb.

Let us now see how the PW structure of (34) might be derived. Observe that the MaPs of line (b) in (34) properly include sequences of one or more PW, shown in line (c), as we expect of a wellformed tree. The prosodic structure of (34) contrasts with that of (36), which is what mapping rules predict. The output of mapping rule (32), shown in (36b), correctly matches the structure of (34b). However, the structure produced by the PW mapping rule (12), shown in (36c), does not conform to the actual parsing into PWs (see 34c). In particular, (12) fails to insert a PW break before the postverbal preposition, 'laq.

(36) a. V [P   N   Prt   N   ]$_{NP}$
     b. (   )(   )(   )
     c. (LH LH)(L   H   L)(L H)
        'z   'laq 'zawNhe   'geq 'njitsz
        'be the son (who is) in Shanghai'

Clearly, our parameterized mapping rules do not alone determine the prosodic structure of an utterance. In fact, taken together, the bracketings in lines (b) and (c) of (36) produce an illformed prosodic structure. In particular, the first PW of line (c) is dominated by two different MaPs, yielding an impermissible bracketing. In the actual prosodic structure of this sentence, shown in (34), this illformedness is eliminated. (34) retains the major phrasing of (36), and it retains all the prosodic word structure of (36) except that which is implicated in creating the illformedness under discussion. Note, moreover, that it is the higher order phrasing which prevails in (34): it forces into existence a lower order PW constituent break that is not otherwise specified by the PW mapping rule (12). Our hypothesis is that the PW break before the strongly embedded preposition is there in order to satisfy prosodic structure wellformedness, so that a PW edge coincides with the higher order MaP edge imposed by (32) at the left edge of the object NP. We term this constraining effect of higher order phrasing on lower order constituency the Top-Down Effect. (See Selkirk and Tateishi 1988a for evidence of a similar phenomenon in Japanese.)

In Section 4 we laid out a modular theory of the relation between the syntactic and prosodic structure of a sentence. On the one hand, the grammar has principles and rules for generating wellformed syntactic structures. On the other hand, it has principles defining wellformed prosodic structures (cf. (11)). And it has a set of parameterized rules specifying the allowable mapping(s) between the two (cf. (10)). The prosodic structure of a particular sentence must therefore satisfy two conditions: (a) it must be consistent with the syntax-phonology mapping rules, (b) it must be prosodically wellformed. We may view the generation of the heretofore 'puzzling' prosodic structure of (34) and related cases as evidence that the principle of prosodic structure wellformedness indeed plays a role in the derivation of the prosodic structure of sentences.

This modular approach to defining prosodic structure has a distinct advantage. It allows us to retain the eminently simple end-based theory of the mapping, instantiated in Shanghai Chinese by the two mapping rules (12) and (32). It also allows us to preserve what appears to be a rather profound generalization about the nature of prosodic structure, namely the wellformedness constraints in (11). The complexities of the mapping, seen in the 'puzzle' sentences, are derived through the interaction of these simple, discrete principles.

Sentences with weakly and strongly embedded postverbal prepositions do not constitute the sole evidence from Shanghai for the Top-Down Effect. Prepositions may be strongly embedded in other environments as well. For example, Jin 1986 points out that a preposition following the subject NP of a sentence is not in the same domain of Obligatory Tone Deletion as the subject. The Top-Down Effect explains this phenomenon, too. To see why consider (37):

(37) a. [N   ]$_{NP}$[[P   [N   ]$_{NP}$]$_{PP}$ V   ]$_{VP}$

   b. (   ) (   )(   )

c. (LHMH) (LH   )(MH HL)   (MH)   Underlying
   'lisz   'zaw   poqtsiN   tsou.

d. (L H   ) (LH   )(M   H)   (MH)   Normal
   'lisz   'zaw   poqtsiN   tsou.

e. (L H   ) (LH   )(M   H)   (MH)   Focused
   'lisz   'zaw   poqtsiN   tsou.
   Li Si   toward Beijing   walk

'Li Si walks toward Beijing.'

This example illustrates a function word, 'strongly' embedded within a VP. The relevant preposition, *'zaw*, retains its own. The reason is that the MaP mapping rule (32) requires the left edge of a major phrase to coincide with the left edge of VP, a Lex^{max}; the Top-Down Effect then locates the preposition in a separate PW from the subject.

Other sorts of function words may be strongly embedded as well. For example, the complementizer *'we* 'for' in (38) does not undergo tone deletion rules. It keeps its own tone for the same reason: It is 'strongly' embedded in a VP. The left edge of a MaP coincides with the left edge of VP; the Top-Down Effect prevents the underlying tone of the complementizer from being deleted.

(38) a.

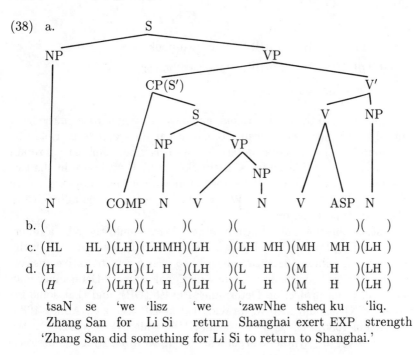

b. (   )( )(   )(   )   )(   )
c. (HL   HL)(LH)(LHMH)(LH   )(LH MH)(MH   MH)(LH)
d. (H   L)(LH)(L H)(LH   )(L   H)(M   H   )(LH)
   (*H*   *L*)(LH)(L H)(LH   )(L   H)(M   H   )(LH)

tsaN se   'we 'lisz   'we   'zawNhe tsheq ku   'liq.
Zhang San for Li Si   return Shanghai exert EXP strength
'Zhang San did something for Li Si to return to Shanghai.'

5.2   A Solution to Puzzle Two

The second puzzle cited at the end of section 3 was the contrast in tonal behavior between two instances of the same NP specifier element, depending on whether or not it was interpreted as an indefinite. When used as indefinite or 'weak' specifiers, the morphemes *'liq* and *'ljaN* (17a,b) and *sa, tsi* (18a,b) form a PW with the preceding verb and lose their tone. But when used in their 'strong' capacity (as numerals, in (20a,b), or wh-interrogative determiners (21a,b)) these same morphemes begin a new PW, retaining their tone. Also in the strong class are demonstrative determiners.

Data from Post-Focus Tone Deletion suggest that noun phrases with strong specifiers begin a new MaP, while noun phrases with weak specifiers do not. Consider one of the 'puzzle' pairs, (17b) and (20b), repeated here as (39) and (40). Major phrasing has been added in line (b), as has an additional pronunciation in which the verb is focused (line (d)).

(39) a. V [Q   Cl   N]
  b. (   )
  c. (L   H   L   )(HL)   'buy some books'
  d. (*L*   *H*   *L*   )(L)   '*buy* some books'
   'ma ljaNpeN   sz

(40) a. V [Q   Cl   N]
  b. (   )(   )
  c. (LH)(L   H   )(HL)   'buy two books'
  d. (*LH*)(L   H   )(HL)   '*buy* two books'
   'ma ljaNpeN   sz

In (39) focusing of the verb is accompanied by deletion of tone on the head noun. In (40), however, focusing the verb has no such effect. Both the head noun and the preceding determiner and classifier combination retain their tones. This evidence for a distinction in MaP structure in the two cases permits us to invoke the same top-down solution proposed above for the puzzling difference in PW structure revealed by the difference in Obligatory Tone Deletion.

Another question now arises, however. Why should there be a difference in major phrasing in these two cases? Current developments in the theory of noun phrase structure allow us to offer a very tentative answer. Arguments have been made that the functional category Determiner may head a maximal projection Determiner Phrase (DP), and that some instances of NP should instead be regarded as DP (see e.g., Abney 1985, 1986; Fukui 1986). DP is a functional X^{max}, while NP is a Lex^{max}. We have not as yet any syntactic arguments for drawing a distinction between

DP and NP in Shanghai Chinese, but feel compelled to point out that if the noun phrases with 'weak' determiners were instead analyzed as Determiner Phrases, while those with 'strong' determiners retained their NP analysis, then the major phrase mapping rule (32), which attends only to the left edge of Lex^{max}, would generate just the MaP structures given above in (39) and (40). This suggestion opens an interesting avenue for further research.

17

Syntax and Semantics in Phonology

IRENE VOGEL AND ISTVÁN KENESEI

AS IS WELL KNOWN, the standard T-model of generative grammar allows for only very simple interactions among its various components. That is, syntax interacts with phonology and semantics only in the sense that the output of the syntactic component serves as the input to the other two components. As far as the relation between syntax and semantics is concerned, evidence in favor of the T-model has been increasing. The nature of the relation between syntax and phonology, on the other hand, has come under challenge in a number of instances, and more complex types of interactions have been argued for. Moreover, in recent years it has also been proposed that a connection exists between phonology and semantics, a possibility excluded by the T-model. In this paper we will take stock of the main arguments and linguistic phenomena that have been brought to bear on specific aspects of the interactions among the different components of grammar. In bringing the various points together, we will evaluate their implications not only in relation to the issues they address directly, but also in relation to our understanding of the organization of grammar in general.

1 Phonology and Syntax

The connection between phonology and syntax gives rise to three questions: (a) is there any interaction at all; (b) if there is an interaction, is it direct or indirect i.e., do rules of one component 'see' structures of the other components; and (c) if there is an interaction, is it a two-way interaction or does only one component influence the other.

The answer to (a) is the easiest. In any model of grammar where syntax feeds phonology, all phonological rules that are not limited to applying within individual words will automatically require some interaction between the two components. As soon as the domain of application of a phonological rule involves a string of two or more words, syntax must be called upon to determine what types of words may be involved and how these words must be related to each other. In fact, in recent years numerous phenomena which depend on a connection between phonology and syntax have been adduced within the framework of generative grammar (e.g., Selkirk 1978, 1980a ; Kaisse 1985; Nespor and Vogel 1986).[1] Since the answer to the first question is positive, we must now address the other two questions, both of which relate in some way to the actual nature of the interaction between phonology and syntax. The issues can be represented schematically as in (1).

(1)   phonology-syntax connection

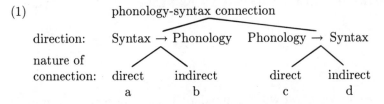

direction: Syntax → Phonology   Phonology → Syntax

nature of
connection: direct   indirect   direct   indirect
               a   b   c   d

If all of the possibilities exist, a grammar would need to allow for the four distinct types of interactions between phonology and syntax indicated by (a–d). In our examination of the issues relating to the nature of the syntax/phonology interaction just mentioned, however, it will be shown that only two of the possibilities occur.

An issue other than the three questions mentioned above that has received attention in the past is whether more than one level of syntax may be subject to phonological (and/or semantic) interpretation. Since it seems to be generally accepted now that only surface structure representations may be taken as input to phonology, we will not discuss this issue further in the present paper.

1.1   Direct Interaction

The most detailed claim of a direct interaction between syntax and phonology is found in Kaisse 1985. In Kaisse's system, the only syntactic information relevant in determining the application of external sandhi rules (ESRs) is the output of a syntactic derivation, complete with the results of all movement and deletion rules. Specifically, it is argued that the output structure of a syntactic derivation must be available to the postlexical phonology, where ESRs apply. In fact, it is precisely on the basis of

---

[1]The syntax-phonology connection has also recently received attention within the framework of Lexical Functional Grammar; however, we will restrict the present investigation to the standard transformational framework.

this syntactic structure that the application of ESRs is determined. In Kaisse's model ESRs apply between two words only when certain syntactic conditions are met. Either (a) one of the two words must lie on the edge of the constituent containing the other or (b) one of the words must c-command the other (p. 155). The operative definition of c-command is the following:

(2) Domain c-command

In the structure [$_{\mathrm{X^{max}}}$...α...], $\mathrm{X^{max}}$ is defined as the domain of α. Then α c-commands any β in its domain (p. 159).

According to Kaisse, the Italian external sandhi rule of *raddoppia-mento sintattico* (RS) applies only when both syntactic conditions are met; that is, when in a sequence of words *a* and *b*, (a) *a* c-commands *b* and (b) *a* and *b* lie at the left edge (i.e., are the first two words) of the constituent containing them. Thus, the rule applies in (3), as indicated by the arcs under the pairs of words involved in the phenomenon, to lengthen the first *g* in *gru* and *gallegianti*, following the stressed vowel at the end of the preceding words.

(3)

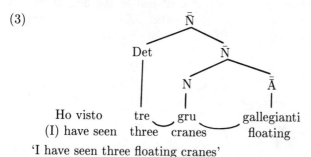

Ho visto   tre   gru   gallegianti
(I) have seen   three   cranes   floating
'I have seen three floating cranes'

According to Kaisse, who bases her argument on Napoli and Nespor 1979, RS is blocked between *gru* and *gallegianti* in (4), as indicated by the slash, since in this case *gru* does not lie on the left edge of the constituent containing it and *gallegianti*.

(4)

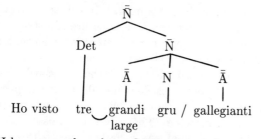

Ho visto   tre   grandi   gru / gallegianti
                large
'I have seen three large floating cranes'

The blocking of RS in (4) poses a problem, however, since in more recent work (Nespor and Vogel 1982, 1986) it has been argued that at least in the variety of standard Italian spoken in Tuscany, RS can, indeed, apply between *gru* and *gallegianti*. The problem could be resolved by relaxing the requirement that the first word involved in RS be at the left edge of the constituent that dominates *a* and *b*. But this would just create other problems, as it incorrectly predicts that RS should take place between *gru* and *poco* in (5), where it must, in fact, be blocked.

(5)

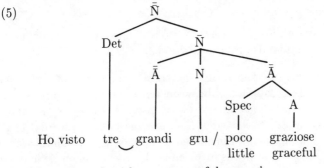

'I have seen three large ungraceful cranes'

A similar problem arises in structures such as the one in (6). Although Kaisse's model would correctly predict RS between *farà* and *già*, it incorrectly predicts failure of RS between *già* and *buio*.

(6)

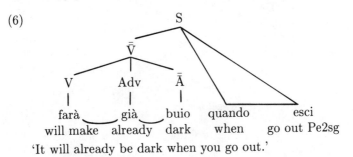

'It will already be dark when you go out.'

Thus, c-command and edge restrictions on external sandhi rules cannot make correct predictions for RS in Italian.

A more general problem with this approach lies in the directness of the interaction between the syntactic surface structure of a string and the application of phonological rules. In order to determine whether a sandhi rule applies, the syntactic relation between a given pair of words must be scrutinized each time to determine whether the necessary conditions exist. As Selkirk 1986 points out, this does not allow for the possibility of sandhi rules which apply throughout a given string whenever their structural description is encountered. The only rules Kaisse claims may apply throughout a string are what she calls fast speech rules. These rules are supposed to apply across the board throughout a sentence, the claim being that no phonological rules apply to substrings which cannot be defined in a pairwise fashion by the two conditions seen above. Thus, since

Kaisse does not identify any independent phonological constituents or domains, she cannot account for the type of external sandhi rules referred to as 'domain span' rules (Selkirk 1980a), of which examples abound in the literature (see, among others, Selkirk 1978, 1980a; Hyman et al. 1987; Rice 1987; Nespor and Vogel 1986).

In addition to Kaisse's proposal, it has been claimed that some sandhi rules apply directly in relation to syntax in yet another sense. Instead of being sensitive to specific syntactic relations between words, these rules are sensitive to the syntactic category of the words involved. One such rule is a vowel deletion rule of Italian which may delete the final vowel of a verb if preceded by a coronal sonorant and followed by another word within a specific domain (Nespor and Vogel 1986:32). Thus, deletion applies (as indicated by the slash through the vowel) in (7a), where the word in question is the verbal head of a phrase, but it is blocked in (7b), where the potential target is a nominal head, despite the similar segmental and structural characteristics of the two phrases.[2]

(7) a.   mangianø tutto   '(they) eat everything'
    b. *un fagianø turco   'a Turkish pheasant'

Rules that need to refer to specific syntactic categories do not appear to be very common, but additional examples are discussed in Welmers and Welmers 1969, Kenstowicz and Kisseberth 1977, and Kaisse 1977b. Unless some more general way to account for such rules is discovered in the future,[3] it seems that linguistic theory must be able to accommodate phonological rules that make direct reference to syntax.

1.2   Indirect Interaction

Within the framework of generative grammar, even the early work of Chomsky and Halle 1968 takes an explicit position with respect to pho-nology-syntax interaction: phonology does not necessarily reflect syntactic structure. While the output of the syntactic component constitutes the input to the phonological component, SPE recognizes that discrepancies may obtain between the syntactic and phonological structures of a sentence. In such cases, readjustment rules convert the surface structures generated by the syntactic component into the structures required by the phonology (SPE:9). This is especially noticeable in intonational phrasing, as has often been pointed out in relation to the following sentence:

(8) This is [the cat that caught [the rat that stole [the cheese]]]

---

[2]The final vowel of a noun may be deleted only in a very restricted set of words. See van Hoorn 1983 and Vogel et al. 1983 for a more detailed discussion of this rule.

[3]Cowper and Rice 1987 argue that at least some 'phonosyntactic' rules originally claimed to require direct reference to syntax can, in fact, be reanalyzed in terms of phonological constituents.

While the brackets in (8) indicate certain aspects of the syntactic structure of the sentence, they do not correctly reflect its phonological structure. Instead, the major phonological breaks should come after *cat* and *rat*. Thus, SPE posits a readjustment rule to convert (8) "with its multiply embedded sentences, into a structure where each embedded sentence is sister-adjoined in turn to the sentence dominating it" (p. 372). Intonation breaks thereby coincide with the beginning of each S.

While the phonology-syntax interaction is a peripheral issue in SPE, it takes center stage in Selkirk 1972. Working within the SPE framework, Selkirk modifies the original proposal by showing that at least in certain types of phonological phenomena, interaction between the two components is only indirect. Word boundaries (#'s) inserted into a string on the basis of syntactic structure determine where external sandhi rules apply. Phonological rules thus do not directly 'see' syntactic structure, but rather access only strings of segments and boundaries. Selkirk also argues that readjustment rules modify the phonological structures arrived at on the basis of the syntactic surface structure, resulting in an even less direct connection between phonology and syntax. For example, words P and Q are in a liaison context in French in the configuration . . . P][#Q. . . (Selkirk 1972:143), as in *les*][#*animaux* 'the animals'. In certain cases, however, readjustment rules change . . . P#][#Q. . . into the appropriate liaison configuration, with only one boundary between the two words. Thus, *un petit*#][#*animal* 'a small animal' is converted to *un petit*][#*animal* so that liaison may apply between *petit* and *animal*.

In subsequent works, Selkirk 1978, 1980a argues for an even less direct relation between phonology and syntax. The model of prosodic phonology advanced in these articles provides two ways for syntax to affect phonology. First, there is a small number of so-called labelled bracket domain rules—phonological rules which mention specific types of syntactic information in their environments. This phenomenon is manifested by the Italian rule of vowel deletion. In addition, syntax interacts with phonology more indirectly, through the application of a set of mapping rules which convert syntactic surface structure into a phonological structure that is not necessarily isomorphic to the former. Certain aspects of syntactic constituent structure are used in order to build up a hierarchically arranged set of (prosodic) phonological constituents, as in (9), where '$\emptyset$/s/p' is the mapping which converts the final syntactic representation of a sentence, S_k, into a phonological representation.

(9) $\{S_1, \ldots S_i, \ldots S_k\}\emptyset/s/p \{P_1, \ldots P_n\}$
     (Selkirk 1980a:108)

In this model, syntactic rules apply from S_1 to S_i, and labelled bracket domain rules apply from S_i to S_k. Subsequently, S_k, the last syntactic representation, undergoes a set of mapping rules to yield P_1, the phonological representation of the sentence. Additional phonological rules, the so-called prosodic domain rules, may then apply to the prosodic constituents comprising this structure.

A typical prosodic domain rule is the rule of *raddoppiamento sintattico*, seen above. RS applies at the juncture of phonological words belonging to the same immediately higher prosodic constituent, the phonological phrase. The application of RS in (10) is indicated by an arc beneath the two conditioning words, while its failure to apply is marked with a slash.

(10) a. Ho visto tre‿gru‿gallegianti.
         'I have seen three floating cranes.'

      b. Ho visto tre‿grandi gru‿gallegianti.
         'I have seen three large floating cranes.'

      c. Ho visto tre‿grandi gru / poco graziose.
         'I have seen three large ungraceful cranes.'

According to the rules proposed by Nespor and Vogel 1986 for constructing phonological phrases in Italian, the string *tre gru gallegianti* in (10a) forms a single phonological phrase. Thus, whenever the appropriate segmental context for RS occurs within this domain, the rule applies. Similarly, in (10b), *tre grandi gru gallegianti* constitutes a single phonological phrase, providing two contexts for RS to apply in. In (10c), on the other hand, *poco graziose* does not form a phonological phrase with what precedes it; RS is, therefore, blocked between *gru* and *poco*. If we try to account for the application of RS by referring directly to syntactic structures, the result is, at best, a list of environments in which the rule may or may not apply. The indirect reference approach whereby syntactic structure only plays a role in the mapping rules that create the phonological phrase (and other phonological constituents) provides a more accurate and insightful account of RS and analogous rules.

In addition to Selkirk's original proposal, a substantial amount of data has been amassed in support of the claim that direct reference to syntactic structures cannot account for the application of a large set of phonological rules. Instead, it has been found in a wide variety of languages that prosodic constituents (from the phonological word through the phonological utterance) are what determine the domains of application of ESRs. (See, among others, Nespor and Vogel 1986, Hyman et al. 1987, Rice 1987, Vogel and Kenesei 1987).

Thus far we have taken for granted the assumption that the connection between syntax and phonology proceeds in one direction only, and have examined only cases in which syntax affects phonology. In the next section, we address the issue of whether this is, in fact, the only direction in which information may pass between the phonological and syntactic components of grammar.

1.3   Phonological Input to Syntax

While syntax automatically has an effect on phonology in any model of grammar that takes the output of syntax as the input to phonology (e.g., the standard T-model), such a model makes no provision for the opposite effect. Rather, it predicts that phonology will not affect syntax. No syntactic operations should make reference to phonological information, nor should any phonological rules be ordered before any syntactic rules. This situation accords with the principle of phonology-free syntax (Zwicky and Pullum 1986a). In the literature, however, a number of phenomena have been argued to be counter-evidence to this claim. That is, it has been proposed that there must, indeed, be a two-way interaction between phonology and syntax, on the grounds that there are phenomena that require the syntax to have access to phonological information.

The types of phonological phenomena which have been argued to affect syntax are typically nonsegmental, e.g., number of syllables, or intonation patterns, as well as identity of adjacent (or close-by) strings of sounds. For example, Hetzron 1972 points out that in Modern Israeli Hebrew the relative position of two pronominal complements following a verb is dependent on the number of syllables each contains. The shorter one appears directly following the verb. If the complements are of the same length, either order is possible. This can be seen in (11), where the complements in question are italicized (Hetzron 1972:253–54).

(11) a.   hu   her?a   *li*   oto
          he   showed   to-me   it-acc
          'he showed it to me'

      b.   hu   lakax   *oto*   *mimenu*
          he   took   it-acc   from-him
          'he took it from him'

      c.   hu   her?a   *oto*   *lanu*
          he   showed   it-acc   to-us
          'he showed it to us'

      d.   hu   her?a   *lanu*   *oto*
          he   showed   to-us   it-acc
          'he showed it to us'

Since the order of the complements depends not on their grammatical function, but rather on their syllabic form (at least in nonemphatic pronunciations), Hetzron argues that the syntactic rule of pronoun placement must have access to phonological information.

In another instance, intonational structure (specifically, stress) has been argued to be relevant for the application of certain syntactic rules, including Auxiliary Shift (AS) in English (see Baker 1971). For example, in sentences such as those in (12), the auxiliary is typically shifted to the left of certain preverbal elements (e.g., *often, never*).

(12)   a. They have often considered moving to Italy.

  b. Archibald is never late.

Baker argues that two circumstances can prevent AS: (a) emphasis on the finite auxiliary verb and (b) deletion of the constituent following the auxiliary. Thus, when the auxiliaries in the sentences in (12) are stressed, AS fails, as indicated by the asterisks in (13).

(13)   a. *They *have* often considered moving to Italy.

  b. *George *is* never late.

Similarly, if AS applies to a sentence such as the one in (14a), the result is ungrammatical, as indicated in (14b).

(14)   a. Clarence has worked more for you this week alone than Charlie ever has ___ for you.

  b.*Clarence has worked more for you this week alone than Charlie has ever ___ for you.

According to Baker, what characterizes these two instances of AS blocking is their dependence on a phonological property of the sentences. That is, the auxiliary is not stressless. Thus, Baker argues, a movement rule of syntax must take into consideration the degree of stress on a word in order to determine whether or not it can apply.

 A third area in which it is argued that syntax must have access to phonological information involves phonological identity (e.g., Eisenberg 1973, Rivero and Walker 1976). For example, Eisenberg 1973 argues that certain syntactic deletion rules in German may apply only if the elements involved are phonologically identical, in addition to being structurally and referentially identical. Thus, deletion is possible in (15b), but not in (16b).

(15)   a. weil Franz das Haus kaufen könnte und ich den Garten kaufen könnte
   'because Franz could buy the house and I could buy the garden'

  b. weil Franz das Haus ___und ich den Garten kaufen könnte

(16)   a. weil Franz das Haus kauft und ich den Garten kaufe
   'because Franz buys the house and I buy the garden'

  b.*Weil Franz das Haus ___und ich den Garten kaufe

 Pullum and Zwicky (forthcoming) and Zwicky and Pullum 1986b argue that examples like these are not, in fact, violations of the principle of phonology-free syntax. For each case, they claim, either (a) something other than what is suggested is actually going on or (b) an alternative analysis is possible. For example, according to Pullum and Zwicky, cases such as the German identity phenomenon can be dealt with by a universal condition on the way in which phonology is allowed to play a role in ellipsis phenomena. Thus, this phenomenon does not require the incorporation of phonological information into syntactic rules.

The problem raised by AS can probably be dismissed as a preference or a tendency, following Pullum and Zwicky's treatment of other so-called stylistic rules. Such rules, it is argued, are not really transformations, but represent preferences for certain orders that depend on more general principles, such as ease of processing. In fact, the sentences marked with an asterisk in (13) and (14) may only be less preferred than the corresponding ones where AS has not applied, rather than actually being ungrammatical. In any case, just because no syntactic account of a rule such as AS can be found, this does not mean that the solution is to bring phonology into the syntactic component. One possible alternative might be to account for the presence of stress on the relevant auxiliaries with a postsyntactic phonological rule. The issue would thus no longer be one of phonology influencing syntax, but the reverse, syntax affecting phonology, the usual state of affairs.

As for the Hebrew problem, and others where it seems that syllable structure has an effect on the application of syntactic rules, several factors may account for the observed restrictions. Again, processing considerations may be relevant, with the preference being for heavier elements to appear closer to the end of a sentence (see Pullum and Zwicky (forthcoming)). Alternatively, there might be some other language specific (or possibly universal) phonological factor involved. Perhaps the overall rhythmic structure of a sentence favors a shorter clitic before a longer one. In this event, different versions of the sentence could be generated by the syntactic component, with the phonology filtering out structures that do not conform to the general phonological constraints of the language.

A somewhat more complex challenge to the principle of phonology-free syntax is raised by Inkelas 1988.[4] On the basis of the distribution of the conversational particle, *fa*, in Hausa, Inkelas argues not only that the phonological phrase is a constituent of the language, but also that syntax must make crucial reference to this phonological constituent. Essentially, *fa* can be found following certain words or syntactic constituents, which it serves to highlight. In most instances, there are also specific conditions that must obtain, namely that the constituent following the site of *fa*-insertion must either be intonationally emphasized or branching (i.e., contain more than one word). It should be noted that it is not enough for there to be two or more words after *fa*; they must actually form a constituent. Thus, *fa* is correctly placed in the sentences in (17), but not in those in (18), where the conditions on what may follow *fa* are violated (see Inkelas 1988).

---

[4]See also Zec and Inkelas (this volume).

(17) a. Ya sayi fa *rigar.*   (italics = intonational emphasis)
          'He bought *the shirt*'

      b. Ya sayi fa babbar riga.
          'He bought a big shirt'

      c. Ya sayi   fa abincin rana.
          He bought   food-of day
          'He bought lunch'

      d. Sun siffanta wa Tanko fa ni da ita.
          'They described to Tanko me and her'

      e. Mun sauka a fa *Kano.*
          'We arrived at *Kano*'

(18) a.∗Ya sayi fa riga.
          'He bought a shirt'

      b.∗Ya sayi fa abinci jiya.
          'He bought food yesterday'

      c.∗Sun siffanta wa Tanko fa ita.
          'They described to Tanko her'

      d.∗Mun sauka fa Kano.
          'We arrived at Kano'

When *fa* follows the first constituent of a sentence, the conditions on the subsequent constituent are no longer necessary, as can be seen by comparing the sentences in (19) with the corresponding ones in (20). This is, in fact, not particularly surprising since initial position automatically signals emphasis in Hausa, thus eliminating the need for it to be expressed intonationally.

(19) a.∗Na sayi   babbar fa riga.
          I   bought big   shirt
          'I bought a gown'

      b.∗Mun rubuta wasiƙa guda fa shida.
          we   wrote letter   unit   six
          'We wrote six letters'

(20) a. Babbar fa riga na saya.
          big   shirt I   bought
          'A gown, I bought'

      b. Wasiƙa guda fa shida muka rubuta
          letter   unit   six   we   wrote
          'Six letters, we wrote'

Inkelas points out that to account for all the environments in which *fa* can and cannot occur in terms of syntactic structure, we would have to provide a list of positions, without being able to capture any generalizations. On the other hand, if the phonological phrase is taken into consideration, it becomes very simple to state the environment for *fa*: it must follow a phonological phrase, as shown in (21).

(21) fa: $[\ [\ \ ]_\phi -]_\phi$

(Inkelas 1988)

The problem this analysis raises is that the syntactic distribution of the element *fa* is not determined directly by syntactic factors but rather depends on phonological factors. Thus, it violates the principle of phonology-free syntax. It is true that the construction of the phonological phrase takes into consideration certain syntactic (and in Hausa, according to Inkelas, also lexical and semantic) information, but once phonological phrases are built, syntactic information is no longer available. Thus, the placement of *fa* is related to syntax only indirectly, via a derived phonological structure. The picture of the interaction between syntax and phonology that emerges from this analysis of *fa* is a very complex one. If syntactic rules are allowed to refer to prosodic structure, this means that they may be sensitive to the result of a mapping which takes place on the basis of the surface structure of a sentence. In other words, such syntactic rules are sensitive to a structure which is derived from a later stage in the syntax than the one at which these rules, themselves, apply. Not only does this type of analysis require that a syntactic rule take phonological structure into account, it also seems to require a type of globality.

The problem of globality might be eliminated by allowing prosodic structure to be built up along with syntactic structure, rather than after all syntactic operations have been carried out. Thus, for any stage in a syntactic derivation there would be a corresponding prosodic structure. This prosodic structure would be modified as needed in relation to modifications in syntactic structure, not unlike the way it has been proposed metrical structure can be built up cyclically in lexical phonology (see among others, Kiparsky 1982a, Booij and Rubach 1984). While such a solution might alleviate the problem of globality, it certainly does not avoid the violation of the principle of phonology-free syntax. To the contrary, it would require a systematic alternation of syntactic rules with, at least, the mapping rules that create phonological structure. Moreover, whether phonological rules that apply in relation to this phonological structure would also be allowed to apply at the various stages of a derivation, interspersed with syntactic rules, is an empirical question that would have to be addressed if such an analysis were adopted.

Alternatively, we could adopt still another solution that would maintain the principle of phonology-free syntax without requiring other major

changes in the model. Specifically, we could allow the syntactic rule of
fa placement to generate structures with *fa* in (almost) any position.
Only subsequently, when such structures enter the phonological and logical form components of the grammar, will those sentences that do not
conform to some appropriate phonological and/or semantic interpretation
be eliminated. For example, all sentences with more than one *fa* could be
eliminated on semantic grounds having to do with how many constituents
may be emphasized in a sentence. All sentences in which *fa* does not follow a phonological phrase could be ruled out on the grounds that they
would violate the phonological requirement that *fa* must follow precisely
this type of prosodic constituent. Thus, rather than violating the principle of phonology-free syntax, we could allow the syntax to generate a
wide variety of structures, many of which must be ruled out at a later
stage. Such a position is not unique to the problem of *fa* placement in
Hausa, but rather is part of any system in which the rule component is
fairly unconstrained and the final task of determining which sentences are
grammatical is left to a set of conditions.

1.4   How Many Types of Phonology-Syntax Interactions Are There?

We have seen in the preceding sections an unquestionable need for syntactic information to affect phonology. Furthermore, this type of interaction
appears to work in two ways. Certain phonological rules require direct
reference to specific properties of the elements involved, such as the syntactic category to which they belong. In addition, other rules do not
apply directly in relation to syntactic structure, but rather depend only
indirectly on syntax. The latter, which appear to be much more common
than the former, apply to prosodic constituents which are built on the
basis of syntactic (and other types of) information, but which are not
necessarily isomorphic to any other constituents of the grammar.

As for the opposite direction of influence, that is, phonology affecting
syntax, the situation is not as clear. A variety of phenomena have been
discussed in the literature as challenges to the notion of phonology-free
syntax. Following arguments made by Pullum and Zwicky, a number of
alternative methods were suggested for handling cases in which syntax appears to refer to such phonological properties as syllable structure, stress
patterns, or segmental identity of two words. This still leaves the problem
raised by Inkelas 1988, though, where syntax is claimed to be sensitive not
to the phonological properties of words, but to phonological constituent
structure. Alternative analyses of the phenomenon of *fa* placement in
Hausa on which Inkelas bases her claim have been considered here, and
at least one can be found which does not lead to a violation of the principle
of phonology-free syntax. On these grounds, we can answer the question
raised at the beginning of section 2 about the number and types of interactions between phonology and syntax. Returning to the figure in (1),

we can conclude that of the four possibilities described, only two actually exist: (1a) and (1b). That is, only those interactions are allowed in which syntax affects phonology. As we have seen, however, limiting the possibilities in this way has required reanalysis of a number of phenomena. In at least some cases, the reanalysis is clearly to be preferred. If and when more data are amassed in which it appears that phonology is affecting syntax, it may become necessary to reevaluate this type of interaction. In the meantime, however, the bulk of the evidence favors a single direction of influence, from syntax to phonology.

2   Phonology and Semantics

While the interaction between phonology and syntax has received much attention in recent years, the interaction between phonology and semantics has attracted much less interest. There are nevertheless areas in which the investigation of the phonology-syntax connection cannot be complete unless semantics is also considered. This is particularly true where intonational phenomena are concerned since they not only involve syntactic structures, but are also intimately connected to certain aspects of the meaning of a sentence. Such issues also bear on the relationship between the syntactic and semantic components of a grammar.

Observing that there seems to be some relation between meaning and intonation (see among others, Bolinger 1972, Halliday 1967, Ladd 1980), in recent years many have tried to capture this relation in terms of one of the constituents of the prosodic hierarchy, namely, the intonational phrase (IP). Semantic factors such as focus and scope are proposed to play a role in creating and/or assigning stress to IPs (Selkirk 1984, Nespor and Vogel 1986, Vogel and Kenesei 1987). The details of how the relation between semantics and phonology is to be encoded, however, give rise to a number of problems. In this section, we will examine some of these problems, primarily in relation to two proposals that attempt to explicitly relate semantics to the IP constituent: Selkirk 1984 and Nespor and Vogel 1986.

2.1   Intonational Phrasing and Sense Units

Of the various options available in a (somewhat extended) framework of Government and Binding Theory, Selkirk 1984 chooses to assign intonational phrasing freely to surface structures as long as the following two conditions are met: (a) intonation phrases do not overlap and (b) they correspond to 'sense units.' A sense unit, according to Selkirk, may consist of any single (syntactic) constituent or group of constituents if the following requirements are met (Selkirk 1984:291):

(22) Two constituents C_i, C_j form a sense unit if (a) or (b) is true of the semantic interpretation of the sentence:

    a. C_i modifies C_j (a head)

    b. C_i is an argument of C_j (a head)

On the basis of this Sense Unit Condition then, (23a) represents a possible intonational phrasing since each bracketed constituent either consists of a head (*Jane*) or of a head and argument (*gave the book, to Mary*). (23b) is not a possible intonational phrasing since *the book to Mary* does not conform to any of the definitions of what may constitute a sense unit.

(23) a. (Jane) (gave the book) (to Mary)

    b.*(Jane) (gave) (the book to Mary)

Such intonational phrasings contribute to the Intonated Surface Structure (ISS) of a sentence, a representation consisting of surface syntactic structure enriched with indications of intonational structure and pitch accents. The latter are tonal elements assigned freely to one or more word-sized units in a sentence. Since intonational phrasing and pitch accent assignment both apply freely, ISS is subject to certain well-formedness conditions. It is precisely at this point that the relation between semantics and phonology is encoded in Selkirk's system since the conditions essentially involve the appropriateness of the match between the phonological structure of ISS, and possible semantic interpretations of these structures. One of the well-formedness conditions is the Sense Unit Condition seen above, which requires that a sentence be divided into one or more sense units, a semantic notion defined in syntactic terms. The other involves the assignment of focus to the relevant constituent(s) of a sentence. The same notions of head, modifier and argument needed to define sense units are also needed in determining the focus structure of a sentence, as can be seen in (24).

(24) a. Basic Focus Rule

    A constituent to which a pitch accent is assigned is a focus.

    b. Phrasal Focus Rule

    A constituent may be a focus if (i) or (ii) (or both) is true:

      i. The constituent that is its *head* is a focus.

      ii. A constituent contained within it that is an *argument* of the head is a focus.

(Selkirk 1984:207)

Thus, in (25a), where *books* bears pitch accent, each of the following may be interpreted as being in focus: N, NP, VP, S. In (25b), however, where *new* bears pitch accent, only this adjective (or AP) may be in focus since it is a modifier of the head noun books, and not itself an argument.

(25)   a. [$_S$ Jane [$_{VP}$ gave [$_{NP}$ the new [$_N$ *books*]] to Mary]]

   b. Jane gave [$_{NP}$ the [$_{AP}$ *new*] books] to Mary

The fact that ISS must be checked for well-formedness in relation to certain semantic principles and provided with an interpretation by the semantic component, i.e., Logical Form (LF), requires that the overall model of grammar be changed somewhat from the standard T-model shown in (26). Specifically, Selkirk proposes to modify the model as in (27), so that ISS is the input to LF, mediated by the necessary well-formedness conditions.

(26) Standard T-model

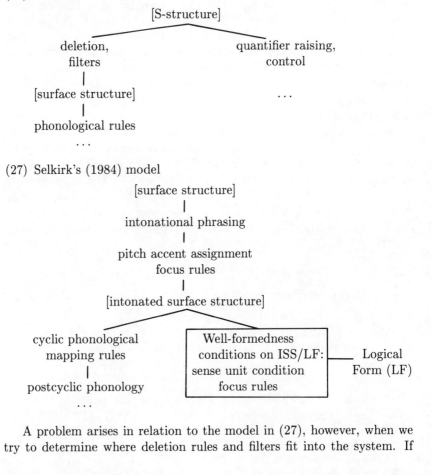

(27) Selkirk's (1984) model

A problem arises in relation to the model in (27), however, when we try to determine where deletion rules and filters fit into the system. If we make the standard assumption that the surface structure in (27) incorporates the results of deletions (and filters), then the input to the intonational phrasing rules must be devoid of certain phonologically 'invisible' material. This material, however, may be needed to contribute to the semantic interpretation in LF of such elements as wh-relative pronouns. Nevertheless, we must maintain that intonational structure is a distinct representation from the syntactic surface structure, given that a bracketing such as the one in (23a) above is perfectly acceptable intonationally, but not syntactically. If such a structure were taken to be a syntactic representation and, as such, subject to the rules of LF, it would violate the Projection Principle, which requires that the theta-marking properties of each lexical item be represented in D-structure, S-structure and LF. What this means is that a dual structure which consists of the intonational phrasing as well as the syntactic structure, i.e., Selkirk's ISS, is the only way to get both syntactic and phonological information into LF. The domain of the Projection Principle in its standard form does not include the Phonetic Form (PF) component. But if the Projection Principle is observed in PF, as required in Selkirk's model, empty categories will have to be part of ISS; deletion rules will not be allowed to delete anything that contributes to LF-interpretation (e.g., wh-relative pronouns, *that, for*). It should be noted, furthermore, that if the Projection Principle is in force at the point of ISS construction, the Sense Unit Condition can be directly observed. That is, heads, arguments (i.e., maximal projections whose theta-roles are determined by a head) and modifiers (i.e., non-subcategorized maximal projections dominated by a projection of the head) can be 'read off' the tree. Thus, the only reason the ISS must be the input to LF is that it provides the necessary information for focus interpretation, at least in the examples given by Selkirk. Note, however, that head-argument relations become less clear in S-structure as a result of movement transformations. So, while *Jane* may be considered an argument of *seem* in *Jane seems t to be intelligent,* it is somewhat more difficult to find criteria for what type of elements may join with a wh-phrase to form an IP (cf. *which boys did Jane see t in the room*).

Although Selkirk does not specify how LF would interpret the dual structure of an ISS, it seems that there must be two types of semantic interpretation. One would apply to the syntactic surface structures and the other would apply to the phonological structures. As far as the latter is concerned, what must be interpreted semantically is the focus structure of those ISSs that are found to conform to the well-formedness conditions regulating the relations among intonational phrasing, pitch accent assignment and focus assignment. For example, a structure such as the one in (28a) would not even reach LF for interpretation since it would be eliminated on the grounds that *the book to Mary* violates one of the well-formedness conditions: the Sense Unit Condition. The structure in (28b), however, conforms to the well-formedness conditions and therefore may be given a semantic interpretation.

(28) a.

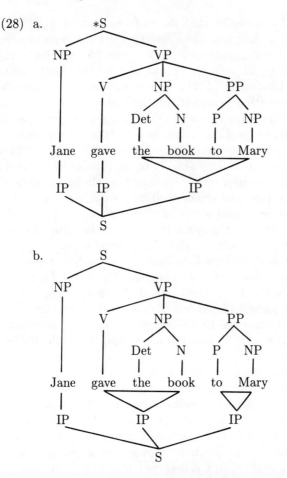

This is not the first time dual structures have been proposed in the generative literature. For example, it has been proposed that they are needed to represent the distinct properties of two levels of analysis in nonconfigurational languages: lexical or virtual structure, and phrase or configurational structure (see Zubizarreta and Vergnaud 1982, Hale 1983, Mohanan 1983). The dual structures of the ISS, however, have significant consequences for our understanding of the interactions among the various components of grammar. Specifically, the proposed analysis requires that the input to semantics be not only the output of the syntactic component, but also a phonological representation. Thus, phonology feeds semantics, and the original notion of the phonological and semantic components being independent of each other cannot be maintained. On analogy to the principle of phonology-free syntax, we can say that the model in question would violate a principle of phonology-free semantics. Furthermore, there is a type of mismatch in the two structures in the sense that LF sees in the ISS a phonological representation derived from the surface structure of a sentence, while at the same time it sees the earlier syntactic form from which the ISS is derived. In the next section, we will consider a different type of approach which we believe resolves the problems just seen.

2.2   Intonational Phrasing and Quantifiers

While Selkirk's model is claimed to incorporate semantics in determining the intonational structure of a sentence, this is done, at best, only indirectly, through well-formedness conditions. In the model proposed in Nespor and Vogel 1986, semantics also plays a role in relation to intonation phrases. Specifically, it is claimed that information about semantic prominence, or focus, is required in order to assign the appropriate relative prominence relations to the phonological phrases contained within an IP. In an extension of this model, Vogel and Kenesei 1987 propose a more direct and substantial contribution of semantics to phonology, arguing that certain semantic notions, such as scope, must be referred to in defining and constructing IPs in the first place.

As in the case of Selkirk's ISS proposal, the proposals of Nespor and Vogel 1986 and Vogel and Kenesei 1987 encounter difficulties in associating the necessary semantic information with a phonological structure. If we assume that S-structure is the input to LF and that surface structure is the input to phonology, as in (29), it will be necessary for the phonological structure of a sentence to be matched somehow with the semantic interpretation of that same sentence.

(29)

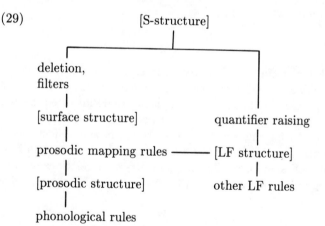

Since it is the semantic information that is relevant to phonology in this approach, the direction of the interaction between these components is the opposite of that seen earlier. Thus, instead of the issue being 'phonology-free semantics', it is 'semantics-free phonology'. In either case, however, the solution conflicts with the standard T-model in that the two interpretive components are not independent of each other. In what follows, we will explore another possibility which would allow us to maintain the autonomy of the phonological and semantic components.

First, consider a proposal made by van Riemsdijk and Williams 1981 with respect to the structure of a grammar. In a discussion of several models, they introduce data on the interaction of pied-piping and *wh*-movement. They argue that these data support a rule of Quantifier Interpretation which 'assigns an index to a quantifier phrase and adjoins a (phonologically null) copy of that index to the S that is the scope of that phrase' (p. 192). In the model van Riemsdijk and Williams propose, NP-movement and wh-movement are relegated to different syntactic levels. The former maps D-structure to NP-structure while the latter maps LF-structure to S-structure. Furthermore, the mapping between NP-structure and LF-structure is regarded as a function of Quantifier Interpretation, as can be seen in (30).

(30)   [D-structure]

            |

            NP-movement

            |

            [NP-structure]

            |

            Quantifier Interpretation

            |

            [LF-structure]

            |

            wh-movement

            |

            [S-structure]

Adducing additional arguments from reconstruction, variable binding and parasitic gaps, Williams 1986 proposes certain modifications of this model. Showing that the rule of Quantifier Raising is not well motivated, he concludes that a separate LF component is not needed. He replaces Quantifier Interpretation with a rule which has essentially the same effect: Scope Assignment. This rule, together with *wh*-movement, allows us to derive S-structure from NP-structure.[5] Thus, quantifier-scope relations are represented by scoped S-structures as in (32), rather than LF-structures as in (31).

(31)   a. $[_{S'}$ which car$_i$ $[_S$ did you see e$_i$]]

       b. $[_{S'}$ every car$_i$ $[_S$ you saw e$_i$]]

(32)   a. $[_{S'}$ which car $[_{S:i}$ did you see e$_i$]]

       b. $[_{S'}$ $[_{S:i}$ you saw every car$_i$]]

---

[5]There is also an another mapping relation between S-structure and NP-structure which, according to Williams, covers certain cases of reconstruction.

Note that in (32) the quantifiers, whether moved or not, are the determiners of their respective NPs. The variables are the indexed argument positions, and the scopes of the quantifiers are defined as the phrases bearing the same indexes.

In the model proposed in Williams 1986, 1988, the functions of LF are thus redistributed between NP-structure and S-structure. Modules defined on the basis of relations between arguments (i.e., NP and trace, Binding Theory, thematic structure) are associated with the level of NP-structure. On the other hand, those modules that depend on relations between arguments and non-arguments (i.e., quantification, the licensing of parasitic gaps, weak cross-over effects) are associated with scoped S-structures. We will not go into further detail here about van Riemsdijk's and Williams's proposals. It is worth noting, however, that their arguments provide independent evidence for assigning quantifier-scope relations to S-structure rather than to LF. This turns out to be crucial to the issue at hand since we are concerned precisely with the interaction between such semantic notions as quantification and focus on the one hand, and phonological structure, especially the IP, on the other hand.

Elsewhere (Vogel and Kenesei 1987), we propose that the IP in Hungarian is dependent on quantifier-scope relations for its construction. Given a flat S-structure for Hungarian sentences, as represented in (33) (see Kenesei 1986, (forthcoming); Marácz 1987), a neutral sentence allows for as many IPs as there are immediate constituents in the sentence.

(33)

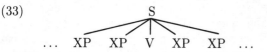

     ... XP   XP   V   XP   XP ...

In sentences containing quantifiers (e.g., universal quantifiers, *even, only,* negation, focus, *wh*-phrases), however, each quantified constituent must be the leftmost element of an IP containing it and any number of adjacent nonquantified constituents to its right. Thus, the rule for constructing the IP in Hungarian can be formulated as in (34).

(34) a. Group the phonological phrase containing the element with the widest scope into an intonation phrase together with all the phonological phrases to its right until another constituent with a logical function, or the end of the sentence, is reached.

b. Each remaining phonological phrase forms an intonation phrase on its own.

Since there may be only one heavy stress per IP in Hungarian, any stresses to the right of the first one in an IP must be reduced. The requisite rule of Stress Reduction has as its domain of application the IP, as defined in (34). This can be seen schematically in (35), where double strokes indicate unreduced stress, and single strokes reduced stress (see Vogel and Kenesei 1987). 'QP' stands for a quantified constituent.

(35) a. *Neutral*

[s[IP ″PP] [IP ″PP] [IP ″PP] ...]

b. *Non-neutral*

[s [IP ″PP] [IP ″QP ′PP ′PP] ...]

Corroboration for the proposed IP construction rule based on the quantifiers present in a sentence comes from another phonological rule: *l*-Palatalization (LP). As demonstrated in Vogel and Kenesei 1987, this rule changes *l* to *j* before another *j* in the same IP.[6] Thus, LP does not apply in the sentence in (36a), where the *l* and *j* are in different IPs, though it may apply in (36b), where the relevant segments are part of the same IP.

(36) a. *Neutral* (*L* = no LP; *l* = LP possible)

[IP ″Pá*L*] [IP ″játszik] [IP az ″ango*l* ′játékkal]
Paul   plays   the English toy-with
'Paul is playing with the English toy.'

b. *Non-neutral*

[IPcsak ″Pá*l* játszik az ′ango*l* ′játékkal]
only
'Only Paul is playing with the English toy.'

The concept of scope also plays a role in another aspect of intonation phrase structure in Hungarian, in particular in the optional rule of IP restructuring. Any IP containing a quantifier which has scope over another quantifier in an adjacent IP may join with it to form a single IP. This can be seen below, where (37a) represents the basic IP division, assuming that *Júlia* is focused, and (37b) represents the structure once restructuring has taken place.

(37) a. [IP ″minden ′nyú*L*] [IP ″Júliát   szereti a   ′legjobban]
every   rabbit   Julia-acc likes   the best
'For every rabbit, it is Julia that it likes best.'

b. [IP ″minden ′nyú*l* ′Júliát szereti a ′legjobban]

Note that in (37a), LP does not apply, but in (37b), where the *l* and the *j* come to be in the same IP, the rule may apply.

The above examples accord with the Sense Unit Condition on intonational phrasing given above in (22). In (36b) and (37b) the IPs are complete sentences; in (36a) each constituent phrase of the sentence is an IP; and in (37a) the first IP is identical with the subject, while the second one contains the verb and its arguments. Recall, however, that the order of the constituents of a sentence is free in Hungarian. It is, therefore, possible for the words in (37a) to occur in a different order, with a slightly different meaning as determined by the scope of the quantifiers.

---

[6]The geminate [*jj*] may subsequently be shortened to [*j*].

(38) [IP "Júliát szereti] [IP "minden 'nyúl a 'legjobban]
'It is Julia that every rabbit likes best.'

Note, however, that in (38) the second IP includes two unrelated constituents: a subject and a degree adverbial. That is, neither one is an argument or a modifier of the other, so that the Sense Unit Condition cannot be invoked here. Furthermore, IP construction must be able to separate constituents of an argument and group one of them with a different head (39) or an adjunct (40).

(39) a. [NP Pál   [N' minden barátja]] [V megérkezett]
     Paul-nom. every   friend-3sg   arrived
     'Every friend of Paul's has arrived.'

   b. [IP "Pál] [IP "minden 'barátja 'megérkezett]

(40) a. [NP Sok   iskola   [N' egyetlen tanára   ]] sem
        many school-nom. one   teacher-3sg not

     [PP a   könyvtárban] olvassa el   a   szükséges irodalmat
        the library-in   reads   perf. the necesary literature-acc.

     'For many schools, for none of their teachers is it the library where they read the necessary literature' (i.e., all the teachers of many schools read the necessary literature at some place other than the library)

   b. [IP "Sok 'iskola] [IP "egyetlen 'tanára sem a 'könyvtárban olvassa 'el a 'szükséges 'irodalmat]

In (39), the quantified head (i.e., *minden barátja*) of the NP (i.e., *Pál minden barátja* 'Paul's every friend') forms an IP with the verb, while in (40), following optional restructuring, the head N' (i.e., *egyetlen tanára (sem)* 'no teacher') of the NP forms a single IP with the focused adjunct (i.e., *a könyvtárban*) and whatever follows it.[7]

---

[7] Observe that in a model of phonology that includes prosodic constituents between the word and the IP (e.g., the phonological phrase), as opposed to Selkirk's 1984 model, it is possible to have NP-internal IPs. This can occur when there is more than one phonological phrase in an NP, and when the end of an IP corresponds to the end of an NP-internal phonological phrase. Consider the potentially ambiguous phrase in (a).

(a) a   fekete   kalapos   nő
    the   black   hat-provided with   woman

   i. the woman wearing a black hat

   ii. the black woman wearing a hat

The syntactic structure and the phonological phrase structure (as proposed in Vogel (forthcoming)) corresponding to the first meaning are as in (b).

(b) [NP a [AP fekete kalapos] [N nő]]   [[a fekete kalapos nő]PP]IP

The syntactic structure corresponding to the second meaning requires two PPs. Depending on the focus structure of the phrase, these will be grouped into either one or two IPs, as seen below.

The conclusion we must draw at this point is that the conditions on IP construction for English and Hungarian differ in that they ultimately rely on syntactic structure in English, whereas they are a function of quantifier interpretation in Hungarian. It should be noted that Selkirk's model is not necessarily incompatible with the data from Hungarian, assuming that scope relations can play a role in the well-formedness conditions on IP-structure. That is, we could allow IPs to be formed freely and then subject them to conditions that determine (a) whether they contain quantifiers, (b) if so, whether they are in IP-initial positions, (c) what the relative scopes of the quantifiers are, and so forth. But such a modification would destroy one of the most significant aspects of Selkirk's model, the ISS-LF interface. Focus rules would have to feed the rules of quantifier interpretation, which in turn feed the well-formedness conditions. Intonational phrasing would have to be part of the representations at LF, and thus the hypothesis of the internal autonomy of the subsystems of grammar would have to be abandoned.

In the alternative model proposed by van Riemsdijk and Williams, by contrast, information about scope relations is available before the mapping from syntactic structure onto prosodic structure takes place; that is, the interface between syntax and phonology is enriched with scope relations, which can be taken directly into consideration by the rules or conditions relevant to prosodic structure (in particular to the construction of IPs). It then follows that the Projection Principle remains unchanged, i.e., it does not include any segment of the Phonetic Form component in its domain. The output of one subsystem serves as the input to another, lending support to the thesis of internal autonomy.

3   Conclusion

Our goal in this paper was to show that a more restricted theory of grammar can be upheld in the face of data and arguments suggesting that there is a two-way relationship between syntactic and phonological rules on the one hand, and, on the other, that semantic interpretation must rely on phonological information. Specifically, we have argued that syntactic rules do not need to take into account phonological structures or the output of phonological rules. The seemingly problematic cases examined can be resolved by freely generating all the possible syntactic structures, of which some may be blocked by a set of phonological conditions. It seems, however, that the two modes in which syntax can contribute to phonological representations and rules cannot be further reduced. Although

---

(c) [$_{NP}$ a [$_{AP}$ fekete] [$_{AP}$ kalapos] [$_N$ nő]]

    i. [[a fekete]$_{PP}$ [kalapos nő]$_{PP}$]$_{IP}$

    ii. [[a fekete]$_{PP}$]$_{IP}$ [[kalapos nő]$_{PP}$]$_{IP}$

indirect interaction between the syntactic and phonological components is more common and theoretically preferable, direct reference to syntactic categories cannot be eliminated in at least a few crucial examples.

There are also two ways in which phonology and semantics can interact: either some aspect of the phonological structure has to be taken into account by the semantic component, or semantic information must be used to construct phonological constituents. Regardless of which position is correct, the standard T-model has to be modified. We have examined the changes suggested in relation to one type of prosodic constituent, the Intonation Phrase. On the basis of data from Hungarian, and van Riemsdijk and Williams's proposal to collapse syntactic S-structure and quantifier interpretation, we have argued that the interface between syntax and phonology must incorporate information about scope relations. It may be the case then that some languages, including English, have 'more syntactic' conditions on IP-structure, while others, like Hungarian, make use of semantic information at this stage, in accordance with more general parameters or properties of the language.

18

Prosodically Constrained Syntax

Draga Zec and Sharon Inkelas

The aim of this paper is to propose a model of the phonology-syntax interface, in which the interaction between these two components is bidirectional. Such a model will not only predict that syntax can exert influence on phonology, as is commonly assumed—but also predicts the reverse effect. This latter claim, that phonology can constrain syntax, is much less widely recognized, and we will support it with data from three unrelated languages.

Under our approach, the bidirectionality of phonology-syntax interactions derives from the nature of the grammatical model itself. We assume a nonderivational model within which all components of the grammar are co-present, and which also allows for a certain amount of interaction between the components. It follows from the architecture of this model that different components can exert influence on each other.

Models that do not allow any phonology-syntax interactions at all are clearly too impoverished to describe the known data. On the other hand, models that allow direct access between the two components are overly powerful. We strike a balance between these two extremes by offering a bidirectional model in which the interaction between the components is highly constrained: all interactions between syntax and phonology are, we propose, mediated by prosodic structure, a hierarchically organized subpart of the phonological component (Selkirk 1978, 1986; Nespor and Vogel 1982, 1986; Hayes 1989) consisting of prosodic constituents within which phonological rules apply. Phonological rules will, therefore, not have direct access to syntactic domains. Likewise, the influence of phonology on syntax will not extend further than prosodic structure, and will at most affect its hierarchical organization.

Thus, although bidirectional, the model to be proposed here is sufficiently constrained to exclude all the undesirable types of interaction allowed by a direct access model. In particular, we have in mind what Zwicky and Pullum 1986a describe as the pernicious consequences of allowing syntax to have direct access to phonological information; an example would be a syntactic rule that "obligatorily moves to the beginning of the sentence the highest constituent that begins *phonetically* with a bilabial consonant" (Zwicky and Pullum 1986a:75). Our model will never allow any interactions of this kind because syntactic rules have access not to the full-fledged phonological representation, but only to its prosodic subpart. This automatically excludes segmental information from the range of information available to the syntactic component. Furthermore, as already mentioned, the model of syntax we assume is nonderivational. The influence of prosodic structure on syntax can thus be expressed as an additional source of constraints on syntactic representations, just as the influence of syntax on prosodic structure is an additional source of constraints on phonological representations.

Precisely because it is bidirectional, this model has the descriptive adequacy, which is by definition lacking in any, even the most powerful, unidirectional model, to handle the prosodic effects on syntax which we will examine. A model which allows no effects of phonology on syntax will rule out the existent cases together with the nonexistent ones. By positing the prosodic hierarchy as a mediator of phonology-syntax interactions, we capture fully the range within which phonology can influence syntax.

1　Sources of Influence

The most widely recognized source of influence on prosodic structure is a mapping from syntactic to prosodic structure, typically captured by phrasing algorithms. In this case the constraints go only in one direction, as is explicitly assumed in the various phrasing algorithms proposed in the literature (e.g., Selkirk 1978; Nespor and Vogel 1982, 1986; Hayes 1989; and others). Less commonly recognized in the literature is the fact that constraints may also hold in the other direction; that is, some syntactic phenomena may be affected by prosodic requirements. Clearly, however, these effects do not result from the phrasing algorithm.

In fact, we view the phrasing algorithm as only the most general, or elsewhere, mechanism for relating syntactic and prosodic structures. It is bypassed by more specific prosodic constraints, among which are some that may also influence syntactic structure.

2   Lexically Based Prosodic Constraints

In this section we argue that prosodic structure can constrain syntactic constituent structure, using as evidence two cases in which prosodic requirements on certain lexical items influence the linear order of syntactic units.

2.1   Serbo-Croatian Clitics

Serbo-Croatian, like a number of other languages, is known for its second position clitics. Second position can actually be defined in two ways: either after a first word or after a first constituent, and speakers generally have a choice between these options, as shown in (1) and (2):

(1) Taj čovek=*joj*=*ga*=*je* poklonio.
    that man=her=it=aux presented
    'That man presented her with it.'

(2) Taj=*joj*=*ga*=*je* čovek poklonio.
    that=her=it=aux man   presented
    'That man presented her with it.'

We will concern ourselves here with the option of locating clitics after a first word. Of particular interest to us is the fact that not every syntactic terminal counts as first for the sake of clitics. While every major category word can host second position clitics (see (3), (4), and (6)), function words such as prepositions and conjunctions systematically fail to do this (as in (5) and (7)). Furthermore, as shown in (4) and (6), a content word counts as first even when preceded by a function word.

(3) Petar=*je*   u kući.
    Petar=aux in house
    'Petar is in the house.'

(4) U kući=*je*   Petar.
    in house=aux Petar
    'Petar is in the house.'

(5)*U=*je* kući Petar.
    in=aux house Petar
    *'Petar is in the house.'

(6) A Petar=*je* u kući.
    So Petar=aux in house
    'So, Petar is in the house.'

(7)*A=*je*   Petar u kući.
    So=aux Petar in house
    *'So, Petar is in the house.'

This asymmetry in the syntactic behavior of function and content words coincides exactly with a systematic phonological difference between the two. As shown in Inkelas and Zec 1988, all lexical words, i.e., content words, correspond to phonological words, and as such receive High tone and stress. But this is not the case with function words, which do not stand on their own as phonological words.[1]

On the basis of what we have said so far, we could characterize the distribution of second position clitics either syntactically or phonologically: following the first content word appears equivalent to following the first phonological word. However, the dichotomy between words which can host second-position clitics and those which cannot is not quite this simple; there is in fact some evidence that a syntactic account alone is not sufficient to capture the entire range of facts.

As mentioned in Browne 1974, two conjunctions, *ali* and *pa*, can optionally host clitics—and when they do, they also surface with 'accent', i.e., High tone and stress. Inkelas and Zec 1988 take this as evidence that these conjunctions optionally form phonological words. The examples below illustrate the behavior of *ali*:

(8) Mi smo zvonili, ali niko=*nam*   nije   otvorio.
     we aux rang   but nobody=us(Dat) neg.aux opened
     'We rang but nobody opened the door for us.'

                        *
(9) Mi smo zvonili, ali=*nam*   niko   nije   otvorio.
                        |
                        H
     we aux rang   but=us(Dat) nobody neg.aux opened
     'We rang but nobody opened the door for us.'

Under a syntactic account we would have no way of characterizing the set of forms that can host clitics without resorting to a disjunction and to diacritic marking of *ali* and *pa*:

(10) a. Clitics can follow any major category word, with the exception of prepositions.

     b. Clitics cannot follow minor category words, with the exception of the conjunctions *ali* and *pa*, which precede clitics only when combined with a High tone.

But under a prosodic account, we can capture all of the clitic facts with one simple statement: clitics follow a phonological word. Following Inkelas 1987, 1989a, we characterize clitics as lexical forms with a prosodic

---

[1]In fact, we take all conjunctions and prepositions to be proclitics. In Serbo-Croatian, it seems that, with the possible exception of a subclass of pronouns, every syntactic terminal is either a phonological word or a clitic; unlike English, Serbo-Croatian does not have a large class of non-clitic function words.

subcategorization frame.[2]   In the case of these Serbo-Croatian clitics, the frame encodes the fact that the unit they subcategorize for is the phonological word.[3] The fact that these clitics cannot be separated from their host by pause is also captured by the frame, which indicates that a clitic and its host together form a single phonological word.

(11) je: $[\ [\quad]_\omega -]_\omega$

It is in order to satisfy the requirements of this prosodic subcategorization frame that the distribution of clitics is restricted; that is, word order in Serbo-Croatian is subject to prosodic constraints.

2.2   Hausa *fa*

Similar constraints on word order are observed by Inkelas 1988 in a description of the possible location of the discourse particle *fa* in Hausa. *Fa* tends to emphasize the immediately preceding material, from which it cannot be separated by pause:

(12) Audu **fa** ya tafi
      Audu   3sg leave
      'Audu (emph.) left'

What interests us about *fa* is that it is allowed to appear only in a subset of the environments which would be licensed by phrase structure rules. Furthermore, the constraint holding over these environments is properly stated in prosodic rather than in syntactic terms.

For example, *fa* may appear between a verb and the following object NP if and only if that NP is branching (i.e., contains more than one word), as in (13b). If this condition does not obtain the construction is rejected, as in (13a) and (13c). Example (13c) is of special interest as it illustrates that *fa* needs to be followed by a branching *constituent*, not just by more than one word.

(13) a.*Ya sayi   **fa** teburin.
        he bought   table-def
        'He bought the table'

      b. Ya sayi   **fa** babban tebur.
         he bought   big   table.
         'He bought a big table'

---

[2]Given this frame, we require no further mechanism for distinguishing clitics from non-clitic words. For discussion of prosodic subcategorization see Inkelas 1989a.

[3]The frame actually encodes two things—that the clitic is sister to a phonological word with which it forms another phonological word. The latter information is relevant in the case where a number of clitics appear 'stacked' in second position, but we will not discuss these facts here (Inkelas 1989a).

c.*Ya sayi   **fa** teburin   jiya.
he bought   table-def yesterday.
'He bought the table yesterday'

Other examples prove this phenomenon to be quite general; in fact, syntactic branching of the immediately following maximal projection is by itself sufficient to license the occurrence of *fa*.

In addition to branching, however, we find that *fa* is also licensed when followed by a constituent that is intonationally emphasized; in this case, we get a well-formed sentence even when that following constituent is nonbranching:

(14) Ya sayi   **fa** *teburin*
he bought   table-def. (emph.)
'He bought the *table*'

Given this set of conditions, any attempt to characterize the distribution of *fa* in syntactic terms will contain the otherwise unmotivated disjunction of conditions listed in (15).

(15) a. No utterance may begin with *fa*.

b. If *fa* immediately precedes any material, then that material must be (i) a branching maximal projection or (ii) intonationally emphasized.

However, when viewed in terms of prosodic structure, the problem becomes simple: *fa* must follow a phonological phrase. Inkelas 1988 develops a simple phrasing algorithm for Hausa, each clause of which is paralleled by phrasing algorithms in other, unrelated languages, that produces phrase boundaries in exactly the locations where *fa* is allowed to occur, and in none of the locations where *fa* is prohibited. This algorithm, which takes into account emphasis and branchingness, is stated in (16). Each clause operates only on unphrased material; where two clauses would produce different results, the more specific overrides the more general. That is, (a) overrides (b), which overrides (c).

(16) Phonological Phrase Algorithm:

a. Prominent elements are mapped into their own phonological phrases.

b. From the bottom up, branching nodes are mapped into phonological phrases.

c. No two phonological words on opposite sides of an XP boundary may be phrased together to the exclusion of any material in either XP.

Below we illustrate the result of applying this algorithm to the example sentences shown earlier in (13) and (14):

(17) a.

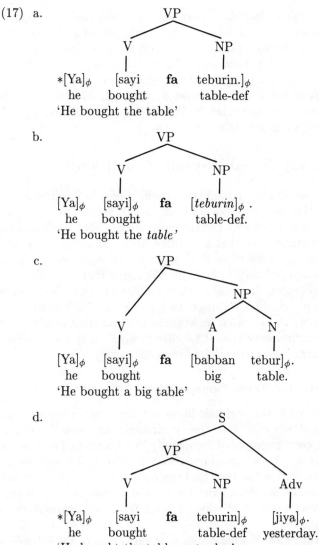

b.

c.

d.

'He bought the table yesterday'

Given this phrasing algorithm for Hausa, which parallels phrasing algorithms in other languages, we can now state the distribution of *fa* quite simply, without requiring a single disjunction: *fa* must follow a phonological phrase.

We encode this generalization formally by lexically assigning *fa* a prosodic subcategorization frame which encodes its dependence on a preceding phonological phrase.

(18) fa: [[   ]$_\phi$ —]$_\phi$

That is to say, we analyze *fa* as a phrasal clitic—where its host is a *prosodic* constituent, the phonological phrase. Note that this analysis captures one additional fact that a syntactic account could not handle, namely that *fa* is not separable by pause from what precedes. As the frame in (18) indicates, *fa* forms a prosodic unit with the preceding material.

In sum, it is precisely because of the prosodic requirements represented by the prosodic subcategorization frame in (18) that the syntactic distribution of *fa* is restricted to a subset of the positions which could be licensed by phrase structure rules; in Hausa, just as in Serbo-Croatian, word order is subject to prosodic constraints.

3   Syntactically Based Prosodic Conditions

In the preceding section we showed that specific prosodic constraints can be associated with particular lexical items. In this section we show that they can also be associated with certain types of dislocated syntactic constituents, in particular those that have often been characterized as topic or focus. We examine here two cases—the topic construction in Serbo-Croatian, and heavy NP shift in English. We argue that, in both cases, special prosodic constraints are at work in addition to those imposed by the phonological phrasing algorithms of each language. The special condition imposed in both cases is what we will refer to as constituent heaviness. We show that this property cannot be characterized in syntactic terms, but obtains natural characterization in prosodic terms.

3.1   Serbo-Croatian Topic Construction

It has been observed in the syntactic literature that certain types of constituents have to satisfy a minimal size requirement, for example, at least two words, or a certain degree of complexity in structure. These are at least the terms in which such cases have been described, although no satisfactory characterization has thus far been obtained. We will claim here that the traditional difficulties exist for a good reason: syntax is simply not the right component in which to look for generalizations about constituent weight.[4]

An analogy that most readily comes to mind is that of the syllable, a prosodic constituent whose weight plays an important role in a number of rules, stress rules in particular. In the recent literature syllable weight has been defined in terms of syllable structure. Internally, the syllable branches into one or two moras, giving the following structures for CV, CVV and CVC syllables:

(19)

_____

[4]The analysis in this section was first presented in Zec 1987.

These three types of syllables fall into two classes: those that have a branching syllable node, i.e., CVV and CVC, and those like CV, which have a nonbranching node. This gives us a way of characterizing syllable weight in a natural fasion: a syllable is heavy if and only if it branches. Weight is thus defined on a prosodic unit in terms of its internal structure, or 'tree geometry' as Hayes 1981 puts it.

On analogy with this case, we will define heaviness of prosodic units such as the phonological phrase and higher in terms of their prosodic structure (henceforth p-structure), i.e. in terms of their tree geometry. That is, we propose the following to be a general condition on constituent heaviness:

(20) A p-constituent is heavy iff it branches.

Constituent heaviness as defined in (20) plays a role in phonological phrasing itself: branching is one of the possible conditions on phonological phrasing. For example, Nespor and Vogel 1986 show that in both Italian and English, a complement immediately following the head forms a phonological phrase either on its own or with the head. The former case occurs, however, only if the complement following the head is heavy, i.e., branching. The same is true of Hausa, as we saw earlier.

We will now discuss one particular case where a prosodic heaviness condition is imposed on a syntactic constituent, the case of the Serbo-Croatian topic construction. Consider the following sentences:

(21) Taj čovek voleo=*je*   Mariju.
      that man   loved=aux Mary
      'That man loved Mary.'

(22)*Petar voleo=*je*   Mariju.
      Petar loved=aux Mary
      'Peter loved Mary.'

Here, the topicalized constituent appears sentence-initially (preceding the constituent that serves as 'first' for the purposes of clitic placement): in (21) and (22) the 'topicalized' constituents are *taj čovek* 'that man' and *Petar,* respectively. A constraint on this topic construction is that the topicalized constituent has to be 'heavy': (21) satisfies this condition but (22) does not. Note that the topicalized constituent branches at c-structure—i.e., syntactic constituent structure—in the former case but not in the latter, as shown in (23):[5]

(23)

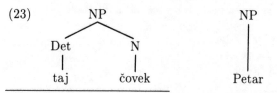

---

[5]For convenience we will continue to use the term 'c-structure' to refer to syntactic constituent structure and 'p-structure' for prosodic constituent structure.

The corresponding p-structures are as follows:

(24)

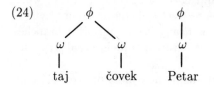

In this case, c-structure and p-structure constituency, and therefore c-structure and p-structure branching, are identical. However, this is not always the case, as shown by the following examples:

(25) Sa   tim čovekom razgovarala=*je* samo Marija.
     with that man   talked=aux   only Mary
     'To that man, only Mary spoke.'

(26)*Sa   Petrom razgovarala=*je* samo Marija.
     with Peter   talked=aux   only Mary
     'To Peter, only Mary spoke.'

In (25) and (26) the topicalized constituent is a PP. Although a PP is a branching constituent at c-structure, it does not necessarily form a branching constituent at p-structure; for example, the branching condition is satisfied in (25) but not in (26). The reason for this is that Serbo-Croatian prepositions can never form independent p-constituents (as shown in section 3.1.).[6] Rather, as clitics, they form a phonological word with the first word of the following NP, which explains why the PP in (26) fails to satisfy the branching condition on the topic construction: it counts as a nonbranching p-constituent. This shows clearly that we are dealing not with c-structure branching but rather with p-structure branching; furthermore, we can conclude that heaviness, defined in terms of branching structure, is a p-structure rather than a c-structure notion. Thus, c-structure branching is not a sufficient condition for heaviness, just as c-structure constituency is not a sufficient condition for p-structure constituency.

In fact, c-structure branching does not seem to be a necessary condition for heaviness, either. To show that this is indeed the case, we need a nonbranching phrasal constituent that branches in p-structure. It is highly suggestive, for example, that both (22) and (26) are well-formed when a first name is replaced by a first and a second name used together.

(27) Petar Petrović voleo=*je*   Mariju.
     Peter Petrović loved=aux Mary
     'Peter Petrović loved Mary.'

---

[6]Non-clitic prepositions in other languages (e.g., English) may form independent p-constituents, as argued in Zec and Inkelas 1987.

(28) Sa Petrom Petrovićem razgovarala=*je* samo Marija.
with Peter Petrović   talked=aux   only Mary
'With Petar Petrović, only Mary spoke.'

It is not clear what syntactic constituency should be assigned to proper
names, in particular whether *Petar* and *Petar Petrović* should differ in
c-structure constituency (for example, both parts get case marking). But
there is one case for which it seems plausible to claim that the two parts
of the proper name form one unit syntactically—but two prosodically.
Consider the following:

(29) a. Rio (Nom) 'Rio'

   b. u Riju (Loc) 'in Rio'

(30) a. Rio de Žaneiro (Nom) 'Rio de Janeiro'

   b. u Rio/*Riju de Žaneiru (Loc) 'in Rio de Janeiro'

We may easily assume, in fact, that the c-structure constituency of
the (a) and (b) sentences in (29) and (30) is identical, i.e., that the NP
structure is nonbranching in both cases. Note that in (30b), only the
second member of the 'compound' obtains case marking; the first member
is marked for case only when it is said in isolation (29b). This suggests
that the entire phrase in (30) is formed in the lexicon and goes through
cyclic morphology as a unit. (29) and (30) should therefore have identical
c-structure constituency, as shown in (31).

(31)   NP   NP
            | |
       Rio de Žaneiro   Rio

However, although *Rio de Žaneiro* forms a single sytactic unit, it contains two phonological words, which makes it a complex prosodic unit:
Rio de Žaneiro is a branching, i.e., 'heavy', phonological phrase. We can
then predict that it will satisfy the heaviness constraint in (22). This is
exactly what happens, as shown by the following:

(32) U Rio de Žaneiru ostali=*su* dve godine.
    in Rio de Janeiro stay=aux two years
    'In Rio de Janeiro, they stayed two years.'

(33)*U Riju ostali=*su* dve godine.
    in Rio stay=aux two years
    'In Rio, they stayed two years.'

Thus, conditions on the Serbo-Croatian topic construction are both
syntactic and prosodic: the syntactic condition is that the topicalized
unit has to be a syntactic constituent of a certain kind; and the prosodic

condition is that it ought to be a *branching* prosodic constituent. This latter condition will be satisfied only if the phonological phrase contains at least two p-constituents; in this case the relevant p-constituents will be phonological words. The mismatches are due to the fact that certain lexical units which are syntactically independent lack phonological independence: they act as clitics.

Thus, the case of the Serbo-Croatian topic construction shows that the 'heaviness' requirement can be stated naturally at p-structure but is unstatable at c-structure.

3.2   English Complex NP Shift

Another case that we believe can be treated as a prosodic condition on weight is the so-called Heavy NP Shift, or Complex NP Shift, in English. This latter term, of course, goes back to the transformational model, where the alternation in (34) (taken from Ross 1968) was attributed to the operation of a movement transformation.

(34)   a. He threw *the letter which he had not decoded* into the wastebasket.

   b. He threw into the wastebasket *the letter which he had not decoded*.

(35)   a. He threw *the letter from the principal decoder* into the wastebasket.

   b. He threw into the wastebasket *the letter from the principal decoder*.

The puzzling property of this alternation is that the shifted NP has to be of some minimal size. For example, the sentence in (36b) is ill-formed because this condition is not met.

(36)   a. He threw *the letter* into the wastebasket.

   b.*He threw into the wastebasket *the letter*.

However, precise syntactic characterization of this condition has proved to be notoriously difficult. At best, we find approximations like that in Postal 1974:83, for example, where 'heavy' is used to mean "roughly, long and/or clause-containing". And Culicover and Wexler 1977 simply resort to the attribute "complex" without further attempting to specify its content. We suggest that the problem lies not in the inadequacy of description but in the incorrect assumption that syntax is the right component to look for the relevant generalizations.

Let us now look at this phenomenon from a different perspective. Rather than examining the syntactic structure of the heavy string, we will look at its prosodic structure. The basis for this discussion is the phrasing algorithm formulated in Zec and Inkelas 1987 for English (whose resemblance to that postulated in section 2.2 for Hausa supports the assumption that phrasing has at least some universal properties.) Below we present the two relevant clauses of the three-clause algorithm:

(37) Phonological Phrase Algorithm:

  a. Branching Clause: From the bottom up, branching nodes are mapped into phonological phrases.

  b. Anti-Straddling Clause: No two phonological words on opposite sides of an XP boundary may be phrased together to the exclusion of any material in either XP.

Consider now the following examples, whose relevant portions have been phrased by the algorithm in (37):

(38) *Mark showed to John [some letters]$_\phi$.

(39) Mark showed to John [some letters]$_\phi$ [from Paris]$_\phi$.

(40) Mark showed to John [some letters]$_\phi$ [from his beloved city]$_\phi$.

On the basis of these sentences one might hypothesize that the generalization is the dislocated NP is licensed when it contains at least two phonological phrases. Thus, (38) is ill-formed because its dislocated NP corresponds to only one phonological phrase. To make sense of this finding, we can refer back to the earlier analogy to syllables, where a syllable counts as heavy if it contains more than one mora. Thus, it seems reasonable to hypothesize that here,again, we are dealing with a branching prosodic constituent:

(41) *Mark showed to John [some letters]$_\phi$.

(42) Mark showed to John [[some letters]$_\phi$ [from Paris]$_\phi$].

(43) Mark showed to John [[some letters]$_\phi$ [from his beloved city]$_\phi$].

The most obvious candidate for this is the constituent immediately dominating the phonological phrase, i.e. the intonational phrase of Selkirk 1978. While we have not investigated this question exhaustively, it is worth noting, in support, that heavy NPs are typically preceded by pause and associated with special intonational effects, correlates of intonational, as opposed to phonological, phrases.

Thus, we have shown that in English, as in the other cases we have investigated, certain phenomena can be described only if we admit constraints holding simultaneously on syntactic and prosodic constituent structure. Furthermore, we again see that what has been characterized as a constraint on minimal size is in fact a constraint on prosodic branchingness, a common parameter which pervades the entire prosodic domain.

4   Concluding Remarks

Prosodic constituency has been motivated by in the past the need to provide proper domains for certain phonological rules, in particular those that apply across words or phrases. But, as has been shown in this paper, the relevance of prosodic constituency is not limited to phonological rule domains. Certain phenomena which belong to the borderland of syntax cannot be characterized in purely syntactic terms. At least part of the burden needs to be shifted to phonology, and this characterization crucially depends on prosodic units and the hierarchy they form. Furthermore, this characterization does not merely depend on the nature of prosodic constituents, but also relies on the relation of the prosodic component to the syntactic one. At least some of the interactions we have motivated would be impossible to describe in a derivational model where syntactic structure is transformationally related to prosodic structure (as in, for example, Selkirk 1980a). This type of model would have to rely on filtering in order to capture the influence of a 'later' component on an 'earlier' one. But although filtering may be able to capture lexical prosodic constraints, it is incapable of capturing prosodic constraints on syntax.

The prosodic component might be viewed as a filter in the case of lexical constraints, in particular, in the case of clitics and their prosodic subcategorization frames, which cannot be satisfied until the relevant type of structure is created; prosodic structure could then itself be a filter which discards strings with clitics whose subcategorization frames are not matched by the surrounding material. However, this type of filtering will give no results with other prosodic effects on syntactic structure, where a piece of the string needs to satisfy both a syntactic *and* a prosodic constraint. In the Serbo-Croatian topic construction, for example, the conjunction of conditions is that a piece of string be a syntactic topic and a branching phonological phrase. The two conditions can be satisfied only if the syntactic and the prosodic information are available simultaneously. A (transformational) derivational model would have have no way of filtering out in the prosodic component those topics which do not have branching structure, since, by that point, all syntactic information, including the information about which constituents are topics, will have been lost— unless we allow a certain amount of globality, which of course is not what is assumed here.

In sum, it would be misleading to say that the phenomena described here could equally well be captured by a derivational model enriched with a filtering device of some sort. Instead of assuming that the syntactic and phonological components are derivationally related, we have posited a model in which the two exist side by side, so to speak, and are able to place constraints on each other.

19

Syntactic Representations and Phonological Shapes

ARNOLD M. ZWICKY

BOTH SYNTACTICIANS AND PHONOLOGISTS tend to see themselves as engaged in framing restrictive theories about these domains. There is much to be said for this attitude—Occam's razor has often been wielded to good effect in linguistics—but it is not an unmixed blessing. The danger is early theoretical closure, in which the theorist fixes on a few fundamental notions, assumptions, or formalisms (because these make plausible candidates for a minimal theory) and then refuses to entertain richer, or simply alternative, possibilities.

Now my purpose here is not to advance any new theory of grammar, or even any new framework within which such a theory might be couched. Instead, my intention is to try to stave off early theoretical closure in both syntax and phonology, and to step back some for a certain amount of pretheoretical stock-taking in both domains, in the hope that this will help to guide future theorizing and so eventually illuminate the nature of the connection between the two domains.

Consider syntactic representations (hereafter, synreps). I assume that each such representation is an assemblage of (at least) all the syntactically relevant information about (one reading of) a sentence. But what makes some particular bit of information, some particular property of an expression, syntactically relevant? The fact that some syntactic rule (hereafter, synrule) distributes this property or is sensitive to it. Synrules, in turn, I view as embodying constructions; they are matchings of semantic content with suites of formal properties—properties that are formal in the sense that they ultimately manifest themselves in phonological substance.

I will not be assuming, then, that synreps encode either constituency or dependency relations but not both. Both, I believe, are relevant in syntax (and in phonology), so that the possibility that one set of properties might be definable on the basis of the other set is beside the point here; both should appear in synreps. Nor will I be assuming that the only properties distributed by synrules are ones that would ordinarily be recognized as 'syntactic' in a narrow sense. In particular, certain properties realized as inflectional forms of individual words serve as marks of specific syntactic constructions and so are distributed by synrules; the same is true of certain properties realized as intonational contours and accent patterns on constituents.

On the other hand, not all observations one might make about the syntax of an expression necessarily find a place in its synrep. Take a Subject-to-Object Raising (SOR) example like

(1) believe Robin to be a spy

It is true that the NP *Robin* must be the sort of constituent that could be the subject of the VP *be a spy,* and the rule describing the SOR construction must incorporate a restriction to this effect. But there is no reason to say that this rule assigns the subject property to *Robin* vis-a-vis *be a spy;* in particular, no other synrule—and, so far as I am aware of, no phonological rule either—treats *Robin* as a subject. As far as the synrep of *believe Robin to be a spy* goes, *Robin* bears the direct object relation to *believe,* period.

1   Organization of This Paper

Section 2 sketches some properties of expressions that (at least sometimes) belong in synreps; I make no claim that this list is exhaustive rather than merely illustrative. In principle, all these properties are available as conditioning factors in phonology.

Section 3 reviews the syntactic properties that are known to have influences on the application of phonological rules. Following Hayes's contribution to this volume, these influences are divided into two gross types—conditions on the distribution of alternative phonological shapes for lexemes and conditions on prosodic domain formation.

Section 4 then begins an exploration of what synreps would be like if they had to serve the purposes only of phonology (rather than also being motivated by syntactic, semantic, morphological, and pragmatic considerations). The suggested scheme of representation involves properties (of several types) belonging to individual words, and relations (also of several types) holding between pairs of words.

This paper is intended to be both integrative and exploratory, incorporating observations from the literature rather than contributing new data to the discussion of the phonology-syntax connection.

2   Syntactic Background

What properties of expressions can synrules distribute and/or be sensitive to?

2.1   Chunking (= Constituency)

The most impressive syntactic evidence for indicating chunking in synreps is that some synrules are sensitive to whether an expression forms a single constituent or not. The rule for WH question clauses in English, for instance, requires that such clauses begin with a single constituent preceding their head verbs. Compare

(2)   a. Which people from California did you introduce to Tracy?

b. To how many of your friends did you introduce people from California?

with

(3)   a.*Which people from California to Tracy did you introduce?

b.*People from California to how many of your friends did you introduce?

2.2   Unit Type

Synrules can be sensitive to various properties of the units they refer to.

Category membership

Little comment is required here, except to point out that the character of particular synrules seems to require a moderately complex organization of syntactic categories (hereafter, syncats), involving cross-cutting taxonomies. Vs, for instance, belong both to one larger syncat comprising Ps as well and to another larger syncat comprising As as well; this is the sort of observation that motivates the familiar decomposition of N, A, V, and P into two cross-cutting category features. But there are still larger syncats, and still smaller ones. As for larger syncats: NP, PP, and AP (vs. VP) group together in English, as the syncats that can be fronted in WH questions, and V, A, and N (vs. P) group together in English, as the syncats that can have PP and clausal complements as well as NP complements. As for smaller syncats: Count nouns constitute a syntactically relevant subclass of N in many languages, and transitive verbs (including ditransitives and also transitives with PP complements) constitute a syntactically relevant subclass of V in many languages.

Rank

I use the term in the Hallidayan sense, with reference to the distinction between W[ord], P[hrase], and C[lause] rank; this is the 'bar level' property of many current syntactic frameworks, but without the attendant arithmetic. Individual synrules can require that a particular constituent be of rank W, as in the WH clefts in English in (4); or of rank P rather than C, as in the objects of prepostions of English in (5); or of rank C rather than P, as in the *that*-complements of English in (6).

(4) What you saw from Antarctica was a penguin

   *What creature you saw was a penguin

   *What from Antarctica you saw was a penguin

   compare the WH questions

   What (creature) from Antarctica did you see?

(5) from the fact you left

   *from you left

(6) I know that they will be at home.

   *I know that they.

   *I know that (will be) at home.

Depth

NPs can be nested within NPs, and VPs within VPs, in many languages, and the depth of a unit within such a nesting can be relevant for synrules. Maximality has been made much of in the recent syntactic literature, thanks to the involvement of maximal projections in the GB notions of 'command' and 'government' (though Pullum 1986:204 maintains that "the relation ... MAX-command has very little support, if any, despite its popularity"). I will assume that both maximality and minimality are syntactically relevant properties of units—the latter, in my dialect at least, serving as a condition on the VP fronting construction:

(7) Watching television they might have been

   *Been watching television they might have

   *Have been watching television they might.

2.3 (Grammaticized) Functions

Under this heading I refer both to grammatical relations (hereafter, grels), which I view as grammaticizations of participant roles in events, and to pragmatic roles (hereafter, proles), insofar as these latter are grammaticized.

Grels

I take it as amply demonstrated that grels like subject, direct object, and so on are syntactically relevant. The English subject-auxiliary inversion rule, for instance, picks out rank-P constituents that are subjects, and so allows inversion both of NPs and PPs

(8) a. Have you finished?

b. Is under the rug a safe place to hide your money?

but not when these serve in a non-subject grel:

(9) a.*Have home I gone?

b.*Did under the rug go your money?

What has perhaps not been appreciated, despite the work of (several varieties of) dependency grammarians and relational grammarians, is the number of distinct grels that can be justified and the complexity of their organization. In both respects the world of grels seems to be entirely comparable to the world of syncats. In particular, the organization of grels involves cross-cutting taxonomies: The intransitive subject grel groups with transitive subject (in the larger subject grel) for some purposes, but with direct object (in the larger absolutive grel) for other purposes; all three together make a nuclear term grel, while direct object also groups with indirect object and oblique object, in an object grel; all these together with various others form a complementing (as opposed to complemented, modifier, and modified) grel; and the complementing and modified grels together make an argument (vs. functor) grel, the complemented and modified grels a head (vs. adjunct) grel.

Proles

Much the same is true, I believe, in the world of proles. There are two very large divisions in this universe, separating topic expressions from others and focus expressions from others, and each has a complex internal organization, which is only beginning to be mapped out by syntacticians. It seems clear, for instance, that contrastive focus, emphatic focus, and question focus must be distinguished in the syntax of at least some languages, but many other details are quite unclear.

2.4   Order

I scarcely need to point out that synrules can determine the linear sequence of constituents.

2.5   Conditions on Contained Unit(s)

Synrules describing expressions of type X routinely place conditions on some unit(s) contained within these expressions.

Head unit

A synrule can require that the head W within an expression must have some property, as when the English rule for passive VPs requires that the head W appear in its past participle form:

(10) (My chickens are) often attacked by wolves.

Edge unit

A synrule can require that the first (or last) W (or P) within an expression must have some property, as when the English rule for possessor NPs requires that the last W appear in its possessive form:

(11) my friend from Chicago's (crazy ideas).

Some unit(s)

A synrule can require that within an expression there must be one or more occurrences of a unit with some property, as when the English WH question rule requires that the clause-initial expression contain one or more WH-question Ws:

(12) Which people from which cities (did you meet?).

Exactly one unit

A synrule can require that within an expression there must be exactly one occurrence of a unit with some property, as when the rule for an English comparative AP requires that exactly one of its constituents be itself comparative:

(13) more handsome, handsomer, *more handsomer.

2.6   Stipulated Properties of Contained Unit

Beyond the obviously 'syntactic' properties listed above in 2.2, several other types of properties of a contained unit can be relevant for synrules. Some of these have already been illustrated.

Lexeme subcategories

In principle, whenever a synrule licenses a unit of rank W and category x in some slot, there is a special class of lexemes (a subclass of x) available for occurrence in that slot; this is the 'subcategory' (or, as I shall say, lexcat) associated with the rule. The unit in question is often the head— in English, the V in the prepositional indirect object construction

(14) *donate* money to the campaign,

for instance, or the V in the subject-auxiliary inversion construction ('auxiliaries' in English being simply the verbs available for occurrence in this slot), or the V that occurs with a passive VP complement, as in

(15) *be/get* attacked by wolves.

But it does not have to be the head. The English WH question rule requires one or more units of rank W within the clause-initial constituent; the 'WH question words' are simply those that can occur in this slot. The rules for WH exclamations, WH clefts, restrictive relatives, appositive relatives, and free relatives all make reference to rank-W units, and the lexcat of WH words is somewhat different for each of these rules.

Grammatical categories

Synrules of several different types distribute properties that are realized in some instances via (inflectional) morphology and in other instances via lexemes specialized as grammatical markers, which I shall refer to as particlexemes. Some such rules involve 'vertical' distribution of properties, in which a construction relevant to some constituent is marked by an inflection or a particlexeme within that constituent (as when clausal negation in English is marked either by negative inflection on an auxiliary—*don't, won't,* and so on—or by the particlexeme *not* following the auxiliary). Other such rules involve 'horizontal' distribution of properties—government and agreement, essentially—in which one unit determines properties of, or imposes properties on, some adjacent unit, and these properties are themselves marked via inflections or particlexemes.

Particlexemes   To say that such a lexeme—the preposition *to* marking indirect objects in English, the auxiliary verb *to* marking infinitival VPs, the definite article *the,* the negative adverb *not,* the degree adverbs *more* and *most,* and so on—is specialized as a grammatical marker is to say, first, that it is available, so to speak, as a counter in the game of syntax, that it can be distributed by several different synrules (with different corresponding semantics), so that it will not necessarily be possible to assign a single meaning to it in all of its occurrences; and, second, that its default meaning—the meaning contributed by the lexeme so long as this is not contradicted by the semantics for a particular synrule—is not like the meaning of an ordinary lexeme, but instead involves two steps, each involving a default association rather than a simple translation: a default association of the lexeme with an assemblage of 'grammatical categories' (hereafter, gramcats), plus a default association of each gramcat with meaning. The second point here—that gramcats of case, gender, number, definiteness, tense, aspect, finiteness, polarity, degree, and so on are not themselves meanings, though they are not unconnected to meanings—I take to be a familiar one. The first point is in fact conceded (though perhaps inadvertently) whenever syntacticians write rules that introduce particlexemes as acategorial words picked out by their phonological shape (see Pullum 1982) or by some arbitrary index.

Note that the 'same' item can serve sometimes as a particlexeme and sometimes as an ordinary lexeme, as when *to* serves both 'grammatically,' as a marker of indirect objects, and 'locally,' as a directional preposition:

(16) We sailed to China.

Some lexemes, including many particlexemes, function as ('bound word') clitics; they serve as independent words from the point of view of syntax but combine with adjacent (inflected) words to form units that are word-like from the point of view of morphology (Zwicky 1987b); but not all particlexemes work this way, and not all bound word clitics are particlexemes. It is also true that many particlexemes are phonologically dependent (and form prosodic units with adjacent expressions); but not all are, and not all phonologically dependent words are particlexemes.

Inflectional categories   Inflectional morphology is, in most respects, parallel to particlexemes. An inflectional category is available as a counter in the game of syntax (dative case forms might mark indirect objects in one synrule, direct objects in another, possessors in another, subjects in still another, for instance) and its default meaning is a matter of gramcats, these serving in fact to name the category. The 'same' category can serve sometimes grammatically, as when the German dative case marks indirect objects, and sometimes locally, as when the German dative case conveys location (rather than direction) with a set of prepositions (dative *hinter dem Hause* '(at) behind the house,' versus accusative *hinter das Haus* '(to) behind the house'). And some inflections function as ('phrasal affix') clitics, located in a layer of morphological structure outside ordinary inflections, as is the English possessive in *children's*.

Note that gramcats—like syncats, grels, and proles—are organized into cross-cutting taxonomies for the purposes of syntax and morphology. The accusative case category of a language, for instance, might group with a nominative category (as a 'direct case') for one generalization but with a dative category (as a 'spatial case') for another.

Shape properties

Gramcats provide one route by which synrules determine phonological shape, but according to the usual story for ordinary lexemes it is not a direct path: Synrules distribute gramcats, ultimately to individual words, and morphological rules describe how gramcats are realized as 'the (inflectional) forms of' those lexemes, where each such form has phonological content. It seems clear, however, that direct determination of aspects of phonological representation ('shape properties,' or shaprops), with no mediation by gramcats, must also be allowed for in synrules.

Emptiness   To describe constructions like gapping, pseudogapping, and VP ellipsis in English, synrules must be able to stipulate that certain anaphoric constituents are phonologically empty. Gap-filler constructions like the WH question and topicalization constructions in English call for the same sort of direct determination of phonological shape. In neither case is there any reason to say that there is some gramcat of the constituents in question that is itself realized as a phonological zero.

Prosodies (in the strict sense)   Accent patterns and intonation patterns not infrequently serve as marks of syntactic constructions, though this fact tends to be obscured by other grammatical and extragrammatical uses of such patterns. I would maintain, for instance, that there is a default accent pattern for N+N combinations in English, with accent on the first member, a pattern that is overridden by a second-member accent pattern that is one of the marks of a construction in which the first member denotes the material of which the object denoted by the second is composed; compare the default

(17) PAPER box   'box having to do with paper(s)'

with

(18) paper BOX   'box made of paper.'

And I would also maintain that the rising terminal intonation of the English yes-no question is one of the conventional marks of this particular construction. In neither instance is there any reason to say that there is some gramcat of any of the constituents involved that is itself realized as an accent or tone. Instead, the accents or tones are distributed by synrules without the mediation of gramcats.

Prosodies (in the wide sense)   The phonological features distributed in this fashion do not have to be suprasegmental (or 'prosodic' in the narrow sense), but can in fact be segmental. The Welsh mutations of word-initial consonants, for instance, serve in a number of instances as marks of particular syntactic constructions (see Zwicky 1986a:310–12 for a compact review); there is no reason to say that the lenition of the first word of a feminine singular nominal under the triggering of a preceding definite article involves some mediating gramcat of the affected word, rather than being directly determined. Similar remarks hold for a number of the other phenomena treated by Lieber 1987 (who is, however, interested in the phonological description of mutation and harmony rather than in the syntactic distribution of these phonological effects).

3   Syntactic Influences on Phonology

I now summarize the types of contributions that syntax appears to make to phonology.

I assume here a division between two types of phonology, essentially the fundamental distinction of natural phonology (Donegan and Stampe 1979) between automatic phonology—involving rules applying within 'prosodic' (that is, phonological) domains and subject only to phonological conditions—and nonautomatic phonology; this division corresponds roughly to that between the P1 and P2 rules of Kaisse 1985. That is, I assume that there are rules of automatic phonology, P2 rules, which associate 'prosodophonological' (P2) representations (phonological representations organized entirely within prosodic domains, of the sort treated by Nespor and Vogel 1986) with phonetic representations; rules of nonautomatic phonology, P1 rules, which associate syntactic and morphological representations with 'tacticophonological' (P1) representations (phonological representations organized in part within morphosyntactic domains); and 'prosodic domain formation' (PDF) rules, which match P2 with P1 representations.

3.1   PDF and P1 Rules

Within this framework of assumptions, there are two ways in which syntax could influence phonology: via conditions on individual PDF rules, conditions referring to the syntactic properties of P1 representations; or via conditions on individual P1 rules.

Syntactic conditions on PDF rules are familiar from the literature on 'phonological readjustment.' A typical instance is the set of syntactic conditions on the English infinitive particlexeme *to* when it lacks its complement VP (Zwicky and Levin 1980, Zwicky 1982), conditions that for many speakers prohibit accented *to* in

(19) You don't have TO (*vs.* You don't HAVE to)

and for some speakers prohibit even unaccented *to* in

(20) I don't want PAUL to (*vs.* I don't WANT to).

Syntactic conditions on PDF rules also stand at the center of 'end-based' approaches to phonological domain formation (Selkirk 1986, Chen 1987c, Hale and Selkirk 1987, Cowper and Rice 1987), in which one end of a phonological domain is constrained to occur at the edge of a syntactic constituent of a specified sort.

The garden-variety P1 rule is exemplified by the alternation between *a* versus *an* as shapes for the English indefinite article. Almost anyone who considers such a phrase-phonological alternation is inclined to label it as a 'lexical' (item-specific) dependency on adjacent words. There is something right in this impulse, but there are at least three reasons for not dismissing the matter once a label has been assigned.

The first is that the epithet 'lexical' has been applied so widely and variously in the recent theoretical literature of linguistics that it is not clear that it conveys any real content anymore; I list here a small sample of these uses, without attribution: lexical (= basic = underlying) phono-logical representation, lexical redundancy rule, the Lexicalist Hypothesis (whether 'strong' or 'weak'), the Lexical Integrity Hypothesis, Lexical-Functional Grammar, lexical (vs. syntactic) rules, Lexicase, Autolexical Syntax, lexical (vs. phonetic vs. underlying) phonological representation, lexical (vs. postlexical) rules, morpholexical rules, Lexical Phonology and Morphology, Radical Lexicalism, lexical (= derivational) versus phonolog-ical (= inflectional) rules, lexical insertion, lexical exceptions, nonlexical versus lexical items.

A second reason for pausing over the label 'lexical' for the *a/an* alter-nation is that the English indefinite article is one of the items to which the (apparently oxymoronic) term 'nonlexical item' has been applied.

A third is that the label alone is worthless without some account of the phonologically relevant information about lexemes and of the character of the P1 rules involved. At the very least, we need a distinction between four levels of paradigmatic organization: the lexeme (for instance, the verb *hit*); the (inflectional) form (for instance, the base form /hɪt/, the first-singular present /hɪt/, the first-singular past /hɪt/, the present par-ticiple /hɪtɪŋ/), a phonological representation paired with an assemblage of gramcats; the form set (for instance, base/present *hit,* past *hit,* present participle *hitting*), a class of systematically identical forms; and the shape (for instance, the present participle shapes /hɪtɪŋ/ and /hɪtɪn/), a P1 rep-resentation matched with a form. Rules of inflectional morphology, or 'realization rules,' are responsible for the description of the forms and form sets for lexemes (as in Zwicky 1985c), while P1 rules assign shapes to forms. Hayes's contribution to this volume suggests a scheme for P1 rules; the framework of Zwicky 1986a divides these rules into two types— 'shape' rules that override, or preclude, the effects of realization rules and 'morphonological' rules that alter, or are superimposed upon, the rep-resentations provided by realization rules—but this potential refinement should not obscure the general claim that phonologically relevant infor-mation about a lexeme must be organized in a fairly complex way: one or more stem representations for the lexeme, forms organized into form sets, and shapes for each form.

3.2   Syntactic Influences

What aspects of syntactic organization are relevant for the applicability of P1 and PDF rules?

Adjacency

Obviously, adjacent material is relevant for the applicability of P1 rules, and the literature on such rules routinely assumes that their triggers are adjacent to their targets. Lieber's 1987 approach is, in fact, designed to maintain this position for all P1 rules, via the positing of floating autoseg-ments, which on occasion must (apparently) be distributed syntactically. I have been glossing over some complications here. To begin with, the targets of P1 rules are syntagmatic 'words' in either (or both) of two distinguishable senses, as we have been taught by works like Sadock 1985 and Di Sciullo and Williams 1987: expressions of rank W in the syntax, which is to say 'syntactic words' (synwords); or the word-like units of morphology, which is to say 'morphological words' (morwords). *Kim's going*, for instance, is three synwords, but only two morwords. The sec-ond complication is that synwords can contain synwords and morwords can contain morwords; compounds like *abstracts committee* are in fact complex in both ways. I will continue to gloss over both complications in this paper, though a careful discussion of the phonology-syntax connec-tion cannot refer simply to 'words,' without differentiating synwords from morwords, and complex words of either type from elementary ones.

Distinguished words within constituents: edges, heads/bases

P1 rules have a demarcative and/or culminative function, just as many P2 rules do, but P1 rules serve to tick off the units and mark the boundaries of morphosyntactic, rather than prosodic, organization. Following the lead of Selkirk 1980a, we could say that rules of these two sorts apply within domains (morphosyntactic or prosodic, respectively) of certain types, at the edge of a domain of a certain type, or between domains of certain types. At any rate, both P1 rules and (insofar as prosodic domains depend upon syntactic constituency) PDF rules must be capable of being sensitive to whether some word is within a syntactic constituent (of some type) or at one of its edges.

I leave open the possibility that edge location for phonological pur-poses might be like edge location for clitic placement (see Zwicky 1987b and the references cited there), in that there might be four possibilities rather than only two: last word (word at right edge), penultimate word (word before right edge), first word (word at left edge), second word (word after left edge).

The culminative function of some P1 rules is evidenced by their picking out a single (not necessarily edge) word within a syntactic constituent—a word that counts as the 'head' for some phonological purpose as well as for syntactic or morphological purposes. For instance, "Shortening applies to the head [word] of the phrase" in Kimatuumbi (Odden 1987:20).

Now what is to count morphosyntactically as a head is not always clear (see Hudson 1987 for the latest in a series of discussions on this point). My current inclination is to say that there is not just one grammatically relevant notion here, that at the very least we must distinguish between, on the one hand, the word that is the *head* for the purposes of feature sharing (as in the Head Feature Convention of GPSG) and for the deter-mination of government and agreement within its constituent and, on the other hand, the word that is the syntactic *base* within that constituent, in the sense that it is the obligatory element and the one whose lexcats determine the external syntax of the constituent. Usually the head and base coincide, but in certain types of constructions—most notably, those involving 'specifiers,' like VPs composed of a (specifier) auxiliary V and its complement VP—the two sets of properties are allocated to different words; in the VP *am to go,* it is the auxiliary V that exhibits the (person, number, and tense) features belonging to the VP as a whole, and it is the auxiliary V that governs, or determines, gramcats on its sister (infinitival) VP rather than vice versa, but it is the V slot instantiated here by the lexeme *go* that is the obligatory element (a VP without an auxiliary is just a VP, but a VP composed only of an auxiliary is elliptical) and that is involved in subcategorization with an external subject argument:

(21) I am to go.

    *There is to go.

    There is to be trouble.

It is not entirely clear to me whether references to 'head of a phrase,' as in Odden's formulation for Kimatuumbi Shortening, are in fact to heads in the narrow sense, to bases, to words that are both, or sometimes to one and sometimes to the other. Our current data base seems too scanty for the matter to be decided now, so that I will leave open the possibility that both heads and bases (as well as edges) might be distinguished words for the purposes of phrase phonology.

Distinguished constituents containing a word: homes

The rather confusing literature concerning command relations and their relevance to phrase phonology (see especially Kaisse 1985 (chapter 7) and the formal discussion in Pullum 1986) has searched among the configurational properties of expressions for the factors that are crucial to whether two adjacent words count as part of the same unit, or instead as being at the edges of adjacent units, for the purposes of specific P1/PDF rules. Many of the crucial examples in this literature involve contrasts like those between *happy bear,* in which the A *happy* will count as being part of the same unit as the N *bear,* and *very happy bear,* in which the same A will count as ending an AP unit separate from N; or between *fierce bears,* in which the A *fierce* will count as being part of the same unit as the N *bears,* and *fierce bears and lions,* in which the same A will count as ending a unit separate from the coordinate NP *bears and lions.*

I believe there is some virtue in taking the contrast here to be primitive, rather than trying to define it from syntactic configurations. The intuitive notion is that for any word there is a rank-P constituent that is 'its phrase,' in much the same way that for any word there is a rank-C constituent that is 'its clause.' I will call such a distinguished constituent the *home* (of rank P or C) for the word in question. A P1/PDF rule might then require that one word be an edge or head/base of an adjacent word's rank-P home constituent, or that one word stand in a specified grel to the rank-P home constituent of an adjacent word. Conditions of this sort require only a function that assigns to each word in an expression its rank-P home, rather than making large-scale reference to configurational properties.

Gramcats of individual words

One effect of synrules is to locate gramcats on individual words (the heads or edges of some units), and P1/PDF rules are routinely sensitive to these gramcats. In particular, the targets of P1 rules are often specific particlexemes (the indefinite article in English, for instance) or inflectional affixes (the realization of the nominative singular masculine in Sanskrit, for example), and these are often implicated in PDF rules as well.

Syncats and lexcats

As Hayes observes in section 2 of his contribution to this volume (notably, with reference to Ewe and Hausa), the syncats of both target and trigger words can be crucial to the applicability of P1 rules. There is some question as to whether the syncats of the constituent that a given word is at the edge of, is the head of, or is adjacent to is ever relevant—"cross-categorial behavior being the rule," as Kaisse and Zwicky 1987:7 have it—but I will not deny the possibility.

The lexcat of a word can also be relevant, as when the constraint that bars certain occurrences of accented *to* in English (Zwicky and Levin 1980) is only part of a more general constraint applicable to non-finite forms of auxiliary verbs.

Rank

Reference to (being at the edge of) a rank-P constituent is commonplace in P1/PDF rules; Chen's 1987c PDF rule for Xiamen, for instance, constructs a tone group from the right end of XP. Indeed, references to 'non-branching' constituents (as in Cowper and Rice 1987 on Mende) and to 'unmodified' constituents (as in Zwicky 1984 on Yiddish) can be treated as references to rank P, for a non-branching or unmodified constituent is one that comprises a single word—that is, a word that is both the left edge of some constituent i of rank P and also the right edge of i.

Depth

Reference to maximality, at least, is also commonplace. Hale and Selkirk's 1987 PDF rule for Papago, for instance, constructs a tone group from the right end of X^{max}.

Grels and proles

Both are obviously relevant for P1/PDF rules, but the extent to which they are relevant has been, I believe, grossly underappreciated. My discussion here is programmatic and tentative, but I hope at least to draw attention to the potential importance of grels and proles in phrase phonology.

Given my discussion in section 2.3 above, not only do references in P1/PDF rules to subjects ("A personal pronoun subject can form a prosodic phrase with the VP following it" in English (Zwicky 1986b:107)) and objects ("A verb-final long vowel is shortened immediately before an object NP" in Hausa (Hayes, this volume)) count as references to grels, but so do certain references to heads (for the appearance of *mon, ton, son* instead of *ma, ta, sa* in French, "the trigger must be the head noun in the NP" (Zwicky 1985d:435)) and to the distinction between arguments and modifiers (as in Chen's treatment of a Xiamen PDF rule, which marks off tone groups for rank-P arguments but not modifiers (Chen 1987c:118)). In other work, not yet published, Chen has suggested that reference to specific constructions might be necessary in describing tone sandhi in Chongming Chinese, but his summary statement of the rules—one sandhi effect in subject+predicate combinations, another in numeral+classifier combinations, a third elsewhere—suggests reformulation in terms of specific grels rather than specific constructions.

Other languages might have P1/PDF rules referring to specific proles, rather than specific grels. In fact, since proles are grammaticizations of discourse and context-dependent properties (such as aboutness, givenness, identifiability, foregrounding, and contrast), mediation by specific proles in phrase phonology could provide one way in which the effect of reference to semantics/pragmatics might be achieved in P1/PDF rules.

Shaprops

As pointed out in section 2.6 above, synrules can distribute shaprops directly; these will ultimately be associated with individual words. This scheme provides a direct way in which specific constructions could determine phrase phonology, and another way in which the effect of reference to semantics/pragmatics might be achieved in P1/PDF rules: Each synrule has an associated scheme of compositional semantics and an associated set of pragmatic values, so that if it also distributes shaprops, these are then indirectly tied to semantics and pragmatics.

4   Phonologically Based Syntactic Representation

My text for this final section is from Kaisse and Zwicky 1987:4:

> "whether syntax conditions some phonological rules directly
> or whether its influence is entirely on principles of prosodic

domain formation, the phrase phonology of a language can tell us a good bit about what a syntactic description of a language should be like, and so about what syntactic theory should be like. Syntax, after all, must provide the information that is relevant for phrase phonology (be this constituent boundaries, category membership, c-command, headship, bar level, grammatical relations, or whatever), either by representing such information explicitly in syntactic structures or by representing syntactic properties from which it can be derived."

What, in fact, will a scheme for synreps be like if it is designed entirely for the purposes of phrase phonology? Various theoretical frameworks for syntax have posited representations motivated entirely by syntactic considerations; some syntactic theorizing has been guided in a fundamental way by the needs of semantic interpretation or of pragmatics, discourse organization, and stylistics; morphological considerations play an important role in other frameworks; but syntacticians are not accustomed to viewing phonology as a source of information about the nature of their domain. What happens if we adopt the strategy of taking such a scheme as the basis on which a fully adequate theory of synreps is to be constructed?

Notice that I am being careful here, as in section 1, to separate an account of synreps from an account of synrules. The latter concerns itself with the nature of language-particular generalizations about the objects that are the concern of the former. As a first approximation, I want to say that synrules are associated with semantic interpretation (and pragmatic values), while synreps are associated with phonological interpretation—a position that is recognizably a descendant of the one in Chomsky 1965, where semantics interprets deep structure and phonology interprets surface structure.

Now, standard tree representations might be inadequate in various respects—see the inventory of possibilities in Zwicky 1985a, and note especially that grels do not appear in the standard two-dimensional trees—but they are also (from the point of view of phonology) over-rich in a number of ways. In particular, syntacticians are accustomed to thinking of trees as global representations, in which constituents are apprehended as wholes, even though it is a hallmark of P1 and PDF rules that they involve local determination of phonological features. The usual mathematical treatment of tree representations, as in Wall 1972:144–52, builds on relations and properties—immediate dominance, linear precedence of sisters, and category membership of constituents—which, as will be clear from the discussion of section 3, are for the most part not the ones that play roles in phrase phonology; alternatives such as those in Lasnik and Kupin 1977 and Chametzky 1985 are no improvement in this respect.

4.1 A Scheme for Syntactic Representation

In the scheme I sketch here, six types of information about an expression are to be encoded.

The word list

First, there is a list of the words in the expression, each assigned some arbitrary index.

Word properties

Second, for each word w there is an assemblage (which itself might be internally complex) of properties: syncats, lexcats, gramcats, and shaprops, whether these belong inherently to the lexeme instantiated in w or belong to w by virtue of the application of synrules.

Adjacency

Third, there is information about which words are adjacent to which others. All that is needed is a list of pairs (w_1, w_2) of immediately adjacent words.

Distinction lists

Fourth, for each word w there is information about which constituents w is a distinguished word of: which ones it lies on the left edge of, which it lies on the right edge of, and which it is the head/base of. This can be managed by providing 'distinction lists' for w, each such list consisting of a set of arbitrary indices, where each index c is paired with a set of properties (syncats, rank, depth, proles) for constituent c.

I have already pointed out, in section 3.2, that from the left edge and right edge lists for a word we can determine whether that word constitutes a phrase on its own, so that references to 'non-branching' or 'unmodified' constituents can be reconstructed in this system.

Homes

Fifth, there is information about the rank-P home for at least some words. I will assume that this is represented by further distinguishing one of the constituents on a distinction list.

Grels

What this scheme still lacks, for its sixth type of information, is a place for relations between words, other than the relation of linear ordering—a place for grels, in particular. The question then is: When should a grel be listed as holding between two adjacent words? Do we list a grel, for instance, between *Antarctica* and *can't*, or between *fly* and *distresses*, in

(22) That penguins from Antarctica can't fly distresses me?

There are several ways in which such questions might be answered—I am about to suggest two—and I am not in a position now to commit myself.

It might be said that insofar as *Antarctica* bears any relation to *can't* (at least for phonological, if not also for syntactic, purposes), it does so by virtue of being at the right edge of a constituent that is the subject of the constituent that *can't* is at the left edge of, and that insofar as *fly* bears any relation to *distresses*, it does so by virtue of being at the right edge of a constituent that is the subject of the constituent that *distresses* is at the left edge of. Speaking this way would pick out what we might call the 'top grel' connecting two words—the grel of the sister constituents that lie, speaking in global tree terms, at the tops of the two chains of nodes dominating the words.

Another possibility would be to say that word w_1 is listed as bearing a grel g to adjacent word w_2 if and only if w_1 itself really bears g—that is, if and only if w_1 is the head of a constituent c that bears g to a constituent on one of w_2's distinction lists. On this interpretation, *Antarctica* bears no grel to *can't*, but *can't* bears to *Antarctica* the grel of expressions with subject complements, and similarly for *fly* in relation to *distresses*.

4.2   Nonstandard Synreps

I note here that without further conditions this scheme is compatible with various sorts of nonstandard synreps, including those with unattached interior constituents (as in Rotenberg 1978), with multiply attached constituents (as in Sampson 1975), and with discontinuous constituents (as in McCawley 1982). Ojeda 1987 discusses the latter two extensions in the standard tree representation framework.

However, it is not clear to me that there is motivation for these extensions in a reasonably rich scheme that incorporates grels. Consider, for instance, 'loosely adjoined' constituents, like the adverbial in

(23) You are, obviously, loony.

One possibility would be to represent it Rotenberg-fashion as an unattached constituent entirely surrounded by the clause

(24) You are loony.

Another possibility would be to represent it McCawley-fashion as a daughter of the top node in a tree, sister to a discontinuous clause. But another possibility would be to represent it as a sister of the constituents *are* and *loony*, but as forming a constituent with neither of them and as bearing a grel to neither of them.

4.3   The Relationship Between Synrules and Synreps

I have left unexplored here the question of how the six types of information in this scheme of synreps are determined from the application of synrules. Though the details are of considerable interest in themselves, it is enough to point out that there is reason to think that the information associated with individual words and with pairs of adjacent words can be derived by recursive definitions building on the (strictly local) information in synrules. The model for this sort of recursive definition is the way individual words are ordered with respect to one another in the standard framework of phrase structure grammar: Each rule orders a set of daughter constituents, and the recursive definition for precedence stipulates that if c_1 precedes c_2, then c_1 precedes all the daughters of c_2, and all the daughters of c_1 precede c_2.

I realize that this is only a promissory note, but it is impossible to be more concrete without making decisions about what I view as still-open questions, questions both about the nature of synrules and also about the nature of synreps as they are relevant to phonology. The exploration of the phonology-syntax connection is still in its infancy; as Kaisse and Zwicky 1987:4 have it,

"At the moment theories must be advanced on the basis of data that are, from the language-internal point of view, rich and complex, but are also, from the cross-linguistic point of view, sparse and diverse."

Bibliography

Abercrombie, D. 1967. *Elements of General Phonetics.* Edinburgh University Press.

Abney, S. 1985. Functor theory and licensing: toward the elimination of the base component. Manuscript, MIT.

Abney, S. 1986. Functional elements and licensing. Paper presented at GLOW colloquium, Barcelona.

Anderson, S. R. 1969. *West Scandinavian Vowel Systems and the Ordering of Phonological Rules.* Bloomington: Indiana University Linguistics Club.

Anderson, S. R. 1975. On the interaction of phonological rules of various types. *Journal of Linguistics* 11:39–62.

Anderson, S. R. 1982. Where's morphology? *Linguistic Inquiry* 13:571–612.

Anderson, S. R. 1985. *Phonology in the Twentieth Century: Theories of Rules and Theories of Representations.* Chicago: University of Chicago Press.

Anderson, S. R. 1988. Morphological theory. In F. J. Newmeyer (Ed.), *Linguistics: The Cambridge Survey,* Vol. 1. Cambridge, England: Cambridge University Press.

Aoyagi, S. 1969. A demarcative pitch of some prefix-stem sequences in Japanese. *Onsei no Kenkyuu* 14:241–247.

Archangeli, D., and D. Pulleyblank. forthcoming. *The Content and Structure of Phonological Representations.* Cambridge, Mass.: MIT Press.

Aronoff, M. 1976. *Word Formation in Generative Grammar.* Cambridge, Mass.: MIT Press.

Baker, C. L. 1971. Stress level and auxiliary behavior in English. *Linguistic Inquiry* 2:167–181.

Bangboṣe, A. 1965. Assimilation and contraction in Yoruba. *Journal of West African Langauges* 2:21–27.

399

Beckman, M. E., and J. B. Pierrehumbert. 1986. Intonational structure in Japanese and English. *Phonology Yearbook* 3:255–309.

Berendsen, E. 1985. Tracing case in phonology. *Natural Language and Linguistic Theory* 3:95–106.

Bickmore, L. 1989. *Kinyambo Prosody*. PhD thesis, University of California, Los Angeles.

Bickmore, L. forthcoming. Trigger-target distance effects in Kinyambo. In L. Tuller and I. Haik (Eds.), *Current Approaches to African Linguistics*, Vol. 6. Dordrecht: Foris.

Bolinger, D. 1972. Accent is predictable (if you're a mind reader). *Language* 48:633–644.

Booij, G. 1985. Coordination reduction in complex words: a case for prosodic phonology. In H. van der Hulst and N. Smith (Eds.), *Advances in Nonlinear Phonology*, 143–160. Dordrecht: Foris.

Booij, G., and J. Rubach. 1984. Morphological and prosodic domains in lexical phonology. *Phonology Yearbook* 1:1–27.

Booij, G., and J. Rubach. 1987. Postcyclic versus postlexical rules in lexical phonology. *Linguistic Inquiry* 18(1):1–44.

Borowsky, T. 1986. *Topics in English phonology*. PhD thesis, University of Massachusetts, Amherst.

Bresnan, J., and J. M. Kanerva. 1989. Locative inversion in Chicheŵa: a case study of factorization in grammar. *Linguistic Inquiry* 20(1):1–50.

Bresnan, J., and S. A. Mchombo. 1987. Topic, pronoun, and agreement in Chicheŵa. *Language* 63(4):741–782.

Broselow, E. 1979. Cairene Arabic syllable structure. *Linguistic Analysis* 5:345–382.

Browne, W. 1974. On the problem of enclitic placement in Serbo-Croatian. In R. D. Brecht and C. V. Chvany (Eds.), *Slavic Transformational Syntax*, no. 10 in Michigan Slavic Materials. Ann Arbor: Department of Slavic Languages and Literatures, University of Michigan.

Byarushengo, E. R., L. M. Hyman, and S. Tenenbaum. 1976. Tone, accent, and assertion in Haya. In L. M. Hyman (Ed.), *Studies in Bantu Tonology*, no. 3 in Southern California Occasional Papers in Linguistics, 183–205. Department of Linguistics, USC.

Cassimjee, F. 1986. *An Autosegmental Analysis of Venda Tonology*. PhD thesis, University of Illinois, Urbana.

Chametzky, R. 1985. Coordination and predication: a 3-d view. In *Proceedings of the Second Eastern States Conference on Linguistics*, Vol. 1, 165–80. Department of Linguistics, Ohio State University.

Chang, S.-J. 1986. The reflexive CAKI reconsidered: a micro to macro view. In *Proceedings of SICOL-86*, Seoul.

Chen, C.-Y. 1984a. Neutral tone in Mandarin: phonotactic description and the issue of the norm. *Journal of Chinese Linguistics* 12:299–333.

Chen, M. Y. 1984b. Unfolding latent principles of literary taste – poetry as a window onto language. *Tsing Hua Journal of Chinese Studies* 16:203–240.

Chen, M. Y. 1986a. An overview of tone sandhi phenomena across Chinese dialects. In W. Wang (Ed.), *Proceedings of Conference on the Languages and Dialects of China*, Oakland, California.

Chen, M. Y. 1986b. The paradox of Tianjin tone sandhi. In *Papers from the Twenty-second Regional Meeting of the Chicago Linguistics Society*, 98–114, Chicago. Chicago Linguistic Society.

Chen, M. Y. 1987a. Must phonology directly access morphosyntax? Manuscript, UC San Diego.

Chen, M. Y. 1987b. A symposium on Tianjin tone sandhi: introductory remarks. *Journal of Chinese Linguistics* 16:203–228.

Chen, M. Y. 1987c. The syntax of Xiamen tone sandhi. *Phonology Yearbook* 4:109–49.

Chen, M. Y. 1988. Accent, tone and phrasing. Manuscript, UC San Diego.

Cheng, L. 1987. On the prosodic hierarchy and tone sandhi in Mandarin. *Toronto Working Papers in Linguistics* 7:24–52.

Cheng, R. 1968. Tone sandhi in Taiwanese. *Linguistics* 41:19–42.

Chierchia, G. 1986. Length, syllabification and the phonological cycle in Italian. *Journal of Italian Linguistics* 8(1):5–34.

Cho, Y.-M. 1987a. The domain of Korean sandhi rules. Paper presented at the annual meeting of the Linguistics Society of America.

Cho, Y.-M. 1987b. Phrasal phonology of Korean. In S. Kuno et al. (Eds.), *Harvard Studies in Korean Linguistics*, Vol. 2. Cambridge, Mass.: Harvard University.

Choe, H. S. 1985. Remarks on configurationality parameters. In S. Kuno et al. (Eds.), *Harvard Studies in Korean Linguistics*, Vol. 1. Cambridge, Mass.: Harvard University.

Choi, S.-Y. 1984. A contrastive analysis of Korean postpositions '-nun' and '-ka'. *Language Research* 20(3).

Chomsky, N. 1965. *Aspects of the Theory of Syntax*. Cambridge, Mass.: MIT Press.

Chomsky, N. 1971. Deep structure, surface structure, and semantic interpretation. In D. D. Steinberg and L. A. Jakobovits (Eds.), *Semantics: An Interdisciplinary Reader in Philosophy, Linguistics and Psychology*, 183–216. Cambridge, England: Cambridge University Press.

Chomsky, N. 1986. *Barriers*. Cambridge, Mass.: MIT Press.

Chomsky, N., and M. Halle. 1968. *The Sound Pattern of English*. New York: Harper and Row.

Clements, G. N. 1978. Tone and syntax in Ewe. In D. J. Napoli (Ed.), *Elements of Tone, Stress, and Intonation*, 21–99. Washington, D.C.: Georgetown University Press.

Clements, G. N. 1981. Akan vowel harmony: a nonlinear analysis. In G. N. Clements (Ed.), *Harvard Studies in Phonology*, Vol. 2, 108–177. Bloomington: Indiana University Linguistics Club.

Clements, G. N., and K. C. Ford. 1979. Kikuyu tone shift and its synchronic consequences. *Linguistic Inquiry* 10:179–210.

Clements, G. N., and J. Goldsmith. 1984. *Autosegmental Studies in Bantu Tone.* Dordrecht: Foris.

Clements, G. N., and S. J. Keyser. 1983. *CV Phonology: A Generative Theory of the Syllable.* Cambridge, Mass.: MIT Press.

Clements, G. N., and E. Sezer. 1982. Vowel and consonant disharmony in Turkish. In H. van der Hulst and N. Smith (Eds.), *The Structure of Phonological Representations (Part II)*, 213–255. Dordrecht: Foris.

Cooper, W. E., and J. Paccia-Cooper. 1980. *Syntax and Speech.* Cambridge, Mass.: Harvard University Press.

Cowper, E. A., and K. D. Rice. 1987. Are phonosyntactic rules necessary? *Phonology Yearbook* 4:185–94.

Culicover, P., and K. Wexler. 1977. Some syntactic implications of a theory of language learnability. In P. Culicover, T. Wasow, and A. Akmajian (Eds.), *Formal Syntax*, 7–60. New York: Academic Press.

Culicover, P. W., and M. S. Rochemont. 1983. Stress and focus in English. *Language* 59(1):123–165.

Dauer, R. 1983. Stress-timing and syllable-timing reanalyzed. *Journal of Phonetics* 11:51–62.

de Manrique, A. M. B., and A. Signorini. 1983. Segmental durations and rhythm in Spanish. *Journal of Phonetics* 11:117–128.

Dell, F. 1984. L'accentuation dans les phrases en français. In F. Dell, D. Hirst, and J.-R. Vergnaud (Eds.), *Forme Sonore du Langage: Structure des Representations en Phonologie.* Paris: Hermann.

den Os, E. 1988. *Rhythm and Tempo in Dutch and Italian; a Contrastive Study.* PhD thesis, Utrecht.

Di Sciullo, A.-M., and E. Williams. 1987. *On the Definition of Word.* Cambridge, Mass.: MIT Press.

Dixon, R. M. W. 1977. *A Grammar of Yidiɲ.* Cambridge, England: Cambridge University Press.

Dixon, R. M. W. 1980. *The Languages of Australia.* Cambridge, England: Cambridge University Press.

Dois-Bienzobas, A. 1988. The interaction between phonology and syntax in Basque. Manuscript, UC San Diego.

Donegan, P. J., and D. Stampe. 1979. The study of natural phonology. In D. A. Dinnsen (Ed.), *Current Approaches to Phonological Theory*, 126–73. Bloomington: Indiana University Press.

Downing, L. 1988. Tonology of noun-modifier phrases in Jita. *Studies in the Linguistic Sciences* 18(1):25–60.

Dresher, B. E. 1983. Postlexical domains in Tiberian Hebrew. Paper presented at the annual meeting of the Canadian Linguistic Association, University of British Columbia.

Eisenberg, P. 1973. A note on 'identity of constituents'. *Linguistic Inquiry* 4:417–420.

Emonds, J. E. 1976. *A Transformational Approach to English Syntax: Root, Structure-preserving, and Local Transformations.* New York: Academic Press.

Fukui, N. 1986. *A Theory of Category Projection and Its Applications.* PhD thesis, MIT.

Goldsmith, J. 1984. Meeussen's rule. In M. Aronoff and R. Oerhle (Eds.), *Language Sound Structure.* Cambridge, Mass.: MIT Press.

Goldsmith, J. 1987a. Tone and accent, and getting the two together. In *Berkeley Linguistics Society,* Vol. 13.

Goldsmith, J. 1987b. Vowel systems. In A. Bosch, B. Need, and E. Schiller (Eds.), *Papers from the Parasession on Autosegmental and Metrical Phonology.* Chicago: Chicago Linguistic Society.

Goldsmith, J., et al. 1986. Tone and accent in the Xhosa verbal system. Manuscript, University of Chicago.

Gowlett, D. 1967. Morphology of the verb in Lozi. Master's thesis, University of the Witwatersrand.

Gussenhoven, C. 1984. *On the Grammar and Semantics of Sentence Accents.* Dordrecht: Foris.

Guthrie, M. 1967. *Comparative Bantu.* Farnsborough: Gregg International Publishers.

Hadzidakis, G. 1905. *Meseonika ke Nea Ellinika.* Athens.

Hale, K. 1976. On ergative and locative suffixial alternations in Australian languages. In R. M. W. Dixon (Ed.), *Grammatical Categories in Australian Languages,* 414–7. Canberra: Australian Institute for Aboriginal Studies.

Hale, K. 1983. Warlpiri and the grammar of non-configurational languages. *Natural Language and Linguistic Theory* 1:5–47.

Hale, K. 1985. Preliminary remarks on configurationality. In *Proceedings of NELS 12,* University of Massachusetts, Amherst.

Hale, K., and E. O. Selkirk. 1987. Government and tonal phrasing in Papago. *Phonology Yearbook* 4:151–83.

Halle, M. 1973. Prolegomena to a theory of word formation. *Linguistic Inquiry* 4:3–16.

Halle, M., and K. P. Mohanan. 1985. Segmental phonology of Modern English. *Linguistic Inquiry* 16:57–116.

Halliday, M. A. K. 1967. *Intonation and Grammar in British English.* The Hague: Mouton.

Hasegawa, N. 1979. Fast speech vs. casual speech. In P. R. Clyne, W. F. Hanks, and C. L. Hofbauer (Eds.), *Papers from the Fifteenth Regional Meeting of the Chicago Linguistic Society*, 126–137, Chicago. Chicago Linguistic Society.

Hayes, B. 1981. *A Metrical Theory of Stress Rules*. Bloomington: Indiana University Linguistics Club.

Hayes, B. 1984. The phonology of rhythm in English. *Linguistic Inquiry* 15:33–74.

Hayes, B. 1986. Inalterability in CV phonology. *Language* 62:321–351.

Hayes, B. 1989. The prosodic hierarchy in meter. In P. Kiparsky and G. Youmans (Eds.), *Rhythm and Meter*. Orlando: Academic Press.

Hetzron, R. 1972. Phonology in syntax. *Journal of Linguistics* 8:251–262.

Hong, K.-S. 1988. A pragmatic account of Korean pronouns. Paper presented at the International Circle of Korean Linguistics.

Hou, J. 1980-82. Pingyao fangyan de liandu biandiao [tone sandhi in the Pingyao dialect]. *Fangyan*. 1980,1-14; 1982, 7-14 and 85-99.

Householder, Fred, K. K., and A. Koutsoudas. 1964. *Reference Grammar of Literary Dhimotiki*. Bloomington: Indiana University.

Hudson, R. A. 1987. Zwicky on heads. *Journal of Linguistics* 23(1):109–32.

Hung, T. 1987. *Syntactic and Semantic Aspects of Chinese Tone Sandhi*. PhD thesis, UC San Diego.

Hyman, L. M. 1978. Tone and/or accent. In D. J. Napoli (Ed.), *Elements of Tone, Stress, and Intonation*. Georgetown University Press.

Hyman, L. M. 1985. Word domains and downstep in Bamileke-Dschang. *Phonology Yearbook* 2:45–83.

Hyman, L. M. 1987. Direct vs. indirect syntactic conditioning of phonological rules. In *Proceedings of the Fourth Eastern States Conference on Linguistics*. Department of Linguistics, Ohio State University.

Hyman, L. M. 1989. The phonology of final glottal stops. In *Proceedings of the West Coast Conference on Linguistics*. California State University, Fresno.

Hyman, L. M., and E. R. Byarushengo. 1984. A model of Haya tonology. In G. N. Clements and J. Goldsmith (Eds.), *Autosegmental Studies in Bantu Tone*, 53–103. Dordrecht: Foris.

Hyman, L. M., F. Katamba, and L. Walusimbi. 1987. Luganda and the strict layer hypothesis. *Phonology Yearbook* 4:87–108.

Hyman, L. M., and N. Valinande. 1985. Globality in the Kinande tone system. In D. L. Goyvaerts (Ed.), *African Linguistics*, 239–260. Amsterdam: Benjamins.

Inkelas, S. 1987. Prosodic dependence in the lexicon. Paper presented at the annual meeting of the Linguistics Society of America.

Inkelas, S. 1988. Prosodic effects on syntax: Hausa 'fa'. In *Proceedings of the Seventh West Coast Conference on Formal Linguistics*. Stanford Linguistics Association.

Inkelas, S. 1989a. *Prosodic Constituency in the Lexicon*. PhD thesis, Stanford University.

Inkelas, S. 1989b. Representing invisibility. Paper presented at the Eighth West Coast Conference on Formal Linguistics, Vancouver, B.C.

Inkelas, S., W. R. Leben, and M. Cobler. 1986. Lexical and phrasal tone in Hausa. In *Proceedings of NELS 17*, University of Massachusetts, Amherst.

Inkelas, S., and D. Zec. 1988. Serbo-Croatian pitch accent: the interactions of tone, stress and intonation. *Language* 64(2):227–248.

Innes, G. 1962. *A Mende grammar*. London: Macmillan.

Innes, G. 1967. *A Practical Introduction to Mende*. London: School of Oriental and African Studies, University of London.

Innes, G. 1969. *A Mende-English Dictionary*. Cambridge, England: Cambridge University Press.

Itô, J. 1986. *Syllable Theory in Prosodic Phonology*. PhD thesis, University of Massachusetts, Amherst.

Jackendoff, R. S. 1972. *Semantic Interpretation in Generative Grammar*. Cambridge, Mass.: MIT Press.

Jackendoff, R. S. 1977. *X' Syntax: A Study of Phrase Structure*. Cambridge, Mass.: MIT Press.

Jin, S. 1986. *Shanghai Morphotonemics*. Bloomington: Indiana University Linguistics Club.

Kageyama, T. 1982. Word formation in Japanese. *Lingua* 57:215–258.

Kahn, D. 1976. *Syllable-based Generalizations in English Phonology*. Bloomington: Indiana University Linguistics Club.

Kaisse, E. M. 1977a. *Hiatus in Modern Greek*. PhD thesis, Harvard University.

Kaisse, E. M. 1977b. On the syntactic environment of a phonological rule. In W. A. Beach, S. F. Fox, and S. Philosoph (Eds.), *Papers from the Thirteenth Regional Meeting of the Chicago Linguistics Society*, 173–185, Chicago. Chicago Linguistics Society.

Kaisse, E. M. 1985. *Connected Speech: The Interaction of Syntax and Phonology*. Orlando: Academic Press.

Kaisse, E. M. 1986. Locating Turkish devoicing. In *Proceedings of the West Coast Conference on Formal Linguistics*, Vol. 5. Stanford Linguistics Association.

Kaisse, E. M. 1987. Rhythm and the cycle. In *Papers from the Twenty-third Regional Meeting of the Chicago Linguistic Society*, Chicago. Chicago Linguistics Society.

Kaisse, E. M., and P. A. Shaw. 1985. On the theory of lexical phonology. *Phonology Yearbook* 2:1–30.

Kaisse, E. M., and A. Zwicky. 1987. Introduction: syntactic influences on phonological rules. *Phonology Yearbook* 4:3–12.

Kameyama, M. 1985. *Zero Anaphora: The Case of Japanese.* PhD thesis, Stanford University.

Kaye, J., J. Lowenstamm, and J.-R. Vergnaud. forthcoming. Constituent structure and government in phonology. In *Proceedings of GLOW 1987*, University of Venezia. Annali di Ca' Foscari.

Kenesei, I. 1986. On the logic of word order in Hungarian. In W. Abraham and S. de Mey (Eds.), *Topic, Focus and Configurationality.* Amsterdam: J. Benjamins.

Kenesei, I. forthcoming. On the interaction of lexical structure and phrase structure in pronominal binding in Hungarian. In P. Muysken and L. K. Maracz (Eds.), *Configurationality.* Dordrecht: Foris.

Kenstowicz, M. 1987. Tone and accent in Kizigua–a Bantu language. Paper presented at the Cortona Workshop on Phonology.

Kenstowicz, M., and C. Kisseberth. 1977. *Topics in Phonological Theory.* New York: Academic Press.

Kenstowicz, M., and C. Kisseberth. 1979. *Generative Phonology.* New York: Academic Press.

Kenstowicz, M., and J. Rubach. 1987. The phonology of syllable nuclei in Slovak. *Language* 63:463–97.

Kidima, L. 1987a. Objects and object agreement in Kiyaka. *Studies in African Linguistics* 18(2).

Kidima, L. 1987b. Tone and accent in Kiyaka. Manuscript, UCLA.

Kidima, L. forthcoming. *Tone and Accent in Kiyaka.* PhD thesis, UCLA.

Kim-Renaud, Y.-K. 1987. Fast speech, casual speech, and restructuring. In S. Kuno et al. (Eds.), *Harvard Studies in Korean Linguistics*, Vol. 2. Harvard University.

Kinyalolo, K. 1987. Agreement and clausal structure in Kilega. Manuscript, UCLA.

Kiparsky, P. 1973a. Abstractness, opacity, and global rules. In O. Fujimura (Ed.), *Three Dimensions of Linguistic Theory*, 57–86. Tokyo: TEC.

Kiparsky, P. 1973b. 'Elsewhere' in phonology. In S. R. Anderson and P. Kiparsky (Eds.), *A Festschrift for Morris Halle*, 93–106. New York: Holt, Rinehart, and Winston.

Kiparsky, P. 1977. The rhythmic structure of English verse. *Linguistic Inquiry* 8:189–247.

Kiparsky, P. 1979. Metrical structure assignment is cyclic. *Linguistic Inquiry* 10:421–442.

Kiparsky, P. 1982a. From cyclic to lexical phonology. In H. van der Hulst and N. Smith (Eds.), *The Structure of Phonological Representations (Part I)*, 131–175. Dordrecht: Foris.

Kiparsky, P. 1982b. Lexical morphology and phonology. In I.-S. Yang (Ed.), *Linguistics in the Morning Calm*, 3–91. Seoul: Hanshin.

Kiparsky, P. 1984. On the lexical phonology of Icelandic. In C.-C. Elert et al. (Eds.), *Nordic Prosody III: Papers from a Symposium*, 135–162. University of Umea.

Kiparsky, P. 1985a. The role of quantity in Finnish and English meters. Paper presented at the Eleventh Annual Meeting of the Berkeley Linguistic Society.

Kiparsky, P. 1985b. Some consequences of lexical phonology. *Phonology Yearbook* 2:85–138.

Kisseberth, C. 1984. Digo tonology. In G. N. Clements and J. Goldsmith (Eds.), *Autosegmental Studies in Bantu Tone*. Dordrecht: Foris.

Kisseberth, C. 1989. Chizigula tonology. Manuscript, University of Illinois, Urbana.

Kisseberth, C., and M. I. Abasheikh. 1974. Vowel length in Chimwi:ni—a case study of the role of grammar in phonology. In M. M. L. Galy, R. A. Fox, and A. Bruck (Eds.), *Papers from the Parasession on Natural Phonology*, Chicago. Chicago Linguistics Society.

Klavans, J. L. 1982. *Some Problems in a Theory of Clitics*. Bloomington: Indiana University Linguistics Club.

Klavans, J. L. 1985. The independence of syntax and phonology in cliticization. *Language* 61:95–120.

Koopman, H. 1984. *The Syntax of Verbs*. Dordrecht: Foris.

Korzen, I. 1980. Il raddoppiamento sintattico e la geminata nella variante toscana dell'italiano standard risultati di un'indagine sperimentale. *Studi italiani di linguistics teorica e applicata* 9(3):333–366.

Korzen, I. 1986. Syntactic gemination and open juncture: distinctive and phonematic units? *Journal of Italian Linguistics* 8(1):53–66.

Kraft, C. H., and A. H. M. Kirk-Greene. 1973. *Hausa*. London: Teach Yourself Books, Hodder and Stoughton.

Kuno, S. 1973. *The Structure of the Japanese Language*. Cambridge, Mass.: MIT Press.

Ladd, Robert D., J. 1980. *The Structure of Intonational Meaning: Evidence from English*. Bloomington: Indiana University Press.

Lapointe, S. G. 1981. The representation of inflectional morphology within the lexicon. In *Proceedings of NELS 11*. University of Massachusetts, Amherst.

Lasnik, H., and J. J. Kupin. 1977. A restrictive theory of transformational grammar. *Theoretical Linguistics* 4:173–96.

Lasnik, H., and J. Uriagereka. 1988. *A Course in GB Syntax: Lectures on Binding and Empty Categories*. Cambridge, Mass.: MIT Press.

Leben, W. R. 1971. The morphophonemics of tone in Hausa. In C.-W. Kim and H. Stahlke (Eds.), *Papers in African linguistics*, 201–18. Edmonton, Alberta: Linguistic Research, Inc.

Leben, W. R. 1978. The representation of tone. In V. Fromkin (Ed.), *Tone: A Linguistic Survey*, 177–219. New York: Academic Press.

Lehiste, I. 1979. Perception of sentence and paragraph boundaries. In B. Lindblom and S. E. G. Ohman (Eds.), *Frontiers of Speech Communication Research*, 191–201. New York: Academic Press.

Liberman, M. 1975. *The Intonational System of English*. PhD thesis, MIT.

Liberman, M., and A. Prince. 1977. On stress and linguistic rhythm. *Linguistic Inquiry* 8:249–336.

Lieber, R. 1980. *On the Organization of the Lexicon*. PhD thesis, MIT.

Lieber, R. 1987. *An Integrated Theory of Autosegmental Processes*. Albany: State University of New York Press.

Lightner, T. 1972. Problems in the theory of phonology. In *Russian Phonology and Turkish Phonology*, Vol. 1. Edmonton, Alberta: Linguistic Research, Inc.

Lin, T. 1962. Xiandai hanyu qingzhongyin he jufa jiegou de guanxi [the relationship between the strong/weak accent and sentence structure in modern Chinese]. *Zhongguo Yuwen* 7:301–11.

Lloyd, J. A. 1940. *Speech Signals in Telephony*. London.

Mackridge, P. 1985. *The Modern Greek Language*. Oxford University Press.

Maes, T. 1988. Pause insertion as a phonological rule. Paper presented at the Phonology-Syntax Connection workshop, Stanford University.

Malikouti-Drachman, A., and G. Drachman. 1978. Mi phonologikoi periorismoi se phonologikous nomous boreion idiomaton (non-phonological constraints in phonological rules of northern dialects). In *B΄ Symposio Glossologias tou Boreioelladikou Chorou: Praktika (Proceedings of the second symposium on linguistics of the northern Greek area)*. Institute of Balkan Studies, Thessaloniki.

Marácz, L. K. 1987. On the projection principle in Hungarian. In I. Kenesei (Ed.), *Theories and Analyses*, Vol. 2 of *Approaches to Hungarian*. Szeged: JATE.

Marotta, G. 1986. Rhythmical constraints on syntactic doubling. *Journal of Italian Lingusitics* 8(1):35–52.

Martin, J. G. 1970. On judging pauses in spontaneous speech. *Journal of Verbal Learning and Verbal Behavior* 9:75–78.

Martin, S. 1951. Korean phonemics. *Language* 27:519–33.

Matthews, P. H. 1972. *Inflectional Morphology: a Theoretical Study Based on Aspects of Latin Verb Conjugation*. Cambridge: Cambridge University Press.

McCarthy, J. 1986. OCP effects: gemination and antigemination. *Linguistic Inquiry* 17(2):207–264.

McCawley, J. D. 1982. Parentheticals and discontinuous constituent structure. *Linguistic Inquiry* 13(1):91–106.

McHugh, B. D. 1981. Towards a theory of Hausa tone. Undergraduate honors thesis, Department of Linguistics, Yale University.

McHugh, B. D. 1986. Cyclicity in phrasal phonology: evidence from Chaga. In *Proceedings of the West Coast Conference on Formal Linguistics*, Vol. 5, 154–164. Stanford Linguistics Association.

McHugh, B. D. 1987. Syntactic structure, empty categories and phrasal phonology in Chaga. In D. Odden (Ed.), *Current Approaches to African Linguistics*, Vol. 4, 247–65. Dordrecht: Foris.

McHugh, B. D. forthcoming. *The Phonological Interpretation of Syntax: Phrasal Cyclicity in Kivunjo Chaga*. PhD thesis, UCLA.

Meeussen, A. E. 1971. Zur morfotonologie des yaka. In V. Six et al. (Eds.), *Afrikanische Sprachen und Kulturen — ein Querschnit*. Hamburg: Deutsches Institut für Afrikaforschung.

Meng, Z. 1982. Yixie yu yufa youguan de beijing hua qingsheng xianxiang [some syntax-related neutral tone phenomena in the Beijing dialect]. *Yuyanxue Luncong* 9:25–59.

Mercado, I. 1981. Vowel sandhi in a Spanish dialect. Master's thesis, University of Washington.

Mohanan, K. P. 1982. *Lexical Phonology*. PhD thesis, MIT.

Mohanan, K. P. 1983. Lexical and configurational structures. *The Linguistic Review* 3:113–139.

Mohanan, K. P. 1986. *The Theory of Lexical Phonology*. Dordrecht: Reidel.

Mohanan, K. P., and T. Mohanan. 1984. Lexical phonology of the consonant system in Malayalam. *Linguistic Inquiry* 15:575–602.

Morin, Y.-C., and J. Kaye. 1982. The syntactic bases for French liaison. *Journal of Linguistics* 18:291–330.

Mtenje, A. D. 1986. *Issues in the Nonlinear Phonology of Chicheŵa*. PhD thesis, University College London, London, England.

Napoli, D. J., and M. Nespor. 1979. The syntax of word initial consonant gemination in Italian. *Language* 55:812–841.

Napoli, D. J., and J. Nevis. 1987. Inflected prepositions in Italian. *Phonology Yearbook* 4:195–209.

Nespor, M. 1987. Vowel degemination and fast speech rules. *Phonology Yearbook* 4:61–85.

Nespor, M. 1988a. Aspects of the interaction between prosodic phonology and the phonology of rhythm. In P. M. Bertinetto and M. Loporcaro (Eds.), *Certamen Phonologicum*, 189–230, Torino. Rosenberg and Sellier.

Nespor, M. 1988b. Rhythmic characteristics of Greek. In *Studies in Greek Linguistics.* Thessaloniki: Ekdoseis Kiriakidi.

Nespor, M., and M. Scoreretti. 1985. Empty elements and phonological form. In J. Gueron and J.-Y. Pollock (Eds.), *Grammatical Representation.* Dordrecht: Foris.

Nespor, M., and I. Vogel. 1979. Clash avoidance in Italian. *Linguistic Inquiry* 10:467–482.

Nespor, M., and I. Vogel. 1982. Prosodic domains of external sandhi rules. In H. van der Hulst and N. Smith (Eds.), *The Structure of Phonological Representations (Part I),* 225–55. Dordrecht: Foris.

Nespor, M., and I. Vogel. 1983. Prosodic structure above the word. In R. Ladd and A. Cutler (Eds.), *Prosody: Models and Measurement.* Berlin: Springer-Verlag.

Nespor, M., and I. Vogel. 1986. *Prosodic Phonology.* Dordrecht: Foris.

Nespor, M., and I. Vogel. 1988. Arhythmic sequenes and their resolution in Italian and Greek. In *Proceedings of GLOW 1987.* University of Venezia: Annali di Ca' Foscari.

Nespor, M., and I. Vogel. 1989. On clashes and lapses. *Phonology 7.*

Newman, P. 1973. Grades, vowel-tone classes and extensions in the Hausa verbal system. *Studies in African linguistics* 4:297–346.

Newton, B. 1972. *The Generative Interpretation of Dialect: A Study of Modern Greek Phonology.* Cambridge: Cambridge University Press.

Odden, D. 1981a. The phrasal phonology of Kimatuumbi. Manuscript, the Ohio State University.

Odden, D. 1981b. *Problems in Tone Assignment in Shona.* PhD thesis, University of Illinois, Urbana.

Odden, D. 1985. Three dialects of Kipare. In G. Dimmendaal (Ed.), *Current Approaches to African Linguistics,* Vol. 3, 257–280. Dordrecht: Foris.

Odden, D. 1986a. On the role of the obligatory contour principle in phonological theory. *Language* 62:353–383.

Odden, D. 1986b. The ordering of lexical and postlexical rules in Kimatuumbi. Paper presented at the annual meeting of the Linguistic Society of America.

Odden, D. 1987. Kimatuumbi phrasal phonology. *Phonology Yearbook* 4:13–26.

Ojeda, A. E. 1987. Discontinuity, multidominance, and unbounded dependency in generalized phrase structure grammar. *Syntax and Semantics* 20:257–82.

Parsons, F. W. 1960. The verbal system in Hausa. *Afrika und Uebersee* 44:1–36.

Pesetsky, D. 1985. Morphology and logical form. *Linguistic Inquiry* 16:193–246.

Pierrehumbert, J. B., and M. E. Beckman. 1986. Japanese tone structure. Manuscript, AT&T Bell Laboratories and the Ohio State University.

Pierrehumbert, J. B., and M. E. Beckman. 1989. *Japanese Tone Structure.* Cambridge, Mass.: MIT Press.

Pike, K. 1945. *The Intonation of American English.* Ann Arbor: University of Michigan Press.

Poser, W. J. 1984. *The Phonetics and Phonology of Tone and Intonation in Japanese.* PhD thesis, MIT.

Posner, R. 1987. Non-agreement on Romance disagreements. *Journal of Linguistics* 21:437–51.

Postal, P. 1974. *On Raising.* Cambridge, Mass.: MIT Press.

Pratelli, R. 1970. Le reinforcement syntactique des consonnes en italien. *La Linguistique* 6:39–50.

Prince, A. 1983. Relating to the grid. *Linguistic Inquiry* 14:19–100.

Pulleyblank, D. 1983. *Tone in Lexical Phonology.* PhD thesis, MIT.

Pulleyblank, D. 1986. *Tone in Lexical Phonology.* Dordrecht: Reidel.

Pullum, G. K. 1982. Syncategorematicity and English infinitival *to. Glossa* 16(2):181–215.

Pullum, G. K. 1986. On the relations of IDC-command and government. In *Proceedings of the West Coast Conference on Formal Linguistics,* Vol. 5, 192–206. Stanford Linguistics Association.

Pullum, G. K., and A. M. Zwicky. 1988. The syntax-phonology interface. In F. Newmeyer (Ed.), *Linguistics: the Cambridge Survey,* Vol. 1. Cambridge, England: Cambridge University Press.

Pullum, G. K., and A. M. Zwicky. forthcoming. *The Syntax-Phonology Interface.* Orlando: Academic Press.

Riad, T. forthcoming. *Tracing the Foot.* Arkiv for Nordisk. Filologi.

Rice, K. D. 1987a. On defining the intonational phrase: evidence from Slave. *Phonology Yearbook* 4:37–59.

Rice, K. D. 1987b. Review of ellen kaisse (1985). *The Canadian Journal of Linguistics* 32(3).

Rice, K. D. forthcominga. *A Grammar of Slave (Dene).* Berlin: Mouton de Gruyter.

Rice, K. D. forthcomingb. Vowel-initial clitics and suffixes in Slave. In D. Gerdts and K. Michelson (Eds.), *Canadian Native Languages in Theoretical Perspective.* Albany: SUNY Press.

Rivero, M. L., and D. C. Walker. 1976. Surface structure and the centrality of syntax. *Theoretical Linguistics* 3:99–124.

Robins, R. H. 1959. In defence of WP. *Transactions of the Philological Society* 116–144.

Rochemont, M. S. 1986. *Focus in Generative Grammar.* Amsterdam: Benjamins.

Rooth, M. E. 1985. *Association with Focus.* PhD thesis, University of Massachusetts, Amherst.

Ross, J. R. 1968. *Constraints on Variables in Syntax.* Bloomington: Indiana University Linguistics Club.

Rotenberg, J. 1978. *The Syntax of Phonology.* PhD thesis, MIT, Cambridge, Mass.

Rubach, J., and G. Booij. 1985. A grid theory of stress in Polish. *Lingua* 66:281–319.

Sadock, J. M. 1985. Autolexical syntax: a theory of noun incorporation and similar phenomena. *Natural Language and Linguistic Theory* 3(4):379–439.

Sagey, E. C. 1986. *The Representation of Features and Relations in Nonlinear Phonology.* PhD thesis, MIT.

Sampson, G. R. 1975. The single mother condition. *Journal of Linguistics* 11(1):1–11.

Schlindwein, D. 1985. Downstep in the Kipare verb complex. *SAL Supplement* 9:285–289. Precis from the 15th conference on African linguistics.

Selkirk, E. O. 1972. *The Phrase Phonology of English and French.* PhD thesis, MIT. Distributed in 1981 by the Indiana University Linguistics Club, Bloomington, Indiana.

Selkirk, E. O. 1978. *On Prosodic Structure and its Relation to Syntactic Structure.* Bloomington: Indiana University Linguistics Club.

Selkirk, E. O. 1980a. Prosodic domains in phonology: Sanskrit revisited. In M. Aronoff and M.-L. Kean (Eds.), *Juncture (Studia linguistica et philologica 7),* 107–29. Saratoga, Calif.: Anma Libri.

Selkirk, E. O. 1980b. The role of prosodic categories in English word stress. *Linguistic Inquiry* 11:563–605.

Selkirk, E. O. 1981a. On prosodic structure and its relation to syntactic structure. In T. Fretheim (Ed.), *Nordic Prosody II,* 11–40. Trondheim: TAPIR.

Selkirk, E. O. 1981b. On the nature of phonological representation. In J. Anderson, J. Laver, and T. Myers (Eds.), *The Cognitive Representation of Speech.* Amsterdam: North Holland.

Selkirk, E. O. 1984. *Phonology and Syntax: The Relation Between Sound and Structure.* Cambridge, Mass.: MIT Press.

Selkirk, E. O. 1986. On derived domains in sentence phonology. *Phonology Yearbook* 3:371–405.

Selkirk, E. O., and T. Shen. 1988. Tone deletion in Shanghai Chinese. In *Sentence Phonology,* Vol. 1. Amherst: University of Massachusetts.

Selkirk, E. O., and K. Tateishi. 1988a. Constraints on minor phrase formation in Japanese. In *Papers from the Twenty-fourth Regional Meeting of the Chicago Linguistic Society,* Chicago. Chicago Linguistics Society.

Selkirk, E. O., and K. Tateishi. 1988b. Syntax and phonological phrasing in Japanese. In C. Georgopoulos and R. Ishihara (Eds.), *Studies in Honour of S.-Y. Kuroda*. Amsterdam: Reidel.

Sezer, E. 1981. The k/∅ alternation in Turkish. In G. N. Clements (Ed.), *Harvard Studies in Phonology*, Vol. 2, 354–382. Bloomington: Indiana University Linguistics Club.

Shen, T. 1985. The underlying representation of Shanghai tones. *Yuyan Yanjiu* 2:85–101.

Shen, T. 1986. The formation of tone groups in Shanghai. Manuscript, University of Massachusetts, Amherst.

Shen, Y. 1988. A tentative hypothesis regarding trisyllabic tone sandhi in Pingyao. Manuscript, UC San Diego.

Sherard, M. 1972. *Shanghai Phonology*. PhD thesis, Cornell University.

Shih, C.-L. 1985. *The Prosodic Domain of Tone Sandhi in Chinese*. PhD thesis, UC San Diego.

Silverman, K., and J. B. Pierrehumbert. forthcoming. The timing of prenuclear high accents in English. In J. Kingston and M. E. Beckman (Eds.), *Papers in Laboratory Phonology I: Between the Grammar and the Physics of Speech*. Cambridge, Mass.: Cambridge University Press.

Sohn, H.-M. 1980. Theme prominence in Korean. *Korean Linguistics* 2.

Spencer, A. 1988. Arguments for morpholexical rules. *Journal of Linguistics* 24:1–29.

Sproat, R., and C.-L. Shih. 1987. Adjective ordering. Manuscript, AT&T Bell Laboratories and Cornell University.

Steriade, D. 1988. Greek accent: a case for preserving structure. *Linguistic Inquiry* 19:271–314.

Sweet, H. 1913. Words, logic and grammar. In *Collected Papers of Henry Sweet*. Oxford.

Tateishi, K. 1987. Consonant mutation in Mende, Loma, and Gandi and its implications. Manuscript, University of Massachusetts, Amherst.

Tateishi, K. 1988. A morphological analysis of Mende consonant mutation. Paper presented at the 19th Annual African Linguistics Conference, Boston University.

Thomas-Flinders, T. 1981. Initial lenition in Celtic: evidence for inflection as a phonological process. In T. Thomas-Flinders (Ed.), *Inflectional Morphology: Introduction to the Extended Word-and-Paradigm Theory*, 72–83. UCLA.

Thumb, A. 1912. *Handbook of the Modern Greek Vernacular*. Edinburgh: T. & T. Clark.

Triandaphyllidis, M. 1941. *Neoelliniki Grammatiki*. Organismos Ekdoseon Scholikon Vivlion.

van den Eynde, K. 1968. *Elements de Grammaire Yaka*. Kinshasa: Presses Universitaires.

van Hoorn, H. 1983. Cancellazione della vocale finale prima di consonante. University of Amsterdam.

van Riemsdijk, H., and E. Williams. 1981. NP-structure. *The Linguistic Review* 1:171–218.

Vandersande, A. 1968. *Myungdo's Korean.* Seoul: Myungdo Institute.

Vogel, I. 1977. *The Syllable in Phonological Theory: With Special Reference to Italian.* PhD thesis, Stanford University.

Vogel, I. 1984. On constraining prosodic rules. In H. van der Hulst and N. Smith (Eds.), *Advances in Nonlinear Phonology,* 217–233. Dordrecht: Foris.

Vogel, I. forthcoming. Prosodic constituents in Hungarian. In P. M. Bertinetto (Ed.), *Proceedings of the Cortona Workshop on Phonology, 1987.* Scuola Normale Superiore.

Vogel, I., M. Drigo, A. Moser, and I. Zannier. 1983. La cancellazione di vocale in Italiano. *Studi di Grammatica Italiana* 191–230.

Vogel, I., and I. Kenesei. 1987. The interface between phonology and other components of grammar: the case of Hungarian. *Phonology Yearbook* 4:243–263.

Wall, R. E. 1972. *Introduction to Mathematical Linguistics.* Englewood Cliffs NJ: Prentice-Hall.

Welmers, W. E., and B. F. Welmers. 1969. Noun modifiers in Igbo. *International Journal of American Linguistics* 35:315–322.

Whitman, J. 1986. Configurationality parameters. In T. Imai and M. Saito (Eds.), *Issues in Japanese Linguistics.* Dordrecht: Foris.

Whitman, J. 1987. Local and long-distance binding of null elements. Paper presented at the Harvard Workshop on Korean Linguistics.

Whitney, W. D. 1889. *Sanskrit Grammar.* Cambridge, Mass.: Harvard University Press.

Williams, E. 1981. On the notions 'lexically related' and 'head of a word'. *Linguistic Inquiry* 12:245–74.

Williams, E. 1986. A reassignment of the functions of LF. *Linguistic Inquiry* 17:265–299.

Williams, E. 1988. Is LF distinct from S-structure? a reply to May. *Linguistic Inquiry* 19:135–146.

Woodbury, A. 1987. Meaningful phonological processes. *Language* 63:685–740.

Wright, M. S. 1983. *A Metrical Approach to Tone Sandhi in Chinese Dialects.* PhD thesis, University of Massachusetts, Amherst.

Yip, M. 1980. *The Tonal Phonology of Chinese.* PhD thesis, MIT.

Yip, M. 1988. The obligatory contour principle and phonological rules: a loss of identity. *Linguistic Inquiry* 19(1):65–100.

Zec, D. 1987. Interactions of prosodic and syntactic constituency. Manuscript, Stanford University.

Zec, D. 1988. *Sonority Constraints on Prosodic Structure*. PhD thesis, Stanford University.

Zec, D., and S. Inkelas. 1987. Phonological phrasing and the reduction of function words. Paper presented at the annual meeting of the Linguistics Society of America.

Zee, E., and I. Maddieson. 1979. Tones and tone sandhi in Shanghai. *UCLA Working Papers in Phonetics* 93–129.

Zhang, H. 1988. A syntactic or prosodic domain? – on tone sandhi in Chongming. Manuscript, UC San Diego.

Zubizarreta, M. L., and J.-R. Vergnaud. 1982. On virtual categories. In A. Marantz and T. Stowell (Eds.), *Papers in Syntax*, Vol. 4 of *MIT Working Papers in Linguistics*.

Zwicky, A. M. 1972. On casual speech. In P. M. Peranteau, J. N. Levi, and G. C. Phares (Eds.), *Papers from the Eighth Regional Meeting of the Chicago Linguistic Society*, 607–615, Chicago. Chicago Linguistic Society.

Zwicky, A. M. 1977. *On Clitics*. Bloomington. Indiana University Linguistics Club.

Zwicky, A. M. 1982. Stranded *to* and phonological phrasing in English. *Linguistics* 20:3–57.

Zwicky, A. M. 1984. 'reduced words' in highly modular theories: Yiddish anarthrous locatives reexamined. *Ohio State University Working Papers in Linguistics* 29:117–26.

Zwicky, A. M. 1985a. The case against plain vanilla syntax. *Studies in the Linguistic Sciences* 15(2):205–25.

Zwicky, A. M. 1985b. Clitics and particles. *Language* 61:283–305.

Zwicky, A. M. 1985c. How to describe inflection. *Berkeley Linguistics Society* 11:372–86.

Zwicky, A. M. 1985d. Rules of allomorphy and phonology-syntax interactions. *Journal of Linguistics* 21:431–6.

Zwicky, A. M. 1986a. The general case: basic form versus default form. *Berkeley Linguistics Society* 12:305–14.

Zwicky, A. M. 1986b. The unaccented pronoun constraint in English. *Ohio State University Working Papers in Linguistics* 32:100–13.

Zwicky, A. M. 1987a. French prepositions: no peeking. *Phonology Yearbook* 4:211–27.

Zwicky, A. M. 1987b. Suppressing the *z*'s. *Journal of Linguistics* 23(1):133–48.

Zwicky, A. M., and N. S. Levin. 1980. You don't have to. *Linguistic Inquiry* 11:631–6.

Zwicky, A. M., and G. K. Pullum. 1983. Cliticization vs. inflection: English 'n't'. *Language* 59:502–13.

Zwicky, A. M., and G. K. Pullum. 1986a. The principle of phonology-free syntax: introductory remarks. *Ohio State University Working Papers in Linguistics* 32:63–91.

Zwicky, A. M., and G. K. Pullum. 1986b. Two spurious counterexamples to the principle of phonology-free syntax. *Ohio State University Working Papers in Linguistics* 32:92–99.

Index